The Psychology of Emotion

THIRD EDITION

The Psychology
of
Emotion

THIRD EDITION

K.T. STRONGMAN

*Department of Psychology, University of Canterbury,
Christchurch, New Zealand*

JOHN WILEY & SONS

Chichester · New York · Brisbane · Toronto · Singapore

Library of Congress Cataloging-in-Publication Data:

Strongman, K.T.
  The psychology of emotion.

  Bibliography: p.
  Includes index.
  1. Emotions.   I. Title. [DNLM: 1. Emotions.
BF 531 S924p]
BF531.S825   1987   152.4   86-28187

ISBN 0 471 91143 7
ISBN 0 471 91433 9 (pbk.)

British Library Cataloguing in Publication Data:

Strongman, K. T.
  The psychology of emotion.—3rd ed.
  1. Emotions
  I. Title
  152.4   BF531
ISBN 0 471 91143 7
ISBN 0 471 91433 9 Pbk

Typeset by David John Services Ltd., Maidenhead, Berks.
Printed in Great Britain by St Edmundsbury Press, Bury St Edmunds.

For Lara and Luke

Contents

Preface to First Edition

In spending some years teaching an advanced undergraduate course on the psychology of emotion, I increasingly felt the need for a book which gathered together some of the very different approaches which have been made to the subject. Our knowledge of emotion has been gained in diverse ways; it is discussed in most areas of psychology and, indeed, permeates the whole subject. This inevitably means that its study within a single course is difficult—the relevant sources and their evaluations are spread very widely throughout the psychological literature. The present book is an attempt to simplify matters by drawing together and comparing representative examples of the better thought and research on emotion. In that it presupposes some knowledge of psychology, the book is not directed at the beginning student. It is meant for the second- or third-year undergraduate who wishes to gain a more specialized knowledge of the subject.

Although the basic aims of the book are to provide a broad coverage of emotion and to suggest guidelines for its study and research, it is not completely unbiased. It quite self-evidently reflects two fundamental viewpoints. First, emphasis is laid on research which is reasonably sound methodologically, and on theory which is reasonably well anchored to such research. Second, there is more than a faint leaning towards the behavioural (although not necesarily behaviouristic) approaches to the subject. In spite of this, it should be simple enough for the reader who is antipathetic to these types of analysis to skim over them or miss them out altogether. In any case, he should certainly forgo the last few pages of the book. However, I make no apologies for such biases, since I believe them to lead to research strategies which are important to the overall study of psychology.

Finally, I would like to express my gratitude to all those who have tolerated my vagaries during the writing of this book. In particular, I thank my friends and colleagues Philip Wookey and Robert Remington for their help, advice and encouragement, and my wife, Thelma, without whose support I should never have finished.

Preface to Second Edition

There were a number of reasons why I welcomed the opportunity to produce a second edition of *The Psychology of Emotion*. Naturally, since 1973 more research on various aspects of emotion has been carried out and some of the more important parts of this have been included in this new edition. Also, there were a number of errors of omission in the first edition which I hope have now been rectified. Doubtless, there are still some ideas and research findings which have been forgotten, although I have tried to keep these to a minimum. Similarly, there were some parts of the original edition which both hindsight and critical comment tell me to have been poor. It was a relief to attempt to improve them.

More important than new research findings, there have been a number of recent publications which, in my opinion, have somewhat changed the direction of research and theory in emotion. Broadly speaking, a greater emphasis has been placed on analysis of cognitive factors in emotion and on the significance of emotional expression and recognition. In large measure this is due to the work of Izard, reflecting ideas and approaches which I suspect will become very influential. In consequence I felt it necessary to allow these new emphases to partly replace the rather behavioural orientation of the first edition.

Finally, since the publishers have allowed me a few more words in this edition, I have been able to expand some sections of the book a little. This was particularly enjoyable in dealing with the chapter on theories of emotion, which is now more representative of the many directions which these have taken. Also, I have been able to include an entirely new chapter on the phenomenology of emotion—a subject too often neglected by experimental psychologists, yet which can have much to offer.

To sum up, the aims of the second edition are precisely the same as those of the first. It is merely that I have attempted to realize them in slightly different ways.

Preface to Third Edition

It is a considerable privilege to be asked to write a third edition of a text, even though some aspects of the task are daunting. Since there is an obvious sense in which the first two editions of *The Psychology of Emotion* seemed to have been reasonably successful in realizing their aims, these aims remain unchanged. They are to present a critical overview of past and present theory and research into emotion.

Between the first two editions of this book a great deal changed in the study of emotion, but it was on a small scale in comparison with what has happened since the second edition appeared in 1978. There has been a mild explosion in investigations of emotion. New ideas, fresh theories and innovative research techniques have begun to open up the field in a way which has never happened before. This has even led to the development of new areas of study such as emotion and memory, lateralization, and emotion considered in the total life-span. Also, there has been a proliferation of research into emotional expression. Throughout the 1970s the balance of power behind attempts to understand emotion began to change from the behavioural to the cognitive. That change is now complete, the behavioural approach to emotion has virtually disappeared and every aspect of emotion appears to depend on cognitive considerations. All of these changes and developments are reflected in the present text.

As well as a necessary change in emphasis, this edition of *The Psychology of Emotion* also embraces a considerable change in style. A criticism which was levelled at the previous editions by successive generations of students was that they (the books, that is) were too dense. References came thick and fast and made a vast amount to remember. Reviewers of the proposed third edition made similar comments and suggested that I aim at being less exhaustive and cautious and more didactic—in other words, to stop being so careful and over-inclusive and to try to be a little more interesting. I have made the attempt, cut out many of the less important references, made more evaluative comments and included discussion of more naturally interesting although less secure topics, such as the links between emotion and culture.

Finally, some thanks are due and are most willingly offered. Once again, Thelma, Lara and Luke have had to cope with my many vagaries during the writing of this book. They have done so with fortitude and I thank them for this as well as for their encouragement. I also thank the very many students who have listened and been critical. Similarly, I would like to thank my colleagues and friends at the University of Canterbury for their support and tolerance, particularly Brian Haig with whom it is always a pleasure to discuss things. Finally, I thank many postgraduate students, both in England and New Zealand, who have put up with me and who have been unfailingly stimulating. They began in the first edition of this book with Philip Wookey and Robert Remington whom I wish well at a distance, and end in this edition with Carol Parrott, Jan Watt, Malcolm Fletcher, and many others. I would also like to extend my thanks to Don Locke, Professor of Philosophy at the University of Warwick, who stretched my thinking.

Acknowledgments

The author wishes to acknowledge the co-operation of the following for granting permission to reproduce diagrams from their publications:

Academic Press, Inc.
Figures 4 and 5 (M. Arnold, Ed. *Feelings and Emotions,* Academic Press, New York, 1970, pp.10–11).

American Psychologist Association
Figure 10 (V.H. Denenberg, *Psychol. Rev.,* 1964, **71**, 235–351). Copyright 1964 by the American Psychological Association and reproduced by permission.

McGraw-Hill Inc. and Appleton-Century-Crofts
Figure 7 (from *Psychological Psychology,* 3rd edn. by G.T. Morgan © 1965 McGraw-Hill Inc., adapted from *Bodily Changes in Pain, Hunger, Fear and Rage,* by W.B. Cannon, published by Appleton-Century-Crofts).

New York Academy of Sciences
Figure 3 (D. Bindra, 'A unified interpretation of emotion and motivation', *Ann. New York Acad. Sci.,* 1969, **159**, p.1073).

1

Introduction

'So many learned men have treated of the Passions, that nothing more can be added on the subject . . . .'

(Charles Lebrun, 1734)

As it is commonly conceived, emotion is bound up with feeling. Were you to produce an off-the-cuff definition of the term, it would probably make some reference to subjective feelings. Go one stage further and consult a dictionary, and yet again the word feeling would be prominent. For example, the *Shorter Oxford English Dictionary* defines emotion (in psychology) as a 'mental feeling or affection, distinct from cognitions or volitions'. Clearly, one thing we mean if we use the word emotion is personal subjective feeling. We describe this feeling as pleasant or unpleasant, mild or intense, transient or long-lasting, and as interfering with or enhancing our behaviour.

In his *Dictionary of Psychology,* Drever (1952) is a little less subjective in his definition. He describes emotion as a complex state of the organism involving widespread bodily changes. Mentally, this is accompanied by strong feelings and impulses to behave in particular ways. He has added two more ingredients to the mixture—bodily states and behaviour. To return to your off-the-cuff definition, it may well have included some reference to palpitations or trembling. Or it may have referred to some behaviour such as fighting or running, or to some strained facial expression. Emotion then also involves physiological and behavioural change; again, such change may vary along several dimensions—it may, for example, be great or small, acute or chronic; we may enjoy it or we may not.

To take the exercise one stage further, were you to define a specific emotion, such as anger or fear, you might well begin your definition with some phrase like 'It is when . . .' or 'Yesterday I was with . . .'. In other words, you would escape the definition by giving an example, and that example would describe some environmental situation that you had experienced.

Emotion is feeling, it is a bodily state involving various physical structures, it is gross or fine-grained behaviour, and it occurs in particular situations. When we use the term we mean any or all of these possibilities, each of which may show a wide range of variations. This points to the major difficulty which besets the academic study of the subject. Different theorists have taken different starting points. Any theory of emotion or any empirical research on emotion deals only with some part of the broad meaning that the term has acquired. Some theorists stress psychological factors, some behavioural, some subjective, some deal only with extremes, some say emotion colours all behaviour. There is no consensus of opinion.

In an attempt to get to grips with the great difficulty involved in defining emotion, Kleinginna and Kleinginna (1981) categorize many types of the hundreds of definitions there have been. Consider the following, chosen from amongst the more cogent or understandable.

'It is my basic assumption that the labels one attaches to a bodily state, how one describes his feelings, are a joint function of . . . cognitive factors and of a state of physiological arousal'.

(Schachter, 1970)

'Emotion . . . the association between certain widespread changes in ongoing operant behaviours and the presentation or removal of reinforcers'.

(Millenson, 1967)

'conflicting interruptive (mental and environmental) events play an important role in emotion and many even play an important role in generating the visceral substration. Conversely, it is recognised that mere visceral response is not a sufficient condition for emotional phenomena, though it may be necessary; other mental or cognitive, events are also required'.

(Mandler, 1979)

'An emotion may be defined as a patterned bodily reaction of either destruction, reproduction, incorporation, orientation, protection, reintegration, rejection, or exploration or some combination of these, which is brought about by a stimulus'.

(Plutchik, 1962)

'I am aware of no evidence for the existence of a special condition called 'emotion' which follows different principles of action from other conditions of the organism . . . . Emotion has no distinguishing characteristics. It represents merely an extreme manifestation of characteristics found in some degree in all responses'.

(Duffy, 1941)

'The 'emotions' are excellent examples of the fictional causes to which we commonly attribute behaviour. The names of the so-called emotions serve to classify behaviour with respect to various circumstances which affect its probability'.

(Skinner, 1953)

'In general, it appears that emotional behaviour is so complexly determined that a consistent characterisation is at present elusive. It would appear, then, that little is gained by retaining the concept of emotion in psychology'.

(Fantino, 1973)

In the end, Kleinginna and Kleinginna (1981) tried to put everything together in one all-embracing definition.

'Emotion is a complex set of interactions among subjective and objective factors, mediated by neural/hormonal systems, which can (a) give rise to affective experiences such as feelings of arousal, pleasure/displeasure; (b) generate cognitive processes such as emotionally relevant perceptual effects, appraisals, labelling processes; (c) activate widespread physiological adjustments to the arousing conditions; and (d) lead to behaviour that is often, but not always, expressive, goal-directed, and adaptive'.

This definition suffers because it embraces all possibilities, it includes too much. In the end the investigator has to be bolder than this, to make some definite decisions, to make some firm suggestions about the conditions which are necessary to emotion and those which are merely very important. For now, the range of definitions mentioned will help to set the scene. At this point, rather than add another to these, it will be reserved for the final chapter, by which time I hope there will be a certain inevitability about it.

In a recent discussion, Hinde (1985) considers problems of the definition of emotion via the assumption that human emotional behaviour and animal signal movements have elements in common. He describes problems with many of the ways in which emotion has been conceptualized. Regarding emotion as input, it is difficult to say what is and is not emotional. Similarly, the common view of emotion as a state has many attendant problems. Is it a motive, a state or a trait? Is it an intervening variable or a hypothetical construct? What is its mode of action? Is it specific or general? What is the status of the subjective experience of emotion? If emotion is regarded as output, what is the difference between emotional and nonemotional behaviour?

Hinde argues that emotion is best defined in terms of chains or loops, with emotion and cognition closely linked. There are many ways in which emotion affects experience and experience affects emotion, the whole being made very complex by cognition. He suggests that emotional input is determined by the physical characteristics of the input and the responses of the individual, plus interruptions to and discrepancies in the external situation and the internal state. He also argues that there is a complex relationship rather than a one-to-one correspondence between emotional behaviour and emotional state. Finally, Hinde suggests that emotion should be considered simultaneously as an independent variable, an intervening variable and a dependent variable.

FOUNDATIONS OF THE STUDY OF EMOTION

Leeper (1965) puts forward an interesting hypothesis to account for the rationalist, commonsense doctrine of the emotions which was generated by the early philosophers. Briefly, this doctrine contrasted reason and emotion by proposing that man is basically knowing and rational, but to achieve this must minimize his baser, emotional elements. Reason was equated with choice and emotion was regarded as an inbuilt response to significant environmental stimuli—we hear the roar of the lion, feel afraid and run, rather than coolly and rationally shooting it between the eyes.

Leeper argues that there are parallel trends in everyday thought about emotion and in its pre-scientific study. He suggests that these trends come from the emphasis which is usually laid on palpable factors in any new field of study. He describes palpable factors as tangible, highly variable, and showing close relationships between cause and effect. He believes that stress on such factors led pre-scientific thought to focus on conscious, intense emotions, particularly those capable of strongest expression. Also, emotion (as a process underlying behaviour) was viewed as having its effects mainly by increasing the intensity and duration of primitive behaviours such as fighting, and as producing socially irresponsible actions.

Leeper suggests further that much of the present-day scientific thought is still caught in this basic philosophy. For example, despite Freud, there is not much credence given to possible unconscious emotions, although it is quite clear that emotions can be experienced pre-consciously. Emotions are still often thought of only as strong experiences, and it is mainly the negative ones which receive attention. Emotions continue to be regarded as fundamentally opposed to realistic, adaptive functioning.

Although the rationalist philosophy of the emotions began with Plato and Aristotle, it received its fullest expression by Descartes in the seventeenth century. Descartes' was the extreme dualistic philosophy, separating mind and body. In animals, he thought that there is simply an environmental input and a bodily output. In man, reason (or choice) intervenes. Emotions (or passions) were vital to his viewpoint since he thought of them as changing the flow of animal spirits, the basic determinant of action. Descartes suggested that there are six primitive emotions: admiration, love, hate, desire, joy and sadness. These combine to produce the introspective feelings which we regard as emotion. However, he also drew attention to the place of physiology and bodily functions in emotion. He regarded overt emotional behaviour as the result of instinctive attempts at achieving suitable responses to given environmental conditions.

Descartes believed emotions to have four main functions. They cause: (1) the appropriate flow of animal spirits in the body; (2) the body to be held ready for the various environmental goal objects which come its way; (3) the soul to desire these objects, which nature has already told us are of use; and (4) a persistence of the desire for these objects.

Descartes regarded the actual course taken by the emotions as beginning with an object in the environment which, via the sense organs and nerves, creates an impression in the pineal gland. This causes the soul to apprehend the stimulus and also causes the animal spirits in the brain and nerves to become active. These spirits act on the pineal gland to convert the feeling which is already there into a passion (emotion). Thus Descartes distinguishes between passions (in the soul), bodily commotion (in the viscera) and action (overt movement). However, although his view of emotion is considerably more sophisticated than previous ideas, and although he lays much emphasis on emotion as basic to behaviour, the problem of the relation between emotion and reason (and also between mental and bodily factors in emotion) is still very apparent. His theory of emotion can be summarized as suggesting that emotion intervenes between stimulus and response, causing the response to be less rational than it otherwise would have been.

After Descartes, the next significant discussion of emotion is to be found in Darwin's *Expression of the Emotions in Man and Animals* (1872). He stressed overt action as the biologically significant aspect of emotion and emphasized the importance of causative environmental stimulation. Also, of course, his theory of evolution pointed to the continuity between man and animals with respect to emotion, as well as in every other way. Shortly following this, James (1884) brought together the ideas of Descartes and Darwin and with a neat reversal of the commonsense view produced what was effectively the first psychological theory of emotion. James's theory will be discussed at length later, but, in summary, he suggested that the perception of emotional stimuli leads both to visceral reactions and to overt muscular reactions. The feeling of these reactions (i.e. cortical feedback from them) *is* the emotional experience. We hear the lion roar, run and then feel afraid. James's theory was important in that it pointed to a relationship between emotional stimuli, emotional behaviour and emotional experience. In fact, it is James who provided the obvious and necessary stimulus to academic thought about emotion. He removed the emphasis from considerations of how emotion might function.

MODERN APPROACHES TO EMOTION

Since James, the experimental and theoretical work on emotion has diversified considerably. Bindra (1970) provides a concise breakdown of the various experimental approaches. These have been clearly related to emotion as feeling, emotion as response, and the stimuli which produce emotion. (1) Emotional experience (or recognition): this refers to emotion as subjectively reported by man and as inferred by him about other men and about animals. (2) Emotional arousal: referring to changes in internal bodily processes, i.e. visceral, somatic and neural function, as produced by environmental stimuli. (3) Emotional action: referring to overt response patterns, obvious behaviour. (4) Emotional stimuli: here the stress has been on the stimulus features of the physical or social environment that produces (1), (2) and (3). This last line of attack carries an immediately obvious problem, its implicit circularity; it is difficult to define emotional stimuli independently of emotional responses. However, it has led to two research strategies—first, one aimed at finding what stimuli will produce a given range of emotional responses; and second, the selection of a particular stimulus pattern and a determination of what responses this will elicit under various organismic conditions, such as hormonal change.

Theoretically, the aim over the last 80 years or so has been to define emotion and to find a place for it in behaviour theory. Bindra again provides a cogent analysis of the three major approaches which have developed. The most common of these specifies emotion as a *unique* process. However, ideas on the workings of this process have taken many forms. As we have seen, James (1884), for example, viewed it as a 'feeling' of bodily changes stemming from a perception of an 'exciting' fact. Wenger (1950) regarded it as visceral reaction, Cannon (1927) as neural thalamic impulses which are generated by the release of cortical inhibition. Or Arnold (1950) regarded it as an appraisal in the brain of sensory stimuli, resulting in an 'emotional attitude' which produces the 'emotional experience', and Lindsley (1951) as behavioural activation due to arousal of the brain-stem reticular formation. There are many such theories, some of which will be discussed in detail later. However, none has gained general acceptance. This is probably because the idea of emotion as a single process cannot cater for all the data which have been gathered from empirical studies. And the studies themselves have been concentrated on very different aspects of emotion.

Emotion has sometimes been analysed as an intervening variable, anchored to observable stimuli and responses. McDougall's (1928) instinct theory, for example, posits an 'emotional impulse' which links stimuli and responses. Or Brown and Farber (1951) describe emotion within a Hullian framework. The third approach has the advantage of immediately fitting emotion into general behaviour theory. It explains all emotional phenomena without any theoretical recourse to emotion; a single set of processes are hypothesized to account for emotion, for motivation and for perception. Bindra (1969) and Leeper (1965) provide examples of such theories. If the theories which adopt this broad strategy can be judged as 'good' theories (see below) they are perhaps to be preferred since they make considerable gains in parsimony. However, this remains to be seen.

The more recent theories of emotion can also be analysed in terms of their main emphasis. Such a breakdown points to at least five major approaches: (1) emotions as conscious experiences, differentiated subjectively (for example, the psychoanalytically oriented theories); (2) emotions as psychological states (particularly cognitive) emphasizing either the autonomic nervous system and/ or the limbic system (for example, Lindsley; Arnold); (3) emotions as concerned with adaptation (for example, Plutchik); (4) emotions as motivational (for example, Leeper); (5) emotions as one aspect of behaviour (for example, Millenson).

Finally, an even broader analysis, and one which will be used in this book, is simply into those theories which are primarily cognitive, those which are primarily physiological, those which are primarily behavioural, and to some extent those which are primarily experiential.

It should be clear from what has been said so far that rather than simplifying the layman's view of emotion, modern academic psychology complicates it even further. Theory and research have stemmed from and developed the many intuitive meanings which emotion already has. More complexity is added to this increasingly complex picture by each line of enquiry appearing in several contexts. Most aspects of psychology are relevant to emotion. As will be explained below, it is hoped that the structure of this book will aid understanding of these various areas and approaches. However, before this, mention must be made of some more general issues. In considering emotion it is necessary to evaluate many theories. There will follow a discussion of some problems which should be borne in mind in any appreciation of emotion. Some of these are germane to particular approaches such as the cognitive. Others occur with regularity across the whole sphere of emotion and indeed throughout much of psychology. Also, recent ideas have begun to complete the circle and to take views of emotion from academic psychology back to intuitive meanings and their everyday input.

SOME BASIC PROBLEMS

At present, there are no right or wrong answers to the problems discussed below. Although they are pressing and important to the study of emotion, they have tended to be dealt with in idiosyncratic and arbitrary ways. Each investigator produces equally good solutions and an equally cogent supportive argument. For this reason they are problems that the reader should bear in mind throughout this book and then draw personal conclusions.

Terminology

Within the literature on emotion many terms are employed quite freely. Their usage is inconsistent and they are seldom adequately defined. Not least of these is 'emotion' itself. Other words which have high association value but which nevertheless denote little are 'feeling', 'affect', and 'emotionality'. A similar lack of precision surrounds terms which refer to specific emotions, jealousy, fear, love, anger, for example (and, particularly, anxiety). To concentrate on 'emotion' it has sometimes been defined, for example, as a state of the organism which affects behaviour, and sometimes more directly as a response. When defined as a state, it is sometimes regarded as mentalistic, and sometimes as physiological. When defined as a response, it is sometimes seen as physiological and sometimes as behavioural. The particular everyday connotation of emotion which has provided the starting point for any one theorist or researcher has led to an individualistic and biased definition.

Occasional inconsistencies are even evident *within* as well as between those who study emotion.

When words such as feeling and affect are found in this book, it will be made clear whose usage is being followed. Otherwise they will be avoided. For the most part, the term emotion will itself be used broadly. In this way it is hoped that the reader will build up a general concept of emotion, and one which in fact reflects its everyday usage. It clearly does embody many different aspects at many levels of function. It is a large part of a complex subject.

Levels of discourse

The problem of the various levels of discourse to be found in the psychology of emotion has already been described. It devolves from the continuing division of emotion into experience, behaviour, physiological substrates and eliciting stimuli. Those who study emotion have their own preference for the terms in which they can most comfortably converse and presumably in which they regard emotion as most appropriately expressed. They may be restricted to one of the above types of discourse or they may be happy to handle them in combination. Whichever way, it is frequently difficult to compare the work and ideas of various researchers.

Subsuming the type of problem to be discussed here under the rubric of levels of discourse is perhaps mistaken since it implies that some 'levels' are higher (more worthy) than others. This in itself must be an arbitrary matter, since each level brings its own problems. However, as will become apparent throughout this book, it is now obvious that in attempting to account for emotion some aspects of it are less easy to ignore than others. Put another way, some levels of discourse are considerably more helpful than others.

The problems of regarding emotion primarily as a matter of personal experience are the most self-evident; they concern the validity and reliability of data. It is many years since the introspectionist approach to psychology was thrown into disrepute; however, it may be that the subject has grown enough to give something approaching introspection its place once more. The subjective report of 'how a person is feeling' or of what emotion a person is experiencing may provide useful information, and in some circumstances might well be essential. Ways have to be found of assessing the reliability of verbal report and to decide whether one person's 'anger' is the same as the next's. From one viewpoint, results from any studies of emotion which stress subjective experience can be regarded as no more than indicative, as productive of hypotheses which can be more rigorously tested. From another viewpoint, accounts of the subjective experience of emotion should not be cast aside too easily. They may have much which is of value to the psychologist.

These are problems which are also an integral part of any discussion of emotional stimuli. How can we know that a stimulus is 'emotional' without finding that it leads to emotional behaviour or emotional experience? It is difficult to define the stimulus independently of the response. For example, commonsense or intuition (i.e. everyday observation) tells us that if we jostle a man in the street he is likely to become angry, that is, he may shout at us or perhaps hit out. More systematic observations may confirm us in this belief. We would happily maintain our hypothesis until we met the man who ignored our jostling or who ran from it. Is jostling no longer an anger-producing stimulus? Did our man 'feel' anger but not show it in the usual way (statistically speaking)? Does jostling also act as a fear stimulus? It is difficult to break the circle between stimulus and response. Of course, if a definition of emotional stimuli can be made independently of the responses which they produce then these problems fade away. But this has not usually been done. It is similar to the problem which, for example, has faced learning theorists in their considerations of punishment.

Research and theory into the physiology of emotion has produced a vast literature, but has been beset by the insoluble problems of reductionism. As will be seen in Chapter 3, the physiological approach to emotion has been focused largely on the possible emotional functions of the autonomic nervous system (ANS) and the central nervous system (CNS)—mainly the limbic system. Subjectively, the reason for this emphasis is easy to see. For example, we can 'feel' our pulse rate increase and our face become red when we are experiencing what we have been taught to call anger. However, if this approach is taken too far, then psychology (as the study of behaviour) becomes reduced to physiology. It is conceivable that this is all to the good, though there are many psychologists who would not agree. Clearly, psychology can gain much from physiology, and physiological fact may well lead to useful psychological predictions. Basically, there are two important questions which require an affirmative answer before we can argue that a reductionist approach is justified: (1) *Can* we reduce whatever we are studying to another level? (2) Is it useful to make this reduction? In studying the physiology of emotion these questions have usually received scant attention. The physiology has often been far removed from behaviour, and the physiological speculations have been frequently far removed from physiological fact. And, of course, there are the inevitable problems which vitiate most attempts to compare results from psychological physiological studies of emotion—essentially different languages are being used and different experimental techniques followed. Emotion can be *studied* physiologically, but as this is but one of its many aspects it is unlikely that there could be any justification for reducing it entirely to this level. Also, as will be seen later, there is even some doubt about whether physiological arousal is necessary to emotion.

Finally, there is a large body of work on emotion in which the main emphasis or level of discourse is on overt behaviour. Such work can have the advantages of increased objectivity. It is methodologically 'purer' to deal with observable behaviour than with more hypothetical experiences or feelings. However, this level of discourse is often criticized for oversimplifying complex problems.

Internal feelings which we 'know' subjectively to exist are disregarded and little notice paid to physiological changes. The behavioural approach is good from the viewpoint of sound investigation, but gives less than the whole picture. It omits cognitive accounts, the significance of which has been pointed to recently with increasing frequency.

Animals or humans—artificiality

Studies of emotion have been carried out on a large variety of species—from mice to man—and in the earlier days the primary emphasis was by no means on human investigations. The reasons for (what at first sight might seem to be) the surprisingly large number of animal studies in this field are quite straightforward, as they are in other areas of psychology. The first is rooted in the problem of artificiality. Are human 'laboratory' emotions, emotions at all? it is notoriously difficult to evoke human emotion in a laboratory setting, even with powerful, intense stimuli. The subjects' responses are tempered by the situation. In passing, it is worth noting that this idea brings out the 'language problem'. For example, we can say that the laboratory nature of a study will change the stimuli used from what they would otherwise have been in real life. They become fresh stimuli evoking new responses. Or we can say that the subject 'knows' that it is only an experiment and cuts down the tenor of his reactions accordingly. Either way, however, the result is artificiality.

The most obvious way around this problem is to use stimuli which are intense or powerful enough to produce responses which approximate to our everyday observations of emotion (although there is some circularity in this argument). Alternatively, the subjects may be so completely deceived that they are unaware that they are taking part in an experiment. The ethical objections to each of these solutions are immediately apparent. The other possibility is to use infrahuman subjects. Here, any objection that artificiality will lead to distorted results is weakened, particularly if laboratory-raised animals have been used; their 'natural' home is the laboratory. With such subjects a much closer control can be legitimately exercised over their emotional behaviour, making it that much more likely that its determinants will be found.

However, many psychologists would question the validity of using animal subjects at all in the study of emotion. Are 'animal' emotions emotion? They might argue that animals do not have emotions, or if they do then they may be so different from human emotion as to make comparison fruitless. Such an attitude would be most likely to be held by those who view emotion primarily at an experiential level. How can we meaningfully speak of the subjective experiences and feelings of animals? Conversely, it can be argued that if the determinants of emotion can be elucidated by well-defined and methodologically sound animal studies then they will lead to hypotheses which will be more easy to test at the human level. So the argument twists on, and it is for the individual to reach personal conclusions.

The relationship of emotion to other fields of study

The difficulty in defining emotion and the problem of its general breadth as a concept have led it to overlap considerably with some of the other equally wide concepts with which psychology abounds. Four in particular will be met frequently in this book: cognition, drive, motivation and arousal. Three of these will be briefly discussed below, leaving cognition for later, since it has become so integral to an understanding of emotion that it will be returned to many times.

In some form or another the concept of motivation has existed for as long as humans have been attempting to account for their own behaviour. It makes no reference to experience or to any behavioural fact, but is used as a *hypothetical* cause of behaviour. It is conceived of as a force which lies behind behaviour and which therefore aids in our understanding of it. Although not an essential construct in explanations of behaviour, motivation has tended to appear in most accounts of behaviour and has frequently led to highly productive investigations.

An attempt to give a firm theoretical and empirical basis to motivation is embodied in the idea of drive, taking over as it did from instinct. Like instincts, drives were first seen as basic to motivation, as a way of objectifying the subjective, and as of biological importance. These three qualities were itemized as a result of the idea that drive has a solid physiological foundation (in bodily need). If this were in fact the case then the concept of motivation would become less hypothetical than it is. From these hopeful, if vague, formulations four main lines of research developed. (1) Hunger and thirst were studied as central dynamic states, not just as stimuli. (2) It was demonstrated that animals become more active with increases in biological need, i.e. drives have general energizing effects. (3) Evidence accrued to support the idea of specific hungers. (4) Drive strength was measured. Although each of these avenues of research provided interesting information in its own right, it did not lead to any generally acceptable definition of drive. Instead there were many definitions, each of which could be objected to in some way. Some were too loose and others too tight; sometimes drive was regarded as a stimulus, sometimes as a central state.

At this point in the development of the drive concept, two further problems came to light. (1) How many drives are there? There may be just one which has a general effect, or there may be many. Should we invoke a new drive to account for every new sort of behaviour which is observed? (2) Do drives add to the direction of behaviour, or to its energy, or to both?

In the midst of this confusion, Hull (1943) gave drive a much firmer theoretical basis. Briefly, he related it to physiological need and viewed it as similar to, but independent of, habit. He regarded it as energizing behaviour and, when it was reduced, as reinforcing behaviour. He saw it as nonspecific and nondirectional. Recent evidence concerning these and other defining characteristics of drive point to it as a not very robust concept. However, Hull's formulations were the most far-reaching, and so when the term is used in the present text it will be in the Hullian sense.

The other concept which inevitably keeps popping up within this book is that of arousal (or activation). Some psychologists (for example, Duffy, 1941) altogether replace 'emotion' with 'arousal'. This is yet another hypothetical construct, and one which is closely related to drive. Various theorists (for example, Duffy, 1951; Bindra, 1969; Lindsley, 1951) believe the basis of drive to be the hypothetical physiological state of arousal. The fundamental suggestion is that the diffuse projection system in the reticular formation of the brain enhances the reception of specific stimuli and thus serves to influence any learning that is occurring at the time. Although, like drive, arousal is a heavily used concept, hard evidence to support it is not abundant. This state of affairs is worsened by the theoretical structure on which the concept of arousal is built. This depends on the notion that for a behavioural task of a given complexity there is an optimum level of arousal for optimal performance. Thus is derived the notorious inverted U-shaped function relating arousal to performance. It is approaching the optimal level or retreating from it. Overall, we are ignorant of any individual response patterning in arousal and there is little evidence for any individual differences.

Although there is little empirical support for the validity of a unitary concept of arousal, it has been frequently used in accounts of emotion. it is often accepted that emotional behaviour occurs with high levels of arousal and that different emotions enjoy different positions on the arousal continuum. If physiological arousal involves pushing the sympathetic nervous system into action, then this is a reasonable idea, but it does not account for all emotional reactions or experience. A necessary condition for emotion to occur must be an aroused organism, but arousal need not imply emotion. A similar set of physiological changes may be seen in hard physical exercise. The general view adopted here is that arousal as a unitary concept is not very useful, particularly to our understanding of emotion. It is difficult to define and awkward to measure. As will be seen, people differ in their physiological response patterns and different situations may have similar or different physiological effects.

THE STRUCTURE OF THE BOOK

The various problems described above led to the form taken by the previous editions of this book. The form of the present edition evolved from these together with the far-reaching changes which have taken place since 1978. The aim is to put emotion into a perspective for the reader. As so much of the area is characterized by theories or models, Chapter 2 presents a number of these in summary form. Although many of these appear again in their specific contexts later in the book, some points of criticism and some attempts at co-ordinating comments are made. Mainly, they are collected together to give some idea of the development of theoretical viewpoints of emotion and to allow a comparative basis for their evaluation.

Following Chapter 2 are three chapters which each emphasize different approaches to the study of emotion: physiological, cognitive, behavioural, philosophical and phenomenological. After these are three further chapters which deal with the study of emotion as it cuts across psychology. These are emotional development, the social-psychological approach to the expression and recognition of emotion and emotion in social relationships, and abnormal emotion.

Throughout these six chapters an attempt is made to present the major empirical facts and wherever possible to fit these into the existing theories. Also, where appropriate, critical comment is made. Chapter 9, is more speculative, giving consideration to individual differences in emotion, the emotional impact of the environment and the relationship between emotion and culture or art. Finally, Chapter 10 offers an overview, some implications and personal conclusions.

The major aim of the remainder of this book is to present a balanced view of research into emotion, be it theoretical or empirical. Also, it is hoped to give an indication of the richness of the subject and of the considerable advances which have occurred in the general understanding of it during the last few years.

2

Theories of Emotion

There are many theories of emotion. They stem from various fundamental assumptions, they stress various problems, and they can be distinguished in their breadth, and in the degree to which they are anchored to empirical fact. The present chapter contains summaries of some of these theories. At this stage, no evidence will be presented either for or against them and evaluation and criticism will be kept to a minimum. The aim is to provide some idea of the breadth of thought which has been put into theorizing about emotion. Also, it is intended that this chapter may be used as a comparative reference guide to representative aspects of the many approaches which have been made to the subject. To describe all theories of emotion would necessitate a book in itself, so the number has been restricted. Those included have been chosen either because they are centrally important to modern thought in emotion and/or because they illustrate the breadth of the subject. Many of the theories which are described here will be analysed in greater detail later in the book. There, when appropriate, they will also receive criticism. Others, judged to be of less importance, will only be encountered in this chapter and the interested reader should study the references given for a fuller exposition ot them.

Any sample of theories of emotion could be organized in a number of ways—according to the type of approach or emphasis which they take, their chronological order of appearance, the extent of their influence, and so on. Whichever way is followed leads to some confusion. The plan used here was devised to minimize such confusion and to allow similarities and differences between the theories to be seen as easily as possible. The earlier theories are arranged in rough chronological order and the more recent are gathered into a broad classification according to the type of approach on which they depend and the assumptions which they share. There are examples of theories which highlight arousal, motivation or physiological mechanisms those which stress behaviour, those which stem from the psychoanalytic and experiential traditions, those which emphasize cognition, and finally those which could be termed grand theories since they combine a number of approaches and even in some cases relate emotion to personality theory.

As will be seen the divisions are not always distinct. There are a number of reasons for overlap between them. First, the confusion inherent in some theories makes them difficult to categorize. Second, some theories place equal emphasis on more than one aspect of the subject, making classification somewhat arbitrary. When this is the case and where there are obvious grounds for comparison, it will be indicated. Finally, the theories to be described differ from one another in their breadth of approach, some being very narrow and biased, others broad and all-inclusive.

When reading the summaries which follow it is worth keeping in mind the problems mentioned in Chapter 1. It is here that they will first become evident. Also, it is instructive to note that many of the ideas expressed by the early theorists have been echoed in the last few years, although in more sophisticated form.

1. EARLY THEORIES

W. James (the James–Lange theory)

The James–Lange theory of emotion is probably the most famous of all in that it generated a lasting controversy amongst psychologists. Also, it has acted as a stimulus for many more recent theories and a great deal of research (see Chapters 3 and 4). The theory is usually attributed to James and to Lange since it put forward separately by each (James, 1884; Lange, 1885), although James was its main and clearest exponent.

James began by limiting his field of consideration to those emotions which have 'a distinct bodily expression'. He was attempting to distinguish between mental processes which have no obvious physiological concomitants and those in which straightforward, easily observable changes occur. He suggested that the everyday way of regarding these grosser emotions is: (1) we mentally perceive some fact, (2) this produces some mental affect (called the emotion) and (3) this in turn produces the bodily expression. His view was the converse of this:

> 'the bodily changes follow directly the PERCEPTION of the existing fact, and that our feeling of the same changes as they occur IS the emotion'. (1884, p.189; italics and capitals his)

So, for example, rather than face some public performance to which we are unused *at this point we become anxious* and then have 'butterflies in our stomach', tremble and stutter; in James's terms we face our public performance, have 'butterflies', tremble and stutter and *as a result feel anxious*. He was therefore (as have so many emotion theorists in lesser ways) making a *volte face* on what had gone before, the nub of his theory resting on the notion that the visceral discharges associated with some environmental situation actually lead to the emotion as we know it.

The argument based largely on introspection which James used to support this theory can be reduced to a few main points. He asserted that any sensation has extremely complex physiological manifestations and that these are all felt, some obviously, some more obscurely. He suggested that we imagine some strong emotion and then try to push from our consciousness all of the feelings of the bodily symptoms associated with it. He maintained that if we do this successfully there will be nothing left; we shall have completely exorcised the emotion. Finally, he cited many examples of how everyday situations lead directly to these complex, strong (bodily) feelings (seeing a friend peering over the edge of a cliff, for example) and argued support of his case from the idea of how easy we find it to classify both abnormal and normal behaviour according to bodily symptoms.

The James–Lange theory can be summarized simply as in Figure 1. This represents in diagrammatic form the way in which emotions are experienced as James saw it. (It is worthwhile to compare this figure with Figure 2, which represents the Cannon–Bard theory in a similar way.)

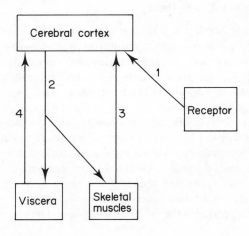

Figure 1.   Diagrammatic representation of the James–Lange theory. Arrows show direction of function

The main points of James's theory then is that afferent feedback from disturbed organs produces the feeling aspect of emotion. The implication is that the cortical activity which comes from this feedback is the actual feeling and that the conscious awareness of this feeling is the emotion itself. It is important to bear in mind Izard's (1972; 1977) reminder that as well as emphasizing the role of the viscera in emotion, James also afforded a similar role to the voluntary muscles. In so doing he laid the groundwork for a search for general bodily patterns and facial expressions in emotion, the latter recently assuming more and more significance in research and theory (for example, Ekman, 1984; Izard, 1977).

Overall, James may be fairly said to have produced the first theory which assumed the existence of discrete emotions, these having an instinctive basis and being separable from certain feelings. Thus for example stimuli which come from colours and sound lead to non emotional feelings on a pleasant/

unpleasant dimension, and equally nonemotional feelings of interest/excitement that come from intellectual activity. These points have all had an influence on more recent theories of emotion.

W.B. Cannon (the Cannon–Bard theory)

Cannon's ideas were the first of any note to appear after those of James. His approach usually took the form of criticism of James (see Chapters 3 and 4) and then a statement of an alternative theory (1915; 1927; 1931; 1932). At different times, Cannon's theory has been referred to as a thalamic theory, the first of the emergency theories, or as a neurophysiological theory. This last gives the clue as to which it is often described as the Cannon–Bard theory, since much of the experimental work on which it was based was carried out separately by Bard (for example, 1928; 1934; 1950).

Cannon's attack on James will be left for later. For now it is enough to say that he based his own theory on evidence (for example, Bard, 1928; Cannon and Britton, 1927; Head, 1921) which could be best interpreted as suggesting that the neurophysiological side of emotional expression is subcortical, or, more particularly, thalamic. He argued that all emotions depend on a similar chain of events. An environmental situation stimulates receptors which relay impulses to the cortex. The cortex, in turn, stimulates thalamic processes which act in particular patterns corresponding to particular emotional expressions. Cannon believed that nothing more specific is required than that the neurons in the thalamus be 'released'. He maintained that the nervous discharge from the

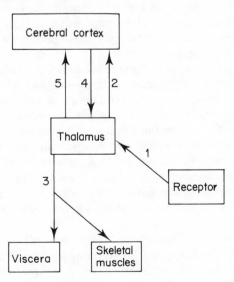

Figure 2.   Diagrammatic representation of the Cannon–Bard theory. Arrows show direction of function.

thalamus has two functions, first to excite muscles and viscera and second to relay information back to the cortex. Thus in Cannon's words:

'the peculiar quality of the emotion is added to simple sensation when the thalamic processes are aroused'. (1927, p.119; italics his)

This implies that when the thalmus discharges, we experience the emotion at almost the same time that bodily changes occur.

Cannon's theory of emotion is diagrammatically summarized in Figure 2. Basically, Cannon brought into regard the importance of the thalamus and in so doing produced some cogent arguments against James, although these have since been seriously questioned. However, as will be seen later, the neurophysiological picture is far more complicated than Cannon painted it. At least he drew attention to the neurophysiology of emotion and hence acted as the progenitor of much research and theory.

W. McDougall

McDougall (1910; 1923; 1928) attempted to distinguish between emotions and feelings, an endeavour made somewhat similarly by the few of the more Gestalt-based European psychologists (for example, Klages, 1950; Krueger, 1928). His theory also depended on some basic biological considerations (compare with Plutchik's theory). McDougall believed that the capacity to approach beneficial goals is fundamental to psychology and that all behaviour stems from seeking food and escaping or avoiding noxious stimuli. He argued that what we call emotions and feelings occur as adjuncts to these basic processes; they come from the way in which we perceive our environment and our various bodily changes.

McDougall proposed that two feelings—pleasure and pain—modify all of our goal-directed behaviour. However, he also regarded human beings as more complex than this; they are cognitive and have expectations, they fuse together many experiences and have odd concentrations of feelings. McDougall suggested that it is these cognitions that set us apart from other organisms and direct that we no longer alternate between pleasure and pain but continually range over a complexity of feelings. McDougall believed that through everyday usage these complex feelings have become known as the various emotions. He then argued that in fact these are not 'real' emotions and that science would profit if the term were not used in their description (see Duffy for a similar argument).

As is well known, McDougall put instincts foremost in his accounts of psychology, seeing them as providing the impetus for all thought and action. He also argued that all instincts have knowing, feeling and striving components, with some emotional excitement in evidence as well. Doubtless depending to an extent on James and Cannon, he suggested that this emotional facet of instinct is reflected by discreet visceral and bodily changes. He also felt that emotions can be distinguished from the cognitive processes which go with them. McDougall was implying that perception triggers emotion. For example, an organism might perceive a threatening stimulus; this would provoke it both to flee and to feel fear, the whole process reflecting a basic survival need or instinct. But McDougall is by no means clear how the instrumental and emotional aspects of such reactions become connected, and in his descriptions usually made little precise reference to the matter of bodily responses or cognition.

McDougall's schema for emotion proper began with a statement that throughout the evolution of man goals became more specific and goal-directed behaviour became more specialized. The result was more precise and particularized bodily adjustment. The experience of each of these well-differentiated strivings gave the clear quality of a 'primary emotion'. If two or more of these main bodily reactions conflict, from the experiential point of view this results in 'the secondary or blended emotions' (1928), such complexities as shame or reproach.

McDougall also made these main points of comparison between complex feelings (not really emotions) and emotions proper (whether primary or secondary). (1) Complex feelings are conditioned by success or failure in our strivings and therefore colour any subsequent impulse that may be similar. 'True' emotions are quite independent of this. They are simply what makes each impulse distinctive and so do not affect any later strivings (2) McDougall believed that complex feelings were restricted to man since they depend for their appearance on the development of cognition. Real emotions must however, have appeared much earlier on the evolutionary scale. (3) Finally, named complex feelings such as hope and anxiety are not entities. They just reflect ill-defined ranges of experience and feelings in which there is no blending. Conversely, McDougall viewed each primary emotion as long-lasting; it is 'an enduring feature of the mental strucure of the organism' (1928). Each emotion is only associated with desire and therefore unlike complex feelings, conflicting desires may produce blends of emotion. Allowing that this was a very subjective analysis, it is possible to appreciate what McDougall was suggesting by comparing, in an everyday sense, the behaviours that tend to accompany 'complex feelings' of anxiety and hope with those that occur with 'true' emotions of, say, fear and curiosity.

J.W. Papez

After Cannon, Papez's (1937) theory of emotion was the next to have a neurophysiological basis. His starting point was the idea that in lower vertebrates there are anatomical and physiological connections on the one hand between the cerebral hemisphere and hypothalmus, and on the other between the cerebral hemisphere and the dorsal thalamus. These relationships become further elaborated in the mammalian brain. Papex believed emotion to be mediated by such cortico-hypothalamic interconnections.

Papez state simply that emotion implies behaviour (expression) and feeling (experience or subjective feeling) and quoted Bard's (1929) results as showing that emotional expression depends on the hypothalamus. But he viewed the cortex as being necessary for the mediation of subjective emotional experience. And further, he suggested that emotional expression and emotional experience are phenomena which can be dissociated from one another in man. Papez also provided a general anatomical picture of the possible structures involved in a corticothalamic mechanism of emotion. Because by now this is a somewhat dated view it is not worth describing in detail. However, Papez believed that his hypothesized circuits could account for emotion as arising either from cortical or from hypothalamic activity.

Clearly, Papez's theory depended heavily on neurophysiologizing. However, it was couched in terms such that it could account for the apparently different origins of emotion, for emotion felt and emotion expressed, and for the emotional colouring which seems to be present in many other nonemotional experiences.

J.B. Watson

Watson (1929; 1930) provided the first of the clearly behaviourist theories of emotion. However, he stressed the physiological aspects of emotion as well as the behavioural. Thus:

> *An emotion is an hereditary "pattern-reaction" involving profound changes of the bodily mechanism as a whole, but particularly of the visceral and glandular systems'.* (1929, p.225; italics his)

Given this definition, Watson went on to distinguish between emotional and instinctive reactions. He did this by asserting that an emotional stimulus shocks an organism into a state of chaos, at least. So, to Watson, emotions were disorganizing.

On the basis of observational work with children, Watson postulated that there are three types of fundamental emotional reaction—fear, rage and love. However, he maintained that such words often cause confusion and that it might therefore be better to term them X, Y and Z. He suggested that the X (fear) dimension is caused by: (1) sudden removal of support from an infant, (2) loud sounds, and (3) mild but sudden stimuli when an infant is just falling asleep or awakening. Typical responses are breath-catching, hand-clutching, eye-closing, lip-puckering and crying. He viewed the Y (rage) dimension as caused by 'hampering an infant's movements'. Responses to this include crying, screaming, body-stiffening, limb-slashing and breath-holding. Finally, he saw the Z (love) dimension as caused by any gentle manipulation, particular of the erogenous zones of the body, responses to which include smiling, gurgling and cooing. Watson believed each of these patterns of reaction to be built-in and evident from birth.

Watson's main contributions to the study of emotion were to offer this three-dimensional theory and to place emphasis on behaviour rather than on internal states and feelings. This, and his classic study with Rayner (Watson and Rayner, 1920) on Little Albert, proved to be the foundation on which later behavioural concepts of emotion have been built. In the way in which Watson was the general father of behaviourism, so he was the particular father of the behaviourist approaches to emotion.

General points

The five theories of emotion discussed so far might by now be reasonably described as the classical theories. Perhaps the most interesting point about them is that they contain in one form or another most of the ideas and concepts which can be found in the more modern theories and models. This will become clear throughout the remainder of this chapter. For now these ideas can be listed quite simply. Some or all of the early theorists: (1) saw emotion as a system which both affects and is affected by other systems; (2) saw both similarities and differences between the various emotions; (3) viewed some emotions as fundamental or primary and others as derived or secondary, hinting at a nature/nurture division; (4) tended to suggest that emotions have ranges of intensity which changes their quality when beyond certain levels; (5) viewed emotions as energizing or motivational in their effects; (6) suggested intricate links between emotion and cognition; (7) in occasionally stressing voluntary muscle involvement and the expressive side of emotion hinted at the possibility of emotional control.

Even though the theories of emotion which appeared in the first part of this century now inevitably look a little naive, they clearly provided the foundation for present views. Also, by being concerned with such a large range and variety of behaviours, feelings, cognitions and physiological changes, they highlighted the enormous complexity of emotion. With one or two not especially noteworthy exceptions, the more recent theories of emotion have added to this complexity.

2. THEORIES BASED ON MOTIVATION, AROUSAL AND/OR PHYSIOLOGY

E. Duffy

Duffy has expressed her view of emotion many times (for example, 1934; 1941; 1962) but probably put it best in her 1941 paper, which she began:

'For many years the writer has been of the opinion that "emotion", as a scientific concept is worse than useless'.

This sets the scene perfectly, for Duffy tries to explain away emotion rather than to account for it, her argument being couched in terms of a behaviourally oriented activation theory. Her views on activation in general can be read in *Activation and Behaviour* (1962).

Duffy's first (1934) reason for suggesting that the term emotion be dropped from scientific usage was that it had been used mainly to refer to the extreme end of a continuum of behaviour, but one which anomalously involved a sharp non-continuation between emotion and nonemotion. She argued that a behavioural continuum and discreet categories of behaviour are likely to have different underlying constructs. Duffy preferred the idea that emotional phenomena are separate aspects of responses occurring in continua.

In 1941, Duffy developed her argument further. She suggested that emotion as it is commonly conceived refers to how we feel and act towards a situation which we expect to be important; our expectations may be positive or negative. So, we shall feel angry and perhaps afraid only if we are blocked from attaining some goal. Duffy hypothesizes that such a state of emotion must involve a change in energy level; excitement represents a higher energy level and depression a lower energy level. Energy level itself is dependent on the stimulus situation. It will increase either when we are blocked or when a block is removed; conversely, there is a decrease only when a goal is so effectively blocked that we give up altogether.

Duffy then widened her argument to include the idea that all behaviour is motivated. She suggested that without motivation there would be no activity, and that what is called emotion simply represents an extreme of motivation, i.e. energy, to argue which, Duffy must have been ignoring her own experiences. But, she then asked, how do we know when behaviour is extreme enough to be called emotional? Her answer was that there is no criterion for this, since emotion-producing behaviour does not differ in kind from other behaviour—to Duffy other responses follow the same principles. In her terms, all responses are adjustive responses which enable the organism to adapt.

From Duffy's standpoint, the second characteristic of emotion as commonly conceived is that it is disorganizing (see Leeper). However, she thought that this apparent disorganization is a function of behaviour which occurs at very high or at very low energy levels. This is not a function of 'emotion' since disorganization is also found at energy levels not extreme enough to be normally called emotions, for example the stammer of an enthusiastic child or the double fault of the over-involved tennis player. This, of course, is representing emotion in terms of the hypothetical inverted U-shaped function relating arousal to performance (see Chapter 1).

Finally, Duffy set out to deal with what she regarded as the commonly proposed fact of its conscious awareness. We tend to feel that our conscious experiences of emotion are different from our conscious experiences of anything else. Duffy argued that such a conscious awareness involves awareness of the environmental situation which leads to the emotional state, awareness of bodily changes, and awareness of a set for response in the situation. Duffy maintained that these factors also make up any nonemotional state of consciousness.

To summarize, Duffy breaks down emotion (and in fact all behaviour) into changes in: (1) level of energy, (2) organization and (3) conscious states, and suggests that each of these occurs on a continuum. The final stage in her argument is that it is meaningless to try to study emotion at all, because it is something which 'has no distinguishing characteristics' (1941). Instead, she suggests that *any* response should be considered according to its energy level (activation), how well it maintains goal-direction (organization-disorganization) and the environmental situation in response to which it occurs. Duffy's is a theory of non-emotion and has been so far overtaken by more sophisticated theorizing as to make it as hollow as she attempted to make emotion.

D.B. Lindsley

Lindsley's theory of emotion first appeared in 1950 and 1951. More recently (1957; 1970) he has extended it to broader aspects of behaviour. Essentially, it is similar to Duffy's theory in that it is based on the concept of arousal. However, it is expressed in neurophysiological rather than behavioural terms.

Lindsley's (1951) theory depended on his belief in five empirical findings. These are summarized below, although it should be borne in mind that some doubt has been cast on them by more recent thought and empirical work. (1) In emotion, the electroencephalogram (EEG) is characterized by desynchronization, i.e. alpha-blocking or activation. (2) EEG activation can be produced by stimulation of the brain-stem reticular formation, or of the sense modalities. (3) Synchrony is restored and EEG activation is abolished by destruction of the basal diencephalon. (4) The behaviour which occurs, at least in cats, if lesions appropriate to (3) above are produced is described by Lindsley as being opposite to that which is usually seen in emotional arousal. It is apathy, somnolence, etc. (5) Overlapping the cortically arousing EEG mechanism is that of the basal diencephalon, which is the substrate for the objective part of emotional expression.

Although Lindsley (1957; 1970) has added some empirical support to these basic points and has also revised some of the details of his theory, the fundamental idea remains the same: arousal/motivation mechanisms underlie emotion. He suggests that the mechanisms of arousal are the brain-stem reticular formation interacting with the diencephalic and limbic systems via the ascending reticular activating system. He also maintains that the limbic systems control emotional expression and emotional and motivational behaviour. He regards emotion as being expressed in three ways: (1) through cortical channels, for example thought, worry anxiety (cortical arousal); (2) through visceral channels, for example sweating, crying, in fact ANS function (cortical, diencephalic and brain-stem arousal); (3) through somatomotor channels, for example facial expression, muscle tension (somatomotor arousal).

Lindsley is a wide-ranging neural arousal theorist. Although his research and theory are important to emotion, he also takes in such phenomena as sleep wakefulness, alerting, attention, selective attention, vigilance and, of course, motivation. Such is the postulated ubiquity of function of the descending and ascending reticular systems, and of those other CNS structures with which they interact.

P.T. Young

Young's (1961) theory is unusual in that it is relatively modern, American, and yet somewhat isolated; it differs both in conception and language from many of the other theories described here. Although he leans heavily on the concept of arousal, Young distinguishes it from what he terms an hedonic dimension. He seems to be the last of the hedonic philosophers, although simultaneously an experimental psychologist.

Young does not speak of emotion *per se* but rather of affective processes and an hedonic continuum. He regards affective processes as varying in sign, intensity and duration. Thus, if naive organisms develop approach behaviour, he postulates that an underlying positive central affective process is at work; similarly, a negative affective process underlines withdrawal responses. Further, he suggest that affective processes can vary from maximally positive intensity to maximally negative—as shown by the development of preferences. And lastly, he maintains that affective processes can differ in duration. Young views these affective processes as spread along an hedonic continuum which ranges from extremely negative through an area of indifferences to extremely positive. Hedonic changes can occur in either direction, and from time to time may even be in opposition. This scheme leads to four possible types of affective change: increasing positive, decreasing positive, increasing negative and decreasing negative. (In some ways this is similar to Millenson's behaviourist ideas.)

Young proposes that affective processes are quite distinct from sensory processes and that their essential role is motivational, having a regulatory influence on behaviour. He postulates a series of principles and functions concerning affective processes. First, the principles: (1) stimulation has affective as well as sensory consequences; (2) affective arousal points the organism towards or away from a stimulus; (3) affective processes lead to motives; (4) the strength of a recent motive is related to various aspects of previous affective arousals (duration, intensity, frequency and recency); (5) motives also depend on learning—affective processes determine what will and will not be learned, but learning itself is simply practice, neurobehavioural change due to exercise; (6) affective processes can be conditioned—we learn 'how to feel' in given situations; (7) affective processes exert their regulatory function by influencing choice; (8) the final principle is very wide-ranging—neurobehavioural patterns themselves follow a pattern of organization which maximizes positive affective arousal and minimizes negative affective arousal.

Young suggests that affective processes have four main functions. (1) They activate. (2) They sustain and terminate behaviour. (3) They regulate behaviour. (4) They organize.

Essentially, Young is speaking of pleasantness and unpleasantness rather than emotion. These are affective processes arranged on an hedonic continuum which itself has an arousal function. The affective processes accompany all behaviour to some degree and themselves work according to a set of underlying principles, and in turn exercise various influences on behaviour.

D. Bindra

Bindra (1968; 1969) puts forward a neurophysiological theory of emotion, or more strictly, of emotion and motivation. He suggests that both emotional and motivational phenomena can best be accounted for in terms of one construct, that of the central motive state (CMS).

Bindra begins by denying that any useful distinction can be made between emotion and motivation and speaks instead of 'species typical', biologically useful actions. He suggests that such actions are an interaction between environmental stimuli (which he terms incentives) and physiological change. Bindra believes this interaction to take place in the brain and to involve joint environmental and physiological action on a common group of neurons. He maintains that this produces a CMS; this is not in itself a drive but is simply a

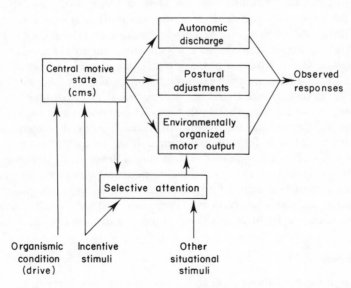

Figure 3. Bindra's central motive state mechanism taken from Bindra (1969). The figure shows two ways in which the hypothetical CMS can bring about species-typical action: (1) via organismic conditions and incentive stimuli from the environment, i.e. selective attention; (2) via effects on ssensory and motor mechanisms, i.e. motor facilitation or response bias

functional change in neurons which needs *both* an environmental stimulus and a physiological change before it will occur. Thus, for example, physiological hunger and sight, smell and taste of food are not by themselves enough to produce a CMS; they must occur together.

The hypothetical notion of how a CMS produces a species-typical action is shown in Figure 3. A CMS is thought to increase the probability of a response to certain environmental stimuli by altering the effectiveness of the sensory input—shown as 'selective attention' in the figure. Or a CMS may increase the likelihood of a particular action by altering neural discharge to appropriate autonomic and somatic motor sites—'motor facilitation' or 'response bias'. Bindra argues that this scheme is equally apposite to considerations of both emotion and motivation. This leads him to the view that many words traditionally used in discussions of emotion and motivation can be replaced by common terms. For example, CMS instead of emotion or emotional state and motive or motivational state; physiological condition instead of emotional predisposition and drive.

Two further aspects of Bindra's CMS ideas are worth summarizing. (1) He believes that CMSs can be classically conditioned. Their nature depends on the actual physical state and environmental stimuli involved in this conditioning stimulus and the unconditioned stimulus (incentive). (2) Bindra asserts that the CMS can be used to resolve many of the long-enduring problems in the study of emotion. For example, the occurrence of emotion has often been thought to depend on external stimuli, whereas that of motivation has been seen to depend on internal stimuli. CMS analysis puts these together and implies that the traditional distinction has been drawn because of a differences in the value of the determining conditions—a very wide environmental stimulus can create an emotional CMS, whereas physiological states for motivational CMSs are very specific. To take another example, emotional behaviour has often been thought of as disorganized (but see Leeper) and motivational behaviour as organized. Bindra argues that both types of behaviour can be organized or disorganized depending on when they are observed during individual development. Thus a lack of experience with a particular environmental stimulus will lead to disorganized responding. However, he also suggests that motivational patterns start early in development and occur frequently, whereas emotional patterns occur less frequently and involve more unusual situations. In this sense, he views motivation as organized and emotion as disorganized, but there seems to be little justification for this in terms of the CMS.

General points

Although the four theories described in this section differ in the degree to which they emphasize physiological mechanisms of emotion, they have a number of points in common. They each put emotion on a sort of continuum, be this of arousal, activation, motivation or pleasantness, and in so doing bracket emotion with motivation. Given the usual awkwardness of deciding where one is on an arousal curve, and in this case of deciding where emotion begins and all else finishes, the implication is that the concept of emotion should be done away with altogether. Indeed, Duffy states this overtly and Bindra replaces both emotion and motivation with central motive state. Lindsley almost casts emotion out as well, although not quite, and Young, even though allowing for more subtleties in emotion than the other three theorists, is basically speaking in terms of an all-embracing pleasantness/unpleasantness continuum.

Enough is not known about emotion to render the approach exemplified by these theorists neither pertinent or useful. As will be seen throughout the remainder of this book, emotion is very rich, complex and subtle, and appears to be subjectively, cognitively and behaviourally different from other experiences and acts. Even if emotion often does involve extremes of arousal, it would seem cavalier to throw out the concept entirely for this reason. Nothing would be achieved by this, either conceptually or empirically. On the other hand the theories discussed here are useful in that they help to draw attention to the physiological bases of emotion and to point to some of the problems of arousal with which the more general theorist of emotion has to contend. Also, of course, they point to possible links between emotion and motivation, both of which are of theoretical significance in attempting to account for psychological functioning.

3. BEHAVIOURAL THEORIES

H.F. Harlow and R. Stagner

It is difficult to categorize Harlow and Stagner's 1933 theory of emotion. It was quite clearly based on a conditioning model and owed much to Watson's behaviourism, and yet retained overtones of Cannon's physiologizing while maintaining a distinction between feelings and emotions. Briefly, they suggested that at the root of emotion are unconditioned affective responses (central physiological changes experienced as feelings). All emotions occur through becoming conditioned to these responses. The effect of this is to modify the original unconditioned affective state in two ways: (1) the range of eliciting stimuli is widened; (2) the violence of the original responses is dampened.

Harlow and Stagner made a number of extensions of their theory. (1) They suggested that although the basic emotional states are feelings, emotions may also reflect other conscious states. (2) Feelings are controlled thalamically, and sensations cortically. (3) Emotions are not innate; Harlow and Stagner simply suggested that there are unconditioned responses from which emotions develop. They believed the innate part of emotion to be the 'four fundamental feeling tones, pleasure, unpleasantness, excitement and depression'. (4) Emotion is distinct from feeling in that in emotion there is cognition of the outside situation. We are born with the capacity to feel but have to learn the various emotions.

Finally, Harlow and Stagner suggested a behaviouristic way in which the various emotions become differentiated from the original amorphous mass of feeling states. They argued, via introspective analysis, that the emotion labels which we attach to various experiences simply reflect our cognitions of the external stimuli involved and the meanings which they have for us. Any name which becomes appropriate to describe an affective state must therefore result from social conditioning. Harlow and Stagner viewed fear and rage, for example, as basically the same states. However, the situation which brings them about is one of threat, and if it is appropriate to attack then we call the state rage, whereas if it is appropriate to run we call it fear.

To summarize, Harlow and Stagner suggested that there are innate, undifferentiated, basic feelings. Emotions are the conditioned form of these which we learn to refer to in particular ways. The feelings, the emotional conditioning and the social learning of labels are each mediated cortically and subcortically.

J.R. Millenson

Millenson (1967) provides the closest approximation to a modern behaviourist theory of emotion, although he himself admits it is not more than a model. It is rooted in Watson, owes much to Plutchik and is inspired by Estes and Skinner's (1941) experimental paradigm for studying conditioned emotional behaviour.

Millenson's model rests on the fundamental proposition that emotional changes which he believes comes about through a process of classical conditioning, either enhance or suppress other, nonemotional behaviour. He argues that: (1) some emotions differ only in intensity; and (2) some emotions are basic and others are compounds of these. From this Millenson produces a three-dimensional system to describe all emotion, each dimension representing variations in emotional intensity. Dimension 1 is terror, anxiety or apprehension, such emotions sometimes suppressing and sometimes facilitating operant behaviour. Dimension 2 is made up of emotions of pleasure which enhance operant behaviour. Dimension 3 is anger; this facilitates some operant behaviour and leads to a greater likelihood of attack and destruction. Clearly, these dimensions are close to Watson's X, Y and Z factors.

Millenson suggests that more complex emotions develop from mixtures of these three dimensions, which he regards as primary. For example, we feel 'guilt' if we steal a book. In Millenson's terms such behaviour would possibly lead to both positive (possession of the book) and negative (being caught) consequences. This is psychological conflict, which Millenson views as often underlying our more complex emotional reactions. Also, he argues that at the human level emotional reactions often become complex owing to the very involved history of conditioning and reinforcement which we all have. Occasionally, great changes can be wrought in the mass of interrelated reinforcers which are controlling our behaviour at any time. For example, a friend may die, or we may suffer a loss of status. In either case we have suddenly been deprived of many reinforcers. We label our emotional reaction to this as sorrow. This argument leads Millenson to an interesting conjecture concerning a possible difference between human and animal emotion. He suggests that we may well be correct in believing certain emotions (such as sorrow) to be essentially human. There are simply no conditions in the infrahuman world which are complex enough to produce them—it is not necessarily that animals are incapable of them.

Millenson's view of emotion is extremely behaviouristic. He concerns himself with little more than observable behaviour and the environmental conditions which he believes to control it. In this singlemindedness, Millenson's ideas are unique amongst the more recent formulations of emotion and have been of little influence.

J.A. Gray

Gray (1971) also puts forward a theory of emotion in the behavioural tradition. As will be seen later it is a theory which is relevant to the development of emotion and which has implications for abnormal emotion.

Gray views emotion as comprising three distinct systems each of which is grounded in relationships between reinforcing stimuli and response systems. (1) When *approach* predominates the reinforcing stimulus is a conditioned stimulus for reinforcement of non-punishment. (2) When *behavioural inhibition* predominates the reinforcing stimulus is a conditioned stimulus for punishment or non-reward. (3) When the *fight/flight* system predominates the reinforcing stimulus is unconditioned punishment or non-reward.

Gray arrives at this conceptualization of emotion via a useful and cogent analysis of innate fears and early conditioning and an initial distinction of emotional states in the common language. He is taking the position that emotions are internal states which are mainly caused by external events (an idea which endorses that of Weiskrantz (1968)) and distinguishes them from drive. When the relationships between external events and emotional states become confused then pathological reactions result. This leads Gray to a pertinent discussion of anxiety and neurosis, psychosis and depression. However, as Mandler (1976) points out, it is a discussion which poses considerable problems in accounting for sex and hunger for example. He describes feeling sexy as nonemotional and love by contrast as emotional. Whilst not wanting to deny that love involves emotion, it can surely be argued that sexual arousal is also emotional, as also might be extreme hunger or thirst (again, see later).

General points

The three behavioural theories or models of emotion described here clearly have much in common. Equally clearly they owe their derivation to Watson, although they go much further than his primitive theory. Of course their greatest point in common is that they dwell almost entirely on behaviour, and then tend to view emotion as dependent on the nature of reinforcing stimuli and the complexities of classical conditioning. That it is possible to conceptualize some aspects of emotion behaviourally is beyond dispute, a point to which Chapter 5 below attests. However, whether or not it is appropriate to do this is another question. By now, there is an impressive array of evidence and thought pointing to the significant role of cognitive functions in emotion (see Izard, Mandler, Schachter, Lazarus and Zajonc, for example) which cannot be ignored. Also, whether or not one assigns a causal role to cognitions and subjective experiences in emotion, they surely exist and consequently attempts should be made to understand them if we are to obtain a full picture of emotion. A purely behavioural analysis, for all the scientific rigour which it promotes, does not permit this and is therefore somewhat wanting. This is reflected in the recent decline in influence of behavioural approaches to emotion.

4. PSYCHOANALYTIC AND EXPERIENTIAL THEORIES

D. Rapaport (psychoanalytic theory)

Rapaport (1950) provides a good general introduction to the psychoanalytic approach to emotion. The reader who is interested in pursuing this line of study will find worthwhile analyses of the Jungian idea of emotion in Hillman (1960; 1970) and of the neo-Freudian in Arieti (1970).

As one might expect, Rapaport's first major point is that the Freudian concept of emotion is unclear. On some occasions, Freud considered affects to be *a* or *the* form of psychic energy, on the others he viewed affect as an implied attribute of other psychoanalytic concepts. Hence: 'affects regulated from the unconscious are defined as discharge processes of energies of instinctual origin' (Rapaport, 1970, p.29).

Rapaport considers that the old problem of the time sequences involved in feeling and the expression of emotion (see James and Cannon) detracted from the possible idea that 'felt' emotion and physiological changes are both the result of some common variable. Naturally, any investigation of this underlying variable would be difficult, since in Freudian terms it is concerned with the unconscious. For Freud, emotions may be psychic energies or they may be discharge processes associated with these energies, but either way one is squarely within the murk of the unconscious and its instinctual origins. Psychoanalytic theory is not concerned with possible sequences of emotional events. Perception occurs and therefore anything might happen; the emotion 'felt', or the bodily process, or both, or neither.

In his account of the psychoanalytic theory of emotion, Rapaport continues by drawing attention to some of the neo-Freudians and showing how their views on emotion differ from Freud's original ideas. For example, he mentions

Brierley (1937) as concluding that affect is some kind of tension phenomenon which leads to an inner and outer discharge. Brierley also believed affect to show what will happen to the basic impulse. According to Rapaport, this notion is in accord with Freud's idea of pleasantness and unpleasantness. These are the conscious parts of decreasing and increasing tension. And further, Rapaport draws from Federn (1936) to demonstrate the importance of conflict theory in the psychoanalytic consideration of emotion. Affect, or emotions, result when difference drive cathexes are in conflict. (A cathexis is an amount of psychic energy which is associated with an idea.)

This is but a taste of the psychoanalytic theories of emotion. To summarize, as far as this is possible, they assert that the substrates (psychic processes) underlying emotion are unconscious and that affects have been variously viewed as psychic energies, discharge processes of psychic energies, discharge processes of psychic energies, and manifestations of instinctual conflict. It is best to let this discussion rest here, since if it is taken any further the writer will become more lost than the reader no doubt already is.

J. Hillman

Although basically a Jungian analyst, Hillman (1960) gives what is arguably the fullest non-existential but nevertheless phenomenological account of emotion (although see discussion of Fall's theory in Chapter 5). He bases his theory on Aristotle's four causes.

(1) *Efficient cause.* Hillman argues that the stimuli which might cause emotion, that is, which function as efficient causes are either representations, conflicts and situations or those with a physiological basis, such as arousal, instinct, constitution or energy. He integrates these with the idea of the symbol which he characterizes as a mixture of inner and outer, conscious and unconscious representations. Thus a situation will arouse emotion if it is perceived symbolically. 'Emotion is thus the symbolic apprehension of the subjective psyche . . .' (1960, p.253).

(2) *Material cause.* In dealing with material cause, Hillman asks the question: 'What is the stuff of emotion?', and then applies six criteria used since Aristotle to establish evidence for the existence of material cause. He concludes from this analysis that material cause in emotion is energy. To be able to say that emotion is present, there must be gross bodily changes plus representations of these in consciousness. At the same time, however, emotion *is* the body as it is experienced here and now. The body becomes the material cause of emotion and the order of its energy is a person's homeostatic balance.

(3) *Formal cause.* The formal cause of emotion must be its essential defining qualities, that which distinguishes it from all else. In Hillman's view this is the psyche, emotion being its total pattern, a combination of expression and inner states. Thus to this point in his theory, Hillman has symbol and form corresponding to each other and only occurring when there is energy.

(4) *Final cause.* Aristotle's concept of final cause can be viewed as the purpose or goal of something or simply as the end of some operation. Hillman reconciles these two possibilities by suggesting that the finish of any emotional process is an achievement; this is its purpose. Such an achievement need not be final in time. Hence, in Hillman's view, emotion can be an event in which the final cause is contemporaneous with the efficient, material and formal causes. The final cause of emotion is its value which comes about through change, particularly if this change leads to survival or improvement. One is immediately led to ask, 'How can emotional change be distinguished from any other sort of change?' In answer, Hillman argues that the distinction can be made using the idea of transformation. Emotion is the transformation of conscious representations in terms of symbolic reality; it is a transformation of energy, of the whole psyche.

This still does not amount to a clear statement of the possible value of emotion; when is emotion good? Hillman is even less clear on this matter than on others. He suggests that *true* emotion (not just deep feelings or concentrated willing, or abortive emotion) always achieves its purpose; it is always good. Its results on the other hand may be good or bad, although emotion itself is always an improvement of some sort. This is somewhat of a miasma through which it is difficult to pick a way.

In summary then, Hillman argues that the efficient cause of emotions is the symbolic perception of the objective psyche, the material cause, or body, emotion is energy, the formal cause, or essence, of emotion is the total pattern of the psyche (or soul), and that the final cause, or value of emotion, is change or transformation which is always and inevitably good.

J.-P. Sartre

Sartre (1948) provides the most completed account of emotion that there is from the existential viewpoint. He argues that the emotional subject and the object of the emotion are inextricably bound up. Emotion is a manner of apprehending the world. For example, if a man believes that his wife is losing interest in him then he sees his every action in terms of what he should do about this. If he fails in his attempts then again his perceptions are coloured.

A second important point of Sartre's theory is that he believes emotion to involve a transformation of the world. If paths to particular goals are blocked or too hard to follow, then a person will try to change the world. If one cannot deal with the world as it is, one might be able to if it is changed. The impetus for making this emotional transformation of the world comes simply from the impossibility of solving the problem with whatever is already available.

Emotion then to Sartre is an attempt to make a qualitative change in an object, to give it an altogether new quality without changing it substantively. Directed by consciousness, the body changes its relationship with the world— and the world is suddenly seen with new qualities. Sartre is not, of course, saying that emotions change the world in reality; the real, external world is as static as ever. Rather, emotions create a magical transformation.

The example of fear might help to clarify these ideas. Sartre states that if a man is afraid and runs away from the source of his fear then he is usually reckoned to be behaving rationally. However, Sartre maintains that this is not rational behaviour. In his terms the man is not running to gain shelter, security or protection, but because he cannot 'annihilate (himself) in unconsciousness'. His fear and running away bring about a magical change in the world so that the dangerous object, with which he can deal in no other way, is negated. It is as if by running away in fear, he is pretending that he is in a world in which the dangerous object does not exist. So, as Sartre views it, fear is consciousness magically negating or denying something which substantively and dangerously exists in the external world.

In developing his tentative theory of emotion, Sartre also makes the point that simple behaviour is not, and can never be, emotion. Emotion always involves a qualitative transformation of the world. He argues that there are some behaviours which at first sight look to be emotion, the pretence of anger or joy, for example. But he characterizes these as spurious or false emotions. He urges that real emotion is always accompanied by a belief. In his terms a person uses his will to give new qualities to objects in the environment and then believes these qualities to be real. So to be defined as real, an emotion must be experienced; it is not something which can be stopped at will, or which can be cast off because it is unpleasant. Also, Sartre regards the physiological concomitants of emotion as the phenomena of the type of belief just described. It is these that can be used to distinguish between false and real emotion. Thus, although a man can stop running, he cannot stop trembling.

Finally, it is worth making the point that Sartre suggests that not all emotions are fully fledged. Subtle emotions can give momentary glimpses of the unpleasant or the excellent. These are dim intuitions which are nevertheless full of potential and give a vague sense of disaster or of something very good. Sartre views the social world as full of such potentials; it is always edging on the magical.

General points

The types of theory exemplified in this section could not contrast more strongly with the behavioural theories considered above. The psychoanalytic and phenomenological theories are concerned with a conceptual analysis of emotional experience and abound with terms such as consciousness, will, and even, in Sartre's case, magic. They are dealing with non-observables and cannot be considered to provide the basis of scientific investigation.

Nevertheless, it can be argued that theories which deal with emotional experience have their place. For example, as will be seen in the cognitive theories which are to be described next, a great deal of emphasis is placed on the idea that emotion involves an appraisal of significant stimuli. This is a process which it is believed to occur almost instantaneously. It may be that theorists such as Hillman and Sartre have insights to offer about what such a process might involve. However, more recent analyses by cognitive theorists offer clearer insights and it should be remembered that it is not easy to put psychoanalytic or phenomenological ideas into a framework which approximates conventional scientific endeavour. At best, they function to stimulate further analysis.

5. COGNITIVE THEORIES

N. Bull

Although involving a straightforward modification of James's ideas, Bull's (1951) theory of emotion is unique in its central concern with motor behaviour. However, it also has enough of a cognitive orientation to be best included within this section. Bull's pivotal idea is that emotion is mediated by an attitude of preparedness to respond, to cry or to run, for example. She views this as an involuntary motor attitude which leads to a series of incomplete movements which occur in invariant sequences. Such incomplete motor sequences are latent, being dependent on predispositions which come from neural organization.

Bull suggests further that not only is there a motor or bodily readiness but also a mentally oriented awareness, this being the emotion as it is experienced. Emotion is then *reduced* by action, especially if this action is consummatory. Bull regards emotion as occurring only when the individual is less than fully aware of the motor aspects of his or her readiness to respond. The argument is that when the individual is fully aware of the possibility of a complete sequence of motor behaviour then he or she gets a feeling of purpose and does not therefore experience emotion.

Bull's theory of emotion, then, lays great stress on motor action but also implies that consciousness or cognition sets limits on emotion, almost by default. Thus, if a person consciously realizes the full implications of a potential motor sequence, no emotion is possible. Whereas if one is less than fully aware then the sequence of motor behaviour is fragmentary or incomplete and emotion is experienced.

P.V. Siminov

Although Siminov's (1970) theory of emotion is brief and simple, it is described here since it reflects a similar approach to that of Leventhal (below); it is presented directly in terms of information theory. Siminov begins with a definition of what he calls negative emotion:

$$E = -N (I_n - I_a)$$

where emotion equals need times the difference between the necessary information and the available information. In this context, information is the possibility of reaching a goal due to a particular communication. Thus, if an organism cannot organize itself appropriately through lack of information then the nervous mechanism leading to negative emotions start to act. Siminov suggests that this has three main implications. (1) 'Dominant' reactions occur—i.e. previously neutral stimuli begin to be reacted to, and ineffectual (as regards any usual goals) activity is maintained. (2) This ineffectual activity leads to physiological changes typical of emotion. (3) The emotions themselves have a strong physiological activating influence. Consequently, if this mechanism becomes active, then some habitual response must have been disrupted.

Siminov views positive emotions in a similar way. When an organism's needs are satisfied it is emotionally quiescent, but if there is a surplus of information over and above that which is necessary for this satisfaction then positive emotion is the result. In the terms of the formula, $I_a > I_n$. Such positive emotions endure in the same way as do negative emotions and may facilitate behaviour.

Finally, Siminov suggests that emotions may be classified by taking into account: (1) the strength of the need; (2) the extent of the information deficiency or redundancy; and (3) specificity of the action which is aimed at satisfying the need. He believes that it is only when 'action at a distance' is necessary (i.e. defence or struggle rather than just pleasure or displeasure brought about by immediate contacts) that emotions proper are seen. Thus he is viewing emotion from a standpoint which involves information theory directly and motivation by implication.

H. Leventhal

Starting with the general cry that to understand emotion fully it is important to come to terms with subjective experience, Leventhal (1974) proposes an information processing model of emotion. He states that such a model must integrate four mechanisms or systems: (1) an interpreting mechanism which turns on emotional reactions; (2) an expressive system, feedback from which will define the subjective quality of emotion; (3) an instrumental action system; (4) a bodily reaction system which maintains the instrumental system. In this statement it seems that Leventhal is simply emphasizing in information processing terminology the same points that many others have stressed before him, namely, that a theory of emotion should take account of how emotion is instigated, and deal with its subjective, behavioural and physiological aspects.

In an attempt at the suggested integration, Leventhal proposes a two-phase model of emotion. In the perceptual/motor phase he suggests that the cognitions which promote emotion and expressive reactions are necessary for feedback to occur, and in its turn the feedback is necessary for subjective feelings. He argues that this process must involve an appraisal of meaning and hypothesizes that this is achieved by two types of decoder. The first is an automatic, built-in decoder and the second a discrepancy decoder which is involved in sorting out discrepancies from a person's expectations.

Leventhal is therefore arguing for the presence of innate perceptual mechanisms which are sensitive to particular features of stimuli—the usual feature analysers of information processing models. These instigate feelings *before* expressive reactions can occur. However, he does not see these feelings as falling into precise categories of emotion, but as merely being positive or negative. More specific emotional discriminations occur later and involve feedback from the expressive and autonomic systems. All of which can be automatic or deliberate, but only with a contribution to subjective feeling when it is automatic (a point with which Izard (1972; 1977) would disagree.

The second component of emotion according to Leventhal is that which is concerned with action. He argues that the over-activity involved and any associated autonomic and visceral activity are clearly separated from feeling states. He makes this point to the extent of saying that the action system will detract from feeling; if one is aware of one's actions then one will be less aware, or even unaware, of one's feelings. But, to have the best of both worlds, his final point is that if action and the feeling state which precedes it are closely associated then the action may enhance the feeling.

In a more recent attempt to place his theory within a discussion of cognition and emotion, Leventhal (1982) makes the following assumptions. (1) It is best to begin the study of emotion with the verbal report of subjective experience. (2) Emotional states are a form of meaning, so if cognition is meaning, emotion is a form of cognition. (3) There are several types of cognitive process. (4) Meanings develop in the perceptual processing system. (5) Emotion can interact with both perceptual and abstract cognition. (6) Meaning systems develop and change. (7) To understand mechanisms underlying emotion and cognition, it is necessary to study specific meaning systems.

Following these assumptions, Leventhal outlines a hierarchy of three levels of processing: (1) expressive motor; (2) a schematic or perceptual memory in which there is a record of emotional situations, experiences and reactions; (3) a conceptual or abstract memory for processing emotional experience and volitional behaviour.

Leventhal views emotion as being attached to single perceptual areas, to perceptual or schematically organized experiences, or to more organized meanings. Above all, emotion is integrated with meaning systems. It is worth noting that Leventhal's perceptual motor theory is compatible with Bower's (1981) views of the links between emotion and memory (see below). Both assume that there is an emotion generator with emotion connected to specific cognitions. Also, both suggest that emotion is experienced as a reaction to an object and as a reaction within the experience.

Within this type of theoretical framework, Leventhal regards emotion as informing us about feelings which are attached to perceptions and thoughts and about momentary internal states. In this sense, it is akin to all illness in informing us of the our state and of the impact on it of the environment. So, to Leventhal, emotion is a meter of internal condition and provides a capacity for particular types of action, awareness of which establishes new goals.

K.R. Scherer

Somewhat similarly to Leventhal, Scherer (1982) and Scherer and Ekman (1984) regard emotion as a dynamic process, which involves cognitive appraisal, physiological arousal, motor expression, motivational tendencies and subjective feeling. It functions between the person and the environment to evaluate the personal relevance of the environment. It then helps in the preparation of coping actions and in communicating the states that result.

Scherer views emotion as making behavioural adaptation flexible, but through cognitive evaluations. In this sense, his theory has evolutionary overtones, with the original role of emotion as preparing the ground for the development of cognition, in that it gave time to think before acting. At the present stage of evolution though, there is no emotion without prior cognition, putting Scherer squarely in the Lazarus side of the Lazarus–Zajonc debate (see Chapter 4).

Scherer's process model of emotion depends on the organism going through a rapid sequence of hierarchically arranged steps of stimulus processing. He terms this a sequence of evaluation checks (SEC), checks on meaning which he deems necessary for survival. These are concerned with: (1) novelty or unexpectedness; (2) the central component of pleasantness/unpleasantness; (3) goal-relevance, (4) possibilities of copying, a step which involves causal attributions; (5) a comparison of the stimuli with social norms and the self-concept.

Each SEC which is experienced helps to further differentiate an emotional state. Eventually, *discrete* emotions may be the modal result of the SEC process. Scherer argues that from this it should be possible to predict the appearance of emotional states within a species from a knowledge of its information-processing capacity. This, in turn, is important because emotion has important functions in social signalling, which suggests the significance to society of emotion control and modification. Scherer's process theory relating emotion and cognition then has important implications, some of which will be returned to later.

S. Schachter

This brief section on Schachter is included since no collection of summaries of the influential theories of emotion would be representative without his name. However, much of Schachter's contribution is through a cunningly devised series of experimental situations and the interpretation of the results which they have produced (see Chapter 3).

For an overview of Schachter's ideas the best sources are Schachter (1959;

1964; 1970). He develops what he terms a cognitive/physiological view of emotion. In fact, however, he suggests that emotional states are mainly determined by cognitive factors. He argues that emotional states are characterized by a general arousal of the sympathetic nervous system (SNS) and that from state to state this may differ slightly in its pattern. He maintains that we interpret and classify these states by clues from the situation which brought them about and also from our typical mode of perception. Physiological arousal occurs and is given its precise direction by our cognitions of what brought it about.

This formulation led Schachter to make three propositions. (1) If we are physiologically aroused but cannot explain why or what caused the arousal, then we will give this state a name and react to it in whatever cognitive way is open. Thus any *one* state could be labelled in many ways depending on the individual and the situation. (2) If we are physiologically aroused and have an entirely reasonable explanation of this available, it is improbable that we will entertain any alternative cognitive accounts. (3) The third proposition involves approaching the theory from the opposite direction. If from time to time we experience the same cognition, we will only describe our feelings as emotions if we are also in some state of physiological arousal. Hence, Schachter's basic idea is that emotions are controlled through a very close inter-relationship and interaction between physiological arousal and cognitive appraisal.

M.B. Arnold

Arnold's theory of emotion developed for more than three decades (see, for example, 1945; 1960; 1968; 1970a; 1970b) and is a mixture of phenomenology, cognition, and physiology. It depends on the assumption that we can gain most knowledge about brain function in emotion (which to Arnold is of fundamental importance) by a cognitive analysis. This will enable us to identify the physiological mediation of the process running from perception to emotion and action.

Arnold's cognitive analysis of emotion depends very much on the construct of appraisal. She suggests that we immediately, automatically and *almost* involuntarily evaluate, with respect to ourselves, anything that we encounter. As long as no other appraisals interfere, this leads us to approach everything appraised as 'good', and to avoid what is 'bad' and to ignore what is 'indifferent'. When we have a 'good' object we may well reappraise it and on the basis of this perhaps alter our behaviour. So Arnold regards appraisal as complementing perception and producing a tendency to *do* something. When this tendency is strong it is called emotion, although to Arnold all appraisals at least have the status of affective experiences.

Arnold suggests that in most new experiences memory is at the basis of our appraisals (the exceptions are 'simple' experiences such as taste or pleasure/pain). Anything new is evaluated in terms of our past experiences. She argues that the new object also evokes a memory of the *affect* associated with the previous experience. These affective memories are relivings of our past appraisals. Arnold regards them as continually distorting our judgement and therefore to be guarded against. It is only within the last few years that the idea of emotion memory has been explored in any depth. Discussion of this and of the influential analyses made by Bower (1981) and Bower and Cohen (1982) will be reserved for Chapter 4.

The final link in the appraisal chain comes from our imagination. Before we act, Arnold believes that the situation plus any relevant affective memories lead us to guess at the future. We imagine whether what will happen will be good or bad for us. Our appraisal then becomes dependent on memory plus expectation. From this we devise a plan of action which involves various possibilities for coping with the situation; we choose which is the best. It is worth pointing out again that Arnold suggests that this whole complex process of appraisal *may* well occur almost instantaneously.

For the most part, the remainder of Arnold's theory is concerned with hypothetical neural pathways which may mediate the hypothetical appraisal processes. However, she also distinguishes between feeling and emotions. Emotional action patterns arise from positive or negative appraisal of perceived or imagined objects, whereas feeling action patterns are viewed as resulting from appraisals of something which may be either beneficial or harmful for our functioning. Although drawing this distinction, Arnold regards the hypothetical sequence of events involved in feeling as being much the same as that for emotion. For example, if I am sitting in a comfortable chair enjoying an amicable discussion, I may well be driven away if a pneumatic drill starts up in the roadway outside. Here is involved perception of the situation, appraisal, feeling, and finally a desire for action; just the same as if I had perceived a situation which had led me to be afraid and run away (emotion).

Arnold also discussed deliberate actions, which involve neither feeling nor emotion. Thus, I may sit writing this summary of Arnold's ideas on emotion without any desire to do so. Any plesure comes when it is finished, not from the fairly mechanical progression of physically writing one word after another. Each successive word has no special attraction for me. If I were to express any emotion at all in the situation it would occur because I had had a period of difficulty in expressing myself, or alternatively had just completed a fluid two thousand words.

Arnold regards such deliberate action as: (1) making up the bulk of our everyday behaviour; (2) involving what we could call rational judgement; and (3) that which distinguishes us from the animals. So we judge situations both in terms of short-term (emotional) possibilities and long-term, more abstract, goals. And we often relinquish the former, which seems more immediately attractive, for the latter, which are better for us in the long run. Animals do not have this capacity; they can only make immediate, emotional appraisals. With her distinction between emotional action patterns and deliberate action patterns, Arnold believes that in reality she is separating emotion and will. In fact, she is nicely maintaining the traditional rationalist doctrine.

R.S. Lazarus

Basically, Lazarus stresses the importance of cognitive factors in emotion. However, in addition to this he also considers the significance of factors which stem from biological and cultural perspectives (see Lazarus (1966; 1968) and Lazarus *et al.* (1970)). Lazarus suggests that although concepts of emotion are important in the description and classification of behaviour, they are not necessarily of use in its explanation. This idea bears comparison with those of both Duffy and Leeper. Lazarus asserts that the development of the concept of emotion has been hampered by difficulties in description and classification. Since there is no one thing to which emotion can be meaningfully and unequivocally said to refer, Lazarus suggests that it is a 'response syndrome'. This is a directly drawn medical analogy, with emotions viewed as having causes, symptoms and a number of courses. In Lazarus's view, the overall pattern of relationships between causes, symptoms and courses permits the descriptive use of the word emotion and also allows the possibility of classification.

As already mentioned, Lazarus dwells on biological and cultural aspects of emotion. But he finds them lacking. He maintains, for example, that emphasis had shifted away from the role of the viscera and other such peripheral 'biological' structures in emotion and has moved towards more central mechanisms. Even within the CNS, the emphasis has been on the evolutionarily more primitive subcortical structures. He argues, however, that these structures have themselves undergone evolutionary change, as have cortical structures, and that they also play an important part in our cognitive functions. Similarly, Lazarus believes that cultural influences on emotion can be just as easily stressed. He suggests that culture affects emotion in four ways: (1) through the manner in which we perceive emotional stimuli; (2) by directly altering emotional expression; (3) by determining social relationships and judgements; (4) by highly ritualized behaviour such as grief. Should we stress the evolutionary, biological viewpoint or the cultural? Lazarus believes that this problem can be resolved by taking a more individual, cognitive perspective.

To Lazarus we are evaluators: we evaluate each stimulus that we encounter, with a view to its personal relevance and significance. Lazarus regards this as cognitive activity with emotion as part of it. Hence:

'each emotional reaction . . . is a function of a particular kind of cognition or *appraisal*'. (Lazarus *et al.*, 1970, p.218; their italics)

Lazarus recognizes emotional reactions at three levels, the behavioural, the physiological and the cognitive or subjective. He views each of these as important in its own right and suggests that the particular pattern which may obtain between them is a distinguishing feature of emotion.

Lazarus extends his ideas with the suggestion that we have dispositions to search for and respond to or attend to particular stimuli, and that these dispositions shape our interaction with the environment. Our cognitive appraisal of these stimuli produces the emotional response. The stimuli themselves are constantly changing and we are continually 'coping' with them; so our cognitions alter, as do our emotional reactions. Lazarus (1966; 1968) argues that there are two sorts of coping process. We may deal with threat or harm by direct action, the urge to which he regards as an important part of emotion. Since the success or failure of this direct action constantly fluctuates, our cognitive evaluations and hence our emotional reactions also fluctuate. Lazarus terms the second type of coping 'reappraisal'. This is solely cognitive, involving no direct action. We may reappraise from positive to negative or negative to positive, and may do so realistically or distortedly. We (and animals) appraise and reappraise all incoming information, each twist and turn of which is shown in emotional reactions.

Lazarus realizes that he has only presented the outlines of a cognitive theory of emotion and that there must eventually be some attempt to point to the detailed cognitive aspects of any individual emotional response. He suggests, however, that a cognitive/phenomenological approach, linked with biological and cultural considerations, will have the effect of putting emotion back into the forefront of psychology. Also recently (1982, 1984) he has entered into considerable debate with Zajonc (1980, 1984) on the relationship between emotion and cognition which will be discussed in detail in Chapter 4.

Averill et al. (1969) put a slightly different perspective on Lazarus's basic views. They describe emotion as a complex response system made up of three subsystems. (1) Stimulus properties. They argue that a stimulus may be influenced by the response which is made to it. So an emotional response may be a stimulus in its own right, which helps to add to the quality of emotion. (2) Appraiser subsystem. The brain appraises and evaluates stimuli, the primary appraisal reducing the stimulus array to a unitary concept such as threat and the second appraisal being appropriate for coping behaviour. (3) Responses. These are categorized into cognitive, expressive and instrumental, which are poorly correlated. Here, cognitions are being viewed as defence mechanisms, expressions are mainly facial, and instrumental responses are seen as symbols which signal the presence of affect. In this context they also speak of operators which are complex goal-directed acts, and conventions which are culturally determined operators.

The emotional response system can interrupt and modify ongoing behaviour and is self-contained. Hence Averill et al. suggest that emotions can only be distinguished through their eliciting conditions, their patterns of response, and via any developmental changes—not through their structure. However, more recently, Averill (1982) has put forward his own very full theory of emotion which is described at the end of this chapter.

General points

The theories which are grouped together in this section have various origins. This can be seen in the emphases they place on motor responses, the processing of information, perception, motivation and physiological reactions in emotion. However, the point which binds them together is that they give cognition a crucial role to play in emotion—a role which is sometimes causal, sometimes not. It is this which gives the theories a richness which is not often seen in the theories discussed so far.

The idea which most often occurs in the cognitive theories of emotion, whether it is explicit or implicit, is appraisal. This is a process of cognitive evaluation, usually regarded as virtually instantaneous which the cognitive theorists believe to be a necessary component of emotion. Thus, in stressing cognition they are not trying to come to terms with emotional experience, but less ambitiously endeavouring to speculate about the cognitive mechanisms which they believe to mediate emotion. Whether cognitive mediation *is* a necessary idea in an understanding of emotion remains to be seen. However, it has become increasingly obvious that it would be foolish, not to say churlish, *not* to discuss cognition when attempting to account for emotion. Such progress has been made by cognitive emotion theorists that the place of emotion can no longer be conveniently forgotten by psychologists as it was for so long. The cognitive influence is also evident in the broader theories which are described in the next section, all of which have a place for cognition as well as for many other processes.

6.   THE GRAND APPROACH

R.W. Leeper

Leeper (1948) put forward a strong argument against the long-held idea of emotions as having a disorganizing influence on behaviour. He maintained instead that emotions pervade all behaviour by organizing and motivating it. Later (1962a; 1962b; 1965; 1970), he added considerable refinement to this basic idea.

Leeper (for example, 1970) suggests that emotions act as motives since they are mildly aroused most of the time. They control our behaviour without our awareness. Emotions give behaviour (and mental activity) its goal-directedness in, for example, allowing us to choose between alternatives, or solve problems, or endure sanctions to obtain a reward. He believes that the traditional emphasis has been antipathetic to the view of emotions as motives since they have been studied in ways indicated by everyday considerations, often leading to study only of the extreme or the sensational.

The most recent idea extended by Leeper (1970) is that emotions function not only as motives, but also as perceptions. By this he means that emotions are cognitive in that they convey information to the organism. In fact, they are perceptions, perhaps longstanding, of situations. Again, Leeper suggests that this view is breaking with tradition. He suggests that, in the past, motivation and perception have been regarded as distinct. He puts forward arguments to explain this dichotomy, similar to those which he uses to account for the division between emotions and motives.

Leeper develops his ideas with the assertion that emotional motives depend for their function on a similar mechanism to that of the more obvious physiologically based motives. He believes that there are 'emotional mechanisms' which function through signals that indicate the favourability of environmental circumstances. These mechanisms act like reflexes.

These developing ideas on emotion have sprung from two aims. Leeper has attempted to dispel the more traditional view of emotion as disorganizing, chaotic and interfering in its effects on behaviour. Also, he maintains that emotion is an active force involving motivation and perception, which organizes, sustains and directs behaviour.

K.H. Pribram

Pribram's ideas concerning emotion overlap with many other theories. He begins from a neurophysiological viewpoint, takes into consideration ideas of appraisal and motivation and develops a cognitive/information theory position. Originally, Pribram (1970; Miller *et al.*, 1960) regarded emotion as Plans, these being 'neural programmes which are engaged when the organism is disequilibriated'. Pribram states that, normally, motivationally based Plans change because they are carried out, but if their execution is blocked then emotion results. Whether this emotion closes or opens the organism to more input (Pribram allows both capacities) the Plan involved is stopped. When a Plan is held up in this way for a long period then 'regression' tends to occur. Pribram (Miller *et al.*, 1960) goes on to argue that emotional expression is more primitive and basic than rational behaviour although emotions need not be expressed at all. Thus, there are emotional Plans as well as motivational Plans, both of which are altered by experience. Pribram (1970) maintains that this idea of emotions as Plans brought with it too many problems. As an alternative, he speculates about feelings rather than emotions.

Pribram distinguishes between the 'objective' world of sense data and the subjective world of feelings, and proposes that where we have no evidence which will allow us to construct the objective world then we must rely on the subjective. In other words, if we have no good evidence that we are faced with something which we can see, hear, smell, taste or touch, then we must be feeling it inside. These feelings Pribram describes in his usual capitalized way as 'Feelings as Monitors'. He develops good, empirically based neurophysiological arguments to support such subjective feelings and affirms that this viewpoint is more fruitful than his previous idea of Plans.

We do not plan to be happy or sad or angry; rather, Pribram suggests, we simply *feel* happy or sad or angry. We construct Plans and implement them. They may be very easily executed, or they may fail, miserably or otherwise. We evaluate or appraise their success, and this process of appraisal is monitored, i.e. it is felt. Thus Feelings as Monitors are regarded as Images not Plans. Plans are merely constructed within the matrix that Images provide. A final contribution (and slight confusion) to the language of emotion suggested by Pribram is that 'go' Plans equal motivations and 'no-go' Plans equal emotions.

In summary, Pribram's most recent suggestion is that the study of emotion will benefit by distinguishing between feelings and emotions, and then concentrating on the former. Feelings are Monitors and Images are appraisals of the degree of success attached to the execution of Plans. The Plans themselves may allow the organism to go ahead, in which case they are motivation, or they may be blocked, in which case the organism is thwarted and we have emotion. Although expressed in a somewhat idiosyncratic language, Pribram's theory of emotion is quite similar to Arnold's: basically, it is cognitive-phenomenological in nature and yet it draws on neurophysiological evidence for empirical support. However, it appears to have had little direct influence in more recent theorizing.

R. Plutchik

Plutchik's theory of emotion has involved over many years (1962; 1965; 1966; 1970; 1980; 1982). It has led him to define emotion as an inferred, complex sequence of reactions. This includes cognitive evaluation, subjective change, autonomic and neural arousal impulses to action. It results in behaviour which is designed to affect the original precipitating stimulus.

Plutchik regards emotion as multidimensional, the dimensions being those of intensity, similarity and polarity. Any emotion can vary in its intensity (for example between pensiveness and grief); any emotion varies as to its degree of similarity to any other emotion (for example joy and anticipation are more similar than loathing and surprise); and all emotions are polar (for example disgust is the opposite of acceptance).

Plutchik represents these three dimensions in the form of a model shown in Figure 4. Vertically on the inverted cone in this figure intensity is represented, whereas each section portrays a primary emotion. Figure 5 shows a cross-section through the cone, with the area in the centre denoting the conflict which Plutchik believes to be involved in mixed motives.

In developing his ideas, Plutchik discusses the problem of the language used in any analysis of emotion. He maintains that we normally use everyday, subjective language of the sort employed in the figures to describe emotion. However, he suggests that there are two other possible sorts of language—a purely descriptive one based on behavioural observation and a functional one based on the adaptive function of what the organism does. Hence, in Plutchik's terms, we may be experiencing joy or ecstasy, whilst behaviourally we are mating or possessing and functionally we are reproducing. He argues that the

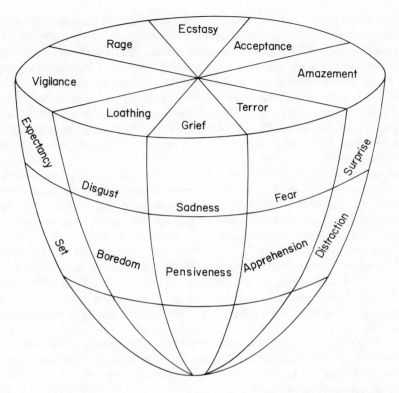

Figure 4.   Plutchik's three-dimensional model of emotion (taken from Arnold, 1970)

Figure 5.   A cross-section through Plutchik's emotional solid (taken from Arnold, 1970)

functional/adaptive language is the best to use when discussing emotion since he views it as varying along the same three dimensions (i.e. intensity, similarity and polarity) as a number of basic adaptive functions. Adaptively speaking, an organism can protect, destroy, reproduce, deprive, incorporate, reject, explore or orient—four pairs of what Plutchik regards as opposites which can vary in intensity and in similarity to one another. Clearly, a behavioural language could also be generally applicable, and a subjective one could only be used with humans (and with caution). However, Plutchik prefers his adaptive language, simply viewing emotion as a bodily reaction of one of the types mentioned above.

Overall, Plutchik regards subjective feelings as sufficient conditions for emotion, but not necessary; in other words a person may have an emotion although be unaware of it. By the same token, physiological changes are necessary but not sufficient for emotion to occur. They can come about through exercise, for example, in which emotion is not involved.

Emotion to Plutchik is a patterned bodily reaction which has its correspondent underlying adaptive processes which are common to living organisms. Primary emotions are short-lived and usually triggered by external stimuli and there are frequently mixtures of physiological and expressive patterns. It is therefore only possible to infer discrete patterns approximately.

Plutchik's most recent (1980, 1982) explication of his theory contains a clear role for cognitive evaluation of the potential benefit or harm of a stimulus. This intervenes between stimulus and feeling. Plutchik regards cognitive capacities to have evolved as the brain has evolved, specifically to predict the future to aid emotions and biological needs.

Within this framework, emotions are triggered by events important to the organism, the emotions themselves being adaptive reactions. However, it is only evaluated events which lead to emotion. Since there are some problems which are common to all organisms, so there are some universals in emotion.

From Plutchik's psychoevolutionary viewpoint, emotion has two functions: (1) to communicate information about intentions or probable behaviour, and (2) to increase the chances of survival when faced with emergencies. Various aspects of emotion can be modified by learning with emotion finally seen as mediating a type of behavioural homeostasis.

This is a very broad, biological way to account for emotion. Its major facets are: (1) emotion involves a prototypical adaptation; (2) emotion involves cognition; (3) emotion involves evolution; and (4) from a different viewpoint, emotion should be studied by specially devised methods—some of which, such as the Emotional Profile Index, Plutchik's suggests.

T.D. Kemper

Kemper (1978) outlines a thoughtful sociological theory of emotion which is worthy of inclusion here since it has some points in common with many of its psychological counterparts. Kemper asserts that 'events in the social environment instigate emotion' (1978, p.26). Taking this back a stage, Kemper believes that people relate via two orthogonal social dimensions of actual and expected power and status. This is a view of interaction as social exchange with outcomes expressable in terms of gains and losses, all of which have emotional consequences.

Sociological analysis leads Kemper to suggest that there are three types of emotion—structural, anticipatory and consequent. To give one example, Kemper argues that combinations of excesses, adequacies, and insufficiencies in one's own power and status can lead to the six structural emotions of security, guilt, fear/anxiety, happiness, shame and depression. If the other person's power and status are also considered then anger and contempt are added to this list.

Kemper analyses the implications of his theory of emotion in the areas of sociophysiology, distressful emotions and positive emotions. On the physiological side, he suggests that we feel emotions that are appropriate to their current conditions of social relations. This allows an interpretation of response specificity through social relations. Similarly, distressful and abnormal emotions are seen as acquired through the patterns of punishment experienced during socialization, the relevance of power and status to this being self-evident.

On the positive side of emotion, Kemper again analyses socialization and derives from it predictions for the avoidance of distressful emotions and the consequent experience of positive emotions. The argument adds power and status relations to the basic biological and occupational division of labour.

Kemper puts forward a well-argued, internally consistent, but idiosyncratic theory of emotion. It suffers a little through the descriptions of the various emotions being somewhat phenomenological, and the nature of the relationship between emotion and power and status remains hazy. However, it has the merits of bridging the chasm which sometimes yawns between psychology and sociology and of ending with a brave attempt to analyse love. Finally, since Kemper's theory hinges on the concepts of power and status it implies the significance of cognition, albeit social cognition.

S.S. Tomkins

Tomkins (1962; 1963) speaks of affect rather than emotion and provides a broad-based, ingenious, but again somewhat idiosyncratic, theory. This means that his theory is not well related to others, although it did provide some of the impetus for Izard's (1972; 1977) approach—an approach which, by contrast, is better, fuller and more easily linked to empirical findings.

Tomkins argues that the affect system is primary, that is it has innate determinants and interacts with the drive system (which is secondary or learned) to give drive its urgency. Further, he suggests the affect has no necessary constraints in time or intensity and hence gives drive its insatiable and very changeable aspects. At the outset, then, he is suggesting very strong links between emotion and motivation.

Like Izard, Tomkins argues that affects are mainly reflected in facial responses, the feedback from which, if it is self-conscious, can be rewarding or punishing. There are organized patterns of facial response which are innate and which are triggered by subcortical mechanisms in the central nervous system. He does not deny that affect is also reflected in bodily responses but simply regards these as less significant than facial expression.

Like many other theoriests who aver that there is a strong innate component to emotion, Tomkins lists what he regards as the eight primary affects. These are: interest/excitement, enjoyment/joy, surprise/startle, distress/anguish, disgust/contempt, anger/rage, shame/humiliation and fear/terror. He postulates that the instigation of these affects is dependent on changes in the rate of neural firing in the central nervous system.

The final point of Tomkins's theory which should be mentioned now is that the instantaneous responses which he believes to occur to the sources of affect require a feedback mechanism. From this he argues that it is very rare for a person to gain precise control over his emotional state.

Tomkins's theory of emotion is very widely based, ranging from a conceptual analysis of motivation to physiological possibilities, and stressing the importance of innate factors. Although it is an interesting theory, it is very speculative, does not relate well to most other theories, and, apart from some work on the facial expression of various primary emotions, is not well anchored to empirical data.

G. Mandler

In two well-argued books, Mandler (1976; 1984) offers a summary statement of what he terms a system of emotion. In Mandler's view the three integral aspects of emotion are *arousal, cognitive interpretation* and *consciousness*. He refers to undifferentiated arousal as the perception of activity in the sympathetic nervous system. Conditions for its presence depend on cognitive interpretation, particularly with respect to interruption and blocking. It has the functions of maintaining homeostasis and of the seeking of information.

Cognitive interpretation involves structures which promote innate reactions to events, plus evaluations of perceptions of self. Mandler argues that expressive movements produce automatic cognitive reactions which are altered by reinterpretation. The experience of emotion and emotional behaviour result from an interaction between autonomic arousal and cognitive interpretation. Arousal gives the visceral quality and intensity of emotion and cognitive interpretation provides a category for the experience. Mandler also argues that emotional experience occurs in consciousness and outputs from this are coded appropriately into conventional language.

In some detail Mandler goes into the means and the effects of interaction between arousal and cognitive interpretation. His general thesis is that autonomic nervous system arousal necessarily sets the stage for emotional behaviour and experience and provides for its intensity. The quality of the emotion then comes from meaning analysis which is engendered by arousal, the general situation and cognitive state. From this point on there are outputs to both consciousness and action.

Arousal, Mandler argues can be produced in two ways: first by pre-programmed release from the ANS and second that which is mediated by meaning analysis which makes mental stimuli into ANS releasers. Thus Mandler is speaking of a continuum from innate to experiential factors. Any perceived input from arousal leads to automatic meaning analysis. This generates a search for structures that can assimilate input, its analysis plus perception of arousal. If the search is successful it stops and the particular structure is put into consciousness.

Without going into too many of the complexities which Mandler introduces at this stage of the argument, summary can be made by saying that *continuous feedback* is involved. Hence environmental stimuli lead to cognitive interpretations which lead to perception of arousal which leads to emotional experience which leads to perception and evaluations of the experience, which changes the original cognitive interpretation, and so on.

An essential aspect of Mandler's view of emotion concerns the analysis of meaning. He argues that the complexity of inputs in emotion makes emotion very rich, its meaning being given by the structure of the input and its relation to other inputs and existing mental structures. Meaning analysis tells us where we are and what our surroundings are. Any discrepancies between available evidence and expectations from existing schemata lead to arousal and then an emotional synthesis. Some meaning analyses are automatic and others require deliberate elaboration.

Mandler makes two interpretations of the interaction beteen cognition and arousal in meaning analysis. In the *passive* view emotion is given by the total relational network from the two sets of structures. For example, an interaction between the autonomic arousal perception and the evaluation of a situation as positive and joyful gives the feeling of joy. In the *active* view, which Mandler believes to be more appropriate, the inputs from either system are fed into existing structures based on past experience and innate factors. Of course, both systems may operate and the same set of events may act as arousal releasers and has to be cognitively evaluated.

In a little more detail, Mandler suggests that structures give analyses of inputs and initial identification of emotion. These are stored, meaning analysis gives further interpretation and then arousal is produced which, with cognitive appraisal of the situation gives a specific emotional reaction. He argues further that a hierarchy of meaning nodes could give various effects, from repression to virtually any emotional experience, all depending on past experiences. So, whether or not an input leads to emotional experience depends on whether or not an arousal switch is triggered, which itself depends on a particular meaning analysis of the input.

Finally, a brief description must be given of Mandler's complex analysis of the role of consciousness in emotion. He makes the necessary point that events in consciousness are unique and sensitive indicators of the individual but are not open to the observer. Therefore any consideration of consciousness must needs be speculative. Mandler suggests that some emotions may *only* be experienced in consciousness and also that many of the determining functions of emotion may occur in consciousness. He argues that emotional consciousness develops from basic processes which involve both arousal and cognition.

Mandler emphasizes consciousness for a number of reasons, not least of which is that arousal and consciousness seem to arise from similar mental conditions—the need to select and alter the current stream of action. Emotional states push for priority and occur at important choice points in our lives and intentions. Mandler goes so far as to describe them as guideposts of human existence. Thus it is not surprising that they depend on consciousness.

Although Mandler is tentative and unpretentious about his ideas on emotion it is quite clear that he has constructed the beginnings of a far-reaching theory or system of emotion which has many implications. Within it are all the usual considerations and facets of the more recent, particularly cognitive, theories of emotion. And perhaps most interestingly, it provides a place for the role of consciousness in a context of ideas and data which derive from conventional science. Whilst this is interesting it does pose problems if emotion is viewed from a psychoevolutionary perspective. Do animals have consciousness (emotions)? Did man experience emotion before the development of consciousness, if theorists such as Jaynes (1976) are correct in suggesting that it developed in relatively recent times?

C.E. Izard

In a full and elegant discussion of emotion, Izard (1972; 1977) puts forward the all-embracing differential theory of emotion. The details of this theory are intricate and will be examined again later, although Izard's influence on the present book is considerable. For now, a summary of his theoretical viewpoint will suffice.

Izard's theory has broad aims: (1) to account for the great complexity of emotion; (2) to deal with neural activity, glandular, visceral and psychophysiological responses, subjective experience, expressive behaviour and instrumental responses; (3) to provide a framework within which to look at innate and learned characteristics of emotion and patterns of emotional–cognitive–motor responses; (4) to fit in with a general theory of behaviour.

Izard regards emotion as a motivational system, a personality process that gives meaning to human existance or which determines behaviours ranging from rape to personal sacrifice. It is one of five interrelated subsystems of personality and is made up of ten fundamental innate and unique emotions, which produce the main human motivational system. These emotions are: interest, enjoyment, surprise, distress, disgust, anger, shame, fear and contempt. He maintains that these emotions are discrete, subjectively and in neurochemistry and behaviour, but that their particular discretion comes from feedback from facial and bodily activity. Also, although discrete, they interact.

In Izard's view, the emotional elements of personality themselves form an interrelated system, which through certain innate influences may be organized hierarchically. There is apparent polarity between some pairs of emotions and certain regular relationships between others. All of which can combine to become like traits and personality patterns. Also, *all* emotions have some common characteristics. They are non-cyclical, have unlimited generality and flexibility as motivators, and influence drives and other personality subsystems.

Izard's great stress on the importance of facial expression in emotion will be discussed later. For the present it is important to see how this fits in with his general analysis of the emotional process. He suggests that emotion is made up of three intertwined components; neurophysiological activity, facial–postural activity and subjective experience which gives immediate meaning. Also important are two auxiliary systems: the reticular arousal system which amplifies and attenuates emotion, and the visceral system which helps to prepare the ground for emotion and also to sustain it. The general emotion process usually functions in an integrated way with the cognitive and motor systems, personality depending on the balance between the three. All emotions have some aspects in common, their non-cyclicity for example, as well as infinite generality and flexibility as they influence and regulate drives and personality.

Izard describes three person–environment interactions and five intra-individual processes which he believes can activate emotion. The person–environment interactions are: (1) obtained perception; this follows stimuli from selective activity of the receptors or sense-organs; (2) demanded perception in which an environmental/social event demands attention (the basic orienting reflex for example); (3) spontaneous perception, which is the indigenous activity of a perceptual system.

The intra-individual processes are: (1) memory which may be obtained (active), demanded (reminded) or spontaneous (indigenous cognitions); (2) imagination; (3) proprioception of facial–postural or other motor activity, taking the form of habitual striate action, spontaneous striate action or motor responses for adaptive behaviour; (4) endocrine and other autonomic activity which affects neural or muscular mechanisms of emotion; (5) spontaneous activity of any or all of the neuromuscular systems.

Izard affirms that once emotion has been instigated, its further phases depend on the site and nature of the original activity. There is no fixed number or order to these phases and very many possible mechanisms and interactions are involved, from perception, through neurophysiological reaction to subjective experience, and emotion–cognition–motor interaction.

Finally, Izard suggests that for any given emotion there are three levels: (1) electrochemical or neural activity which for the fundamental emotions is innate; (2) efferent aspects of emotional activity innervate striate muscle involved in *facial–postural* patterning; patterning which normally gives cues and information to the individual and to the observer; (3) for cues to be useful there must be *feedback* to the association areas of the brain, although an awareness of this process is not inevitable. It can be interfered with in many ways. However, if it is normal it generates the subjective experience of emotion, which in itself is independent of cognition. Izard believes that the emotion process can operate independently of any cognitive process, even though there is usually constant interaction. To Izard, cognition is not a *necessary* part of emotion, although it is very important, a point which will be returned to in Chapter 3.

Izard's conceptualization of emotion has far more implications than can be discussed here. In particular, it has led to the creating of a very interesting theory of emotional development (see Chapter 6). For now, there are a number of points which are too important to forgo.

(1) If feedback is distorted and nonveridical then so will be awareness. (2) Each level of emotion has particular functions which must be taken into account. (3) A given emotion is a subsystem of the whole system and has the qualities of the whole. (4) The emotional system has changed with evolution and also changes within individual development. (5) Emotion is continually present in consciousness. (6) Once an emotion is activated, the life systems are involved and we eventually become aware of the facial expressions *as* the subjective experience of emotion. (7) Autonomic or visceral arousal can occur without emotion. (8) Emotion can be initiated although facial expression is inhibited and there can be facial expression without emotional experience reaching consciousness.

As implied at the outset, Izard has probably had a greater influence on emotion than any other theorist. His ideas will be returned to on a number of occasions.

P. Ekman

Ekman's main contribution to emotion has come from his extensive research with Friesen on facial expression and on the matter of involuntary nonverbal leakage and voluntary masking (see Chapter 7). However, more recently (1984) the results of this research have led him to put forward some theoretical suggestions about the nature of emotion.

Ekman believes that he has evidence that there exist three differentiated systems of emotion—cognition, facial expression and ANS activity, which must interrelate. He admits the possibility that any aspect of emotion might be mediated by cognition, but emphasizes the significance of facial expression. Simply changing facial expression changes how one feels. Endorsing this, Ekman stresses pattern changes in expression and physiology, arguing that language is inadequate to account for the boundaries of emotion. A particular emotion might be highly differentiated in one language and yet entirely missing in another.

According to Ekman, emotion has ten major characteristics, a study of which permits certain theoretical assumptions to be made. (1) There is a distinctive pan-cultural signal for each emotion. (2) These are distinctive universal facial expressions of emotion which can also be traced phylogenetically. (3) Emotional expression involves multiple signals. (4) The duration of emotion is limited. (5) The timing of emotional expression reflects the details of a particular emotional experience. (4) Emotional expressions can be graded in intensity, reflecting variations in the strength of the subjective experience. (7) Emotional expression can be totally inhibited. (8) Emotional expressions can be convincingly simulated. (9) Each emotion has pan-human commonalities in its elicitors. (10) Each emotion has a pan-human pattern of ANS and CNS change.

From his belief in these characteristics, particularly of universality, Ekman's facial expression theory of emotion rests on three general assumptions. Emotion has evolved to manage the fundamental tasks of life. To be adaptive, there must be different patterns for each emotion. Finally, there is a general coherence in that within each emotion an interconnected pattern in expression and physiology is linked to appraisal. Like many recent theorists then, Ekman ultimately stresses cognition.

J.K. Averill

In writing a very closely worked treatise on a single emotion, anger, Averill (1982) has in at least two ways made an extraordinarily important contribution to our understanding of emotion. He has proved that it is possible to analyse a single emotion and to do it well, in itself a unique achievement. More than this, he has demonstrated that it is possible to gain theoretical insights into emotion in general from a study of a single example. In the discussion which follows it should be remembered that Averill's *Anger and Aggression* contains a full, rich and complex thesis which is almost certainly done an injustice here.

Anger, as characterized by Averill, is a conflictive emotion which is biologically related to aggressive systems and to social living, symbolization and self-awareness. Psychologically, it is aimed at the correction of an appraised wrong and socioculturally at upholding accepted standards of conduct. The remainder of this section concentrates on those aspects of this analysis that are germane to emotion more generally.

Averill regards emotions as social syndromes or transitory rules, as well as short-term dispositions to respond in particular ways and to interpret such responses as emotional. He distinguishes between conflictive emotions, impulsive emotions (inclinations and aversions) and transcendental emotions, which involve a breakdown in the boundaries of the ego.

Some emotions can have all three of these characteristics, but complex behaviour usually involves conflicts. These lead to particular emotions that are essential compromises that help to resolve the conflict. At the biological level, aggression is linked to anger but can not be equated with it. Averill argues that there is a biologically based tendency in humans to formulate and follow rules, an argument which echoes one in the psychology of language. Similarly, there is a biologically based tendency to become angry and upset when the rules are broken. All of which means that anger, and of course other emotions are highly symbolic and although biologically based depend very much on appraisals. To continue with the example of anger at the psychological level it is concerned with the correction of a perceived wrong. So any emotion will have its object, part of which is instigation, the other parts being a target and an aim. In this case, the instigation is an appraised wrong.

At the broader, sociocultural level, Averill suggests that anger is concerned with upholding accepted standards of conduct, perhaps unwittingly. Any emotion is concerned with such standards, rules which guide behaviour some of them again being to do with appraisal. The other rules relevant to emotion concern its expression, its course and outcome and the way in which it is casually attributed. To give one of Averill's examples, a fairly self-evident rule of anger is that it should be spontaneous rather than deliberate.

Averill's general view is that any theory of emotion should not be restrictive, but should relate to all of the pertinent phenomena, however complex they might be, if they are seen as part of emotion in everyday langauge. The implication is that everyday emotion concepts can be scientifically useful. The aim would be to try to uncover what Averill terms the prototypic attributes of various emotions and to try to determine the rules that guide them. Averill then views emotion very much as a social construction based on an intricate mixture of biologically determined aspects and a number of levels of cognition, from perception through appraisal to symbolic rules and standards.

GENERAL CONCLUSIONS

Having now described over thirty theories of emotion, representing most psychological approaches to the subject, and varying in their spheres of influence, it remains to withdraw any common threads that there might be. First it would seem reasonable to discard theories which suggest that emotion should not exist as a discrete topic but is merely one aspect of arousal. These theories only seemed to typify a state of quiescence, or perhaps disenchantment with research into emotion which existed some years ago. And they are clearly untypical, though having the saving grace of drawing attention to the role of physiological arousal in emotion. Linked to this of course is a long history of ideas which intertwine emotion with motivation.

Arguably the main common ground between most theories of emotion is the explicit or implicit belief that discrete emotions and emotional expressions exist—a point made with some force by Izard (1972; 1977). This seems to be so whether emotion is viewed primarily as a response or as a motivational process. Then it commonly follows from the idea of discrete emotions that some of these are primary (perhaps innately determined) and others are secondary (learned combinations of the primary emotions).

Other points in common were also shared by the early theories of emotion and have changed little in the half-century or more since they appeared. Emotion is still regarded by most theorists as a system which affects and is affected by other systems, and emotions are usually thought of as varying in range and intensity. Also the implication is often made that the control of emotion possible, a point which has obvious importance in therapy.

In the more recent and increasingly influential theories there are a number of interesting developments to be seen. Importance is now squarely attached to the expressive side of emotion, especially when this is facial rather than postural. This is reflected in a recent proliferation of work (see Chapter 7) as well as ideas. This emphasis harks back to the enormous influence that James has had on emotion.

The role of consciousness in emotion is beginning to be explored, as it relates to arousal and cognition, via hypothetical feedback mechanisms. If such analyses lead to the development of techniques which allow something more than speculation about consciousness, they could be crucially important not only to an understanding of emotion but also to psychology in general.

Each of these points is made in a context in which emotion is viewed as an integral system of the normally functioning individual, a system which interrelates with other systems and which is necessary to the development of personality. So rather than being given a back seat or even being left out altogether, emotion is now being given far more of a central position.

However, the most telling aspect of the recent theories of emotion, whatever specific form they take, or whatever their point of origin or sources of influence, is cognition. All theorists now view emotion as intricately and intimately intertwined with cognition. As will be seen in Chapter 4, this is not only increasing our understanding of emotion, at last, but is also improving our knowledge of cognition. It is also leading to new ways of looking at both of these basic aspects of human functioning and is allowing new questions to be asked.

3

The Physiology of Emotion

From the subjective viewpoint it appears that different emotions involve distinct bodily changes. It seems obvious, not only subjectively but also from observing the reactions of other people, that emotion is physiologically arousing. Many theorists, from the time of James and Cannon onwards have recognized this and have had an important, if not a central, role for physiology in their accounts of emotion. It is probably indisputable that physiological change is frequently involved in emotion, but whether or not physiological arousal is *necessary* to emotion is more debatable. However, leaving aside this theoretical knot, it is reasonable to say that the *significant* place of physiology in emotion has prompted many decades of empirical investigation. From its beginnings though, research into the physiological substrates of emotion has been burdened by problems enough to make conclusions difficult to draw.

There are three basic research strategies within physiological psychology. (1) The most common involves the making of lesions in some part of the nervous system and observing any effects that these might have on behaviour. The lesions may be very restricted in extent or may be complete transections or ablations. There can be great difficulty in the interpretation of any data which derives from this strategy. (2) The second method is that of electrical or chemical stimulation. This type of technique has long been used to record changes in the ANS. However, since the development of a technology which allows the chronic implantation of electrodes, it has also been much used in CNS measurement. (3) The final strategy is fundamental to psychophysiological research. It involves the record of ongoing changes in such peripheral physiological measures as respiration, heart rate, etc. Each of these research methods has produced a wealth of data.

Naturally, physiological studies of emotion often employ behavioural measures. Although the independent variable in such studies is usually physiological, it is always the resultant changes in behaviour which have been of interest although recent ideas might prompt a harder look at links between physiology and cognition. There are two types of behavioural measure of emotion commonly taken in physiologically based studies. The more frequent, and more naive, is the direct behavioural description of 'typical' emotional reactions, usually in infrahuman subjects. For example, fear in cats is thought to be indicated by freezing or by dashing away, rage by violent lashing, arching movements, thrusting, jerking, snarling, biting, and so on, pleasure by purring.

Although such measures appear to be simple, on occasion they have been developed into complex systems. Brady and Nauta (1953), for example, describe a six-component rating of emotionality, including resistance to handling, vocalization, startle and flight, urination and defecation.

The other behavioural measures used in physiological studies of emotion are considerably more sophisticated. They derive largely from techniques designed to study conditioned emotional responding (CER) and active and passive avoidance. Briefly, the CER technique is based on the indirect recording of the 'emotional' influences of signalled uncontingent stimuli as these affect some ongoing operant baseline of behaviour. Active avoidance involves the making of a (fear-motivated) response in the presence of a neutral stimulus to avoid some forthcoming aversive stimulus. Passive avoidance can be defined as learning to avoid some aversive stimulus by *not* making a response.

The first of the behavioural measures mentioned above points to two of the problems encountered in this field. In many studies, although the physiological manipulations are reasonably sophisticated, the behavioural observations are naive, poorly controlled and somewhat subjectively judged. Also, such studies frequently use infrahuman subjects. The difficulty in extrapolating from animals to man has already been discussed. In the search for the physiological substrates of emotion, it is even more of a difficulty. Presumably, the precise functions of, and interconnections between, various parts of the nervous system differ from species to species.

However, there is a more fundamental set of problems involved in studies of CNS ablation and stimulation. There are a number of technical difficulties: for example, how to separate the brain into distinct areas, how to determine the precise location and extent of a particular lesion, how to confine a lesion or an electrical or chemical stimulation to a given area. Also, there is the question of localization of function. The majority of studies of emotion which have dwelt on the CNS depend on this concept. Its meaning, however, is difficult to pin down. The implication is that some structurally well-defined area of the brain is (causally) responsible for some well-defined behavioural function. This cannot be so. At best we can say that some area of the brain may be a necessary condition for the occurrence of some behaviour; it cannot be a sufficient condition. Also, even to this extent, we cannot say that function is localized until we understand how the system works, which at present we do not. What can we say if, on removing one area of the brain or stimulating another, we achieve certain behavioural effects? No more than that these parts are necessary to that function. Too little is known about the precise function of the CNS to determine the neurophysiological extent of our manipulations. It may be that the interconnections within the CNS are such that a stimulus or lesion in one area may produce unexpected changes in behaviour. This, of course, could indirectly affect whatever behavioural measure we might be taking. The picture is complicated in at least three other ways. (1) There are large individual differences in behavioural reaction. (2) The effects of a particular

58

ablation may only become apparent under certain criterial conditions. (3) There is some evidence for mass action in the brain, or of a degree of equipotentiality between various areas. At present, there appears to be no solution to this set of problems. However, they should be borne in mind when evaluating the research and theory to be found in this chapter. Most of this research relies unquestioningly on a belief in localization of function.

Those interested in the physiology of emotion have naturally followed diverse paths to the subject. These have frequently been dictated by that part of the nervous system which the investigator believes to be of particular importance. Hence, there is much pertinent information to be found in studies of the ANS, the subcortex and the cortex. The present chapter will cover these approaches systematically and will also include brief mention of research involving glandular function and neurochemistry, as well as giving consideration to the relationship between laterality and emotion.

Finally, it may be useful to refer to Figures 6 and 7. They represent in simplified form the structural relationship in the nervous system. Much of the text which follows concerns the functional relationships (of emotion) which are hypothesized to cut across these.

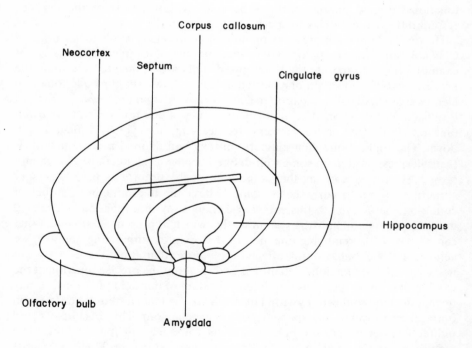

Figure 6. Diagrammatic representation of the limbic systemic (shaded areas)

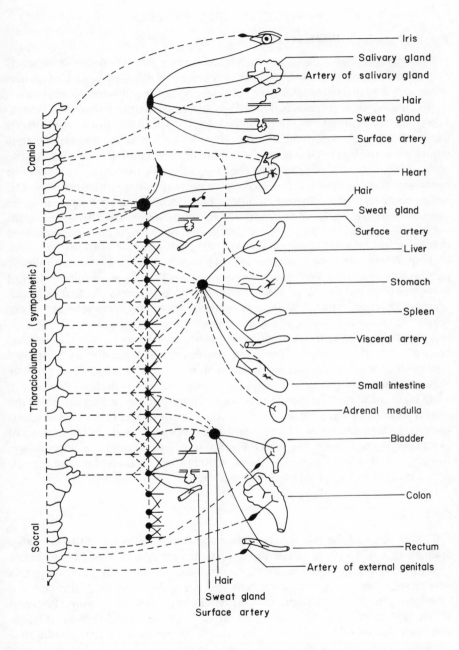

Figure 7. Diagrammatic representation of the autonomic nervous system and the
bodily structures that it serves (from Morgan, 1965)

PERIPHERAL MECHANISMS

Psychophysiological measures

Psychophysiology is the term which has come to be used to describe the study of peripheral measures of ANS activity, such as respiration or cardiovascular change. It is appropriate to begin a consideration of the physiology of emotion by discussing such responses, since they are basic to the influential James–Lange theory. Initially, the psychophysiological approach looks promising: if there are physiological concomitants of emotion, then introspectively they would seem to be reflected in our breathing or blood flow or sweating, and so on. Subjectively, we can *feel* such changes; when we are angry or afraid our breathing may become fast and shallow or we may sweat more profusely. Or, for example, the physiological changes which occur when we engage in some vigorous sport are superficially similar to those which stem from emotion-producing stimuli, but they 'feel' different bodily. Also, it might be expected that any peripheral changes would perhaps occur in orderly patterns corresponding to the various emotions. However, a somewhat disappointing picture has emerged. With a few important exceptions, psychophysiological measures have not produced evidence for any clear patterns. At first sight this seems odd, since, intuitively, peripheral feedback would seem relevant, if not crucial, to our experiencing of emotion. With hindsight, however, it is perhaps less surprising. Psychophysiology relies quite heavily on the idea of general arousal, indeed it is one of the main sources of evidence for its existence. Although arousal is a subjectively reasonable concept, it leads to notoriously imprecise predictions about behaviour or physiological function. Bearing in mind these difficulties, some of the main psychophysiological measures and the results which they have led to will be briefly discussed. The interested reader is referred to Grossman (1967) and Sternbach (1966) for good overall reviews of psychophysiology, and the Ciba Foundation Symposium on Physiology, Emotion and Psychosomatic Illness (1972) for a discussion of specific developments in the physiology of emotion.

Circulation

Circulation and the circulatory system are important both to the everyday maintenance of bodily function and to any emergency which may arise. There are two equally significant mechanisms involved: (1) the heart, pumping; this may change both in rate and strength and is regulated by central reciprocal links between the parasympathetic and sympathetic nervous systems (PNS and SNS); (2) the relative dilation or constriction of the blood vessels; dilation increases the blood which is available to a particular area and results in a consequent constriction elsewhere. The main measures are blood pressure and pulse rate. Although circulatory changes are correlated with behavioural changes, for example in the patterns of sleep and waking or in reaction to sudden, intense stimuli, we cannot use them to discriminate between the various emotions although Lacey and Lacey (1970) provide a possible exception to this. However, cardiovascular changes may represent changes in general arousal. Also, although some circulatory disorders are clearly psychosomatic (for example eczema), there is no evidence for particular dysfunctions stemming from particular emotional problems.

Galvanic skin response

Galvanic skin response (GSR) refers to the electrical resistance of the skin to the flow of electromotive current. Skin resistance (or its reciprocal, skin conductance) fluctuates constantly, but any strange or novel stimulus superimposes immediate although transitory changes on these fluctuations. The problem hinges on whether *all* new, sudden or intense stimuli lead to particular emotional reactions or whether these changes in the electrical activity of the skin just reflect general activation. The GSR allows little differentiation between emotions. There are only poor relationships between changes in skin reactivity and (1) the intensity of the stimuli which produced them, (2) reports of emotional reactions, and (3) distinctions between pleasant and unpleasant emotions.

Respiration

The rate and depth of breathing must be quite directly and closely related to our basic needs. Yet again, this indicates that respiration should provide a fair measure of general arousal. By the same token, respiratory changes would appear likely to accompany any emotional reactions, but, as with the other psychophysiological measures, no methodologically adequate study has successfully used respiratory changes to distinguish between emotions or even between emotional and nonemotional situations.

Other peripheral measures

The remaining psychophysiological measures present essentially the same picture as that given by circulation, skin resistance and respiration. Muscle potential, for example, providing an index of muscular tension, also simply reflects general alertness or arousal but no relationships are seen with specific emotions. An early exception to this general rule was seen with gastrointestinal activity and various biochemical measures. Brunswick (1924), for example, showed there to be a loss of gastrointestinal tone during a number of emotional reactions, fear, envy, disappointment, etc. Distress, surprise and startle had the opposite effect of augmenting it.

Electrical activity of the brain

Although the electrical activity of the brain is clearly not a peripheral response like respiration or muscle potential, it is included here because it is often measured peripherally, and recorded as the electroencephalogram (EEG). When a person is at rest or relaxed the brain is characterized by regular 10 per second waves of electrical activity (alpha). This rhythm tends to disappear with the input of sensory stimulation. This is usually termed alpha-blocking; it seems to depend on the novelty of the stimulus and, in fact, may rapidly habituate.

As with the psychophysiological measures, arousal has a prominent part to play in the thinking of those investigators concerned with EEG activity. For example, it is argued that anxiety may produce nonspecific arousal and in so doing activate electrical activity in the brain (for example Darrow *et al.*, 1946). Also, the stimulation of the brain-stem reticular formation elicits cortical arousal (Moruzzi and Magoun, 1949) and the general autonomic and somesthetic responses which tend to accompany emotion (Ranson and Magoun 1939). Such relationships led to Lindsley's (1951; 1970) activation theory of emotion which is couched sheerly in terms of cortical arousal. To be viable, this theory would require fine shadings of cortical arousal; at the moment there is no evidence for these. Also, as with other psychophysiological measures, there is no evidence for relationship between specific emotional reactions and cortical EEG.

Relationships between the ANS and CNS—response patterning

From what has been said so far, it can be seen that work involving psychophysiological measures of emotion has not produced definitive results. However, there is one tenuous line of evidence which looks more promising. This will be described in greater detail. Most of the work in this area has sown only a generalized psychophysiological response to any emotion-producing stimuli. However, Wolf and Wolff (1947) carried out extended observations of a man with a gastric fistula. They found that there were two types of gastric change with emotional disturbance. (1) With reported anxiety and the wish to escape there was a reduction in the output of acid, vascularity and gastric motility. (2) With reported anger and resentment there was an acceleration of gastric functions. This was the first evidence for any form of physiological response patterning in emotion.

The discovery of epinephrine and norepinephrine (adrenaline and noradrenalin) reinforced the idea of physiological response patterning. Both increase systolic blood pressure, but epinephrine by increasing cardiac output and norepinephrine by increasing vascular resistance. These differences led Ax (1953) to devise an ingenious study, the results of which clearly show physiological differentiation between emotions. When connecting subjects to a polygraph recorder, he made them afraid or angry either by handling them roughly and criticizing them or by 'accidentally' giving them mild electric shocks, becoming alarmed himself and hinting at danger. He found a rise in diastolic blood pressure, muscle potential and in the number of increases in skin conductance, and a fall in heart rate. These effects were all more extreme in the anger than in the fear condition. Also, skin conductance and respiration rate both rose more in the fear condition. The fear pattern was similar to that which follows an epinephrine injection, the anger like that which follows a norepinephrine injection.

The only study directly to confirm Ax's results is Schachter's (1957). Any further attempts, including those of Lacey (1950; 1956) and Lacey and Lacey (1958), although demonstrating that there are various autonomic response patterns, have not shown that any of these correlate with particular emotional responses. However, Lacey and Lacey's (1970) work rests on a far more sophisticated and definitive approach to the psychophysiology of emotion than that of any previous studies. Their research depends on the fundamental idea that organs innervated by the ANS are important to emotion and that the various phenomena which they mediate can be brought together by the concept of arousal. Also, they suggest that ANS responses are usually regarded as effector events which may be modified by the CNS. However, they point out that ANS responses are also different and affect brain function accordingly.

Lacey and Lacey emphasize the cardiovascular system. They suggest that this provides negative feedback to the CNS, which causes *inhibitory* electrophysiological effects. They quote many studies which show increases in heart rate and blood pressure to cause electrophysiological change. Briefly, the argument is for an inhibitory CNS mechanism which produces an inhibitory control of the duration and course of internally and externally stimulated muscular, autonomic and cortical responses. This hypothesized area (centred on the nucleus of the tractus solitarius) is involved with autonomic function and has many cardiovascular afferents. Impulses from this region should suppress any emotional (cortical, motor, autonomic) activity. For example, stimulation of the aortic carotid sinus stops the sham rage usually shown by decorticate cats.

Lacey and Lacey re-evaluated the hypertension (chronic high blood pressure) and tachycardia (chronic high pulse rate) seen in acute emotion as attempts to inhibit an internal 'turmoil' rather than as an index of arousal. Hence, any decrease in blood pressure and pulse rate should lead to an absence of CNS inhibition leading in turn to a corresponding increase in excitation. A test of this proposal involves: (1) a demonstration, following a steady state, of experimental conditions which would *decrease* hypertension and tachycardia whilst other psychophysiological measures are reflecting changes typical of the SNS; (2) an evaluation of whether or not decreases in cardiovascular activity lead to increased behavioural efficiency.

Lacey and Lacey offer four lines of experimental evidence. (1) Lacey *et al.* (1963) gave subjects a series of tasks. Cardiac deceleration was produced by those tasks which required subjects to pay attention to the stimuli. Others which required concentration (for example, mental arithmetic) led to cardiac acceleration. A combination of both types of task produced intermediate changes in heart rate. Broadly speaking, 'cognitive' tasks led to a rise in heart rate and 'perceptual' tasks to a fall. Other psychophysiological measures did not reflect this pattern but simply showed the usual arousal. (2) Lacey and Lacey (1970) extended this work in reaction time (RT) studies. They found a systematic deceleration in heart rate during the warning signal. This was accompanied, for example, by wide variation in respiratory responses and preceded by an early, immediate and transient acceleration in heart rate. These heart-rate changes were intensified in more highly motivated subjects. If the actual RT stimulus was omitted, the deceleration continued (subject 'searching' for the target) and with a longer fore-period, the heart decelerated to much the same level but took longer to do so. Also, the greater the deceleration in heart rate the faster the RT. (3) The third line of evidence uses Walter *et al.'s* (1964) CNVs, a measure of negative EEG variation reflecting the readiness of a subject to respond (RT). Lacey and Lacey (1970) found that the greater the cardiac decelertion, the greater the CNV; this was also related to speed of reaction. (4) Finally, there is some external support. To quote but one example of this, Israel (1969) related cardiovascular change to cognitive style. He regarded people as either levellers (those who make global judgements, do not attend to detail, etc.) or sharpeners (those who do attend to detail). On appropriate tasks, the heart beat of sharpeners decelerated more than that of levellers, a difference not reflected in other psychophysiological measures.

Lacey and Lacey have a more productive approach to the psychophysiology of emotion than many investigators. They emphasize the cardiovascular system, which they view as a specific, delicate response mechanism which does more than reflect nonspecific arousal. Within general arousal, there appears to be some response patterning and perhaps the possibility of emotional differentiation. However, recent ideas from some of the cognitivists suggest that any differentiation between the emotions which is not accomplished physiologically may well be catered for cognitively. (See Chapter 8 on abnormal emotion for a discussion of further links between cognition and physiology in the section on psychosomatic disorders).

Peripheral theories of emotion

As was pointed out in Chapter 2, James's (1884) theory of emotion was the first to be couched in psychological rather than philosophical terms. It was also the first of the 'peripheral' theories. Before James, organisms were thought only to react emotionally after having reacted cognitively. James reversed this in saying that emotion (as felt experience) occurs after visceral discharge and feedback from motor responses; we feel 'happy' because we are laughing. In its inherent untestability, James's theory was not satisfactory. On the other hand, in stressing the significance of the viscera and facial expression it had far-reaching effects.

In that he regarded the thalamus as the seat of the emotions, Cannon (1927) based his theory more on the CNS than did James. Cannon regarded the thalamus as exerting a continuous inhibitory control which is lifted when emotional stimuli arrive at the cortex. Impulses then released by the thalamus proceed via autonomic motor nerves for behaviour and to the cortex for emotional experience. The research which led to this theory and the various points which can be levelled against it will be discussed later. More importantly, however (see Mandler, 1962), Cannon made five major criticisms of James's views. (1) The artificial production of visceral changes does not seem to lead to emotion. (2) There is no evidence for any visceral response patterning in emotion. (3) Visceral organs have little sensitivity; any feedback they give could hardly be used to differentiate emotion. (4) If the viscera are surgically separated from the nervous system by sympathectomy or vagotomy then emotional behaviour still occurs even though no visceral responses can be made. (5) The viscera only react slowly. Emotion could only occur at least one second after external stimulation. Subjectively, it seems to be faster than this.

On the basis of empirical research, Schachter (for example, 1964) has effectively argued against Cannon's points (1), (2) and (3) above, at least as they refer to the general role of the viscera in emotion, rather than especially in vitiating James (see Chapter 3). This work seems to show that the viscera are a necessary, but not sufficient, condition for the occurrence of emotion, although it is difficult to be finally certain that emotion cannot occur without visceral involvement. Also Mandler (1962) argues that points (4) and (5) are accounted for by the fact that after the initial formation of emotional behaviour it may become conditioned to external stimuli, and therefore may occur either before visceral change or without its intervention.

Two further theories also bear on the James–Cannon controversy. Like James, Wenger (1950) equated visceral responses with emotion, but also suggested how these could function in a 'hypothetical robot'. To get away from James's introspectionist sort of approach, he concentrated very much on behaviour. He regarded emotional 'states' as in fact emotional 'complexes', which he saw as explaining why we usually have no language which is adequate to describe them. Wenger also suggested that our perception of an emotional stimulus depends on the pairing of conditioned and unconditioned stimuli, following which the arousal of the ANS leads to visceral responses. These in turn lead to drive stimuli which Wenger regarded as perceptions of visceral action. Appropriately enough, the end point in this chain is overt (muscular) response and verbal report.

Unlike that of James, Wenger's theory is non-introspective and emphasizes behaviour. However, there it lacks sophistication; it is a general mixture of behaviouristic and nonbehaviouristic elements, whilst still pointing to the role of the viscera.

If Wenger's theory bears comparison with James's, then Freeman's (1948) dynamotor theory was dependent on Cannon's. He suggested a concept of 'neuromuscular homeostasis' pointing to a rapprochement between central and peripheral mechanisms. He regarded emotional experiences as 'peripheral meaning structures'. These come from two sources which interact cortically: proprioceptive impulses from learned responses, and unlearned thalamic reactions. Freeman is proposing a combination between proprioceptive stimuli and hypothalamic processes. This allows him the experiential aspects of emotion via proprioception but keeps emotional behaviour distinct from this. This is different from Cannon's view in that the latter postulated distinct physiological substrates for the two. However, Freeman's theory suffers from the same lack of sophistication as Wenger's.

Although it is now some years old, Fehr and Stern's (1970) argument is still the most recent to suggest a renewed emphasis on the periphery in studying the physiology of emotion. Moreover, they suggest that the original James–Lange theory still has much to recommend it. James spoke of 'primary feelings', 'immediate reflexes' and 'secondary feelings'. Fehr and Stern maintain that primary feelings and immediate reflexes might *now* be seen as hypothalamic discharges which inhibit the cortex and excite the ANS (the importance of the hypothalamus to emotion will be seen later). Secondary feelings are perhaps given by afferent feedback from the periphery. This is a similar idea to that of Lacey and Lacey (1970). However, Fehr and Stern deny that there is afferent feedback from the periphery. They argue that behaviour can be produced such that it looks like emotion but without involving visceral mechanisms. Although this may be so, afferent feedback may still occur in 'real' emotion. They also point out that with peripheral feedback cut out there may still be primary feelings and immediate feelings to the object in question. However, as Mandler (1962) suggested, these may be learnt.

Fehr and Stern discuss many investigations which lend support to the importance of the periphery in emotion. For example, Hohmann (1966) described the reactions of 25 adult males with lesions in the spinal cord as being consistent with James's theory. Their reported experiences of feelings of anger, sex and fear were decreased. Hohmann showed that although apparently emotional behaviour might still be seen in these patients if and when it is appropriate, no *feelings* are involved.

As might be expected, Fehr and Stern lay most emphasis on the evidence supporting differential physiological responses to different stimuli. Following Lacey and Lacey (1958) they suggest that there are three aspects to this research, these depending on the type of stereotypy involved: (1) situational stereotypy in which distinct psychophysiological response patterns are related to various empirical conditions, particularly those which simulate various emotions; (2) intrastressor stereotypy, in which for a given stress, an individual shows a reproducible psychophysiological response pattern; (3) interstressor stereotypy, in which the response pattern for one stressor is similar to that for others. This clearly supports Cannon rather than James. But Fehr and Stern argue that all the *different* stress situations which have been studied in this context possibly have fear or anxiety as a common factor. They maintain that any study in this field can be interpreted in this way.

Overall, Fehr and Stern put forward a plea, which is endorsed here, that the periphery should not be ignored in any physiological consideration of emotion. The James–Lange theory was sound insofar as it is now clear that the viscera are important, if not necessary to emotion. Also Fehr and Stern's ideas are relevant to other peripheral theories of emotion (see Goldstein (1968) for a review of these). At present, the significance to emotion of peripheral physiological mechanisms would seem difficult to deny. However, it should not be forgotten that much of the basic work involving psychophysiological measures (including EEG) assigns to them no more than a vague reflection of general arousal, and a very complex role in possible response stereotypy.

INTERMEDIATE MECHANISMS

In heading this section, the term intermediate is used very broadly. There have been some approaches to the physiology of emotion which do not fit readily within a peripheral or a central framework. Their methodology differs from that of the more usual research strategies, and they have not been much pursued within the last decade, but their results are relevant to the general physiological bases of emotion. They should at least be borne in mind in any more theoretically pertinent consideration of possible ANS or CNS mechanisms in emotion.

The endocrines and the ANS

The most interesting study of the interrelationships between the endocrine systems, the ANS and emotion has been made by Brady (for example, 1962; 1970a; 1970b). He views emotion as simply a change, an abrupt immediate disruption in the interaction between the organism and its environment. This leads Brady to a behavioural analysis of emotion, but one that has an overriding emphasis in its psychophysiological and abnormal correlates.

Brady, and others working with a similar viewpoint, have followed three strategies. (1) There has been interest in cardio-respiratory changes which result from acute and chronic emotional stress. Such changes have been found mainly in the results of studies involving behavioural conditioning. (2) Brady (1970a) describes a long series of his own studies concerned with visceral–alimentary and endocrine changes; these are more permanent than the cardiorespiratory effects. (3) Finally, some studies have related gastro-intestinal and infectious disease to emotional stress.

Brady's own studies are of monkeys incarcerated in a complex restraining apparatus. They can be given food, water and foot-shock. They have access to a hand-operated lever, visual and auditory stimuli can be presented to them, and samples of blood and urine collected. Everything is automized, allowing straightforward studies using the CER paradigm or conditioned avoidance, but making it a fairly simple matter to take psychophysiological measures.

Brady's general findings are succinctly summarized in his 1970 papers.

Firstly, they demonstrate relationships between autonomic–endocrine activity and emotional behaviour. For example, there is an increase in the output of the pituitary–adrenocortical system during the acquisition of a CER. Brady suggests that such findings simply reflect the general arousal which is induced by such 'emotional' situations. Brady has also shown the importance of the organism's previous history in determining these reactions, behavioural and autonomic–endocrine activity again being closely related.

Brady's investigations point to many interdependent autonomic and endocrine systems as providing broad patterns of change during more prolonged emotional responding. He speculates that there may be a relationship between such physiological activity and broader aspects of emotion, 'mood' or 'affective dispositions' for example. In that it provides some further evidence for physiological response patterning in emotion, Brady's approach is interesting. Also the work which it has led to is difficult to fault. However, this evaluation is tempered by the relative artificiality of the experimental procedures on which the approach depends and by the gulf between Brady's relatively sophisticated theorizing behaviourally and physiologically and his speculations about concepts such as mood.

Intercranial electrical stimulation (ICS)

Apart from the traditional stimulation of various parts of the brain simply to see what behavioural effects this might have, brain stimulation has also been used as punishment, reward and motivation. Its motivating effects seem to be related to emotion. Delgado *et al.* (1954) and Miller (1958) have carried out many studies on the aversive effects of intercranial stimulation. In a typical experiment, cats would receive electric shock through a grid floor. They could terminate this by turning a wheel. Once this response had been satisfactorily learned, the foot-shock would be substituted with electrical stimulation of the CNS through implanted electrodes. Such studies show that animals learn avoidance responses based on CNS stimulation just as fast as those based on external shock. This lends support to the hypothesis that in avoidance learning fear rather than pain is the motivating agent, as it is thought to be in studies involving external aversive stimulation. Similarly, the well-known studies of reward by Olds and Milner (1954) and Olds (1955; 1958) support the view (see later) that the limbic system is at the physiological core of emotion.

Delgado (1970) describes an interesting technological development in this field. This involves the remote stimulation of the brain with radio waves, whilst recording brain activity telemetrically. So, any subjects are behaving freely. Using cats, monkeys and chimpanzees electrical stimulation of the brain has been found to alter behaviours such as pupillary contraction, food intake, grooming, aggression and general instrumental behaviour. Also, two-way 'communication' has been effected with the brains of people suffering from disorders of the temporal lobe. With the EEG continuously monitored, correlations between electrical activity and behaviour have been observed. It remains to be seen whether or not this type of strategy will have the theoretical or therapeutic significance that it promised.

Intercranial chemical stimulation

A technique which has sometimes been used in the study of the physiology of emotion involves the intercranial administration of drugs. In most cases, this procedure simply has reversible effects on function without causing any permanent structural damage. It is therefore useful in delineating the general relationships between the CNS and behaviour. However, in an early review of this field, Grossman (1970) points to two problems. First, it is difficult to determine precisely either the extent or the rate of diffusion of a drug through the brain. Second, but just as important, the way in which the drug acts is often unknown. For example, it may affect behaviour directly and/or because abnormal conditions are created at that point where it is injected. Of course, appropriate control groups could, and should, be used to take account of these types of confounding influence.

The type of work which has been carried out involves substances such as carbachol, which is parasympathetic-like in action. Grossman (1963), for example, injected it into the amygdaloid complex of cats. The initial reaction was generalized seizures and convulsions, but the EEG gradually became more normal. Everyday behaviour was relatively unchanged except that the animals remain vicious and unhandleable. In some cases this effect was still in evidence after five months. Similar studies with rats have demonstrated altered reactions to punishment, thus making it difficult to establish CERs and passive avoidance responses.

Many similar effects on emotionality have been shown with carbochol injections in the hypothalamus and preoptic areas, the thalamus and the caudate nucleus. But more interesting are the reactions which follow injections into the lower brain areas. For example, an injection of carbachol into the brain-stem reticular formation leads to agitation, and inhibition of avoidance responses, reactions which gradually adjust to repeated injections. However, to date, studies involving intercranial chemical stimulation, although potentially interesting, have not much clarified our knowledge of the physiological substrates of emotion.

Neurochemistry and emotion

In his review of work on the neurochemistry of emotion, Kety (1970) divides it into two major fields of study: (1) that concerned with peripheral biochemical changes which are related to a possible central emotional state; (2) that concerned with those changes in brain biochemistry which are related to emotion.

Work on the neurochemistry of emotion began with the discovery of lysergic acid diethylamide and of its interactions with serotonin in inhibiting the action of smooth muscle. It seemed as though one function of serotonin was the direct control of mood. In addition to this, Kety's (1970) interest was fired by the possible importance of norepinephrine. This will be briefly discussed to exemplify the influence of amines on emotional behaviour. For instance, Thierry *et al.* (1968) showed that severe and mild stress induce the synthesis and use of norepinephrine in the brain. And Reis and Fuxe (1969) demonstrated an increase in norepinephrine when rage occurred in cats electrically stimulated in the amygdala or with brain-stem lesions. And drugs which promote or inhibit norepinephrine also promote or inhibit rage.

Kety (1966) suggests, for example, that drugs which alter our emotions also affect the amines in a way which indicates that they are involved in emotion. Reserpine, for example, often depresses those who take it to combat hypertension. And antidepressants have the opposite effects on norepinephrine. Of course, depression is only one aspect of emotion, but such results are suggestive.

Kety does not maintain that neurochemistry is the final answer to the analysis of emotion. He believes, however, that the amines in the brain possibly provide a system which is 'sluggish, coarse and diffuse' but which parallels the sensorimotor system. He regards it as more primitive and crude but based on survival. It may therefore be influencing all behaviour rather than just emotion.

CENTRAL MECHANISMS

The subcortex

That various subcortical CNS structures are important to the physiology of emotion is almost axiomatic. However, their precise function and inter-relationships are confusing. This is reflected in both fact and theory. At the lowest level of the CNS, the *spinal card* and *medulla* provide the first information. Animals with transected spinal cords show some autonomic emotional behaviour, but animals with cuts just above the cord and the medulla show far better integrated autonomic responses—presumably because the medulla probably controls circulatory and respiratory functions.

The *brain-stem* (that area above the medulla and below the cerebrum) is more interesting. Studies involving decerebration (i.e. brain-stem transection) tend to rely on observations rather than experimentation to concentrate on behaviours such as rage in dogs. Decerebrate animals display some emotion. However, this is usually poorly coordinated and poorly directed. The general rule seems to be the lower the brain-stem transection the poorer the behavioural integration. However, even if it occurs at the highest level, the resultant behaviour is never fully integrated. This suggests that individual emotional responses may be regulated in the lower brain-stem but that the cortex is necessary for their integration. As will be seen later, evidence at the cortical level is regarded as supporting this idea.

The subcortical structures most implicated in emotion are the *hypothalamus* and *thalamus*. The classic study was that of Dusser de Barenne (1920), who found that decorticate animals (i.e. with the hypothalamus and thalamus intact) showed violent rage in response to trivial stimuli. This led to the term 'sham rage'. Results of lesion studies are well exemplified by Bard (1928), who confirmed that the threshold for rage is lowered after decortication (pointing to the inhibitory function of the cortex). However, he also demonstrated that a complex emotional reaction was evident only when the hypothalamus was left intact. The general emotional reactions of decorticates do not tend to be directed towards the source of stimulation. This may be partly due to the increased hypersensitivity which is thought to result from the removal of the forebrain.

Evidence on possible hypothalamic involvement in emotion also comes from studies of electrical stimulation and lesions rather than complete transections. For example, there appear to be distinct systems which mediate attack, defence and flight. In general, electrical stimulation of the hypothalamus produces rage; its destruction should therefore lead to a decrease in emotional behaviour. This was partially borne out by Brady (1960; 1962) for example, with posterior lesions. He also showed, however, that medial lesions may lead to well-integrated but very savage rage and ferocity. And Bard (1960) suggested that emotional behaviour in animals that have been electrically stimulated in the hypothalamus eventually returns to normal.

Work involving the thalamus is even more complex and confusing. For example, stimulation of the posteroventral nucleus elicits a range of emotional activities described as anything from anxiety to attack or defence. And stimulation of the dorsomedial nucleus leads to fear (behaviours such as crouching). Clearly, the thalamus is well positioned to perform a subcortical integrative function, particularly of afferent input, and there is a wealth of early clinical data bearing on its importance to emotion. Such evidence led to Cannon's usefully straightforward thalamic theory of emotion. However, there seem to be two main objections to Cannon's theory. (1) The complete removal of the thalamus does not affect the rage reactions of decorticate animals—it is only removal of the posterior and ventral parts of the hypothalamus which does this. (2) Removal of the thalamus should produce a permanent rage reaction, which it does not. In spite of these objections to Cannon's theory, the thalamus must be involved in emotion to some extent. There are also two difficulties in interpreting any experimental evidence which bears on these issues. It should be noted in fact that these difficulties are of general application to this area of research. (1) The thalamus has extensive projections which make it very awkward to confine lesions or electrical stimulation to specific nuclei. (2) The thalamus has important sensory functions. This makes it difficult to separate effects due to a change in emotional capability from those which might be due to changed sensory function.

To summarize, the subcortex has an important part to play in emotion. This has been indicated with studies involving either complete transections or preparations (experimentally in animals, clinically in humans), lesions or stimulation. The functions and projections of the subcortex are so complex that the overall pattern becomes very confusing. However, in general terms, the higher the position of a subcortical structure within the CNS, the more important to emotion it appears to be. This culminates in the hypothalamus and thalamus.

The cortex and the limbic system

Although there is little doubt that subcortical structures of the CNS are important to the mediation of emotion, it is equally clear that they *alone* do not account for all the facts. The cortex must be involved, particularly those parts of it (i.e. mainly the limbic system) which are interconnected with subcortical areas. For example, general decortication has three main effects on emotion. (1) There is a lowered threshold to those stimuli which usually produce emotion—the organism becomes over-reactive. (2) There tends to be little direction to emotional responses—they are very generalized. (3) The timing of the emotion is changed—it has an unusually rapid onset and offset. These effects point to the cortex as having an inhibitory influence on emotion, which is of course removed when the cortex is removed.

The boundaries of the limbic system are ill-defined and, somewhat like national boundaries, change from time to time. The most recent formulations include all the *allorcortical* and *juxtallocortical* parts of the cerebrum. These are the phylogenetically older areas of the neocortex. Structurally, they are both simpler and distinct from the remainder. These areas are formed by: the cingulate, retrosplenial and hippocampal gyri, the island of Reil, the operculum and that part of the frontotemporal cortex which is not neocortex; also included are the olfactory bulb and tubercle, the diagonal band of Broca, the septal area, the prepyriform and preamygdaloid complex and the hippocampal formation. Finally, the amygdaloid complex is also usually subsumed under the general limbic system heading. This is solely for the sake of functional convenience, since it is actually subcortical. Much of the literature on the limbic system is concerned with its important olfactory functions. However, the main usefulness of this work to the study of emotion has been to point to the extensive interconnections within the limbic system.

Lateral limbic system

From the research viewpoint, the lateral limbic system can be divided into five major structural possibilities. These will be discussed in turn.

1. *Temporal lobe.* It is in the area of the temporal lobe that Kluver and Bucy (1937; 1938) first made their observations which led to the coining of the term Kluver–Bucy syndrome. They made lesions in the temporal lobe involving the hippocampus, amygdala and pyriform and frontotemporal cortex. This made

previously aggressive monkeys tame, active, hypersexual and very oral, a finding which was supported by Bard and Mountcastle (1948) and Bard (1950), who first ablated the neocortex, leaving the limbic system intact. This produced tame, placid, emotionally unresponsive animals. They then produced an increase in emotionality by ablation of the amygdaloid complex and/or cingulate gyrus, suggesting that these areas may have inhibitory functions.

2. *Amygdaloid complex.* As mentioned above, some studies (for example, Bard and Mountcastle, 1948) show there to be an increase in emotional activity following amygdaloid lesions. Others do not (for example, Schreiner and Kling, 1953). Similarly equivocal findings obtain for aggression and dominance. At this point it is perhaps worth re-emphasizing that it is virtually impossible to ascertain from one study to the next whether or not the lesions involved were in precisely the same places. The possibility that they were not might account for any discrepancies in results. However, each of the studies on the amygdaloid complex shows some effect, which suggests that this area is at least sensitive for emotional reactivity. This is supported by studies (for example, Schwartzbaum, 1960) which show that amygdaloid lesions do not interfere with the acquisition of simple discriminations, but block the formation of CERs and non-reinforced response suppression. Also, animals with such lesions are relatively insensitive to changes in reinforcement conditions.

3. *Amygdala–hippocampus.* Both Smith (1950) and Walker *et al.* (1953) carried out studies involving lesions in the amygdala *and* the hippocampus. These produced the tameness and docility part of the Kluver–Bucy syndrome without the hypersexuality and orality. There appeared to be only a *temporary* reduction in emotional reactivity. Stimuli needed to be far more intense to produce the usual fear or rage.

4. *Hippocampus.* Electrical and chemical stimulation of the hippocampus facilitates emotional responses and autonomic reactions similar to those which are found during normal emotion (MacLean, 1954; 1957). Also the hippocampus influences hormonal mechanisms which may affect emotional behaviour. Whether they have been based on naive or sophisticated experimentation, the results of the many studies of hippocampal influences do not lead to any firm conclusions. For example, at the observational level, Orbach *et al.* (1960) showed monkeys with hippocampal lesions to be highly ferocious, and Mirsky (1960) showed no changes in the social rankings of monkeys with such lesions and described them as being less fearful of man. Similarly, at the more formal level, Pribram and Weiskrantz (1957) showed hippocampal lesions to lead to a decrement in active avoidance responses acquired pre-operatively, although Isaacson *et al.* (1961) showed rats with such lesions to acquire an avoidance response faster than control animals and to be more resistant to its extinction. On the other hand, most studies show hippocampal lesions to produce deficits in passive avoidance learning (for example, Isaacson and Wickelgren, 1962) and CER responding (for example, Brady and Hunt, 1955).

All hippocampal studies are difficult to interpret, since lesions and stimulation in this area may have many other effects which could indirectly influence emotional behaviour—such effects could be sensory, motor or motivational. Also, in few studies have the lesions been restricted precisely to the hippocampus; surrounding structures may have been damaged, which again clouds the issue.

5. *Frontotemporal cortex*. Fulton *et al*. 1952) show that ablation of the frontotemporal cortex leads to much of the Kluver–Bucy syndrome, but exluding orality and hypersexuality.

Reading between the lines of the mass of research findings on the lateral limbic system, it can be tentatively concluded that lesions in this area reduce emotional reactivity, especially where fear and rage are concerned.

Cingulate gyrus

In neodecorticate animals, removal of the cingulate gyrus has effects similar to those following ablation of the hippocampus and amygdala—a *rise* in emotional reactivity. In normal animals, removal of the cingulate gyrus *lowers* the threshold for fear or rage (for example, Bard and Mountcastle, 1948). But Pribram and Fulton (1954), for example, show such changes to be only temporary. Also, some studies (for example, Kennard, 1955) report an immediate but transient increase in emotionality following bilateral damage to the cingulate gyrus—there is an increased aggression and viciousness.

Lesions in the cingulate gyrus have often been used in attempts to combat clinical problems of anxiety neurosis and obsession but reports of such work obscure as much as they clarify. There is the usual problem of ensuring that only this area has been damaged and also that of the notorious inadequacy of behavioural testing by many clinicians. However, there have been a few well-conducted analyses of post-lesion behavioural changes, but not in human subjects. For example, Lubar (1964) showed that rats with cingulate lesions learnt passive avoidance better than normal rats, but were worse at active avoidance.

Septal region

Much of the experimental work on the septal region has been concerned with avoidance behaviour. Its beginnings can be found in Brady and Nauta (1953; 1955) and Brady (1958a; 1958b; 1960), who made lesions in the ventral portions of this area. Their general findings were quite clear, namely, increases in general emotional rectivity and in the startle response to loud auditory stimuli. But these effects disappeared within a few weeks, behaviour reverting to normal. In the longer term, there is improved performance in the acquisition of active avoidance responses but interference with these same responses if they have been acquired pre-operatively. Performance is impaired whenever appetitive responding is involved. Also, Harvey *et al.* (1961) found general post-septal lesion impairment of CER behaviour. This complex picture is further complicated by equivocal results from passive avoidance studies.

Four possible explanations of the observed changes in avoidance behaviour following septal lesions have been suggested: (1) an increase in emotional hypersensitivity; (2) faster active avoidance responses through a weakening of the crouching reflex; (3) the septal area may be partially in control of motivation; (4) behaviour may increasingly perseverate since the lesion has destroyed the mechanism which usually suppresses overt responses to non-reinforced or punished stimuli. There is insufficient evidence to judge which, if any, of these possibilities is more likely.

Frontal lobes

Although the frontal lobes are mainly neocortex, they are clearly implicated in emotion. There is a straightforward anatomical and functional relationship between them, the limbic system proper, and the relevant subcortical structures. Also, there are no obvious sensory or motor functions mediated by the frontal lobes and they do receive most of the hypothalamic connections to the cerebrum.

The basic work on the frontal lobes began with Ferrier (1875) who carried out frontal ablations in monkeys. This changed their 'character' and 'disposition'. This type of research eventually led to the development of the clinical technique of frontal lobotomy. Many thousands of lobotomies have been carried out. Analysis of these (for example, Rylander, 1939; 1948) leads to the conclusion that approximately half the cases result in lowered anxiety. However, many individuals also show post-operative intellectual impairment. Different investigators stress the efficacy of the ablation of different areas in the frontal lobes. No further conclusions can be drawn. With the increasing use of drug treatment, interest in frontal operations has declined. The frontal lobes are important to emotion, but how important or in what way is unknown. Arnold (1950) suggests that they are concerned with the sympathetic side of emotion, and (1970a and 1970b) with emotional appraisal. But some studies have found (for example, Kennard, 1955) an increase in emotional responsivity after lobotomy, rather than the more common decrease.

Lateralization

The last few years have included the development of a very promising area of research into the role of the CNS in emotion. This has been concerned with hemispheric lateralization or asymmetry. The two main hypotheses to be addressed are: (1) the right cortical hemisphere (RH) is responsible for the processing of all emotional information; (2) positive emotions are processed by the left hemisphere (LH) and negative emotions by the RH. The general evidence supports RH emotion processing, but psychophysiologically oriented investigators such as Schwarz *et al.* (1979) provide support for the LH positive/ RH negative hypothesis. More generally, this interesting area of research will be covered in some detail (see Campbell (1982) for review) since it has implications for the understanding not just of emotion, but also of laterality and of the relationship between emotion and cognition. The main stimuli used in this area of research have been words and faces, which will be discussed in turn.

Results of studies on emotion and laterality using verbal material are mixed, perhaps because the LH might dominate when words are involved. To take one example, Ley and Bryden (1982) told Ss (subjects) which ear to attend to when reading to them short sentences in different tones of voice (happy, sad, angry and neutral) with similar sentences in a neutral tone used as competing stimuli. Results demonstrated the RH to be mainly involved in judging emotion, i.e. there was a left ear advantage.

Another research strategy (for example, Strauss, 1983) involves comparing the recognition of emotional and neutral words. The results of such studies are confused by inexplicable sex differences, but suggest that emotional words are recognized more accurately than neutral words, even though the LH seems to be more accurate at processing both types. Moreover, research involving lateral eye movements (for example, Ahern and Schwartz, 1979) or comparing the emotional and neutral in the processing of words and faces have produced equivocal results.

Research on faces and laterality and emotion is more advanced than that involving words. Faces are processed in the RH, so any emotion laterality effect may be masked by this. Since faces have a RH advantage, emotional facial expressions have to produce an effect large enough to be apparent over this. A typical finding is that of Ley and Bryden (1982) who showed a clear left visual field (and hence RH) advantage for emotion and character judgements, the more intense and more negative the emotion, the greater the effect. In general there appears to be a RH advantage, supporting the main thrust of the results of the research using verbal material.

Throughout all the recent research on emotion and laterality, there are two abiding problems. Mood change which might be generated by any aspects of the experimental procedures may confound the results. Possibly intertwining with mood, sex differences confuse the interpretation of results, since they do not conform to any obvious pattern.

Four theories of emotion and laterality have been proposed, with some degree of overlap between them. (1) Tucker (1981) suggested that one set of neural arousal processes give rise to both cognition and emotion, processes which are lateralized. The LH is focal and analytic, the RH being diffuse and holistic, different emotions also accordingly being mediated. Disturbances to both emotion and cognition occur when the balance of the two arousal systems is disturbed. Subjectively, LH arousal is anxiety and RH arousal is mood level.

(2) Ley and Bryden (1988) suggest that RH is more sensitive than the LH to (mainly negative) emotional information which may not be conscious. RH

damage will produce euphoria or indifference, whereas LH damage will produce negative emotion and depression.

(3) Ladavas *et al.* (1984) also suggest that the organization of emotion is bilateral, since the hypothalamus and amygdala are not lateralized. Emotion works through a type of interference. For example, they maintain that sadness is RH-mediated and is related to the motor organization which gives expression to this emotion.

(4) This type of interference theory is also in accord with Kinsbourne's (1982) functional cerebral space model. He views emotions as lateralized in a complementary way, with the LH dealing with benefits, linked to approach, and the RH dealing with costs, linked to withdrawal. In this way, emotions and cognition are related through lateralization.

Although this area of study is a very interesting development in the investigation of emotion, it is fraught with methodological and conceptual difficulties. As Leventhal and Tomarken (1986) point out, many of the problems stem from a dearth of knowledge about the links between neural process and electrophysiological and neuropsychological measures. Interpretations of experimental results and test performance therefore must often be ambiguous.

Conclusions

It is as difficult to summarize the results of the more traditional work on the role of the CNS in emotion as it was to summarize evidence from psychophysiological investigations. Much of the work has been reasonably sophisticated on the physiological side, but there is always the problem of the precise locations and ramifications of the lesions or stimulations. Also, no study has produced unarguable evidence in support of localization of function, although most have simply assumed its existence. On the side of the dependent variable, behaviour, the problem has been the usual one of striking a balance between artificiality and the lack of methodological expertise. It is not easy to fault those studies which have taken measures of avoidance learning or CERs, but how relevant are they to emotion as it is commonly conceived? (See Chapter 5 for a discussion of this.) On the other hand, many behavioural measures taken following CNS manipulation have been little more than observational. Can we rely on the observers? Was their reliability checked? Has the investigator given a precise behavioural definition of 'ferocity' or 'pleasure', etc. All too often these questions can only be answered in the negative.

We are left in the position of knowing that various subcortical structures, particularly the hypothalamus and thalamus, and perhaps the brain-stem reticular formation, together with parts of the cortex, the limbic system and frontal lobes, are all implicated in emotion. But how exactly they are implicated, or what the functional relationships are between these structures, at the moment cannot be said. Often it is even impossible to say that they are necessary to emotion, simply that they are implicated. However, recent developments of research into lateralization are providing increasing evidence concerning the balance of the contribution made to emotion by the two cortical hemispheres.

Central theories of emotion

The remainder of this chapter will be taken up with a discussion of five physiological theories of emotion that rely on hypotheses that concern the CNS at least as much as the ANS. The first two are the only truly 'cortical' theories of emotion. The next two represent the more traditional, grander approaches to theory and the final theory is the most promising general psychobiological, physiologically based theory yet to have appeared.

Papez and MacLean

Papez (1937; 1939) and MacLean (1970) are the two major cortical theorists of emotion. Papez suggested that emotional expression and emotional experience may be dissociated and that the experiential aspects require cortical mediation. The physiological details of the theory are not worth describing since they are not supported by empirical data. From this starting point, MacLean suggests that the limbic system integrates emotional experience, although the effector mechanism is probably the hypothalamus. His reasons are: (1) the limbic system has extensive subcortical connections; (2) it is the one part of the cortex which has visceral representation. This accords with the extensive olfactory functions of the limbic system. MacLean argues that olfaction is of prime importance to motivation in lower animals, from food-seeking to obtaining sexual partners. He suggests that although the sense of smell is no longer involved to the same extent in more advanced organisms, their emotional behaviour may be mediated by the same mechanisms.

MacLean regards the hippocampus and amygdala as having especial significance for the subjective side of emotion. Unlike Papez, MacLean does not attempt to trace specific cortical pathways for emotion to follow. All the structures in the limbic system seem in some way to be involved in emotion, but *no* specific mechanisms have been found which mediate particular emotional patterns.

Gellhorn

Over many years, Gellhorn has made a huge contribution to our knowledge of the physiological bases of emotion. His work, however, both in research and theory, seems to have often been passed over by other investigators. Examples may be seen in Gellhorn (1964), Gellhorn and Loufbourrow (1963). The latter gives a good introduction to his erudite approach to the subject and provides a statement of his general theory.

Gellhorn suggests that the basis of emotion is the integration of somatic and autonomic activities, as modified by neurohumours (chemicals liberated at the nerve endings) and hormones, into what he terms ergotropic and trophotropic activities. The former are work-directed and the latter rest-directed. When one of the two systems becomes excited the other is correspondingly diminished, this balance being independent of the stimuli which bring it about. Gellhorn cites the example of the inhalation of carbon dioxide. This increases ergotropic excitability and raises the spindle threshold in the caudate nucleus. This spindle is a series of nervous potentials lasting for a few seconds, and is regarded as a good indicator of trophotropic reactivity. A similar effect is seen if the ergotropic part of the hypothalamus is increased in excitability (for example by electrical stimulation). On the other hand, the spindle threshold in the caudate nucleus drops if the organism receives barbiturates, chlorpromazine or a lesion in the posterior hypothalamus. Also, Gellhorn suggests that both ergotropic and trophotropic effects can be brought about by manipulations of the thalamic reticular system, septum, anterior hypothalamus and medulla—the continuous balance between the two supposedly reflecting emotional reactivity.

Gellhorn evaluates any work on the physiology of emotion in terms of his balance theory. In support he quotes well-established facts; for example, stimulation of the posterior hypothalamus produces rage, whereas lesions lead to somnolence. Or, trophotropic emotion is aroused through stimulation of the touch receptors, the typical picture being a slowing of heart rate, synchronous EEG, pupillary constriction and a tendency to sleep. He also regards broader aspects of emotion, like mood, as dependent on the ergotropic–trophotropic balance. For example, electroconvulsive therapy, like amphetamines, lifts ergotropic activity and mood, whereas the tranquillizers depress mood and diminish ergotropic hypothalamic activity (Gellhorn and Loufbourrow, 1963). Other aspects of Gellhorn's theory of emotion are very broad. He regards emotional arousal and the modification of the ergotropic–trophotropic balance as coming about through afferent impulses, internal environmental changes which act on visceral receptors or the brain-stem, and by direct stimulation of the brain-stem, the limbic system and some subcortical structures. All the relevant physiological mechanisms are in with a fighting chance, including the possibility that similar effects may be brought about by hormonal change. For example, epinephrine acts on the posterior hypothalamus and increases central and peripheral ergotropic discharge. Gellhorn suggests, in fact, that when emotions are aroused, the ergotropic–trophotropic balance must be altered by *both* neurogenic and hormonal processes.

Gellhorn also argues that there is an increasing cognitive involvement in human emotion, implying that a greater part is being played by the neocortex. To this point Gellhorn's theory is reasonably in accord with the facts, but from here onwards it becomes more difficult to accept. He starts by recouching Schachter's results in his own terms. He regards the euphoria and anger produced in Schachter's subjects after they had been injected with epinephrine and experienced the appropriate environmental conditions as reflecting increased sympathetic activity, increased cortical arousal and, in general, increased ergotropic excitation. Gellhorn extends this by introducing the idea of 'tuning'. He suggests that the hypothalamic ergotropic–trophotropic balance controls the 'group-character' of the emotion, but within this the specific emotion results from cognitive factors and experience. For example, he argues that if we consciously relax then we cannot feel rage. So, we can be ergotropically or trophotropically 'tuned', thereby vastly increasing the likelihood of these types of response. Clearly Gellhorn has moved far into speculative realms; a brief quotation will demonstrate how far:

'facilitation of the activity of sensory projection and association areas of the neocortex as the result of emotion plays a part in man's highest intellectual achievements and in the enrichment of his emotional life'. (Gellhorn, 1968)

However, this type of statement does have relevance to recent ideas on the control of emotion (see Chapters 9 and 10).

Arnold

Arnold's theory of emotion depends in equal part on physiological speculation and the cognitive concept of appraisal. Appraisal is discussed in detail in Chapter 4. Here it is mainly the physiological side of her arguments that will be covered. At the outset it should be mentioned that Arnold's theory, although quite complex physiologically, is lacking in empirical support and like many other physiological theories of emotion loses power in becoming too speculative.

Arnold's most recent (1970a; 1970b) formulation begins with MacLean's (1970) notion that there are three 'levels' of brain function—reptilian, old mammalian and new mammalian, and Lindsley's (1970) idea that emotional arousal is reflected in the cortex, diencephalon and brain-stem. Arnold queries how these levels or areas might be related. To answer this, she suggests that we need identification of 'the relays that mediate the sequence of psychological activities from perception to emotion and action'.

Although Arnold's theory is physiological, she clearly states that any physiologizing can only occur after a phenomenological analysis. This will allow us to find out what goes on psychologically in emotion, after which possible neural pathways can be traced. She suggests that there are definite activation patterns for particular psychological activities, rather than any sort of action *en masse,* an idea straightforwardly based on a belief in localization of function within the CNS.

Arnold (1960) defines emotion as a 'felt tendency towards something appraised as good (and liked) or away from something bad (or disliked)'. She regards the limbic system as controlling liking and disliking (i.e. cognitive appraisal) and the hippocampus as the spur to recall of memory and impulse to action. In particular, she suggests that affective recall occurs via a neural pathway from the cingulum, hippocampus, postcommissural fornix and anterior thalamic nuclei, back to the limbic system. Thus the limbic system gives us our experience of liking and disliking both as new appraisals and as remembered affective attitudes. She believes the hippocampus to initiate the emotion in its total form; any pattern associated with a particular emotion (appraisal and affective memory) must be organized before arriving at the motor cortex and being translated to movement. Arnold maintains that action patterns begin at the cerebellum and are relayed to the frontal lobes. When we feel a complete bodily urge to action, then we experience the emotion as an action tendency. Arnold suggests that this experience is mediated by the premotor area in the frontal lobe and that the frontal lobe, in turn, serves motor functions in general. So, any felt urge to action becomes overt action. Arnold proposes that the main function of the cerebellum is that of organization and co-ordination. Impulses arrive from the hippocampus and are made ready for action—action which includes all the more overt aspects of emotion, namely movement, facial and bodily expression and autonomic change.

In distinguishing between emotional and nonemotional behaviour, Arnold argues that there are four main patterns of action: (1) actions resulting from hormonal change; these lead to an approach towards various 'good' objects and are basically instinctual; (2) emotional action patterns; these arise from positive or negative evaluations of either perceived or imagined objects and lead both to action and emotion; (3) action patterns based on feeling, which result from evaluations of something which may be beneficial or harmful 'for our functioning'; (4) deliberate action.

Arnold's instinctive and deliberate actions are of little relevance here; also, she makes little neurophysiological distinction between emotional and feeling action patterns. In analysing particular action patterns, Arnold focuses exclusively on fear and anger. She simply traces neural circuits which could possibly account for behaviours such as anger, fear, rage, escape and avoidance. For example, she suggests that rage is mediated via impulses from the limbic system to the hippocampus, cerebellum, thalamus, hypothalamus, caudate nucleus and frontal lobe. Similarly, she argues that the desire for flight appears to be mediated by impulses from the hippocampus through the lateral ventral thalamic nucleus to the premotor and motor areas and becomes registered in the prefrontal cortex via the anterior and medial ventral nuclei.

Since Arnold engages in even more intricate physiologizing (it is presented here only in brief outline) than most other theorists, it is worth making some discussion of the empirical evidence which bears on her ideas. Grossman (1967) and Izard (1972) suggest that there is not much supporting evidence, and Arnold (1970) herself realizes that hers is a difficult theory to test experimentally. For example, she regards emotion as not only inclusive of a tendency to behave in a particular way but as also incorporating many physiological and hormonal changes. So, cortical stimulation would not be expected to produce any recognizable emotional expression—although subcortical stimulation sometimes has. Also, for example, although Olds's

(1955; 1958) studies show 'reward' and 'punishment' effects from stimulating electrodes placed in limbic system, as we have seen the overall evidence from stimulation and ablation studies is ambiguous.

In attempting to account for the confusing results from studies of avoidance learning, CER and emotional reactivity, Arnold's argument becomes tortuous, subjective and mentalistic. She speaks of hungry animals 'wanting to find food'—making possible an active avoidance response. If sated, they are without the food drive which means that the fear drive is gone and that there is a deficit in avoidance; and so on.

Experiments bearing on the concept of affective memory are more supportive. Arnold (1970a) quotes several studies in which the basic technique involved training rats in successive discrimination tasks in each of the sensory modalities, and also in some passive avoidance. Electrolytic lesions were made either before or after learning in the proposed affective memory circuit to see which lesions in which areas produce what impairments. These studies support the ideas that, for example, the anterior cingulate gyrus mediates the appraisal of head movements, the posterior insula mediates taste appraisal, and so on.

Arnold has produced an odd mixture of good theory and experimentation with seemingly unnecessary subjective aspects to it, especially when it comes to interpretation and evaluation. She makes an honest attempt to combine all of the bodily structures and functions which have been shown to be concerned with emotion. On the other hand, her main contribution on the theoretical side is perhaps her general notion of excitation (1950). She regards the cortex as having excitatory control over emotion. The cortex supposedly focuses on any stimulus appraising a situation by modifying sensory input to fit in with our expectations. Emotional expression and peripheral changes stem from emotional impulses going from the cortex to the hypothalamus or thalamus. Autonomic changes are then reported back to the cortex, where reappraisals are made.

Panksepp

In what is clearly the best-worked and most far-reaching physiologically based theory of emotion, Panksepp (1982) has three aims. To produce a neurobehaviourally derived taxonomy of emotions, to outline a scheme of emotional organization in the brain, and to explore the implications of the theory for learning and for emotional disorder.

Panksepp's theory rests on the unusual belief that there should be a blending of introspection or anthropomorphism and animal brain research. It also springs from the likelihood that mammals share emotional circuits in the limbic system, which provide what Panksepp terms 'obligatory internal dynamics'.

The theory builds from five assumptions. (1) Distinct emotion processes are reflected in specific hard-wired brain circuits. (2) Primitive emotion processes are shared between humans and other animals. (3) There are a limited number of basic emotional circuits but much can be contrived through mixtures and social learning. (4) It is possible to consider neurotaxonomy through introspection. (5) It is possible to gain a scientific understanding of emotion processes through the study of brain organization.

Panksepp also lists a number of major proposals. (1) There are genetically hard-wired unconditioned response made to life-challenging circumstances. (2) There is an adaptive activation or inhibition of classes of related actions. (3) With recurrent feedback, emotion circuits change their sensitivities. (4) Neural activity can go on longer than the circumstances that give rise to it. (5) Reinforcement can condition activity in the emotion circuits to environmental stimuli. (6) There is interaction between the emotion circuits and the brain mechanisms of consciousness.

The evidence on which Panksepp bases his theory concerns behaviour he describes as stimulus-bound. This is well-ordered emotional behaviour which can be seen when various brain areas are stimulated. This is also described as species-typical expressions of class-typical brain circuits that mediate emotion. There appear to be a number of behavioural control or command systems from which an emotional taxonomy can be constructed.

The suggestion is of four emotion-mediating circuits that pass between the midbrain, limbic system and basal ganglia. They are labelled according to the extremes of the emotional experiences they are presumed to mediate in humans—expectancy, fear, rage, and panic.

To take the example of expectancy, this is thought to be mediated in the medial forebrain bundle of the lateral hypothalamus. It is sensitized by homeostatic imbalances and linked environmental incentives and produces motor arousal for exploration and investigation for survival. Fear is mediated in the sites for flight and escape and occur in response to potential harm. Rage sites elicit angry emotional displays and invigorate irritable or restrained behaviour. Panic sites bring about distressed calls and explosive behaviour.

In general, Panksepp puts forward a convincing case based on diverse information for a neurophysiological basis for these four command systems. Anatomically, Panksepp suggests that the systems run from the mesencephalon through the reticular fields of the hypothalamus and thalamus to basal ganglia and the higher limbic areas. Neurochemically, Panksepp believes that the circuits depend on single or multiple command transmitters. He argues for dopamine and acetylcholine having key functions in expectancy and rage and very tentatively for the involvement of the benzodiazepine receptor and endorphin systems in panic and fear. The major brain amines, serotonin and norepinephrine are likely to be generally involved as well.

At the psychological level, Panksepp stresses learning and reinforcement and suggests that much learning is based on the capacity of emotionally neutral stimuli to establish increasing influence over the emotion circuits. Panksepp has confirmed for expectancy that learning ability is an intrinsic property of the emotive circuit. He goes on to make a detailed analysis of learning based on brain emotion circuits and emotive state-dependence for memory retrieval. With experience, in Panksepp's system, the higher brain centres may assimilate some functions of the lower circuits. This may lead to cognitive appraisal as an important influence in the development of adult emotions.

Panksepp indulges in speculation with some supporting evidence that what he terms psychiatric disorders reflect imbalances among the emotional circuits of the visceral brain. For example, schizophrenia and depression would be found on the expectancy dimension and personality disorders and psychopathy on the rage dimension. Anxiety neuroses would appear on the fear dimension and autism and the obsession-compulsions on the panic dimension.

In the end, Panksepp believes that he has proposed a relatively simple physiologically based theory of emotion that depends on two basic assumptions. To some extent, all mammals share the evolutionary pressure for the development of emotive circuits which spring from life-challenging circumstances. Secondly, psychological emotional constructs need to be tied to specific brain circuits. The first of these assumptions is more compelling than the second.

Oddly, given the obvious dependence of Panksepp's theory on biological science, he also stresses the importance of introspection. He argues that the conscious mind can see the dynamics of our subcortical heritage. In his view, this leads to a theoretically based analysis of brain function, linked to identifiable neural systems. Two possibilities for looking at the role of the brain in emotion are as a generalized arousal state which promotes individual emotion through social learning, or as a system of hard-wired representations for every emotional nuance. Panksepp's is a middle course, with classes of behaviours always going together, with the basic control of each in common circuits. These are genetically based but modulated by experience, perceptions and homeostasis, all of which would result in numerous specific behavioural expressions.

In summary, Panksepp's scholarly psychobiological theory of emotion suggests that there are brain emotion systems in the form of a limited number of translimbic command circuits. That such states exist in animals is an assumption based on self-recognition and similarities in mammalian limbic systems. Panksepp believes that subjective experience provides a useful guide for categorizing and analysing emotive brain circuits. He establishes a list of such states and begins to establish their properties.

CONCLUSIONS

The search for the physiological substrates of emotion has produced much research and theory. Inevitably, some of this has been sophisticated, useful and suggestive and some has been naive, poorly conceived and on occasion, even obstructive. Unfortunately, however, the better work is inconclusive. The aims of this approach to emotion are straightforward—to further our understanding by studying the relationship between behavioural and physiological responses. For example, it was reasonable to expect that there might be some peripheral response patterning in the different emotions. It is disappointing that such little psychophysiological evidence has been found to support this idea. We can say very little more than that the viscera are necessary to emotion. Whether this is an accurate assessment of reality or whether it is grounded in inadequate conceptualization and/or measurement remains to be seen. However, it may be that a more appropriate way of distinguishing between the emotions is via cognition.

We can be certain that the brain-stem, the thalamus and hypothalamus, the limbic system and, to an extent, the neocortex are implicated in emotion. We can also say that endocrine changes are important and that the periphery has a part to play and that there are underlying neurochemical changes. However, we cannot say how these possible mechanisms interact although Panksepp's (1982) theory offers some hope. We cannot be sure that the idea of localization of function on which most of the CNS investigations are based is valid. Nowadays, there are few psychologists who would argue for a mass action concept of brain function. On the other hand, those who work from the localization standpoint can rarely be sure of the precise relationshiop between structure and function.

Given the confusing mass of empirical data which have come from physiological studies of emotion, it is perhaps hardly surprising that until recently the physiologically oriented theories are of little help. Often, they have included too high a ratio of physiological speculation to empirical fact. This enables them to be twisted in any way and lowers their straightforward predictive power. Or they are sometimes too narrow, attempting to generalize from a consideration of but one aspect of emotion. Of the better physiological theories of emotion, Arnold's speculations are not well supported by the facts and her cognitive ideas are difficult to test. Gellhorn's theory orders the facts consistently, but eventually becomes speculative in ways which are difficult to test. It is only Panksepp's theory that not only makes good sense of the existing data but also offers a series of testable hypotheses.

It is easy to imagine that physiological investigations could do much to simplify and systematize our understanding of a field of the complexity of emotion. However, within psychology in general this reductionist approach has not been especially noteworthy in the quantity and quality of any solutions it has provided. It is instructive that some of the neurochemical work on emotion seems to be following the same course. It is interesting and looks hopeful, but at the moment is not producing obvious solutions to any of the long-standing problems. They may simply have been reduced to yet another level of analysis. Also in the last few years it has come increasingly apparent that cognitive functions, facial and postural expression and even subjective analysis must be taken into account to give a reasonable picture of emotion.

Perhaps this is the most important final point to bear in mind. Whatever frontiers are passed in research into the physiology of emotion, a complete analysis of the subject cannot be made via physiology alone. That there are important physiological concomitants of emotion (as expressed and experienced) is without doubt, but to affirm that emotion is in some way caused by physiological change is as arbitrary as saying that the physiological responses are caused (over evolutionary time) by behavioural change. However, to gain a full understanding of emotion we must analyse the physiological mechanisms involved in it. To do this accurately, there must be more precision on the side of the independent variable (physiological manipulation) and more sophistication and breadth on the side of the dependent variable (behaviour). At present, however, it is interesting that, those who have recently chosen to study the physiological bases of emotion have ended by stressing the importance of cognition. In some ways, a very consistent picture is beginning to emerge.

4

Cognition and Emotion

'The detailed understanding of the relationship of affect and cognition is perhaps the core theoretical problem of psychology for the 80s' (Kiesler, 1982). This may well be so. Certainly it is by now obvious that the only reasonable route to an understanding of emotion is via an analysis of its links with cognition. Both empirically and theoretically, this is inescapable. Also it is equally clear that the nature of the relationship between emotion and cognition, and in particular, the role of cognition in emotion is the core of the present book.

In recent years, it has been barely possible to read an article or book dealing with some or other aspect of emotion which does not mention cognition. Not only have more and more empirical investigations had a cognitive component built into them but also investigations of emotion–cognition relationships have been made in their own right, as have studies of the links between emotion and particular cognitive processes such as memory. Furthermore it is the cognitive approach to emotion which has been responsible for generating the most cogent and profound theoretical discussions of the topic. It becomes increasingly probable the cognition is the one necessary aspect of emotion.

Those who have stressed cognitive aspects of emotion have done so from a number of possible viewpoints. (1) They have regarded the fundamental problem as involving a study of whatever cues, either internal or external, allow us to identify and name our emotional states. Theories (for example, Schachter's) which have developed on this basis have been less complex and less far-reaching than others within the field. On the other hand, some of the research which they have inspired is intriguing. (2) They have assumed that cognitions cause physiological and behavioural change. Therefore we must study the one to gain knowledge of the others. This proposition typifies the 'appraisal' theorists whose ideas, though resting on rather shaky empirical foundations, are widely quoted. (3) They have considered emotions within a cognitive framework or have developed theories which place emotion in a very broad perspective and give an integral place to cognition and subjective experience in their accounts. (4) They have simply addressed the nature of the relationship between emotion and cognition. As will be seen later, this has led to the most profound discussions to date of the nature of emotion.

INTERNAL AND EXTERNAL CUES IN EMOTION

Although knowledge and understanding has advanced considerably, it is Schachter (1964; 1965; 1970; 1971) who has done most to bring cognition into the study of emotion. He drew the impetus for his work from the apparent *lack* of physiological response patterning between the emotions. He argues that in any emotion there is a diffuse sympathetic discharge; this becomes named and identified through the situation in which it occurs and through the individual's perceptions of this situation. In other words, the cognition guides the arousal.

In the usual, everyday, circumstances, Schachter believes that cognitions and arousal are highly interrelated, one leading to the other, and vice versa. Sometimes, however, they are independent. This is exemplified by Maranon (1924). He injected 210 patients with epinephrine, which is sympathetic-like in its effects, and recorded their introspections. Seventy-one per cent reported only physical effects and 29 per cent reported in terms of emotion, but the labels which they applied to their feelings were the 'as if' kind. They said they felt 'as if' they were afraid. Maranon could only produce 'genuine' emotional reactions in these people by providing them with appropriate cognitions. Schachter suggests that the 71 per cent who did not show this effect in Maranon's study in fact had a perfectly appropriate cognition to explain their altered state—the injection.

This point led Schachter on to the question which guided much of his subsequent research: what would be the result of a state induced by a *covert* (non-explicable) injection of epinephrine? Schachter (1959) suggests that such a state would bring about the arousal of evaluative needs, which lead to feelings being labelled from whatever can be perceived of the immediate situation. This argument results in three propositions. (1) If we are in a physiologically aroused state for which there is no obvious explanation, then we will label it according to whatever cognitions are available to us. So the same state could be labelled in many different ways. (2) If we are in a physiologically aroused state for which there is an obvious explanation, we are unlikely to use any alternative possible explanations to label it. (3) With the same cognitive condition we would behave emotionally only to the extent to which we are physiologically aroused. That is, there must be physiological arousal for emotion to occur.

With these three propositions, Schachter states his case for the intricate relationship between cognitive and physiological variables in emotion, both of which he sees as being necessary for the occurrence of appropriately labelled emotional behaviour. Much of his work involves ingenious tests of these ideas.

Schachter's basic studies

The experimental test of the three propositions mentioned above requires: (1) the manipulation of physiological arousal; (2) the manipulation of the extent to which a subject has an appropriate explanation of his state; and (3) the creation of situations which lead to possible explanatory cognitions. The first study produced to these ends and that which therefore set the procedural conditions for later studies was that of Schachter and Singer (1962). Subjects were led to believe that the experimenters were interested in the effects of Suproxin (a supposed vitamin compound) on vision. They were persuaded to agree to an injection of this. In fact, they were either injected with epinephrine or a saline placebo. Epinephrine mimics sympathetic discharge in its effects: systolic blood pressure rises, as does heart rate, respiration and levels of blood sugar and lactic acid. Cutaneous blood flow is decreased. Subjectively, these effects are experienced as palpitations, tremors, flushing, faster breathing, and so on. In the dosage used, these effects lasted for a maximum of 20 minutes.

Just before the injections were given, subjects also received one of three explanations of the effects, differing in appropriateness. (1) *Epinephrine-informed*. The gist of this explanation was that Suproxin sometimes has side effects which may last up to 20 minutes. Subjects were actually given a description of the subjective effects of epinephrine. This was all endorsed by the physician as he was giving them the injections. (2) *Epinephrine-ignorant*. Here, the experimenters said nothing. The physician, whilst giving the injections, said that they were mild and harmless and would have no side effects. (3) *Epinephrine-misinformed*. Both the experimenters and the physician mentioned possible side effects, but these were described as numb feet, body itches and headaches. Epinephrine could not have such effects. A fourth control group were injected with the placebo and otherwise received the same treatment as the epinephrine-ignorant group.

The second independent variable involved the social manipulation of two emotional states. (1) *Euphoria*. Immediately after the injection, the experimenter took the subject into a room which contained an experimental stooge, supposedly another subject. The naive subject was told that he should wait in the room for 20 minutes to allow the Suproxin to become absorbed, then the vision tests would be run. The room was in a mess, for which the experimenter apologized and left. The stooge behaved in a friendly and extroverted way, engaging in a carefully predetermined sequence of activities: playing basketball with waste paper, flying paper aeroplanes, making a sling-shot, using a hula hoop. The subject's reactions were observed through a one-way mirror. (2) *Anger*. A similar initial procedure was followed as for the euphoria condition, except that both the subject and the stooge were given questionnaires to complete. These were designed such that the questions gradually became more personal and insulting. The stooge paced his answers with the subject's and at predetermined intervals made standard comments. These progressed from innocence to anger and culminated in the questionnaire being torn up and the stooge walking out. The epinephrine-misinformed group was not run in this condition as it was decided that one such control group was enough.

Two measures were taken. The first was simple observation aimed at evaluating the extent to which the subject behaved like the stooge. The second involved a self-report questionnaire; this contained many questions hidden amongst which were the two crucial ones. How irritated, angry or annoyed would you say you feel at present? How good or happy would you say you feel at present? There was a five-point scale for each question.

Schachter and Singer's results showed that subjects were significantly more euphoric when they had no explanation of their bodily states. Differences between the epinephrine-informed and -misinformed groups showed this not to be artificial; the epinephrine-informed group was distinct from the other two, which were similar to one another. The placebo group was less euphoric than either the epinephrine-misinformed or the epinephrine-ignorant, but more so than the epinephrine-informed; this, however, was not a significant result. Much the same pattern was found with both the observations and questionnaires. In the anger conditions, the epinephrine-ignorant subjects were much angrier than the epinephrine-informed, and the placebo subjects were midway.

Except for the awkwardness of the placebo groups, the results conformed to the predictions. Schachter and Singer provided an explanation for the placebo group results in terms of the *injection* itself, by arguing that this must have given a reasonable explanatory cognition to the subjects. (Ideally, of course, they would have liked to produce the physiological state without the injection.) Thus, the fact of having the injection would itself be likely to reduce its effects. From their self-reports it seems that some subjects did in fact explain their feelings in this way, so becoming 'self-informed'. With these subjects removed from the analysis, the differences between the placebo groups and the relevant experimental groups became highly significant. Schachter and Singer continued the argument concerning the placebo groups by pointing out that the injection of placebo does not *prevent* sympathetic activity, even though it might not produce it directly. Sympathetic activity might have come about due to the extraordinary experimental conditions. By good chance, Schachter and Singer took a pulse-rate measure for all subjects before and after the experimental manipulations. Those placebo subjects whose pulse rate rose from before to after could be regarded as showing increased activation. *Post hoc* analysis showed these subjects to be more euphoric and more angry than non-aroused placebo subjects.

Schachter and Singer concluded from these results that they had managed to manipulate, via cognitions, the feelings of someone physiologically aroused but with no explanation for the arousal. Also, they suggested that if such a person had a satisfactory explanation for his feelings then he or she would not use any possible alternative explanations. And, finally, with constant cognitive circumstances an individual will only react if aroused. Clearly, these conclusions were somewhat tentative owing to the relatively *post hoc* and subjective analyses which were made.

Further support for Schachter's original formulations comes from Schachter and Wheeler (1962) in a study which explored the differences between the epinephrine and the placebo groups, and in animal studies (Latane and Schachter, 1962).

Schachter's conclusions

Schachter's (1964; 1965; 1970) first and most important, though tentative, general conclusion from this series of studies is that there may indeed be very little physiological differentiation between emotional states. How we label such states may be largely a cognitive matter. He also suggests that his results would be generalizable to *any* internal states for which there would otherwise be no good explanations. This is partially supported by Nowlis (1965; 1970) somewhat similar studies of mood, and by Valins's (for example, 1970) work on the giving of false information about bodily reactions. However, Schachter also maintains that his results do not support an activation theory of emotion. He suggests that aroused subjects are not necessarily emotional. If the determinants of emotion are cognitive to the extent which Schachter believes, then they should be manipulable by factors similar to those which are known to affect opinions and attitudes.

Schachter (1964) devotes some time to a consideration of whether or not his 'cognitive' ideas allow one to deal with the limitations of the visceral theory of emotion. He suggests that three of Cannon's criticisms of James's formulations are overcome by his (Schachter's) ideas. (1) If visceral changes typical of strong emotion are produced artificially then the emotion does not result. However, Schachter's work also shows that if a 'cognitive' approach is adopted then conditions can be specified in which an injection will produce an emotional state. (2) The same visceral changes occur in different emotional states. Although this seems to be the case physiologically speaking, Schachter's ideas bypass it, since they suggest that cognitive and situational factors determine the labels applied to any state of physiological arousal. He argues that it may well be that emotions are characterized by high sympathetic arousal with little physiological differentiation. (3) The viscera are insensitive. This, although a relevant criticism of any purely viseral formulation of emotion, is not relevant to the cognitive ideas.

Schachter views Cannon's final two points as being awkward for the cognitive interpretation of emotion as well as for James's. Visceral changes are too slow to provide any emotional feeling and if the viscera are separated from the CNS then emotional behaviour is not altered. Both James's and Schachter's views need visceral arousal as a necessary condition for emotional arousal.

However, after considering evidence from studies of sympathetomized dogs and humans with spinal lesions, Schachter concludes that autonomic arousal facilitates the acquisition of emotional behaviour, but if this behaviour is acquired beforehand, autonomic arousal is not necessary for its maintenance. Also, without autonomic arousal, behaviour which appears as emotional will not be experienced as such.

Criticisms of Schachter's view

While not wishing to detract from the novelty of Schachter's experimental procedures, his analysis of results can certainly be criticized for its *post hoc* nature. More importantly several criticisms can be levelled at his general theoretical position and the interpretation he makes of his data. Such criticisms have been most concisely put by Izard (1972), Leventhal (1974) and Plutchik and Ax (1967) of which what follows is an amalgam.

The first and in many ways the most important point is that Schachter has *not* proved that emotion is dependent on sympathetic arousal and cognition. He *has* demonstrated that it is influenced by both, but this could be so whilst it nevertheless remains independent of them. Schachter argues that a person can induce physiological arousal by cognition; it is thus that he accounts for the results of his placebo group in the original study. If this is so, then the subjects in the anger and euphoria groups may also have produced arousal in this way. Also, it is possible to say that the subjects injected with epinephrine could have produced their own physiological tranquillization cognitively.

A similar possibility is that subjects injected with epinephrine may simply become more suggestible and hence more likely to imitate behaviour which is occurring around them. Thus they become more euphoric or more angry depending on their experiences. Also, Schachter shows no good evidence for arousal in *all* of his injected subjects. It is widely known that there are large individual differences in reactions to drugs, pulse rate (used by Schachter) not being the least ambiguous measure of this. This point is made particularly by Plutchik and Ax (1967).

Leventhal (1974) and Leventhal and Tomarken (1986) see the problem as one of showing exactly *how* arousal and cognition combine in emotion. Schachter does not, for example, say when or how arousal contributes to particular states of feeling. Schachter's conceptualization of emotion accords cognitions three possible functions in emotional experience. They allow the interpretation of emotional stimuli, the recognition of arousal and the labelling of emotion.

Leventhal argues that there is much evidence that our expectations are important determinants of our emotional state. The more accurate are these expectations then the more likely we are to become emotional. However, there is no good evidence one way or the other on the recognition of emotional arousal, except some of Leventhal's that supports the idea that expressive behaviour intensifies the subjective experience of emotion, but only when reactions are spontaneous and involuntary.

Further, there is the matter of labelling emotion. Here Leventhal suggests that the important question is: do cognitions label arousal and by so doing create subjective feelings? If this is so, then feelings must be learned. However, Leventhal argues against this viewpoint by questioning how a young child can be capable of feeling anything before he knows the label for the feeling, if it is the label which promotes the feeling. The only way in which this is possible is if the situations are similar in meaning to those for which the child already has labels.

In fact, Leventhal turns this argument round and instead suggests that situations become construed as similar because they generate similar feelings. An innate set of feelings generate meaning. This leads to a final position in which cognitions can be viewed as leading to particular reactions of the CNS and to distinctive bodily reactions, the latter being necessary for feeling. Of course, these bodily reactions mainly take the form of facial expression, thus paving the way for the recent emphasis which there has been on the role of facial expression in emotion.

Cotton (1981) and more especially Reisenzein (1983) provide the most thorough analyses of Schachter's theory of emotions yet to have been made. From these critiques it is clear that only one of the deductions or propositions that derive from Schachter's theory is adequately supported. If an emotional state has arousal attributed to it from an irrelevant source, it will be intensified. However, there has been no study which demonstrates that peripheral arousal is a *necessary* condition for an emotional state.

There is support only for a much lesser form of Schachter's theory. Roughly, this is that feedback from arousal can have an intensifying effect on emotional states and this arousal–emotion relationship is mediated and/or modified by causal attributions about the source of the arousal.

Clearly, Schachter's theory has generated a large amount of research and focused attention on the cognitive aspects of emotion. It also overstates the role of peripheral arousal and the links between arousal and emotion. However, as yet, the theory has not been entirely disproved. Reisenzein (1983) argued that it needs to be tested on children, who have fewer learned reactions to situations, and that other methods of producing arousal should be used.

Finally, it should be pointed out that in their recent review, Leventhal and Tomarken (1986) conclude that Schachter's cognition–arousal theory has generated predictions which, when tested, have yielded disappointing results. They also argue that any misattribution effects that occur are mediated centrally rather than peripherally.

Veridicality and bodily change

Breadth is added to the analysis of internal and external cues in emotion by investigations of what is termed veridicality. Valins (for example, 1970) who gave the impetus to this field devised a general research strategy based on a very similar proposition to that of Schachter. He suggests that when studying the relationship between bodily change and emotional behaviour, any effects due to the subjects' perception of the changes should be separated from effects based on the changes themselves; they may be reasonably independent. Valins divides work in this field into two broad categories: (1) the general cognitive/physiological approach, and (2) the approach which is concerned with the modification of established emotional behaviour. Within these categories, he subdivides the research into that which deals with (1) veridical bodily preceptions, and (2) nonveridical bodily perceptions.

Veridical perceptions

The 'veridical' approach is best exemplified by Schachter's work. Valins views this as dependent on the idea that we try to understand and label any unusual bodily symptoms that we may experience. If we latch on to certain stimuli in our explanations then emotional behaviour will result. Valins argues that although Schachter provides reasonable experimetal support for this idea, there are at least two problems: (1) results may be specific to artificial and extreme autonomic arousal; (2) *how* does cognition about an external emotional stimulus lead to emotional behaviour? Nisbett and Schachter (1966) partly deal with these problems and broaden Schachter's original results suggesting the possibility that an emotional stimulus becomes re-evaluated. It is this re-evaluation which perhaps leads the cognition to affect the emotional behaviour.

Nonveridical perceptions

Valins's own work has usually involved deceiving subjects about their bodily reactions and observing the effects of this on their subjective responses to emotional stimuli. Subjects have been led to believe that their heart rates are being recorded on somewhat archaic equipment; equipment that is so old and crude as to be audible. They are therefore instructed to ignore the sounds from the equipment and simply to look at some slides that they will be shown. In fact, the subjects hear prerecorded heart beats. The presentation of emotional stimuli is carefully timed so that the experimenter can control the subject's perception (audition) of the apparent size of his reaction to them.

The type of result found by Valins (for example, 1966) showed that slides of nude females to which subjects heard their heart rates change were liked more than others, independently of the direction of change. This again points to our apparent need to account for our own bodily changes in some meaningful way. In passing, it is worth noting that in Valins's experiments, actual heart rates rarely changed. This perhaps calls into question the extent to which the stimuli used by Valins had any emotional effects. However, a study by Bloemkolb *et al.* (1971) did more clearly point to the possibility that cognitive events can be used to evoke or reduce emotional experience. Further studies by Valins on systematic desensitization, support cognitive analyses of emotion by implying tentatively that there is no evidence for a physiological substrate to the procedure.

In a very useful review, Harris and Katkin (1975) both criticize and extend Valins's ideas. They argue that two research approaches are important in this area: (1) the significance of cognitive evaluations of ANS feedback in labelling emotional experience, and (2) the role of *actual* ANS activity and its feedback, ignoring cognition. They point out that the necessary, and rather confused, background to the work is to be found in Schachter and Singer (1962). They see Schachter as bracketing both the Cannon–Bard theory and the James–Lange theory in that he does not view individual emotions as being linked to precise ANS patterns and yet does view ANS arousal as necessary to emotion. Of course Valins simply argues that all that is necessary is that we *believe* we perceive our own ANS arousal.

In developing their argument, Harris and Katkin seek to integrate with Valins's work the results of subsequent social-psychophysiological studies. These showed that if external stimuli were not strongly emotional then *actual* heart rate was affected by false feedback. However, with strong emotional stimuli, the ANS system seems to be independent of false feedback and subjects' reports of emotionality were related to actual rather than false heart rates. A further argument is that Valins's effects may have been produced by *actual* physiological changes. Finally, Hirschman (1975) presented *subjects* with very negative emotional stimuli (slides of mutilated bodies) and found that false feedback of increasing heart rate affected the rate of electrodermal responses and tonic electrodermal levels. He also found a relationship between false feedback and the subjective experience of discomfort which was elicited by stimuli associated with the feedback.

Harris and Katkin suggest that this type of ambiguous result leads to two different views of the role of the ANS in emotion. First there is that which stems from the James–Lange theory, namely, that ANS arousal is necessary to emotion. Second is the view promulgated by Valins, namely, that the cognitive perception of ANS arousal (rather than the arousal itself) is necessary to emotion. Research has been concerned with actual and with false ANS arousal.

The various studies on true or false feedback of heart rate appear to show that emotion can be indexed either by the attribution of affect (observable behavioural consequences thought to follow emotional experience) or by the self-report of emotional experience. Harris and Katkin point out that false feedback does not allow subjective experience to be analysed and so may *not* be concerned with emotion at all.

Harris and Katkin go on to integrate these various findings and two views of emotion by recourse to a classification into primary and secondary emotion, terms they use somewhat differently from the way in which they have been used by others. They describe primary emotion as a state which includes ANS arousal as well as the subjective perception of it. Secondary emotion they see as a state which does not necessarily involve ANS arousal but which may include nonveridical perception of that arousal. This may be produced by situational contexts or of course by false laboratory feedback. This analysis leads to a clarification in the way in which Valins's original studies can be interpreted. In these studies the actual emotion (primary) is confused with the 'as if' emotions (secondary) since, although Valins developed an interesting experimental procedure and some significant results concerning false feedback, it is debatable as to how much they were concerned with emotion at all.

Mood

A final line of research which is related to internal and external cues in emotion involves the study of mood. Since 1953, Nowlis and Nowlis have been making a conceptual and empirical analysis of mood, their results partially endorsing Schachter's view of emotion. Nowlis (1953; 1959; 1963; 1965; 1970) regards mood as a 'multidimensional set of temporary reversible dispositions'. It refers to some constancies in behaviour and experience which endure over some time. Nowlis believes the 'entire' individual to be involved in mood. He also suggests that the determinants of mood are often obscure or inaccessible although its main function is to monitor or control behaviour. Hence, in its breadth, the concept of mood is more or less equal to that of emotion. However, it is discussed here since it also overlaps with emotion. In Nowlis's terms, some moods may be emotional, while others are not. In general, though, he regards emotion as more temporary than mood. When both are involved in some behaviour and experience, he views emotion as the onset and mood as the continuing steady state. In this sense, emotion is seen as more intensive and explosive, whereas mood is less intense but more available for inspection. Clearly, Nowlis has a somewhat restricted view of emotion. However, the results he describes add generality to ideas concerning the role of internal and external factors in determining emotion and conditions such as mood which might be linked to emotion.

APPRAISAL

At about the same time that Schachter was emphasizing the role of cognition in emotion, so the concept of appraisal was beginning to be developed. Essentially, appraisals are viewed as the cognitions which intervene between stimulus and response in emotion. They are evaluations of the personal worth of any incoming stimulus. We appraise any stimulus as to whether it is 'good' or 'bad' for us, i.e. whether it is worth our while to approach or avoid it. An appraisal is a hypothetical construct which allows us to give some 'meaning' to our environmental situation. Both Arnold and Lazarus believe appraisals to be essential to the generation of emotion.

Arnold

Arnold's (for example, 1960; 1970a) theory of emotion is a mixture of the cognitive and physiological approaches to the subject. As was seen earlier, her theory depends very much on the concept of appraisal as a determinant of emotion, itself a felt tendency to action. It will be remembered that Arnold regards correct appraisals and consequent actions as requiring: (1) memories, of sensory and motor events; (2) memories of previous positive and negative attitudes; and (3) the rehearsal in imagination of the appropriate actions. She also spends much time in neurophysiological speculation as to the substrates of these hypothetical processes. Enough space has been given to a description of Arnold's theory, so at this point a few words of evaluation will suffice.

Arnold's (1970a) latest starting point is that we know little about brain function, particularly in emotion. To obtain this knowledge, she suggests that we need to identify the physiological mediation of the process which runs from perception to emotion and action. She argues that this is best achieved at first by a cognitive analysis. In support of this plea, Arnold maintains that if we can find out what is going on psychologically between perception, emotion and action, then we are in a better position to hypothesize about possible physiological substrates. This may well be so. However, if we find out in enough detail what is going on psychologically in emotion, then this might be enough to make the necessary predictions. Arnold would argue, though, that knowledge of the physiology would provide a useful check on the psychology, by which Arnold seems to mean cognition.

It is perhaps on the cognitive side that Arnold's theory is found most wanting. Although her physiologizing has led to a number of testable predictions and in that way has furthered the study of emotion, it is difficult to see what predictions can be made from her conception of cognitive appraisal, especially as it is a process which she regards as occurring almost instantaneously. Her theory is well-integrated but very speculative and at the end of the day there are serious questions left unanswered. For example, Arnold characterizes some appraisals as being immediate, intuitive and innate and at the same time gives a very important role to general cognition in emotion. If cognition is so heavily involved, the implication is that man can exercise emotional control. How can this be so, if appraisals are immediate, intuitive and innate? Finally, and perhaps even more fundamentally why should it be assumed that appraisals exist at all? This point will be picked up later in discussion of a recent controversy in this field.

Lazarus

Apart from Arnold, the main proponent of the appraisal view of emotion has been Lazarus (see, for example, Lazarus (1968), Lazarus *et al.* (1970), Lazarus and Opton, 1966). These earlier ideas will be described now but discussion of his more recent (1982, 1984) contributions will be reserved for later. Like Arnold, his basic viewpoint is that cognitive processes are causes which arouse coping processes to deal with an appraised situation; a cognitive/adaptive argument. Before discussing the details of Lazarus's theoretical approach to emotion, his research strategies will be briefly described.

Lazarus's earlier research strategies were mainly concerned with an analysis of the possible determinants of appraisal.

1. *Direct manipulation.* The work for which Lazarus and his coworkers are best known is that involving stressful films. The basic technique is to show subjects stressful films with various soundtracks added to them, or to compare the effects of these films with those of more benign films. (See Lazarus *et al.*

(1965) and Spiesman *et al.* (1964) for reviews of this work). The main film to be used has been on subincision—'a ritual performed by men of an Australian stoneage culture in which the penis and scrotum of male adolescents are cut deeply with a sharpened piece of stone'. In comparison with benign films, the subincision film typically generated far more emotional disturbance. This disturbance was enhanced or reduced as a function of the type of soundtrack added to the film. Lazarus interprets these results as demonstrating that emotional appraisal can be directly manipulated, the different degrees of emotional reaction being regarded as dependent on appraisal. These results were reflected in both autonomic and subjective measures.

2. *Indirect manipulation.* This strategy has involved the manipulation of those variables on which Lazarus believes cognition to depend rather than on 'direct' manipulation of the cognition itself. The main emphasis has been on anticipation. Generally, stress (emotional) reactions increase as confrontation time approaches, although this effect is modified by factors such as the duration of the anticipation, prior experiences, and so on. Lazarus argues that these physiological reactions result from cognitive attempts at coping, an idea, of course, which leads to unlimited speculation about the nature of such appraisals.

3. *Self-report.* There are obvious disadvantages to a methodology which depends on the self-report of thoughts after some stressful experience. However, it may be indicative of other hypotheses which could be tested, or act as support for results gained from other strategies. Lazarus *et al.* (1952) in a film study showed there to be three response patterns observed in self-reports: (1) an emotional flooding, (2) an intellectualized detachment, and (3) a denial (I'm not bothered). However, there were no concomitant autonomic differences in subjects who typically gave one of these types of report.

4. *Dispositional variables.* The final strategy involves the selection of subjects with different emotional dispositions. For example, Spiesman *et al.* (1964) in their film study chose deniers and intellectualizers. Stress reactions were more reduced when deniers heard a film-track expressing denial and when intellectualizers heard an intellectualizing track superimposed on the same film.

Appraisals

As a cautionary note, before discussing Lazarus's initial (1968) theoretical analysis of emotion, it should be borne in mind that a common theme to his research is stress. Many of his studies have been based on comparisons of the effects of stressful and nonstressful stimuli. It is not appropriate in this context to spend time attempting to define stress. It is enough to say that it is probably more interrelated with the extreme types of emotional reaction than with the mild. Strictly speaking, Lazarus's views should be regarded as applying only to the 'strong' emotions. Empirically, he does not much concern himself with the 'weak' or 'mild' emotions.

Lazarus suggests that there are two broad types of appraisal: benign and threatening. Benign appraisals have three possible adaptive consequences. (1) Adaptive, *automatic* coping may occur without the emotion. This is in fact some sort of automatic self-protection, the type of response we may make when crossing the road. (2) A benign stimulus may provide us with more information such that it requires reappraisal. A simple example might be the sight of a favourite dish to a hungry person being reappraised on discovering that it has been burnt. There is a continuous interplay between emotional reactions and appraisals. (3) Positive emotional states may follow from benign appraisals, although Lazarus can cite no evidence for this. He speaks of elation, euphoria and love, although in a subjective way which leans heavily on undefined concepts.

Lazarus suggests further that threatening appraisals involve two possible processes. The primary process deals with an evaluation of threat or non-threat and the secondary deals with how to cope with the threat. This has two consequences, each representing a way of coping with the threat. (1) Direct action—impulses or tendencies to remove the threat. This is essential to emotion since its success or failure or any feedback from it changes the cognition and hence the emotion. Lazarus regards these tendencies to direct action as leading to the usual classifications which are made of emotional behaviour. (2) Benign reappraisal. This is entirely cognitive, might or might not be realistic, and occurs when the stimuli suggest that no direct action is possible. Again, fluctuations in emotion are seen as reflections of this continuous cognitive appraisal and reappraisal.

The particular problem which Lazarus identifies for his theory is that of establishing satisfactory criteria for distinguishing between different emotions. He believes, however, that ultimately emotional states will be distinguished from one another by the identification of specific physiological, cognitive and behavioural patterns, and eliciting events. On the other hand he realizes that at present this is not possible.

Lazarus agrees with Schachter on the importance of cognitive processes in emotion but argues against emotions being a single state of physiological arousal to which a cognitive label has been applied. Lazarus also criticizes Schachter for overemphasizing the labelling of emotion whilst placing little importance on the possible steering functions of cognitive activity. However, his alternative is not very different. He suggests that physiological patterns might be associated with the various adaptive tasks which follow directly from cognitive appraisals. He also argues that what he regards as each emotional response system—the cognitive, the behavioural, the physiological—has its own adaptive function. This implies that there are special transactions between a person and the environment on each of these levels. He suggests from this that we may learn most about emotion where we find apparent discrepancies between the various response systems.

Lazarus's more recent views will be discussed towards the end of this chapter.

EMOTION AND MEMORY

Clearly, the relationship between emotion and cognition is very complex, the two processes interacting at a number of points. It has long been implicit in the analyses of those who have taken the cognitive approach to emotion that memory must be involved. However, it is only in recent years that the nature of the links between emotion and memory have begun to be explored. Previously, there had been little more than speculation by Arnold and others about concepts such as affect-memory.

One way in which the emotion–memory link has been explored is through comparisons of the recall of emotional and mental stimulus material. For example, both Strongman (1982) and Strongman and Russell (1986) have demonstrated some of the conditions under which emotional words are better recalled than nonemotional words. Results are definite enough to suggest that the emotional content of a word (and hence of any stimulus) has special significance in remembering. There are a number of ways of accounting for this.

Posner and Snyder (1975) maintain that there are two independent memory structures, one being an item memory and the other being a more abstract and impressionistic emotion memory. Posner (1978) also suggests that emotion raises the level of alertness of the person. Another possibility is that words (or other stimuli) may acquire their emotional meaning through classical conditioning. However, the information-processing-based associative network theory of Bower (1981) and Bower and Cohen (1982) offers a more powerful account.

According to Bower, clusters of 'descriptive propositions' represent events in memory. Associative connections are established among instances of the concepts. Activation is viewed as spreading from one concept to another by associative linkages between them. In the midst of all this there are emotion nodes which can be activated by many stimuli. So excitation is transmitted to nodes that produce whatever physiological reactions or behavioural expression that might be associated with the emotion. Applying the analysis to the recall of emotional material, it may be that if the particular emotional conditions in which material was originally learned is activated during recall, the activation from a combination of context and emotion make material more accessible. Basically, if emotion nodes are activated they should strengthen the associations for the basic material.

Bower (1981) and Bower and Cohen (1982) offer evidence in support of these views from an ingenious range of studies. For example, Bower demonstrates that Ss recall more experiences that are emotionally congruent with mood during recall than those which are not, using measures of word lists, personal experiences in a diary and childhood experiences. Also, emotion influenced a series of cognitive processes in Bower's studies, free association, imaginative fantasy and social perception, for example. Finally, it was also shown that Ss recall of a narrative is better when its feeling tone agrees with theirs.

Also relevant in any consideration of the links between emotion and memory is Leventhal's (1982) parallel processing model. In this view, there are two simultaneously active, parallel systems, one emotional, one cognitive. These processes are described as having three stages—perceptual, action-planning and emotion memory.

Although these developments in the analysis of the links between emotion and memory are welcome, they are more relevant to an understanding of memory than of emotion. As yet little can be said about the way in which memory might affect emotion itself, and even less can be said about the nature of emotional memory as it relates to the experience of emotion. Part of the reason for this is that there has been a strong reliance on verbal material in studies of emotion and memory. This is of limited relevance to the interpersonal stimuli which generate everyday emotion. Also, as Leventhal and Tomarken (1986) point out, most investigators have made little attempt to indicate which aspects of emotion affect memory or other cognitive processes.

Broad conceptualizations

As is mentioned elsewhere in this text, by the mid-1980s it has become obvious that there can be no understanding of emotion without taking account of cognition. Some psychologists recognized this very early on, have been making the attempt for many years and have developed some very broadly based theories. It is with ä consideration of the more significant of these that the present section will be concerned. However, within the last few years, various investigators have become increasingly concerned with exploring the basic theoretical issues involved in the relationship between emotion and cognition, rather than with constructing their own theories. The following section will be given to an analysis of the most searching of these. Between the construction of grand theories and an analysis of theoretical issues, the links between emotion and cognition are becoming far more firmly established than they were by Arnold and Schachter.

Leeper

For the sake of thoroughness, it is important to begin this coverage of the broader conceptualizations of emotion and cognition with one of the very early writers in the area. Leeper began his analysis of emotion in 1948 with a powerful argument that emotion should be viewed within a motivational framework as having an organized influence on the individual. This contrasted with the long-held traditional view of emotion as disorganizing. Then, in a series of papers, ending in 1970, he updated his views. Leeper suggests that emotions should be seen as part of a continuum of motivational processes ranging from physiological motives through to clearly emotional motives. He also considers that dichotomy which puts emotions and physiological motives together and distinguishes them from perceptual/cognitive processes. The former tend to be viewed as lower processes, evolutionarily, phylogenetically and ontogenetically.

Leeper suggests four reasons for this viewpoint: (1) motivation is relatively old, phylogenetically; (2) arousal theories of motivation have been influential; (3) traditional studies have shown perceptual processes to be transient, brief, end products which are tapped via verbal report; (4) it has been assumed that the brain only operates rapidly, its short-term consequences being the domain of perception; motivations/emotions are long-sustained.

Against these points, Leeper argues that (1) is simply not so. Many so-called older parts of the brain also serve 'higher' functions and the responsibility for emotion/motivation is cortical as well as subcortical. Second, he maintains that arousal theorists do in fact emphasize that behaviour has directional properties but that these can only be predicted when we know an organisms's motivation. Third, Leeper believes that the more traditional ways of studying perception are changing. For example, there is less reliance on introspective report and more emphasis on responses which extend in time such as speech. He therefore suggests that it may be appropriate to subsume motives under the general heading of cognitive processes. Finally, he maintains that the idea of the brain as a transmission device and brain processes as only short-term has been gainsaid.

Leeper's alternative viewpoint is that it is reasonable to look on motives/emotion as perceptual processes. He puts forward three propositions. (1) There was evolutionary advantage in animals responding perceptually to situations in which crucial features stood out. Also, behaviour would be guided by perceiving such situations in terms of anticipations of other perceptual effects which might occur if particular actions were followed. (2) There would be biological advantage in such perceptions being fast. (3) For maximal advantage such perceptions should have some effects on activity. For example, rapid perceptual processes might sometimes make the organism forgo present satisfaction to escape impending danger—it is far more adaptive to have the *fast* perceptual mechanism also as a mechanism of motivation.

Leeper is not saying that all perceptual processes are also motivational, but that the perceptual domain is large, complex and contains many dimensions. Clearly, motives/emotion have much in the way of autonomic and 'older' brain involvement. But even the simplest perceptual processes are dependent on cortical arousal, from the lower brain-stem. Leeper argues that subcortical processes and the viscera influence thought through the contributions they make to cortical processes. He regards such *representational* processes as motivational. Thus, perceptions range from motivationally/emotionally neutral to motivationally/emotionally very powerful processes.

Finally, Leeper proposes that his organizational/motivational/perceptual theory of emotion has three important implications. (1) Our emotional life should become very diverse as time goes on. (2) We must often create our own objective realities, since our perceptions allow us to recognize these and our emotions involve perceptions of life situations (3) Leeper suggests that man has been through two great ages, tool-using and technology/scientific or endeavour/education, and that these have each de-emphasized the emotional aspects of life. He believes that his theory might occasionally edge us towards dwelling on emotional experiences—perhaps leading to the third great age of man. Although Leeper's ideas are interesting and help to focus attention on cognition, they are wanting in many ways, not least of which is that they almost take away the concept of emotion altogether. However, he does leave behind the important point that the milder emotions might well have organizing characteristics.

Mandler

In his erudite books, Mandler's (1976, 1984) aim is to develop a psychological theory of emotion within a framework provided by cognitive psychology. Although his theory was described in Chapter 2, it will be summarized briefly here with some of the considerations he took into account in developing it. Mention of some of these background points is made since it may be useful to apply them to any context in which a theory of emotion is being developed.

Mandler argues that it is important to deal with what he terms the mental requirements needed to account for emotion. He suggests that at a minimum there are four such requirements: (1) inputs from the environment; (2) a structure system which interprets such input events; (3) two output systems, one reflected in action and the other in physiological arousal; (4) feedback, for the perception of arousal and the monitoring of action.

In a way which is simultaneously old-fashioned and yet very modern, Mandler argues that the notion of *mind* best summarizes all the inferences that can be made in emotion concerning the structures of input and output, the relationship between them and their history, be this dependent on genetic or environmental factors. Thus for Mandler, the beginnings of a theory of emotion must involve a consideration of mind and its mechanisms and structures and a discussion of consciousness. Also, because emotion covers a large admixture of mechanisms and processes, any theory of emotion must not make it independent of more general processes.

Mandler presents a view of emotion which at one level is a discussion of the parameters involved, and at another level is a summary of a system of emotion. The three parameters which he emphasizes are arousal, cognitive interpretation and consciousness, with special stress being laid on the interaction between arousal and cognitive interpretation, and the analysis of meaning in emotion.

Briefly, Mandler argues that the perception of ANS activity leads to undifferentiated arousal the conditions for which lean heavily on cognitive interpretations, especially where these involve any interruption or blocking. Such arousal has two adaptive functions, either homeostatis or activity involving the seeking of information. Although somewhat akin to appraisal,

Mandler's ideas on cognitive interpretation go further. He suggests that such interpretation is made up of mental structures, innate reactions to events and an evaluation of self-perceptions. The expressive movements in emotion generate automatic cognitive reactions which are themselves modified by re-interpretation. Emotional experience and emotional behaviour result from a complex interaction between automatic arousal and cognitive interpretation. Arousal gives emotion its visceral quality and intensity and interpretation not only adds to quality but also allows the categorization of the experience. Finally, Mandler argues that emotional experience itself takes place in consciousness, output from which is coded into language thus making possible communication about the experience.

Mandler has made an important attempt to come to grips with consciousness and mental activity in his view of emotion, a consideration which most other students of emotion have left well alone. Yet, in the expression of his ideas he is not very far removed from the other appraisal theorists particularly those like Schachter who also stress sympathetic arousal. Whether or not Mandler's attempt to put consciousness and the mind in a framework of an empirically based and scientifically acceptable theory is successful remains to be seen. Clearly, however, it is a worthy and ambitious endeavour, and could have far-reaching influence on future theory and research in psychology.

Izard and Tomkins

Within the present context, it is important to mention the early work of Izard and Tomkins, since it provided the springboard for Izard's more recent, influential analyses. Izard and Tomkins (1966) rely on four main notions. (1) Affect is motivation (Tomkins, 1962; 1963). (2) Positive affect provides the background motivation to effective functioning and to creativity (Izard, 1960; Izard et al., 1965b). (3) Positive affect is important to learning, perception and personality (Izard, 1965; Izard, et al., 1965a; 1965b). (4) Negative affect is disruptive and suppressive (Izard, 1964; Izard et al., 1965a; 1965b).

Their general theory starts with the suggestion that personality is made up of five interrelated *and* autonomous subsystems: homeostatic, drive, affect, cognitive and motor. By this they presumably mean that these subsystems sometimes function together and sometimes independently. The first two subsystems mainly concern biological maintenance and the remaining three provide the foundation for more complex human behaviour. Affect is the primary motivational system, cognition is the primary communication system and motor is the primary action system. Under different conditions any one of these subsystems can dominate and then become the main determinant of behaviour. If affect becomes dominant, they suggest that behaviour will probably be maladaptive. Affect itself can only be fully understood by looking at personality as a *process* of communication.

Rather like Leeper, Izard and Tomkins view affect as the primary motivational system. They suggest that it has three components: (1) neurological—concerning density of neural firing; (2) behavioural—facial, bodily and visceral responses; (3) phenomenological—affect as a motive. The affect system is seen as relatively independent of the others and as laying down cognition, decision and action.

Izard and Tomkins postulate three neurological activators of affect: (1) an increase in stimulation, leading to surprise, fear and interest; (2) a stable level of stimulation, leading to distress and anger; (3) a decrease in stimulation, leading to enjoyment. Hence, there is emotional sensitivity to novel stimulation, enduring stimulation or waning stimulation. By intensifying neural messages, affect is regarded as slowing all the motivational systems.

Behaviourally, Izard and Tomkins place more emphasis on facial than bodily or visceral responses, although they view feedback from any of them as making us unaware of our response patterns and therefore of our affects. Phenomenologically, the picture is even more complicated. Izard and Tomkins state that an individual's purpose is an image (of an end state), often of doing or achieving something. The affects involved and what is being done may be quite independent. For example, in any habitual action affect definitely has no place. Also, they suggest that on occasion affects do not join with cognitions to form purposes. We sometimes may not act on our preferences for positive and against negative affects. On other occasions we may be unaware of the affect that is driving us. When affects complete, that with the greatest density of neural firing becomes conscious and there is a complex relationship between intensity of stimulation, novelty and the likelihood of the consciousness of affect. The affect system with its learned and unlearned aspects is the main provider of the blueprints for cognition, decision and action. This phenomenological analysis must be seen to be lacking in that it provides for any contingency in a highly speculative way. It is impossible to unravel any firm predictions from it, other than that the normal sequence is emotion, cognition and action, a point which will be returned to later.

Reference to Chapter 2 in which Izard's (1972, 1977) theory is summarized will show that he has developed it considerably from its earlier origins, although the same basic idea of complex interrelated systems is retained. In his more recent formulations, Izard still argues that there are three components in the emotion process, but now labels these as neural activity, facial–postural activity and subjective experience. He also sees these as three levels of emotion.

In particular, in this statement of the theory, Izard goes further than previously in delineating the various person–environment and intra-individual processes which can activate emotion. He also lays great stress on the role of facial expression, discusses the development of emotional expression, and especially makes an interesting case for the control of emotional reactions via therapy.

THEORETICAL ISSUES

Zajonc and Lazarus—independence

The major theoretical issue that must be addressed in any consideration of emotion–cognition relationships is whether or not they are linked at all. Is it reasonable to regard the two systems as independent? This is the central matter which the interesting debate between Zajonc (1980; 1984) and Lazarus (1982; 1984) pivots upon. Amongst other things, Zajonc asserts that, not only does cognition not precede emotion, but also that emotion and cognition are independent, with emotion preceding cognition.

Lazarus argues that Zajonc's view is the result of seeing people as no more than computer-like information processors, instead of as sources of meaning. Personal factors colour the processing of experiences, nor do we have to have complete information before reacting emotionally to meaning, a point which will be returned to later. So, Lazarus asserts that there are no exceptions to the cognitive appraisal of meaning underlying all emotional states. This process might, however, be very rapid with thoughts and feelings being virtually instantaneous.

Part of the problem in this debate is definitional. If the idea of emotion is pushed far enough it appears to bang up against cognition. Similarly if cognitive processes are followed far enough they appear to reach emotion. If, in the end, either one is defined in terms of the other, the question of which precedes which becomes meaningless.

Kiesler (1982) suggests that one of the difficulties in conceptualizing the emotion–cognition relationship is that the empirical areas it embraces overlap, but not exactly. He argues that there is such a large range of emotional reactions that although the simple ones may be without cognitive content or cognitive instigation, the more complex ones must involve them. Kiesler attempts to argue in support of both sides of the debate. He suggests that the data provided by Zajonc fit with the idea of two partly independent systems, without ruling out the possibility that there is only one. In fact, both Zajonc and Lazarus offer powerful arguments, but it is Lazarus's view that is finally the more compelling of the two. It is difficult to conceive of emotion without cognition, even though the two systems might be independent as well as interacting.

Preconscious processing

It was mentioned in the last section that we do not need access to full information before reacting to emotional meaning. This idea suggests the importance of an analysis of preconscious processing to an understanding of the links between cognition and emotion. The emotional aspects of preconscious processing are most cogently discussed by Dixon (1981). He points out that many studies in this area have used emotional responsiveness as a dependent variable because many of the correlates of emotional arousal are outside voluntary control and so provide a useful measure of subliminal effects. Also, emotional processes could give a useful clue to the need related government of the preconscious processing of perception and memory. The basic question he poses is whether the emotional connotations of external stimuli can be reacted to without conscious representation, and if so, what influence might this have?

Dixon points to a considerable body of evidence which confirms the original subception effect of the emotional components of stimuli being reacted to autonomically before they are consciously recognized. The various theories which have been offered to account for this effect have in common the notion that preconscious autonomically based emotional disturbance affects both verbal report and perceptual processes. Dixon argues that in a process of sensory scanning, emotionally significant items have priority. He also suggests that emotional responses could change the phenomenal representation of the input and act directly on the verbal system.

That we can remain wholly unaware of being unaware of why we do what we do, leads Dixon on to a useful consideration of possible subjective concomitants of emotion. He suggests that preconscious information can be signalled by a change in feeling, a possibility which is of adaptive value. Any events, whether external to the organism or memorial are likely to have both conceptual content and emotional significance. When it comes to the conscious representation of this, there are three possibilities. There may be representation of both conceptual content and emotional significance. There may be affective flattening as the conscious content is preserved but the emotion is lost. Or they may occur something like free-floating anxiety if the content disappears but the emotional significance remains.

Dixon maintains that the capacity for experiencing emotion has evolved as a signalling system for drive states and/or the external situation, which demands action. If this is outweighed by the effects of interference it can restrict the entry of conceptual material into consciousness, or it can block emotion. The meaning of stimuli which do not enter awareness may be analysed unconsciously and yet evoke a consciously experienced emotion (or feeling) tone. All of which ends for Dixon in the perceptual defence effect in which recognition thresholds for emotional stimuli are higher or lower than those for mental stimuli. Clearly, these ideas on preconscious processing are relevant to both cognitive and phenomenological aspects of attempts to understand emotion.

Value and Complexity

Much of the discussion of the relationship between emotion and cognition remains based on implicit notions of appraisal, i.e. stimuli are judged or evaluated, amongst other things, as to their worth for us. This suggests that it would be instructive to explore the concept of value a little, although strictly within the context of emotion and without straying into the domain of moral philosophy. However, perhaps not surprisingly, psychologists have been a little reluctant to do this. One exception is Mandler (for example, 1982).

Linking somewhat with Dixon's discussion of preconscious processing, Mandler suggests that we are not necessarily aware of the evaluative aspect of an event unless some other either internal or external event somehow requires that the judgement be made. However, in Mandler's view the major processes that contribute to particular conscious structures are peripheral autonomic arousal and evaluative cognitions. Conscious emotion is then constructed from value and from whatever evidence can be gleaned from ANS feedback. Within this context, cognition and arousal may be experienced as phenomenally distinct.

Mandler suggests that evaluative cognitions include simple positive or negative values plus more complex varieties such as sexual attraction, harm, loss of loved ones, self-enhancement, and so on. Emotional experiences are then made up of these values plus ANS arousal, into something unitary, such as love or fear, if it is reasonable to describe such complex experiences as unitary.

Within Mandler's framework, values are structured from past history and are influenced by society. More specifically, facial expressions are evaluative communications. He regards them as occurring so early, from an evolutionary point of view, that they are likely to be concerned with value rather than being seen as descriptive acts. Thus, when we see an evaluative expression we infer that emotional meaning lies behind it.

Clearly, this is but a beginning in the discussion of value from an emotional perspective. However, it does provide a foundation on which to build future considerations, which at some time it will be necessary to make if the relationships between emotion and cognition are to be fully explored. Further, it should be noted that this aspect of the exploration may well be enhanced by a phenomenological approach.

Linville (1982) takes a tangential view of value in a discussion of the emotional aspects of cognitive complexity. He regards such complexity as having evaluative consequences. For example, he points out that people, who are high in cognitive self-complexity experience smaller mood swings and self-appraisal following failure or success. Generally, greater cognitive complexity is associated with less extreme emotion or evaluation.

This view has a number of implications. For example, some occupations prompt more complex conceptions of self than do others. This should lead to people in such occupations as showing less variability in emotion than others. Also, there is a possible link between self-complexity and clinical depression. If one has a simple self-structure there is a greater probability of negative events spilling over into other areas of life and eventually leading to depression. Although they are speculative, these ideas are plausible and interesting.

Feeling

Izard (1982) comments on the relationship between emotion and cognition via a discussion of feeling. Although the third aspect of the experience of emotion for, for example, Leventhal is meaning, for Izard it is feeling which he regards as invariant throughout the lifespan. Although the cognitions associated with, say, joy differ in the young and old, Izard believes that the feelings associated with joy remain the same.

Izard suggests that the feeling component of emotion exists independently of cognition, and it can occur without any reflective or symbolic processes. Without the feeling component there remains just undifferential arousal. However, although in Izard's view emotion is continuously present in consciousness, with the terms of his Differential Emotions Theory, feelings can exist in different levels of consciousness. This ranges from being barely aware of them through to complete domination by them. Of course, Dixon would probably argue that they also might have effects at the preconscious level.

From his most recent standpoint, Izard believes that there are a number of problems which need to be dealt with by those who are concerned with the relationship between emotion and cognition. For example, they do not provide data on causal links between arousal and emotion, nor do they pay any heed to cortical arousal. Also, the arousal–cognition model assumes that there is no emotion without appraisal. Izard maintains, however, that appraisal is not necessary for pain, sexual pleasure, joy, sadness, anger or fear. However, this is surely a point that Lazarus and others might debate with some vigour.

General critique

In Clark and Fiske's (1982) important book on emotion and cognition, Simon makes some trenchant general comments on the state of knowledge and understanding in the area. He begins with a general discussion of affect, the concept which Clark and Fiske choose rather than emotion to emphasise.

Simon argues that it is important to distinguish between three conditions. First, there are emotions such as surprise, fear and anger which are associated with redirected attention plus arousal of the ANS and the endocrine system that follows from interruption of sensory stimulation, the ANS and/or long-term memory. Second, there are sad or happy moods which stem from diffuse and subtle arousal, without any interruption of attention. These may also stem from long-term memories, with moods establishing contexts that influence cognitive activity. Third there are cognitive evaluations that arise from memories of affect which might have been associated with an object or event, or there are particular cognitive evaluations associated with particular objects or events.

Simon argues that it is very important to distinguish between cognitive evaluations and the affects that may link with them. He sees affect as a generic term, with emotion as affect that interrupts and redirects attention. Mood is affect that provides a context but with no interruption and valuations are positive or negative cognitive labels that are associated with objects or events. Simon's view then is very much based on Mandler's emphasis on the significance of interruption.

From a slightly different perspective, Simon characterizes affect as diffuse, graded and changing gradually although continuously. Cognition he sees as specific, digital (symbolic) and rapid. They interact through interruption and arousal. In this sense, in interruption, long-term memory sets aside the current focus of attention as defined by short-term memory. On the arousal side of the coin, stimulation of the ANS and/or endocrine systems leads to interruption.

Simon believes that there are two-directional causal paths which establish the associations between emotion and cognition. Sensation leads to emotion which in turn prompts a change in cognitive attention. Also arousal may have long-term effects on memory activation and thus lead to a context in which cognitive processes might be modified. This is really a description of mood. For the most part, Simon suggests that emotion and mood can be viewed as independent variables which influence or change cognition, or be seen as dependent variables. However, neatly cutting through the Zajonc–Lazarus debate, he also points out that it is obvious that cognition can induce affect; one only has to consider the effects of reading a novel to recognize the force of this simply made point.

CONCLUSIONS

The inescapable conclusion that must be drawn in this chapter and, indeed, in this book as a whole, is that the links between emotion and cognition have been so firmly established that it would be imprudent not to consider cognition in any attempt to understand emotion. More than imprudent, it would almost be churlish to do otherwise. It is clear that both empirical investigations and theoretical analyses involving both emotion and cognition, are not only possible, but significant, compelling and, it might be argued, necessary.

Following the intricate discussion in this chapter, almost any attempt to make general statements runs the risk of oversimplification. However, the relationship between emotion and cognition is so important that the risk must be taken. Perhaps the best way of characterizing the relationship is with the idea that emotion and cognition are both processes, which are simultaneously independent and interacting. They are similar in that both may be preconscious, but differ, in that of the two it seems to be only emotion which may culminate in subjective experience, although it does not have to.

Since emotion and cognition are independent as well as interacting, sometimes, depending on the circumstances, one can be more important or significant for the individual than the other. However, this is a matter of balance. It is hard to imagine circumstances in which either one is driven out entirely by the salience of the other. In a broader context, however, one is drawn to the conclusion that emotion predominates over cognition, perhaps owing to its primitive fundamental adaptive significance in individual and species survival.

If the assumption is made that emotion and cognition are independent but interacting processes, it remains to explore the nature of the interaction. Of course, it is with this that much of this chapter has been concerned, particularly in considerations of appraisal and evaluation. The cognitive influence on emotion must be via such judgement of the value of stimuli for the individual. However, it is also clear that the links between emotion and cognition are more varied than this alone.

Finally, it is perhaps worth making the firm point that at the present state of knowledge and understanding cognition should be regarded as necessary to emotion. Although it can be debated whether or not behaviour and/or arousal are necessary aspects of emotion, it appears to be more and more difficult not to accord cognition an essential role in emotion. In any event, whether or not in the final analysis cognition does prove to be a necessary part of emotion, it is certainly proving to be more helpful than anything else in improving our general understanding of emotion and in leading to innovative developments in its study.

5

Philosophy, Phenomenology and Behavioural Psychology

To any reader who has the stamina to progress this far, it should be evident that the most promising accounts of emotion are predicated on cognition. Many of them see an important, in some cases, a necessary role for physiological arousal. There are two other aspects of emotion which have, as yet, barely received mention, even though at the everyday level they would be regarded as basic—subjective experience and behaviour. Similarly, there has so far been scant consideration of the ideas of philosophers about emotion, even though the subject had its origins in philosophy.

The problem is that for various reasons, events have passed by the philosophical and behavioural approaches. To deal with these in turn, the recent ideas of emotion theorists have in fact come close to those of some modern philosophers who have given attention to the subject. Then with the relative sophistication of science to back them up, they have gone further than the philosophers, not conceptually, but empirically. However, as much for the discipline of thought as for any other reason, the philosophers of emotion have much to offer the psychologist who is interested in coming to grips with the subject.

That subjective experience is a significant aspect of emotion is self-evident; this is the feeling part. At the everyday level this is the *sine qua non* of emotion. However, whether it is necessary to attempt a description of such experience in order to understand emotion is another matter. In itself, it might be interesting, and it might add to the richness of the subject, but strictly speaking, it is not essential. Of course from the viewpoint of conventional science, there are many problems with the phenomenological approach to psychology, mainly involving measurement. In spite of this, rigorous descriptions of the experience of emotion may well have insights to offer to those who prefer (for good reason) the methodologically more sound approaches.

There is an even greater problem when the behavioural approaches to emotion are considered, particularly since they had their origins in the interesting work of Watson. If anything, the difficulty comes about because those who have taken the behavioural route to emotion made a fundamental mistake—they emphasized the wrong thing. As is made evident in Chapter 7 facial expression and bodily movement and posture is being thrust into a more and more important role in the analysis of emotion. But this is all being done by social psychologists in a cognitive context. It is very rare to find mention of facial expression amongst behavioural psychologists, even though it is obviously behaviour.

Those who have taken the behavioural approach to emotion have stressed some remarkably nonbehavioural concepts such as emotionality and frustration and then attempted to give them respectability by the rigour of the empirical studies they have made of them. In so doing, they have taken away much of their meaning and unwittingly ensured that they no longer seem particularly relevant to human emotion. Alternatively, they have made extensive and well-contrived studies of closely defined topics such as conditioned emotional responding (CER). Whilst the data amassed from this approach are impressive in their apparent reliability, their validity is open to question in the context of emotion. It seems a far cry from a conditioned emotional response in the rat to an angry man or frightened child.

For these reasons, as well as the promising developments in the cognitive approach to the study of emotion, the behaviourally inspired investigation has once again become almost quiescent during the last few years. However, as with the ideas of philosophers and those who study the experience of emotion a study of the behavioural approach has much to offer the student of emotion. Concepts such as emotionality and frustration can be useful and CERs exist and should not be discounted.

This chapter offers an introduction to these three approaches to emotion in the hope that they will help in the general understanding of the topic. They may not be essential, but they are important.

SOME PHILOSOPHICAL ACCOUNTS OF EMOTION

It would of course require a philosophical text to do justice to philosophical accounts of emotion; they have been extensive and derive at least from the time of Aristotle. Rather than attempt to be inclusive, the aim in this section is to give a brief description of the relatively recent ideas of three philosophers and a much fuller account of a fourth, simply on the grounds that they seem more relevant to psychology than many other philosophical analyses.

R.S. Peters

Peters (for example, 1969; 1970) adopts an approach to emotion which seems to be a mixture of psychology, philosophy and common sense, beginning with an attempt to gain information by listing what might 'naturally' be called emotions. He suggests that the main criterion for including a term is that it links emotion and appraisal. Emotions as appraisals stem from external conditions or from things that people have themselves generated or suffered. He argues that an emotion cannot even be identified without knowledge of appraisal. If a list of emotions is generated in this way, Peters suggests that most of them also characterized motive. Thus, in Peters commonsense view, there is overlap between emotion and motive.

However, Peters goes on to draw an important distinction between emotion and motivation. In everyday language we speak of motives in situations in which we are searching for explanations of behaviour—'he criticized what you said *because* he feels a need to be dominant', 'he ate *because* he was hungry'. Whereas, Peters suggests that we speak of emotions in situations where people are passive, where they are being overcome by emotion—'he was blinded by anger', 'he could do nothing to stop himself trembling with anxiety', 'he was overcome by love'. In particular, Peters holds that we tend to view emotions in this way if we judge their antecedents to be dangerous or frustrating. Peters is therefore arguing in support of an everyday conceptual connection between motivation and action, and between emotion and passivity or inaction. Although motivation and emotion are connected in that they each involve appraisals, they are distinct in that emotion is not connected to action. Peters maintains that even when there seems to be a relationship between emotion and activity within the autonomic nervous system, the activity involved is still passive—we go white with fear or blush with embarrassment, responses it is very difficult to control. Such responses tend to occur in spite of our better judgement.

Peters suggests further that there are other linkages between emotion and motivation and emotion and action, but these are rather more indirect. He affirms that emotion can suppress or enhance motor performance. For example, if we are angry then we might well act more vigorously than if we were not angry.

Peters extends this view to suggest that there is a *de facto* relationship between emotion and higher mental processes such as memory and perception. Any appraisal which is connected with an emotion must alter the general assessment which is being made at the time. For example, if we appraise something as unpleasant or bad for us, then under some conditions this will obscure what might be relevant for adaptive behaviour in the situation, and under other conditions will highlight it. Either way, however, there is distortion; an emotion simply comes over us, and there is very little that we can do about it.

As a final stage in his analysis, Peters argues that there is a conceptual connection between emotion and wishing. Motivation is concerned with 'wanting' which leads to action; emotion is concerned with the much vaguer 'wishing', which does not lead to action. Peters cites the example of grief. If a woman is mourning her dead husband, she is in fact wishing he were still alive. However, there is obviously no action she can take which will bring him back to life, so the emotion wells up.

A.R. Louch

Louch (1966) takes an entirely different tack from Peters. He puts forward via an analysis of the difficulties which beset any conceptualization of emotion and which attend the traditional rational/emotional distinction, a strong argument that emotion is firmly linked to action,and indeed can be used to explain it.

Lough's starting point is that pleasure and pain can be regarded as different ways of evaluating objects or qualities. If this is so, then emotion must be viewed in the same way. Secondly, he believes that emotions are both caused by stimuli and are themselves causes of behaviour.

By contrasting his thesis with those of other philosophers, Louch makes a number of points. (1) Emotions are frequently regarded as passions or forces (much as Peters views them) rather than as expressions of behaviour. These are forces which we cannot control. (2) The labels of emotion classify feelings which come about as a result of situations which lead to emotional behaviour. (3) There is a very wide variation in emotional behaviour, with enormous idiosyncrasies involved. Consequently, Louch suggests that it is more appropriate to ascribe emotions to behaviours occurring in particular contexts which have been appraised in particular ways by people.

By these and similar arguments, Louch arrives at a general statement of his views. 'Desires and emotions, pleasures and pains, are identified in ourselves and others, in the light of what we regard or infer or see as desirable, appropriate or entailed by the situation in which we find ourselves' (1966, p.93). Louch uses terms such as these to explain actions, the main purpose of his book, by regarding the situation as in some way entitling the action, in the case discussed above, via emotion. In this Louch's ideas are in obvious contradistinction to those of Peters, although similar in that they again emphasize appraisal.

G. Ryle

Ryle's (1948) starting point is the affirmation that emotions are made up of, or suggest, inclinations (motives), moods, agitations (or commotions) and feelings. Of these, the first three are simply propensities, they are not occurrences in the way that feelings are. He develops his argument by drawing a series of contrasts between these different aspects of emotion.

Ryle begins with what is perhaps the most important comparison, that between feelings and inclinations. He states that feelings are what people describe by phrases such as 'a thrill of anticipation', and they are also names for specific bodily sensations, for example, qualms of apprehension or sickness. Thus we tend to give to some feelings specific locations whilst others are assigned a general coverage of the whole body (a flash of anger or a glow of pride). It is clear then that Ryle is suggesting that feelings can be emotions. But people also tend to characterize emotions as *motives*. For example, the behaviour of a clever leader is explained by saying that he carries with him certain dispositions, to be dominant and resourceful, and so on, and that on occasion these will be manifest in his behaviour. However, he will also be expected to feel certain things, although these feelings do not indicate his leadership as well as does his behaviour.

This analysis is relevant to the way in which we typically explain behaviour. If we say that someone did something because of a particular motive, we are merely saying that in our judgement, he *would* behave in a particular way if . . . . One aspect of this argument is that a person will *feel* something when he or she is engaged in these acts. So, in Ryle's terms, both the motive and the feeling are part of an emotion, but the former is a disposition and the latter an occurrence, albeit a difficult one to pin down for study.

In a similar way, Ryle also makes cogent comparisons between inclinations (motives) and agitations, mood and feelings, and feeling and pleasure. In conclusion, Ryle suggests that there are three major ways in which the idea of emotion is commonly used. In the first two it is employed in an attempt to explain behaviour by referring to emotions. Hence we use emotion in the sense of motives or inclinations on the basis of which more or less intelligent actions are made, or we use it to refer to moods, including agitations or perturbations. The third sense in which Ryle believes emotion to be commonly used is in reference to pangs and twinges. These are feelings and emotions, although this usage clearly does not allow any explanation of behaviour to be made.

W. Lyons

From the psychologist's viewpoint, by far the most useful philosophical discussion of emotion has been made by Lyons (1980). He expounds his causal–evaluative theory of emotions via a series of propositions. These will be discussed at some length; their study is valuable.

(1) Lyons proposed that emotion is an occurrent state rather than a disposition. To exemplify the distinction, one might be fearful of being struck by a particular person or one might be fearful of being struck if one is in any company, that is one is liable to be afraid in certain circumstances.

In choosing to stress emotion as occurrent, Lyons is not exceptional; most theories of emotion are concerned with occurrent states. However, in general reference to emotion, some terms are used in both ways and some are not. For example anger or fear can be occurrent or dispositional, whereas love is only used dispositionally and rage only occurrently. Within this, an emotional disposition can be reasonably focused (an angry person expresses the anger in specific directions) or relatively unfocused (irascibility is a general proneness to react angrily).

Lyons prefers the occurrent account since it gives what he terms the full case of emotion. Whatever might be latent in an angrily disposed person is also present when anger is occurring, particularly when there is physiological arousal. Lyons suggests a progression which starts with our beliefs about the present situation, which form the basis for an evaluation. This in turn causes wants and desires which cause behaviour, physiological change and subjective feelings.

(2) Causal–evaluative theory gets its name from the suggestion that X is an emotional state if and only if it is a physiologically abnormal state caused by a person's evaluation of a situation. So emotion is a psychosomatic state, in which both evaluation and physiological change are necessary conditions for emotion, not individually but together.

To be essential to emotion an attitude must be an evaluation in relation to self, which may be occurrent or dispositional. Also, the physiological change in emotion must be unusual since others are occurring constantly. The abnormality will usually take the form of being in some way more or less than the normal range. Lyons does not expand the nature of the causal link between evaluation and physiological change. If one frequently follows the other closely in time, it is simply likely to be causal.

(3) Differently from many psychologists, Lyons argues that it is not possible to differentiate between the emotions behaviourally, physiologically or motivationally. He proposes that such differentiation is only possible through cognitive evaluations. In his view, we clearly seek clues to a person's emotional state from behaviour or physiological indicants, but to be sure we need to find the person's view or evaluation of the situation. If we do draw conclusions from behaviour, this is because the behaviour is a typical manifestation of an evaluative attitude.

(4) Lyons suggests that there is a complex relationship between emotion and desires. Some emotions would not exist unless the person admits to certain wants or desires. For example, it would make little sense to speak of love without admitting to a desire to be with the loved person. Such emotions need not culminate in behaviour; they can exist without being given into. By contrast, Lyons argues that some emotions have no wants at all attached to them, backward-looking ones such as grief, for example. However, it may be that even this might subsume the desire that an event such as the death of another, had not occurred.

(5) Lyons causal–evaluative theory also proposes that evaluations lead rationally and causally to specific desires which then lead to behaviour. He argues that this type of evaluative theory is better than a motivational theory of emotion since it can explain, for example, how various types of behaviour can be part of one emotion. The diversity of fear cannot be explained with action tendencies resulting from motivational theory. Wants/desires are not tied to particular patterns of behaviour. The evaluative aspect of emotion gives a reason for the emotional behaviour.

(6) Finally, Lyons proposed that if emotions are mainly occurrent, they are tangible, including bodily change, facial expression, gesture, speech and motivated behaviour. For the psychologist, the problem is that a 'mental' event, an evaluation, is the differentiation between emotions. However, Lyons

argues that evaluations are as tangible as behaviour. Further, he makes the frequently considered point that there may be a perfect correlation between the structural/categorical basis of evaluations and brain states. If this were to be so then an evaluative account of emotion could eventually be reduced to a behavioural/physiological account—an argument that could apply to any cognitive analysis.

However, and perhaps more interestingly, evaluations might still provide the way of differing between the emotions, even if they are irreducibly mentalist. In Lyons's view, this does not make his theory any more nonobjective than a theory which involves equally nonobservable electrons for example. In as much as a physicist claims to be able to see traces of electrons, so the psychologist can reasonably claim to see traces of evaluations in the tangible aspects of emotional occurrences.

This has been but a brief summary of the main points of Lyons's theory, which should be sufficient to demonstrate its relevance to psychologists. It is instructive that, similarly to the other philosophers' theories mentioned so far, it relies heavily on cognition, indeed suggesting that in combination, evaluations and physiological change are necessary conditions of emotion—in their stress on cognition, these theories add to the weight of numbers of theories of emotion of psychological origin which are similarly oriented.

Apart from this additional pointer to the importance of cognition in emotion, the views put forward by philosophers who have turned their attention to emotion provide psychologists with a fine example of precision in expressing their ideas. Emotion is a difficult concept, which cannot be glossed over by simple empiricism. For there to be any chance of improving our understanding of it, it must be treated with respect, theoretically. The ways of thinking and manner of expression of writers such as Ryle and Lyons are of great help in this.

SOME PHENOMENOLOGICAL ACCOUNTS OF EMOTION

'phenomenology is that empiricistic philosophy which asserts that the givens of experience are configurational entities having a unique integrity of their own and are, therefore, not reducible to sense contents or to any other elemental structure.' (Turner, 1967, p.60)

In order to describe some of the many phenomenological conceptualizations of emotion it is necessary to set the scene with a brief description of phenomenological psychology. Turner's definition is of the philosophical foundations of phenomenology as conceptualized in the early part of this century by European philosophers such as Husserl (1913). Husserl argued that our thoughts and feelings have a purpose and that this purpose must come from the 'essential' person. Also, a thought or feeling is always about something, it reaches out, and is therefore *intentional*. Husserl believed that our senses give us a direct knowledge of the world, a view of the world as it really is, but suggested that the intent in our perceptions might distort this reality. In other words, what we put into perception may distort the information we gain from our senses. Such a distortion could take many forms, from racial prejudice to the effects produced by simple visual illusions.

This type of reasoning provided a foundation from which modern phenomenological psychology developed. The original phenomenology would be too extreme an approach for the present-day psychologist to human nature, stressing as it does only the unique experiencing individual, at the expense of all else. Of course, by a similar token, radical behaviourism is too extreme to be accepted by most psychologists, assigning as it does no status at all to individual experience.

Phenomenological psychology then is the study of consciousness and experience. It is an individual's perception of the world which is the crucial aspect of psychological investigation. The implication is that each of us perceives the world, or some situation or object within it, in a unique fashion, although there might of course be common elements in the perceptions experienced by different people. *And it is these perceptions or experiences that determine the way in which we react or the way in which we behave.* Clearly, phenomenological psychology is working from a model of man which although empirical is very different from that of the behaviourist, or even that of the middle-of-the-road conventional scientific psychologist.

Although the present aim is to explore the relationship between phenomenology and emotion, it is worthwhile now to point out some of the characteristics of the general phenomenological approach. The main concern is with what a person is experiencing here and now, at this moment, in this place, in his or her present state. What a person experiences can be manipulated by controlling prior experiences in a similar way to that of the experimental psychologist who manipulates behaviour. Naturally, similar controls can be employed as well. But the data of experience are necessarily subjective: they are personal reports of a person's conscious process, of his or her experiences. So for the most part the phenomenological psychologist is dealing with what the behaviourist would call verbal report. But interest centres on the content of the report, not its form. And experience or conscious processes are assigned a *causal* role in determining behaviour.

Apologists who stress the importance of phenomenology in psychology (for example, Giorgi, 1970) argue that phenomenology gives the psychologist the one really special approach he can get for his set of specialized problems. The basis of their argument is that psychology is set apart because its object of study is man, and man has consciousness, which should therefore be the proper and foremost concern of psychologists.

If the subject matter of psychology is consciousness, it follows that psychologists should be concerned with the function of the whole person and not just break him down into isolated processes such as learning and memory. Within limits, man has choice, free will to choose what he will do next. They should be concerned with real-life needs, problems and motivation of fully functioning people. They should devise methodologies appropriate to this subject matter rather than simply continue to apply the techniques of conventional science. Because of their unique subject matter, psychologists should not shirk the making of value judgements. Finally, they should be concerned with aiding people to understand themselves rather than with concentrating solely on the prediction and control of behaviour.

Within this context, it is important to ask if it is possible to produce a phenomenological theory of emotion which has the characteristics of a good theory, i.e. is anchored to the real world, makes an adequate summary of any data, is internally consistent and leads to predictions? Second, is there any common ground between phenomenological theories? Third, are the phenomenological approaches to emotion testable with any sort of empirical research, be it within the methodological framework of conventional science or not?

Brief summaries of Hillman's (1960) and Sartre's (1948) theories of emotion were presented in Chapter 2. Although the original material from which these resumés were made is very full, they are sufficient to demonstrate that it is possible to construct phenomenological and even existential theories of emotion. However, in spite of being laudably ambitious, both of these theories, together with any others that might have been considered, are limited. They are limited to human experience and for the most part depend on intuitive, non-quantifiable data. They are dubious and seem to put psychology back on to a pre-scientific footing. So, rather than consider such theories any further at this point, it might be more helpful to describe the ideas of Buytedijk (1950) who made a serious attempt to describe what should be involved in a phenomenological approach to emotion. This will be followed by a discussion of Fell's (1977) even more cogent analysis, and an attempt to come to terms with phenomenological measurement.

F.J.J. Buytedijk

Buytedijk (1950) points out that science is concerned with facts, but goes on to question what a fact is, and more especially, whether or not feelings are facts. If I say: 'I feel angry whenever I am in the presence of my colleague X', is this factual? Buytedijk's definition of a feeling is that it is an *act* which is intentionally present. The meaning of feelings then comes from what they signify. If we feel happy or we feel angry then this implies that we know the meaning that certain situations will have for us, an idea that has something in common with Mandler's (1984) theory.

The general phenomenological approach begins with the idea that consciousness is always consciousness of something else, and that we are also conscious of existing. This means that we are aware of being in situations in which we must respond, that is, we must have attitudes and feelings and make intentional acts. Feeling and emotion function to assure us of our attitudes in various situations. Each situation has its own special feeling for us. It is a spontaneous response to a situation which transforms the situation into a new world. Some sort of choice must be involved here. Our emotional attitude to a situation is confirmed by a feeling, although we choose (in some nonreflective way) to become happy in some situation in order to alter our feeling towards it.

Within this sort of context, Buytedijk suggests that emotion is *not* intentional, it is akin to sensation or excitation. I am only conscious of myself. If I loath someone then I project myself as loathing and make further projections about the person. This is brought about by feeling. Such projection rebounds and has the character of emotion. Thus we cannot experience emotion without feeling, but emotion is not intentional, it is the quality of our existence which occurs through feeling. Although feeling and emotion, viewed in this light, are spontaneous and unintentional, we can alter our feelings by the situations which we can create with the words we use. So, we use language intentionally to modify, enhance or suppress our feelings.

Buytedijk argues that a phenomenological analysis of the essence of various situations can be used to understand the meaning of emotional expressions. One of his examples is the smile. What is characteristic (phenomenologically) of situations which cause a smile? He suggests that a smile anticipates something in the future. We are moderately excited and know that this excitement will remain moderate in our intentional act. A smile is any easy physical act which springs from a general attitude of active inactivity which points to a relaxation, a threshold of something such as joy or elation. So, with a smile we are making a transformation of the situation which faces us, and at the same time are confronting ourselves with this transformed world, that is, we are aware of it.

Clearly, a truly phenomenological analysis of emotion is not an easy matter. What then is its value? Is it worth pursuing? Buytedijk takes a definite stand on these questions. He points out that the phenomenological approach is not introspection; that is, it is not an inspection of subjective experiences. Rather, it is directed at experienced phenomena and towards different acts such as perception, thinking, feeling and so on, even though these might not be viewed analytically. It is worth noting that this is a very different use of the word 'act' than is found amongst the behaviourally oriented psychologists.

It is irrelevant whether or not the phenomenon being considered is real. The emphasis is on what is termed its *essential structure*. Hence, asking the question, 'What is guilt, or anger?', is asking no more than, 'What is a chair, or a table?' It is not causal relationships that are sought, but an exploration of the inner essential structure, in this case the structure of emotion. A phenomenological approach then needs more and more complete description in these same terms. The aim is to make these analyses of the experience of feelings in various situations, in order to discover patterns and invariances in our usual, normal modes of existence. Whether or not this aim can be realized and, if so, what it would mean is another matter. This might be better understood by a consideration of Fell's (1977) ideas.

J.P. Fell

The basis of Fell's (1977) convincing analysis of the possibility of applying a phenomenological approach to the study of emotion lies in the idea of *pretheoretical* experience. This is concerned with the foundations of both science and knowledge in that the suggestion is made that the starting point for science is that of a person who has a prior understanding of a familiar world. In other words, in order for any type of investigation to be made, the phenomena to be investigated must already be known. For example, fear or anger or happiness mean many things within psychology, but whatever psychologists say of them, they must first recognize what they are studying as fear, anger or happiness.

Fell's analysis derives partly from Husserl's, who quite clearly characterized humans as being in cognitive situations that permit them to find the world patterned, organized and hence intelligible. This cognitive ability is there from the start and allows us to make sense of the world immediately and directly, that is, intuitively. Apart from anything else, we are also able to intuit emotion in this way, we can see other people as angry, afraid or happy. Similarly, from this standpoint, a human emotion is a meaningful relation between a person and a meaningful environment, of which behaviour and physiology are no more than components.

As part of his thesis on emotion, Fell makes some interesting comparisons between phenomenology and behaviourism. First, they differ in that one takes an external viewpoint and the other an intuitive. Behaviourists see an environment made up of reinforcers, while phenomenologists fill it with meanings. Emotions, are responses, from an observational viewpoint, but experientially they are feelings that make sense. Put another way, emotions are a function of the environment, be they conditioned or understood. Emotion might depend on contingencies, but their power, according to Fell hinges on what they mean or how they are understood. Emotions are qualitative experiences, albeit they have behavioural aspects.

Second, the behaviourist is concerned, as in anything else, with the prediction and control of emotion. The phenomenologist, however, is concerned with its description, what exactly is being predicted and controlled. An emotion is an amalgam of the observed and the experienced, of behaviour and meaning.

The final point at issue, in this context, between the behaviourist and the phenomenologist turns on what is considered to be real. Because emotion as a felt experience is difficult, perhaps impossible, to quantify and measure, does this mean that it is not real or does it mean that science should be supplemented by direct experience and understanding? Fell implies that it is nonsense to attempt to restrict what is real, to restrict knowledge, to what can be observed.

The objective scientist must have intuited and experienced emotions to know what is being studied. Pre-scientific experience should not be ignored.

An interesting problem which follows from Fel's argument, and which he acknowledges, is that it is difficult to conceive of a phenomenological theory of emotion, since concern centres on pretheoretical experience. Then the question becomes whether it is possible to describe pretheoretical experience without at least partly theorizing about it. The only measure of this comes from the assent or otherwise of whoever sees the description, a sort of consensual validation.

Although a phenomenological analysis of emotion is according to this argument, problematic, theoretically it is possible to investigate emotion phenomenologically. This would be based on a prior understanding of what emotion is and would subsume six possibilities: (1) emotions considered as meanings in a meaningful environment; (2) emotions considered as events understood by the person experiencing them; (3) emotions considered as 'making sense'; (4) distinctively human emotions and moods considered from a perspective of how they are brought about by the intuitive understanding which characterizes cognition; (5) consideration given to the possibility that emotions which seem common to humans and other organisms, behaviourally and physiologically, might be qualitatively different in humans because of cognition; (6) a consideration of the way in which language might affect emotion.

Fell pursues his argument to the extreme of suggesting that the best way of deciding on the adequacy of the many theories of emotion is by returning to what he terms the original cognitive situation. Whatever a theory of emotion might suggest, whatever types of investigation seem appropriate, a precondition for any or all of this is the preliminary or experiential comprehension of the emotion. Whatever the 'it' is which is being studied is specified by ordinary experience. It is an approach which predicates the investigation of emotion and naive understanding. Understanding or intuition is a necessary precondition for knowledge.

Fell does not suggest that the phenomenological approach to emotion offers final solutions, nor does he see it as offering a challenge to other approaches. However, he does view it as providing an important reminder that any approach must depend on the original cognitive situation. In its way, the phenomenological approach to emotion, stressing, no more than meanings, is as limited as the behavioural or the physiological approaches, particularly if taken alone. In the end, in spite of its limitations, Fell's final justification for the inclusion of a phenomenological approach to emotion, is that it is so fundamental, a necessary prerequisite, that nothing less would do. Although this argument might be compelling, the counter to it is the very pragmatic one that some approaches to an understanding of emotion have actually done quite nicely in ignorance of phenomenology. However, it cannot be denied that to include a phenomenological analysis *might* provide a more complete understanding of emotion.

Measurement

Can the phenomenological perspective on emotion be put to empirical test? Can the sorts of ideas expressed by writers such as Fell, or even Sartre, be placed within the domain of more conventional psychology? Answers to these questions will be sought through a brief consideration of what has been attempted.

Although Mandler's (1984) analysis of the role of consciousness in emotion is broadly relevant here, a more appropriate background comes from Tart's (1972) consideration of measurement in the study of altered states of consciousness (ASC). The general point is that it might be reasonable to add emotion to Tart's list of ASCs which are capable of scientific investigation. When experiencing emotion, the individual is in a particular state, although often only partially, which is different from his normal state of consciousness. Phenomenological psychologists would argue that he is experiencing a new perception of the world, a new series of insights, perhaps even a magical transformation of the world.

The general possibility of the semi-scientific investigation of the phenomenology of emotion can be explored further within the framework of Tart's four major principles of science: observation, public techniques, theory and verifiable prediction. There are a number of ways in which a particular emotional experience can be observed. The investigator can record his or her own emotional experiences or ask others to do so, either whilst they are ongoing or afterwards. Of course, there are standard methodological objections to such techniques. For example, the recording of emotional experiences while the person is in an emotional state might interfere with the experience or if records are made once the experiences are finished then some essential points might be forgotten. However, some objections could perhaps be overcome in the way that Tart suggests, by obtaining a general knowledge of the person and also by insisting on consensual verificaiton.

Consensual validation also helps the personal observation of emotion to be made public. Comparisons could be made of a person's reports during an emotional experience and afterwards and these could be compared with those of other people who are experiencing or have experienced emotions following similar sets of precipitating circumstances. The next major principle of scientific endeavour according to Tart is theory. Within a phenomenological context, this has already been sufficiently discussed through the work of Fell.

Finally, there is the question of verifiable prediction. There is little problem here. If data are gained about the experience of emotional states in various situations then there is no reason why these should not be used to make predictions about other experiences in similar situations. As Tart suggests, prediction here is from experience to experience rather than being empirical in the usual way of science, but it is nevertheless verifiable. This is simply another level or another means of verification.

Having established a possible case in support of investigations of, rather than speculations about, the experience of emotion, there are a number of specific research achievements which exemplify it.

(1) Maslow's (for example, 1972) studies of self-actualization are relevant, in which he gathered data from asking questions or reading about the lives and values of a small group of people. It may be that emotional experience could be studied in a similar way to that followed by Maslow as he gained a composite picture of peak-experiences by questioning people about them.

(2) Block (1957) used the semantic differential to evaluate emotions on a series of bipolar scales. Although Block put forward a powerful argument to suggest that language habits refect the phenomenology of emotion, this technique has not been much extended, except perhaps in the work of Mehrabian and Russell (1974).

(3) A third research possibility for studying the experience of emotion derives from Kelly's (1955) personal construct theory. Repertory grid techniques can be used to investigate the constructs which underlie or represent the individual's view of emotion in general.

(4) The most obvious way of attempting to study emotional experience is through questionnaires. With the exception of the specialized field of anxiety, little has been done in this sphere. However, recent and very promising exceptions are the work of Kammann (1979) on well-being and happiness, and more particularly the work of Izard (for example, 1977) in developing the Differential Emotions Scale (see also Fuenzalida et al., 1981).

More recently, De Rivera (1984) has suggested some very promising possibilities for the development of a qualitative methodology in the study of emotion. These include: (1) analysing the transcripts of interviews about emotional experiences into units of meaning, with the gradual explication of themes; (2) having asked a person to give a specific example of an emotional experience, comparing this with an abstract conceptualization about the experience in discussion with the person; (3) developing ways to make others experience what the investigator has discovered or conceptualized; (4) constructing a story from the observation of everyday events as experienced by people from their particular perspectives.

Conclusions

It should be clear from this brief consideration of the phenomenology of emotion that there is something to be gained from this approach, although it is neither necessary, nor even crucial, in spite of Fell's (1977) arguments to the contrary. As well as providing extra insights into emotion and allowing a future description of it, it is also possible to devise various types of qualitative methodology which have something in common with those of conventional science.

Although the phenomenological analysis of emotion may seem tangential to the approaches which offer the most promising route to an understanding of emotion, there is one point which emerges from the ideas of almost all those who have worked within this tradition. Like those who have put forward philosophically based theories of emotion, they all stress the importance of cognition. For the phenomenologists or those interested in the experience of emotion, like most of the recent emotion theorists cognition is central.

SOME BEHAVIOURAL ACCOUNTS OF EMOTION

For the most part, research and theory in emotional behaviour has focused on what is directly observable and directly measurable. Emotion has been seen as a response, or responses, basic to life and survival, rather than as a state of the organism. The emphasis is taken from either cognition or subjective experience and put instead on behaviour. Emotion *can* with a struggle be defined in terms of the operations necessary to bring it about. This approach has traditionally been of importance to science, but might seem too restricted to apply to emotion.

There are three main lines of research into emotional behaviour; although often conceptually related, these have progressed fairly independently of one another. (1) The observation and measurement of 'emotionality'. Investigators have centred their interest either on behaviour in the 'open-field' or on the perseverative effects of noxious stimuli. Such an approach has its roots in Hullian theory, which in fact provides an important background to the study of emotional behaviour in general. (2) The general role of emotion in conditioning and learning emphasized by such as Miller and Mowrer, and by Amsel in frustration theory. (3) The final approach stems from Watson and Skinner. It owes much to an ingenious experimental technique, developed in the early 1940s by Estes and Skinner (1941), for studying the conditioned emotional response (CER). This has produced a proliferation of research but a paucity of ideas.

Much of this section is concerned with research which depends on developments of Hullian theory made by N.E. Miller and Mowrer. Drive theorists such as Miller have tended to view fear (or anxiety) as the salient emotion; they regard it as a necessary part of theoretical accounts of avoidance learning. In such a context, fear is an acquired drive. To Miller (1951), fear (or emotion in general) is: (1) an unconditioned reflex, mainly an ANS reaction which can be brought under stimulus control; (2) a discriminative stimulus; and (3) a drive—new responses can be learnt by the reduction of fear. This formulation leads to two basic hypotheses: (1) that learnable drives such as fear follow the same laws as overt responses; and (2) that they have the same drive and cue properties as strong external stimuli. This in turn suggests a two-factor theory of avoidance learning. For example, a painful shock produces fear (an unconditioned response as an interoceptive stimulus). Fear then acts as a drive which motivates behaviour. In avoidance learning, a neutral stimulus is paired with shock; by classical conditioning this will come to elicit fear, which will bring about avoidance via drive reduction.

Mowrer (1960a, b) regards emotion as being of central importance in learning, viewing emotions as drives which have particular eliciting conditions.

He suggests that there are four fundamental emotions; fear, hope, relief and disappointment. Fear occurs with the onset of some environmental stimulus which signifies that danger will follow. When this same stimulus ends, there is relief. With the onset of some stimulus which indicates that a period of safety (from noxious stimuli) will follow, then hope is experienced. When the safety signal ends, there is a disappointment. Although there is a reasonable amount of evidence which supports Mowrer's operational definitions of fear and hope, there is less to support relief and disappointment. In general, Mowrer believes that sensations from an organism's own behaviour may signify these four states. This enables emotion to come under instrumental control.

Emotionality

Open field

The study of emotionality in the open-field situation began with Hall (1934). (The basic procedure consists of placing an animal, usually a rat, in a large open space which it has not previously encountered. To begin with, this produces in the animal what, at the everyday level, would be called fear—urination, defecation, crouching, freezing in one position, squeaking, etc.).

The early investigations which stemmed from Hall's work were concerned with issues such as whether defecation and urination are appropriate measures of emotionality, whether habituation was the link between these measures and others, and the possible role of inheritance. Later, consideration was given to whether or not differences in emotionality as measured in the open-field have any wider ramifications, for example as a possible indicator of drive-strength. Research in each of these areas does not permit any firm conclusions to be drawn. In the end, it is difficult to assess whether or not the idea of emotionality is useful in accounting for the behaviour of animals placed in open-fields. The concept is more descriptive than explanatory and emotionality certainly does not energize behaviour.

Amongst the firmer conclusions drawn are those of Gray (1971) on rats selectively bred for high or low defecation in the open-field. He suggests that: (1) changes that occur in open-field defecation due to selective breeding are general, rather than situation-specific, (2) the genetic factors promote a general change in the level of fearfulness, (3) defecation under stressful conditions is a valid measure of fear, (4) changes in behaviour in the area of emotionality through selective breeding are dependent on genetic factors, and (5) fearfulness (emotionality) is to some extent under genetic control.

The results of studies of the effects of early experience on later emotionality do not make matters any clearer. They have usually involved giving young animals electric shock or systematic handling by the experimenter, and testing them as adults in open-field situations. The most general finding (for example, Levine, 1962) has been that increased stimulation of any sort during infancy produces more robust, less emotional adults. Or, to put this another way, that an exposure to stress early in life increases a later resistance to it. This is perhaps working against inherited predispositions.

The most useful analysis of open-field research has been made by Walsh and Cummins (1976). They argue that the usual way of deciding *what* is measured in the open-field test has been intuitive or anthropomorphic, and that this has led to the general use of the concept of emotionality. They describe emotionality as 'an entity underlying the non-specific affective components of behaviour'. From attempts to validate this concept more precisely it can only be concluded that defecation and latency are reasonable indexes. Walsh and Cummins also indicate that in the context of open-field research fear has often been used as an explanatory construct. But they can find no good way of distinguishing between fear and emotionality.

Walsh and Cummins make a number of pertinent prescriptions for future research using open-field techniques. These range from an emphasis on precise description of subjects used, apparatus, and measurement techniques, to a suggestion that multifactorial experiments should replace those in which only one independent variable is manipulated. On the side of the dependent variable, Walsh and Cummins highlight the need for the testing of reliability and validity for broad bands of conditions and subjects. Also they urge that the attempt be made at construct validation via factor analysis and ecological data. Such suggestions are unarguable, and should at least allow a conclusion to be drawn about the explanatory usefulness of the concept of emotionality.

Perseverative effects of noxious stimuli

There have been various studies concerned with the effects of prior or contemporaneous but non-contingent aversive stimuli on ongoing behaviour, either consummatory or instrumental (see Myer (1971) for a review). This area sprang up in an attempt to provide supportive evidence for the hypothesis that fear is a drive which will facilitate behaviour which is based on other drives. However, like research into open-field emotionality, this approach now tends to be of little more than historical interest. Most of the studies have been concerned with the unconditioned effects of aversive stimuli measured indirectly on a behavioural baseline; they seem to be dealing with 'emotionality' in some form, although it is not always referred to as such.

Between 1949 and the early 1970s a series of studies were carried out which explored the effects of an immediately prior shock on eating or drinking in food- and/or water-deprived rats (see, for example, Myer, 1971; Strongman, 1965; 1970). Although such studies began in an attempt to explore Hull's ideas concerning the summation of relevant and irrelevant drives, their results could more simply be seen as due to perseverative emotional effects. Frequently, these effects have been facilitatory. An animal shocked just prior to its normal time of eating or drinking, consumes more than one which is not shocked. These results depend in part on variables such as the nature of the food available, on the degree of novelty in the situation, the similarity between the shock and the testing situation, and so on.

A second line of research on the effects of prior aversive stimulation has dwelt on instrumental rather than consummatory behaviour. However, there is little evidence for facilitatory effects. The typical finding by Strongman (1967) is that prior shock suppresses subsequent bar pressing for water or food.

Also relevant in this context are those studies in which aversive stimulation has been administered *during* ongoing behaviour. The most dramatic results in this field come from Webb and Goodman (1958) and Siegel and Sparks (1961), who showed that flooding a Skinner box with half an inch of water increased the response rate of rats previously working at a stable rate. This again brought attention to the idea that emotionality somehow energizes behaviour. These studies are at one extreme of a fairly large literature on the effect of unconditioned aversive stimulation on behaviour such as aggression or eating. (See Myer (1971) for a review.) The general finding has often been of enhancement of whatever behaviour is occurring at the time of or immediately after the aversive stimulation. It may be that moderate shock (the usual aversive stimulus to be used) simply facilitates whatever behaviour is predominant at the time, or there could be some special (and unknown) relationship between shock and consummatory behaviour.

However, a cautionary note occurs in the work of Deaux and Kakolewski (1970), who suggest further factors which should be taken into account in any research into the basic effects of emotionality. They found a complex relationship between prior *handling* and food and water intake in rats. They propose that handling previously unhandled rats produces emotional excitement or anxiety which increases body-fluid osmolality which induces thirst which in turn induces drinking and delays or eliminates eating. It is important to consider the effects of food and water intake together rather than separately.

It is difficult to draw a definite conclusion from the studies of emotionality. Aversive noxious stimuli affect subsequent behaviour. When any effects are suppressive, as is often the case, they can be easily explained in terms of 'fear' conditioned in one situation generalizing to another. However, studies which have demonstrated facilitatory effects are too numerous to be ignored and are not in any way accounted for simply by recourse to the emotionality–drive idea. It would seem improbable that experience with noxious stimuli leads to some sort of autonomous 'emotionality'. Explanations for both the facilitatory and the suppressive effects of prior aversive stimulation are far more likely to be found by a more detailed consideration of the general testing situations. Such variables as amount of deprivation, type of reward, the relative novelty of the shock-box (if shock is used) or experience with emotion-producing stimuli need careful investigation before anything further can be said. It may well be that exploration of these variables would undermine the usefulness of any explanation in terms of general emotionality. Which, of course, is not to say that they would deny that some form of emotional responses follow aversive stimulation or indeed that animals vary with respect to general emotionality, a condition which to some extent is genetically determined. However, whether or not this approach has much to offer in understanding emotion more generally is debatable. At present, it has certainly fallen from favour.

Frustration—a neo-Hullian approach to emotion

A second line of Hullian-inspired research into emotional behaviour comes from Amsel (for example, 1958; 1962). It is based on a technique which Amsel developed for investigating frustration and also on the theoretical ramifications of the so-called frustration effect (FE). In considering Amsel's work, it should be remembered that it is the *latest* approach to frustration, following hypotheses linking frustration with aggression, regression and fixation (see Lawson (1965) and Yates (1962) for reviews).

It has been known since the 1930s that an animal will often respond with momentarily increased vigour when extinction conditions are first instituted. This is the basic FE.

Amsel's first and most important contribution to this field was to define frustration operationally. He suggested that it is what occurs when an organism experiences non-reward after previous experience with reward. This definition was based on a study by Amsel and Roussel (1952) which has proved prototypical for much of the recent work on frustration. Their apparatus consisted of a two-unit runway with a goal-box at the end of each alley. Rats were trained to run the first alley (A1) to the first goal-box (GB1) where food was available, and then run A2 to GB2 where there was further food. Each trial ended after food had been eaten in GB2. This procedure was followed until running speeds had stabilized. In 50 per cent of the trials during the subsequent period, food was no longer available in GB1. Measures were taken of the start time from GB1 and the running time in A2. Rats showed significantly faster start and run times during those trials when food was withheld in GB1 than during those trials when it was not. This is the FE, and it has held up through various procedural and methodological refinements, including, for example, Wagner's (1959) control for possible response suppression.

Amsel (1958; 1962) put forward the theory of frustrative non-reward to account for the FE. After reward, non-reward will elicit a primary aversive emotional reaction—frustration—which is related to the magnitude of anticipatory reward. Amsel regards the components of such frustration as becoming conditioned to antedating stimuli, resulting in anticipatory frustration. If this is so then the decrement in instrumental behaviour which results from the withholding of reward may be due to: (1) suppression effects of incompatible responses, which are learned via anticipatory frustration; (2) the acquisition of avoidance responses reinforced by a reduction in frustration-associated cues.

With the development of the double-runway technique and the theory of frustrative non-reward, Amsel made two important contributions to the study of frustration. (1) Frustration is defined using one basic operation: non-reward after experience with reward. (2) The idea of anticipatory frustration has been used extensively as an explanation for other problems in learning and motivation: extinction, the partial reinforcement effects and discrimination for example (Amsel 1958; 1962; 1967). The theory contains three fundamental generalizations. (1) Frustration is defined solely by non-rewarded trials in conjunction with rewarded. (2) Anticipatory frustration is seen as being conditioned to specific stimuli within the environment. (3) Anticipatory frustration affects response strength by increasing overall drive strength (motivating immediate behaviour), by acting as a drive stimulus the reduction of which is reinforcing and to which other responses become conditioned, and finally by inhibiting overt behaviour. To date, this is the most rigorous analysis to have been made of frustration. It has generated a great deal of research and thought.

Wagner (1966; 1969) offers an alternative theory of non-reward in terms of aversive events—events that an organism will terminate or avoid. He argues that the transition from non-reward to reward is reinforcing and that this is due either to the initiation of reward or to the termination of non-reward.

Wagner extends his argument with a parallel between fear and anticipatory frustration. He suggests that if fear and frustration are capable of similar 'anticipatory' explanations then the effects of punishers (with fear presumably responsible) will not be very different if frustrative non-reward is the aversive event.

Further, Wagner maintains that if there is some similarity between the anticipatory stimuli produced by fear and those stemming from anticipatory frustration, then behaviour learned in the presence of one emotional response should generalize to occasions when the other is aroused.

Wagner, then, puts forward a convincing argument that frustrative non-reward may have properties which make it, like punishment, a response-contingent aversive event, and also that fear and anticipatory frustration appear to have much in common. His ideas have been discussed as an example of the direction taken following Amsel's original thesis. Research in test of Wagner's views does not allow firm conclusions to be drawn and will not be discussed here.

At the human level and in an initial rush of enthusiasm, Amsel's idea of frustration non-reward was applied to children—it has obvious implications for learning, the building of frustration tolerance, and so on. This work has been thoroughly reviewed by Ryan and Watson (1968). They bring together the literature concerned with the FE and the partial reinforcement effect in children, consider the relationship between non-reward and failure, and mention subject variables such as age, sex, and personality. Some of their conclusions will be briefly discussed.

From studies on children, it is clear that non-reward leads to increased vigour of performance at some tasks, and also that frustration may become conditioned to previously neutral stimuli. In forming discriminations, non-reward may have a greater effect on learning than reward. The reaction of a child to non-reward appears to depend quite heavily on individual variables. For example, reward expectancy is related to both chronological and mental age, but not necessarily directly. Thus it is possible that older children and brighter children react to non-reward by devising various strategies for 'solving the problem', rather than by simply showing increased vigour of responding. Also, non-attainment of social reward has similar effects on performance to those of the non-attainment of more concrete rewards.

Such conclusions are important to any behavioural study of emotion since they suggest that in the end there may be implications for behaviour outside the laboratory. With the FE, however, this is not surprising since it probably originated in commonsense notions; think of your own reactions when, having put money into a vending machine and pressed the button, nothing happens.

There have been two developments which add some generality to Hullian derived analyses of emotional behaviour. The first extends the idea of frustrative non-reward in the double runway by demonstrating similar effects in the Skinner box. The second analyses another 'emotion' using similar techniques.

Staddon and Innis (1966) trained pigeons to respond on cyclic presentations of two identical fixed-interval (FI) schedules separated by a brief TO (time out) period (equivalent to delay in GB1 of a double runway). During test trials, omission of reward after the first FI component led to FEs in the second component—a higher than baseline rate of responding. This type of result, extended in a number of studies, is clearly similar to those found in the double runway (for example, Wookey and Strongman, 1971). They add generality to double-runway effects and emphasize the importance of looking in detail at behaviour which *immediately* follows non-reward.

The other 'emotion' which has been studied within this empirical framework is elation. Work on this developed in an attempt to outline the effects of a reward increase rather than decrease in GB1. Intuitively, this might be expected to have an 'elation' effect in A2, which, like the FE, is reflected by an increased running speed. However, with one exception, results from the relevant studies do not point in this direction.

A typical study is that of Strongman and Wookey (1969). Their procedure included a group of animals which had the reward in GB1 increased during testing on a 50/50 basis. A2 running speed was faster after one pellet than after two. Also, there were no differences between running speeds on trials with increased reward and those of controls always receiving the larger number of pellets. On the other hand, test trials where the reward was as in training produced faster A2 speeds than in any of the control or experimental groups during training. The authors interpreted this as a rapidly developing frustration effect. Karabenick (1969) put forward the idea of comparative frustration to account for similar results—an FE building up during acquisition owing to the different reward in the two goal-boxes.

In spite of the very different parameters used in these studies of reward increase in GB1, it is possible to draw two conclusions. (1) An increase in reward in GB1 of a double runway after training at a lower level of reward leads to within-subject performance decrement in A2. (2) Under some conditions A2 performance does not fall as low as that of unshifted control animals always receiving the larger reward. Such experimental procedures, measurement techniques and results are so far removed from everyday conceptions of elation that no attempt will be made to extrapolate from one to the other.

Conditioned emotional response (CER)

The other behavioural approach to emotion developed from two important advances made by Watson (1929). (1) He asked questions about the *external* causes of emotional behaviour rather than speaking in the necessarily more speculative terms of emotional states. (2) His study with Rayner (Watson and Rayner, 1920) laid the groundwork for the large literature on CER. Watson and Rayner demonstrated that a young child who had previously shown only approach responses to a white rat could be conditioned to 'fear' it. They associated the rat with a sudden loud noise—a stimulus which leads to crying, moving away, etc., in a young child. This 'fear' of the rat was long-lasting and generalized to similar animals and objects. (It is worth noting that although this study formed the background to the Estes and Skinner (1941) CER technique, the two procedures differ in one important respect. Watson and Rayner measured 'emotional' behaviour directly, whereas the CER procedure measures it as indirectly expressed in changes in ongoing operant behaviour (see below).) However, before developing the discussion of CER it should be pointed out that the early classical conditioning of emotional responses is not as simple as Watson and Rayner suggested. For example, Valentine (1930) repeated Watson and Rayner's study on his own daughter. His findings led him to suggest that there are some stimuli which elicit a background fear *innately*. A large reaction can be obtained more easily with such stimuli than with others. It is not therefore a simple matter of classical conditioning.

Through a long chain of empirical research and theoretical discussion, Watson and Rayner's finding has led to the general behaviouristic viewpoint that emotions are names that we can give to the disruptions and enhancements of behaviour which occur as immediate consequences of presenting organisms with positive or negative stimuli (S+ and S−). It is argued (for example, Millenson, 1967) that there are two operations that bring about such alterations in behaviour: (1) the presentation or termination of primary reinforcers; (2) the presentation of previously neutral stimuli which have been associated with primary reinforcers by a process of Pavlovian conditioning. Emotion is regarded as changing the reinforcing value both of primary reinforcers and of general activity. In this it is like motivation, but Millenson (1967) argues that its antecedents are different; for motivation they are deprivation and satiation, for emotion they are abrupt stimulus change.

After Watson, the next major (technological) step was taken by Estes and Skinner (1941) and Hunt and Brady (1951; 1955). It mainly involved the development of a technique for studying conditioned emotion in a methodologically 'tight' manner. The basic procedure consists, for example, of having thirsty rats in a Skinner box bar-pressing for water on a variable-interval (VI) schedule of reinforcement. When their response rate is steady, an occasional conditioning stimulus (CS), a clicker for example, is presented for five minutes, at the end of which the rat receives a brief shock (unconditioned stimulus, US). Initially, the CS has no effect, but the US results in a lowered response rate. After a few pairings of CS and US, the response to the US becomes adapted and response rate is lowered only during the CS. 'Fear' responses originally made to the US have become conditioned to the CS. When the effects were first observed, they were termed conditioned anxiety reactions.

The basic CER paradigm

The basic experimental paradigm for studying CERs can be expressed by the notation: CS - - - US, where CS is neutral at first, US is an unavoidable, inescapable, aversive stimulus, and - - - is a short time interval. This procedure is superimposed on an ongoing operant baseline. Since, typically, there is a suppression of operant behaviour during CS, this basic procedure has become known as conditioned suppression. However, the CS - - - US paradigm *may* lead to acceleration during the CS.

From this it may be seen that the basic CER paradigm leads to a number of logical possibilities for the study of conditioned emotion (see Strongman (1969) for a fuller exposition).

	CS - - - S−	CS - - - S+	CS - - - $−	CS - - - $+
Positive baseline	anxiety	elation	—	anger and aggression
Negative baseline	anxiety	elation	relief	—

In this analysis, positive baseline refers to a steady ongoing operant response maintained by positive reinforcement (for example, food), and negative baseline refers to a steady ongoing operation response maintained by negative reinforcement (for example, shock avoidance). Superimposed on these can be CSs which precede four types of emotion-producing event: S− (for example, shock), S+ (for example, food), $− (for example, TO from shock) and $+ (for example, TO from food). This leads immediately to the six possibilities which are shown; such a breakdown brings about the four 'human' emotional possibilities of anxiety, elation, relief and anger, although Millenson (1967) collapses elation and relief into one. (Of course, no great claim can be made for the validity of these particular 'emotion' names in this somewhat rarefied context. However, they seem to be reasonably appropriate and they can at least function as shorthand descriptions of the basic procedural operations.) The two remaining sections have been left blank since at first sight they appear difficult to establish empirically. However, they can perhaps be regarded as other aspects of relief and anger.

Anxiety—conditioned suppression

There has been a great deal of work on conditioned suppression. It has been well reviewed and analysed by Davis (1968), Hearst (1969), Hoffman (1969), Kamin (1965) and Lyon (1968), for example.

Conditioned suppression is defined as a decrement in response rate during a pre-shock stimulus which has been superimposed on, and is independent of, ongoing operant behaviour. This superimposition is achieved by classical conditioning procedure. This distinguishes it from 'punishment' procedures where the noxious stimulus is response-contingent. Also, the US in conditioned suppression is believed to have its effects on respondents, heart rate for example (De Toledo and Black, 1966). Changes in responses such as these are incompatible with the continuation of normal operant performance. Usually, an appetitive baseline has been used, with shock as the US; its effects are reasonably reliable. When they are used in CER studies, other aversive stimuli, TO for example, sometimes produce an acceleration of responding.

There have been variations on this basic procedure and the effect has been demonstrated in a wide variety of species, excluding humans, for obvious ethical reasons. There is a wide range of variables which affect conditioned suppression, mainly those which stem from operant conditioning, and effects have been demonstrated on a negative baseline.

There have been a number of interpretations of conditioned suppression, each of which is inadequate in some way. For example, first and most obvious is the *interference* hypothesis which suggests that the suppression is caused by conditioned respondents interfering with instrumental behaviour. The problem is that the actual respondents which might or might not be involved have been rarely, if ever, studied.

The punishment hypothesis suggests that conditioned suppression hinges on a chance or adventitious contingency between the behaviour and the aversive stimulus which is highly likely early in the procedure. However, amongst other problems, the punishment hypothesis cannot account for the rapid acquisition of conditioned suppression sometimes seen, nor for the effect when the classical conditioning is conducted in a separate environment. Conditioned suppression then is not a straightforward effect and convincing accounts of it are wanting.

Elation

Within the CER context, the term elation describes the superimposition of a signalled positive stimulus (free reward) on either a positive or negative operant baseline. Studies conducted following this procedure were reviewed by Strongman *et al.,* (1971) and demonstrate both conditioned suppression and enhancement, depending on a variety of variables across a number of species, including humans.

It is clear from the studies of conditioned elation that at least four variables are important. These are whether the CS–US pairing occurs before or during responding on the instrumental baseline schedule, whether the CS is presented against an ongoing operant or during extinction, the nature of the operant reinforcement schedule, and the duration of the CS.

Anger and Aggression

Moving on to anger and aggression and later, relief, the behaviourally derived CER paradigm seems even more removed from what would commonly be thought of as emotion, than is conditioned anxiety and elation. In this context, the terms anger and aggression describe the procedure in which, following a signal, positive reinforcers are withdrawn from or are no longer available to a subject working on a positive baseline. This is generally known as TO. There are only a small handful of studies which followed this procedure, some of which show conditioned suppression and some of which show conditioned reinforcement.

Relief

This refers to that procedure which would involve allowing subjects signalled TO from a negative baseline. Any disruption of the ongoing operant could be termed relief and would probably be predicted to take the form of an increase in response rate. To the writer's knowledge, there has been no work on relief within the CER framework.

To summarize, within the CER procedures, there has been a large amount of work on conditioned suppression (anxiety), but its determinants are far from clear. The basic technique has been extended to the study of conditioned elation and conditioned aggression and has led to some straightforward investigations of human subjects. Conditioned relief is an unknown quantity.

Clearly, there is much scope in this field for further study, particularly of a parametric type manipulating background variables. However, the entire field has been almost quiescent for some years. This is perhaps not surprising. The CER technique has some useful practical applications, and although it provides a good structure for the study of emotional behaviour, it seems a very long way removed from emotion as it is now beginning to be investigated. The CER procedures are interesting in their own right but they do not offer much hope in the analysis of emotion more generally.

Behavioural theory

Strictly speaking, there are no behavioural theories of emotion, although Millenson's (1967) model comes close. For the most part, the theoretical contributions to emotion made by investigators from a learning theory or a Skinner background have been piecemeal, adjuncts to empirical work. Some of these ideas will be discussed briefly below. Also occasional attempts have been made at least to construct a framework in which empirical findings based on similar procedures can be placed. An example is the systematic attempt to structure the behavioural analysis of elation made by Strongman *et al.* (1971). They define elation as a non-instrumental change in the vigour of responding brought about by upward shifts in the conditions of reward and then analyse the logical possibilities for the experimental study of the effects of this procedure in its various forms. Although such an approach might help to clarify thought, it makes little contribution to theory and does not merit further discussion here.

Millenson's (1967) model of emotion was described in Chapter 2, and clearly owes much to Watson and to the CER literature. The usual mix of operant and respondent conditioning leads Millenson to a three-dimensional emotional co-ordinate system, the three basic emotions being anxiety, elation and anger. He overcomes the problem of there obviously being more human emotion than this, by suggesting that the others are mixtures which come about as neutral stimuli become conditioned to various combinations of various intensities of these. Unfortunately, he does not describe at all convincingly, *how* that comes about.

Finally, it might be instructive briefly to consider Millenson's ideas on emotional control and pathological emotion. He proposes, from the behavioural viewpoint, that we use three methods of controlling our emotions: (1) adaptation to the continual presentations of emotion-producing stimuli; this leads to the building of a tolerance to frustration and also to 'good' things losing their effect; (2) masking respondents with opposed operants, for example keeping a 'poker face' or a 'stiff upper lip'; (3) the avoidance of emotion-producing situations. These ideas do bear some similarity to those of investigators working from other perspectives and will be returned to in later chapters. Millenson has an oversimplified and inadequate view of pathological emotion. Prolonged anxiety-producing situations lead to neurosis and drastic disruption to positive reinforcers leads to psychosis.

Weiskrantz (1968) ranges widely in his attempt to account for emotion behaviourally. His basic view is that if reinforcers can be defined as stimuli which are consequent to responses, then emotion can be defined as responses which are consequent to reinforcers. He defines responses very widely and speaks of emotion as a *state* which includes many responses. He also follows Skinner's (1938) distinction between operant and respondents and points to the latter as being the subject matter of the study of emotion.

Weiskrantz makes a number of useful points about emotion in general, taking illustrations from the CER literature. He suggests that in an everyday sense emotion often refers to alterations in characteristic *patterns* of behaviour, for example, not smiling, shoulders drooping, not eating. This implies that the effects of emotion-producing stimuli are to make ongoing behaviour either more or less vigorous. He regards this as supporting the idea of emotion as a state, or perhaps a collection of responses.

In summary, Weiskrantz regards emotion as respondent behaviour, and suggests that emotional states are reflected by alterations in large classes of behaviour. He argues that to speak of emotional states has an heuristic value, as long as the 'situational context' is not forgotten. There is much to be said for this view of emotional behaviour. It is clear, is based on few assumptions and gains reasonable empirical support and at least encompasses the idea of emotion as a state which perhaps enriches the behavioural approach.

As already mentioned in Chapter 2, Gray (1971) argues that it is possible to define three distinct emotional systems by analysing the relationship between reinforcing stimuli and response systems. He describes: (1) an approach system in which the reinforcing stimulus is a CS for reinforcement or non-punishment, (2) a behavioural inhibition system in which the reinforcing stimulus is a CS for punishment or non-reinforcement, and (3) a fight–flight system in which the reinforcing stimulus is unconditioned punishment or non-reinforcement.

Brady (1960) regards appetitive and aversive behaviours as approximately congruent with respondent and operant behaviours. Then, he makes the usual point that there are four possible ways in which classical conditioning procedures can be superimposed on ongoing instrument behaviour. This leads him to define four general categories of emotional behaviour which, he argues, have their commonsense parallels in subjective feelings—joy, fear or anxiety, anger and relief.

Hammond (1970) provides the best synthesis of behavioural work on emotion, bringing together the Hullian and Skinnerian traditions. Hammond regards emotion as a central state (CES) of the organism, which is elicited by both learned and unlearned stimuli. The unlearned stimuli may be rewards and punishments (or their absence); the learned stimuli may be rewards and punishments (or their absence); the learned are those which signed the unlearned and which, through classical conditioning, acquire similar properties. Broadly, this is emotion within a motivational framework.

Hammond's thesis draws on Mowrer's (1960a, b) idea that rewarding events lead to decremental processes (drive reduction) and punishing events lead to incremental processes (drive induction). These are correlated with pleasure and pain and represent unlearned emotional states which motivate the organism. If a neutral stimulus occurs just before an incremental event it is as a 'danger' signal; if it precedes a decremental event it is a 'safety' signal. Also, the nature of the emotional state which is produced depends on whether the signal is turned on or off:

Danger signal: on - - - fear, off - - - relief
Safety signal: on - - - hope, off - - - disappointment

The CESs are learned through classical conditioning with the signals as predictive of reward or punishment.

Such a scheme provides a straightforward way of specifying the development of the signals, with behaviour being simply measured as approach or withdrawal. Motivational behaviour within a test situation gives a measure of whether or not the CES has been produced; hope and relief should elicit approach and fear and disappointment should elicit avoidance.

In providing an analysis of the empirical evidence relevant to emotion as a CES, some of the difficulties Hammond encountered led him to suggest a recasting of Mowrer's original formulations.

(1) Stimuli predicting an increase in the occurrence of an aversive event lead to fear—excitatory.
(2) Stimuli predicting a decrease in the occurrence of an aversive event lead to relief—inhibitory.
(3) Stimuli predicting a decrease in the occurrence of a rewarding event lead to hope—excitatory.
(4) Stimuli predicting a decrease in the occurrence of a rewarding event lead to disappointment—inhibitory.

Hammond goes as far as anyone has in at least providing a reasonably illuminating setting in which to consider much of the empirical work on emotional behaviour. This setting owes much to Pavlov and Mowrer but also leans heavily on the general idea of CER. Hammond goes further and attempts to give the CES a physiological basis. His physiological ideas are interesting but, perhaps because they are so speculative, do not seem to have been much taken up. However, this may simply be a reflection of the general fall from favour of behavioural approaches to emotion since the mid-1970s.

In summary, there have been three main empirical approaches taken in attempts to look at emotion against a background of learning theory or Skinner's avowedly atheoretical behaviourism—studies of emotionality, frustration, and the CER. After a flood of research in these areas in the 1950s and 1960s, it has almost entirely dried up in recent years. In part this may be due to the comparative inadequacies in the behavioural models and conceptual analyses of emotion. These have largely been *post hoc* and hence descriptive rather than explanatory.

Behavioural conceptualizations of emotion, for all their neatness and apparent precision, do not go far enough. They are far removed from the subjective experience of emotion and perhaps more importantly they do not take account of any cognitive influences. Not only does this detract from the qualitative *richness* of emotion, but also seems less than justified in terms of current thought and research. Of course, a behavioural analysis of emotion is by no means incompatible with a cognitive analysis, even though their roots and aims may be different. If there is to be any future analysis of emotional behaviour it should find a place for cognition as well. It would then cease to be a pure behavioural conceptualization but would perhaps be better for it.

GENERAL CONCLUSIONS

This chapter contains an unusual, not to say a bizarre, mixture of approaches to the study and understanding of emotion—the philosophical, phenomenological, and behavioural. As was mentioned at the outset, none of them is essential to the study or to the explanation of emotion, although it is hard to conceive of emotion without subjective experience being involved, or, mostly, without it having behavioural expression. On the other hand, this chapter should have made it clear that each of these approaches has something useful to offer and should not be ignored.

Apart from offering some useful theoretical insights, the approach to emotion taken by some recent philosophers is impressive in its precision of thought. Psychologists who are tempted to make theoretical points about emotion would do well to become familiar with the style of doing this adopted by philosophers such as Lyons. It would make them tread more warily.

The phenomenologists who have turned their attention to emotion have performed the valuable service of at least attempting to come to terms with the subjective experience of emotion, which many people would regard to be its most important aspect. Also, their ideas are not as far from the possibility of something like conventional empirical test as was once thought.

The behavioural approach to emotion has not been noteworthy for its insights even though it seemed 15 years ago to offer some hope. Its concepts, investigations, and the fact that its main objects of study are laboratory animals, seem to put it a long way from complex human emotion. However, the experimental procedures, emphasis on control and the general methodology to which it has given rise provide impressive examples of scientific endeavour. Those interested in the empirical study of emotion would do well to apply this same degree of methodological sophistication and exactness.

However, the most important aspect of the philosophical, phenomenological and behavioural approaches to emotion is that in their own ways, each of them points to the importance of taking a cognitive approach to the subject, or at least taking cognition into account. Most of the philosophical and phenomenological theorists actually have a central, if not a necessary, role for cognition in their accounts of emotion. By contrast, the behaviourists do not, which, in my view, is one of the reasons why the behavioural approach has fallen into relative disuse. Interestingly, it is those behavioural theorists who toy with cognitive concepts such as state, that seem to be the most pertinent. Anyway, apart from having something to offer to the study of emotion in their own right, the three approaches considered in this chapter, somehow bring the emphasis round to cognition again, perhaps with some irony on the part of the behaviourists.

6

Emotional Development

For many years, the received wisdom about emotional development was very limited. It had developed only a little way from the influential work of Bridges (1932). The general idea was that the infant inherits the capacity to experience and express emotion in a broad, undifferentiated form. Thereafter, as a function of age, it becomes increasingly differentiated into discrete emotions. Neither Bridges, nor the textbook writers who spent the next 50 years assiduously recapitulating her ideas, made it clear whether these age-related effects were maturational or environmentally determined. Recently, however, there have been some striking advances in the study of emotional development, which will be discussed in this chapter.

Until the last few years, research into emotional development was a mixture of very well-conceived and poorly conceived studies. The main division was between investigations of animal subjects and those involving humans. For the most part, the animal studies were well controlled, methodologically reliable and provided interesting ideas. Equally, with some exceptions, the human studies were of questionable methodology and illuminated very little, being characterized by a lack of definition and precision. Of course, the problem with the research using animals even though it might be well done, is its relevance to human emotional development.

Again, until recently, research on human emotional development has been scanty as well as poor. One reason for the paucity of work at the human level, presuming it is not simply due to lack of interest, may be concerned with the difficulty of study. Emotional development is difficult to study in any way distinct from the remainder of development. Investigations with children were often conducted from the viewpoint that changes in emotional behaviour may account for other developmental phenomena. Rather than dealing satisfactorily with the problem, this was just pushing it one stage further back. Also, discussions of emotional development frequently degenerated into a consideration of the relative importance of genetic and environmental influences. Whilst not wishing to deny that this is an important consideration, it does seem to be one which often stultifies research and theory rather than promoting them.

Ten years ago, it was reasonable to describe the field of emotional development as confused. It was unsystematized, unintegrated, characterized by a series of relatively unilluminated approaches and strategies and simply did not amount to much. Now that both developmentalists and emotion theorists have turned their attention to it, there have been large-scale advances. Issues have been recognized and addressed and new research methodologies developed. Theories have been developed and empirical research has started to appear in considerable amounts. This has not only vastly improved our knowledge of emotional development, it has also completely up-ended the earlier views.

It has become apparent that there are certain issues that are implicit in the study of emotional development. For many years these were ignored, but in the recent developments of interest in this area are now being faced (for example, Murphy, 1983). The following list of issues is not intended to be exhaustive but, rather, representative. Clearly, some of these matters are more central than others and should more readily be addressed in any future analysis of emotional development.

(1) It is obvious that emotion develops at the same time as many other aspects of psychological functioning are also developing. In particular, as emotions are developing, so are cognitions. What is the relationship between the two, or indeed between emotional and social development. There must be links, but cognitions can presumably occur without emotional implications and social behaviour need not be coloured by emotion. Yet it is highly probable that emotional development depends heavily on both cognitive and social development. Also, it would be unlikely that any researcher into emotional development would not have an implicit model of emotion and of its links with other aspects of development. It is important that such models be made explicit.

(2) There must be some capacities for emotional reactivity present in the neonate, as necessary building blocks for later development. What are these and how extensive are they? Just what is built-in emotionally? For example, there are large individual differences in emotional reactivity. Are these built-in or do they arise from situation-generated experiences? Turning the coin over, if there are initial, inherited patterns of emotional response, how are these modified? What are the developmental influences on emotion? By a similar token, if, as seems likely, there is a relationship between early emotional experiences and later adaptations to the environment, then what is its character?

(3) At an even more basic level, there lies an almost insuperable issue. It is one which naturally applies to the study of emotion at any level, but which is highlighted in considerations of development. How is it possible to determine what an infant is feeling? Or even a child whose verbal, perhaps cognitive, capacities are limited? Linked to this is the problem of whether or not physical expressions have associated feelings and, if so, whether or not these are emotional? For example, what does a smile on the face of an eight-month-old infant mean to it? Also, how important or even relevant to an understanding of emotional development is the state which an infant or child might be experiencing, that is whether it has toothache or is feeling cold, for example?

(4) Returning to the question of individual differences, it is apparent that they are widespread and dependent on complex interactions between the organism and the environment. This would seem to imply that basic studies of emotional development should be ethological, that is, carried out in a child's home environment, and should involve interactions with the significant persons in the child's life. This matter is also important in considering the vast cultural and subcultural differences in emotional *style,* in spite of strong evidence for universalities in expression.

(5) Finally, there are some fundamental facets of emotional development which have been known of for some time, but which still form significant issues that should be faced. For example, it has long been thought, from an evolutionary perspective, that tendencies to approach and withdraw are basic to development. How important are these tendencies to emotional development. Similarly, the importance of attachment for a child's social development has long been recognized. Since there are intimate links between social and emotional development and since attachment has obvious emotional concomitants, how important is it to the course of emotional development? Finally, and prompted by thoughts of attachment, is there any essential difference between the development of positive and negative emotions. Traditionally, research has been concentrated far more on negative than on positive emotions, and has been conducted in a piecemeal fashion. Why should this be? Does it reflect the possibility that the positive side of emotional life is also played down by those who influence a child's emotional development?

It is worth reiterating that the questions that have just been posed do not exhaust the possible matters of importance to emotional development. However, they do represent some of the basic issues that should not be ignored whenever emotional development is being considered.

Methodology

The changes in emphasis in the study of emotional development, and the more staightforward facing of the difficult issues involved have clear implications for methodology. As has already been mentioned, earlier research into emotional development was focused either on humans or nonhuman animals. The child-based research was almost all observational, for the obvious reason of the ethical problems involved in any manipulation of the emotional life of children. However, very often these observations were not carried out with the precision and even flair of the ethological tradition. They tended to be observations made with little control and somewhat haphazardly. By contrast, studies of emotional development in animals have usually been well-contrived and well-conducted, but of dubious relevance to human development.

With the recent upsurge of research into human emotional development, observational techniques have begun to be followed, within a framework of human ethology, in which it is possible to have some confidence. This has also led to some trenchant discussions of the methodological matters involved. For example, Thompson and Lamb (1984) discuss some of the difficulties involved in measuring emotional responsiveness in infants. They argue that the only way to proceed with preverbal infants is via essentially ethological observations. Since human infants are social beings, the methodological route to these observations is via social interaction. As will be seen later, this route also happens to have been followed by most of the investigators of emotional development in recent years. Thompson and Lamb show that infants can do more than just discriminate one emotional expression from the next, they can also understand the meaning of the expressions and use them as sources of information about environmental events. So, observational studies in infants show, for example, that facial expressions of emotion can be viewed as independent variables which effect the behaviour of others.

To take a different methodological issue, Beckwith (1979) addresses the important but difficult question of continuity. The question is whether socio-emotional traits in infancy limit later socio-emotional development to simple derivatives of these, or whether socio-emotional development is a series of reorganizations of personality. Is emotional development continuous or discontinuous?

The difficulty is that many standard developmental measures are not constructed to deal with the continuity issue. Again, the best methods are based on behavioural observation, but even then it is difficult to use them precisely to probe the continuity/discontinuity controversy. There need to be developed methods of study which would allow determinations to be made of whether or not there are regular restructurings between the child and the environment. Also in this context, it is difficult to know whether it is sufficient to study only behavioural expression. If as seems likely, cognition is important, it would seem necessary to develop other methodologies.

Dunn (1982) makes two important points which endorse those made in this section. He argues that in order to paint a more accurate picture of emotional development, a child's behaviour must be studied in ordinary, relaxed playful interaction with his or her mother-father. But, he also argues that emotional and cognitive development should be studied 'as twin aspects of a single process'. Dunn also lays great stress on what particular experiences of emotion *mean* to a child, again thereby implicating cognition in emotional development. He suggests that emotion both organizes experience and provides a sense of meaning, and that changes in emotional tension depend on cognitions from an infant's or child's evaluation of a stimulus. Although these are important points, they not only anticipate later discussions, but also point to methodological problems without solving them.

THEORY

The theoretical understanding of emotional development has improved markedly during the last ten years or so. In order to help in the interpretation of the empirical research to be considered later, this section will be used to explicate the main aspects of the most influential of the theories of emotional development. These range from theories which emphasize approach and withdrawal to those which stress psychoevolution. In style, they range from the speculative to the precision of formal postulates.

In an important contribution to the study of emotional development, Lewis and Rosenblum (1978) suggest that at the broad level there are two opposing models of emotional development. From Darwin onward, the biological approach views emotional behaviour as adaptive, with the focus being on unlearned, complex behaviour. No distinction is made between emotional state and emotional experience and the assumption is of the specificity of the CNS and the unlearned connections within it.

The alternative model is based on socialization with emotional development occurring through the establishment of linkages based on learning. It is inferred that emotion results from responses in the social environment to a child's behaviour in specific contexts. As is usually the case when there are these types of contrasting models, it does not have to be a question of one or the other. Both biology and social interaction may be necessary to emotional development, a point to which the more recent theories attest.

Kagan (1978) suggests that there may be theoretically independent classes of phenomena in emotion with distinct developmental functions. He proposes that it is important to look for coherences in patterns of state change rather than simply assuming the evidence of particular emotions. Kagan argues that there are three possible developmental conclusions that can be reached about emotion: (1) internal states produced by incentives remain the same throughout development, although behaviour differs; (2) incentives and states are changed by a child's altered interpretation (or cognitive classification) of events; (3) incentive events are accompanied by evaluations of an individual's ability to understand, assimilate or deal with incentive and resulting changes in state.

From this, Kagan concludes that the study of emotional development must be in terms of altered interpretations of incentive events and changes in the ability to cope with the total event. He stresses the importance of a child's ability to deal with changes in emotional state, changes that occur through new information. He points out that if emotions are indeed changed by information, they must be dependent on cognitive processes.

Biological theory

The biological approach to emotional development rests on the idea that to begin with emotion is only associated with physiological need—the infant cries when it is hungry or cold. In other words, emotion (or at least negative emotion) is said to be experienced when a drive state is blocked.

Bousfield and Orbison (1952) appear to have initiated two quite profitable lines of speculation concerning the ontogenesis of emotional behaviour. These rest on two assumptions. (1) Neonates are functionally decorticate, cortical control becoming increasingly apparent throughout development. (2) Infants are partially lacking in hormones which are important to stress reactions.

There is little 'downwards' inhibitory cortical influence in the brain at birth. This should mean that the emotional responses of children are similar to those of animals, since as adults the latter are comparatively lacking in cortex. In turn, this suggests that emotions in children, although being quickly aroused, should dissipate rather than persist or reverberate. This certainly is in accord with everyday observations.

Emotional states are thought to increase in vigour with age and this vigour is thought to be largely due to the influence of the adrenal glands. The development of the adrenal glands themselves seem to follow an odd course. By the time the child is two they have decreased to half their weight at birth, following which they rapidly increase in weight up to about five years, increase more slowly until 11 and then accelerate until 20. It is not until the age of about 16 that they are back to their birth weight. Presumably, output is associated with weight.

Funkenstein et al. (1957) provide the most detailed hormone-based ideas on the development of emotion. From the fact that the adrenal medulla secretes both epinephrine and norepinephrine, they suggest that the former is related to passive non-aggressive reactions to stress (and predominates in the rabbit, for example) and the latter to solitary, aggressive reactions (and predominates in the lion, for example). On the basis of their studies. Funkenstein et al. also argue that amongst humans there are two sorts of anger. There is that of the anger-inners (who bottle up everything and blame themselves—a predomin-ance of epinephrine), and that of the anger-outers (who show anger and blame others—a predominance of norepinephrine). They also claim that in childhood there is always a preponderance of norepinephrine, which by adulthood has either balanced out with epinephrine or still carries greater weight. It should be pointed out that, though of considerable interest, these ideas are highly speculative and are also tempered by Funkenstein by bringing in possible influences of upbringing.

Internalization

The concept of internalization embodies a mentalistic approach to human emotional development and rests on the idea that anxiety becomes associated with punished behaviour. On future occasions, this anxiety may suppress the behaviour (thereby reducing the anxiety). If a child learns to suppress some aspects of his behaviour without any obvious external intervention, then he is said to have internalized the behaviour of stopping himself from doing something. Hence, emotional changes mediated by cognitive evaluations are believed to form the basis of self-regulatory behaviour through internalization.

Internalization refers to a child's learning of what we normally term self-control through the cognitive aspects of emotional changes. From the subjective point of view, this means that either pleasure or fear and anxiety become attached to everyday acts, which of course lead to reward and punishment. It is thought that these positive or negative emotions can then become associated with a child's understanding, i.e. cognition, of a situation. In putting forward this argument, Aronfreed (1968) concludes that the child may become happy or afraid when he or she *thinks* of doing something, before actually doing it.

Aronfreed (1968) extends his theory by emphasizing that for internalization to come about all a child need do is experience some emotional change in connection with some behaviour; this may happen simply through observation. In stressing the importance of imitation he suggests that a child imitates as a result of the pleasure gained from observing the model. Hence, feeling good becomes associated with perceptions and cognitions of the model. Aronfreed considers cognitions to be crucial since they allow the expansion of emotional self-control. Memories of social experiences will have emotional components. So the child comes to be able to represent, and hence anticipate, reward and punishment. In the end, the child is acting to produce 'good' feelings and to avoid producing 'bad' feelings. This general thesis is very similar to Arnold's (for example, 1970a; 1970b) ideas of appraisal and affective memory.

Another aspect of Aronfreed's (1968) concept of internalization accords well the possible significance for emotional development of initial social attachments. Internalization is thought to presuppose an initial attachment to some person. This implies that the threat of withdrawal of love or nurturance from the child is important to emotional change and development. Self-criticism is the internalization of this: the child is taking away 'love' from himself.

In a final extension of his argument, Aronfreed suggests that a child learns to reduce the cognitive force of unpleasant emotions by being self-critical. Thus, the rejected or neglected child will have no love to lose, will not become self-critical and may therefore end as a delinquent. In Aronfreed's terms, a child behaves so as to maintain his emotional bonds, an idea which is similar to those on attachment expressed earlier.

To summarize, Aronfreed suggests that emotional development is dependent on the process of internalization. Thus, the child learns to control his or her own behaviour by paying attention to the cognitive aspects of his emotion. Emotional change may come about through direct experience or by the child's imitations of rewarding models. So, internalization is more likely to occur if the young child has formed a good social bond with some adult. This way of analysing emotional development is an odd mixture of a concentrated cognitive approach and a somewhat dilute behavioural theory. The cognitive elements are often untestable and the behavioural aspects are often undeveloped. It would be more useful if the cognitive arguments gave way to a clearer behavioural exposition, or if the cognitive aspects were developed further and in ways more open to empirical test.

Play

A view couched in terms rather similar to Aronfreed's is put forward by Izard (1972) concerning the relationship between children's play and emotion. His basic assumption is that children use repetitive play to help them to cope with situations which would otherwise be overwhelming—to control possible anxiety, for example, He further assumes that play has a significant role in integrating the various components of emotion and hence in the development of a more mature personality. Thus emotions both instigate and sustain play which in its turn has influences on emotion.

Izard develops these views by putting forward a number of propositions. Although he generated them on the basis of his theory of emotion and his work on the development of emotional recognition and labelling, they may still be regarded as hypotheses yet to be tested. They also foreshadow later discussion of Izard and Malatesta's (1984) important theory of emotional development.

(1) Emotion is a primary motivational system which promotes play, although high drive does not bring it about.
(2) Interaction between cognition and emotion enliven play and hence stimulate intellectual development.
(3) Interactions between emotion and states of high drive act to make more likely the disruption and distortion of play.
(4) Play is primarily enhanced by the fundamental emotions of interest and enjoyment.
(5) If play which is motivated by interest is thwarted, negative emotion results, the form this takes being determined by the personality of the child plus the nature of the block. For example, sometimes anger may result or sometimes anxiety.
(6) An interaction between interest and anger leads to aggressive play.
(7) The extent to which a child withdraws socially and/or indulges in make-believe will depend on the relative balance between shame and shyness, and interest and enjoyment in what he is doing.
(8) If a low degree of fear oscillates which interest, excitement is raised. Whereas a high degree of fear will suppress interest and therefore reduce play.
(9) Disgust will lead to avoidance of the activity.

Schneirla

Schneirla's theory of emotional development was one of the few to be put forward in any detail before the last few years. For some time it stood alone and has not been very influential. However, it is worthy of brief mention. He defines emotions as:

'(1) episodes or sequences of overt and incipient somatic adjustment, (2) often loosely patterned and variable, (3) usually with concurrent excitatory sensory effects, perhaps also perceptual attitudes characterisable as desirable or undesirable, pleasant or unpleasant, (4) related to the intensity effects of perceptual meaning of a stimulus, (5) synergic with organic changes of A- or W-types.' (1959, p.26)

Schneirla's A- and W-types are fundamental to his view of emotion. They refer to *biphasic* mechanisms of receptors, central and auxiliary nervous systems and effectors which Schneirla regards as basic to *all* ontogeny. A-type arousal is caused by weak-intensity stimuli and leads to local or general approach to the source of stimulation. W-type arousal is caused by strong-intensity stimuli and leads to local or general withdrawal.

Schneirla argues that a James–Lange type of theory may be useful for studying the early ontogeny of animals when these A- and W-type patterns overwhelm behaviour, depending on stimulus magnitude. Equally, he suggests that a Cannon–Bard approach is more germane to the later stages of emotional development, which are far more perceptual and motivational in nature.

Quite differently from Bridges (1932), Schneirla weights the evidence concerning infant emotion and believes that it warrants the conclusion that the reactions of neonates are essentially biphasic, although the evidence which Schneirla draws on at this point is obscure. Schneirla also argues that emotion and motivation are fundamentally related. He suggests that there are physiologically prescribed biphasic states, which in maturing lead to the advancement of emotion and motivation. He supports these contentions by detailed analyses of smiling and reaching.

Giblin

Giblin (1981) puts forward an equilibrium model of emotional development based on a distinction between feelings and emotions. He describes feelings as unprocessed responses to sensorial qualities and/or physiological changes. These are the first affective responses, and are diffuse and occur in preverbal children. If an individual is overrun by this type of affective life, he or she will be subject to frequent losses of equilibrium. This is dealt with by the formation of emotions, which in Giblin's terms are overt physiological and behavioural responses directed towards changing the environment. They vary in kind, depend on both the situation and appraisals and are an attempt to maintain stability.

According to Giblin's speculations, there are five stages in the development of emotion. (1) From 0 to 8 months disequilibrium occurs from sudden or intense sensory sensations to which there are reflexive adjustments. Any expressions represent pleasure/displeasure and sleep/tension. (2) From 9 to 12 months, the first type of disequilibrium is added to by that caused by the presence or absence of other people. Equilibrium comes about through interaction and a sort of diffuse chaos is gradually replaced by more organized responses. (3) From two to six years, disequilibrium is caused directly and indirectly by stimuli and equilibrium is regained through both representational skills and emotion skills. (4) From 7 to 12 years, disequilibrium occurs through immediate perception and by social comparisons. By this time, emotional responses involve characteristic patterns of behaviour. (5) After the age of 13, disequilibrium comes about through internal comparisons and emotions come to contribute to the stable conception of the self, particularly through enduring moods and attitudes.

Although Giblin's distinction between feeling and emotion and his theory of disequilibrium are interesting, it is not easy to see how they can be developed further, or how they lead to easily testable empirical predictions.

Plutchik

Plutchik (1983) has extended his important psychoevolutionary theory of emotion to a consideration of development. From Plutchik's viewpoint, emotions are attempts to achieve control over survival-related events. Cognitive evaluations occur as survival-related emergencies the effect being to reduce threat or stress and to restore homeostatic balance.

From the evolutionary perspective, Plutchik suggests that there are usually two basic questions: from what did the behaviour evolve, and what is its adaptive significance? Emotion is concerned with the communication of information about internal states, the elicitation of (maternal) help, and the amplification of behaviour. It perhaps originated in defences against heat and cold, or exertion in general. Plutchik also points to the large accumulation of evidence in support of a genetic basis to emotional expression, with obvious communication and survival functions.

Rather than extend these ideas into a fully fledged theory of emotional development, Plutchik is content to suggest certain points which any theory of emotional development must take into account. These are: to use basic information about infant expressive behaviour, to conceptualize emotion as something more than expression, to identify those behaviours which reflect behaviour and those which do not, to provide insights into the development course of emotional expressions, to discuss variables that influence emotional development, and to be explicit about the derivatives of emotion that become part of adult life. Plutchik argues that at the time he wrote, there was no theory of emotional development that dealt with all of these issues, although, as will be seen, there is now one theory which comes close.

Izard and Malatesta

By far the most cogent developmental theory of emotion to have been proposed is that of Izard and Malatesta (1984). The theory is presented as sets of postulates with supporting evidence, all of which is based on the assumption that the emotions form a system which is independent of, but interrelated with, life-suport, behavioural and cognitive systems. They view emotions as discrete motivators of human behaviour, each of which is made up of neurochemical, motoric–expressive and mental processes. They also see emotions as prime movers in development.

The twelve postulates that make up Izard and Malatesta's theory fall into three categories. The first three are neurophysiological.

(1) Each of the 11 (according to Izard) basic emotions has its own neural substrates, but shares brain structures with others.
(2) In the developing emotional system, invariance and developmental change are accounted for by the neurobiological growth processes of canalization and plasticity.
(3) The development and organization of the brain allows the independent functioning of the emotions system. Although this would normally interact with cognition, at this point it is not necessary to have cognitive involvement.

The next three postulates concern the expressive component of emotion.

(4) Expressive behaviour undergoes two main developmental changes. The kinds of events and situations that can elicit emotion change, and there is a shift from reflexive movements to enculturation and learning. This is thought to apply at all points in development, including older people.
(5) Expressive behaviour shifts from an all-or-none, canalized form to the more modulated form seen in later development.
(6) The regulation of emotional expression is important personally and socially and so instruction in this begins early in life and tends to continue, at least throughout childhood. The importance of socialization in emotional development will be seen later.

The remaining six postulates fall within the domain of emotional experience.

(7) In the normal infant, the essential quality of the feeling state of the fundamental emotions is activated when the neuromuscular–expressive pattern of that emotion is encoded. This expression is an index of infant's feelings.
(8) The feeling component of each of the basic emotions has unique adaptive and motivational functions.
(9) Throughout the lifespan, some emotion is always present in consciousness.
(10) The essential quality of an emotion feeling does not vary throughout life.
(11) In late childhood and early adolescence, the ability to symbolize emotions is joined with the capacity to deal with them as abstractions. This increases both the possibilities for conflict and the integration of personality.
(12) Finally, emotions retain their motivational and adaptive functions even when development is not adaptive or when it is psychopathological.

Izard and Malatest's theory is very recent and as yet untried. However, it is complete, obviously derives from Izard's more general theory of emotion and has been predicated on most of the recent empirical research into emotional development. It is likely to give our understanding of emotional development considerable impetus.

RESEARCH—HUMAN

Apart from Watson's (1930) observations of fear, rage and love in children, Bridges (1932) set the scene for the study of emotional development. She considered that a child is born capable of experiencing and expressing only indifferentiated excitement, which by the age of three months or so becomes differentiated into the positive and negative—delight and distress.

Following this, she suggested that there is increasing differentiation until about two years of age, when the child displays most of the complex adult emotions. Although this seems to be a very neat schema, Bridges' data were based on quite unsophisticated observations, her definitions were inadequate and she paid scant attention to neonate behaviour.

Smiling and crying

In the earlier research tradition, the two emotional responses most studied in young children were smiling and crying. These are presumed to be representative of pleasure and displeasure. Research into smiling has mainly been concerned with the degree to which it is learned or innate. If a very young infant is handled he or she will usually smile; this is thought to point to some innate component. On the other hand, at a fairly early age he or she will smile upon seeing a human face, which seems unlikely to be an innate response. Salzen (1963) provides a good example of research into smiling. In observing one child he found that it first smiled to an external stimulus at seven weeks of age ('smiles' which appear earlier than this were then usually regarded as facial grimaces caused by internal discomfort). By eight weeks, Salzen's subject was smiling distinctly and to a human face; this may, of course, have been due to a maturational process. However, the child was then shown three, 13-inch cardboard ovals, one white, one black and one white with a black rim. The child smiled at them all, particularly if they were moved about, a response which was maintained over many presentations, independently of the order in which the child was shown the stimuli. After the eleventh week, he was more likely to smile in response to speech or to noisy, moving stimuli than to anything else. Salzen concluded that smiling in infants can be produced by any type of change in contrast or brightness.

Other research showed that smiling tends to appear earlier in children raised at home than those raised in institutions and that smiling in young children can be extinguished by simple non-reinforcement. There was a good deal of this sort of research and conjecture—but it allows little in the way of definitive statements. However, as with all heredity/environment questions, the conclusion is that they interact.

Research into infant crying has followed much the same course as that for smiling, with the general conclusion that there is a large innate component to it, but one which is capable of easy modification by experience. At one time it was thought that crying in the very young, would only occur to noxious (pain-producing) stimuli. However, a number of studies have shown that from quite an early age various non-painful stimuli which are presumed to bring about anxiety and fear may also instigate crying (for example, West and Farber, 1960).

Research into the negative displeasure side of infantile emotion also allows no definitive statements to be made. Like the positive aspects, it has necessarily been bedevilled by the nature/nurture question. Indeed, in the case of crying, it would seem likely that two distinct responses are involved. The first to appear is respondent crying—a reflexive type of response to stimuli of pain or discomfort (for example, hunger). Operant crying would seem to appear a little later in the course of development—here the response is clearly dependent on its consequenes (for example, receiving adult attention). Many parents believe that they can easily distinguish between the sounds of these two types of crying. It is reasonable to support that respondent crying is innately determined. Also, although it never entirely disappears, it would seem to lead to the development of operant crying which is then under environmental control.

Deprivation and attachment

From the early 1950s to the mid-1970s a tradition was established of comparing the development of children raised in institutions with that of children raised under the usual family conditions (for example, Bowlby, 1951; 1960; Spitz and Wolf, 1946; Yarrow, 1964). This work is clearly related to that of Harlow on chimpanzees (see below). It has generally been claimed that in comparison with their more fortunate peers, institutionalized children are often intellectually impaired and emotionally flat, even to the extent of showing 'anaclitic depression'. However, these claims are often not justified by the research on which they are based, and the studies themselves are frequently of dubious methodology. Be this as it may, there have been various proposals to account for the possible effects of early deprivation. Some of these ideas and investigations are relevant to an understanding of emotional development.

The most frequently suggested aetiological argument in this field stresses the significance of breaking the social/emotional tie which exists between a parent (particularly the mother) and a child. This tie is regarded as rooted in the initial feeding situation, although the Harlows' (for example, 1970) work with animals extends the limits of this idea where ethically it would not be possible with human subjects. Schaffer (1958), for example, demonstrated what he termed over-dependency in infants who by chance had been removed from their homes and then returned after varying periods of time. If removal occurred before they were seven months old then they were simply depressed, staring 'anxiously' at everything. Similarly, Yarrow (1964) suggested that by six months of age, 86 per cent of the infants he studied were showing serious emotional disturbance following permanent separation from their mothers. Bowlby (1960) went further and suggested that an emotional reaction may occur within a few hours if separation is experienced within the latter half of the first year of life. He argued that this is expressed by frequent crying and depression, and even happens to a limited extent if the parents go out for a few hours and the child remains with babysitters. Bowlby maintains that the child in this situation has been emotionally hurt by his parents and may therefore be hostile to them when they return.

A permanent separation quite commonly experienced by young children results from adoption. Scott (1968) suggests that any adverse effects of adoption depend more on breaking the old relationship than beginning the new. He believes, basing this largely on evidence from animal studies, that once the primary social relationship has developed—by about seven months in children—then there is a fear reaction to strangers. This in turn increases the likelihood of a more severe reaction to adoption. Thus, adoption is best pursued before this age, since, according to Scott, if it is not maladaptive 'emotional damage' may occur.

There is then support for the idea that emotional disturbance may result from the breaking, even temporarily, of attachments to familiar individuals and places. It is likely that temporal factors are important in this, but it is as yet unclear in exactly what way. Any effects must also depend on such variables as the type of relationship which existed beforehand. Although attachment remains an important issue in development psychology, the institution/home comparison investigations are no longer common.

According to Sroufe (1979) and Sroufe and Waters (1976) attachment represents an enduring affectional tie between an infant and a caregiver. It is not merely social learning but is an organized behavioural system plus a bond. It is through cognition that attachments become emotional.

The argument is that the emotional behaviours seen following long separations between an infant and caregiver suggest an enduring construct lying behind attachment. A typical finding is that a securely attached infant in an unfamiliar environment is attracted to any available toys but with occasional checks back to the caregiver. There are, however, broad individual differences in this largely adaptive pattern. Sometimes maladaptive behaviours develop after separation, but in Sroufe's terms these are best understood by hypothesizing stable categories and organization underpinning the behaviours.

It is clear that much of an infant's early pleasure and distress depends on the caregiver and the attachment, patterns of attachment being dependent on the sensitivity of the caregiving. The caregiver can provide a secure base for exploration and act as the first permanent object for a secure infant. As will be seen shortly, much of the most recent research into emotional development has been concerned with explicating the details of these earliest interactions.

Organization

Again it is Sroufe (1979) who provides a cogent structure from which to view some of the more recent research into emotional development. He is convinced that emotion is organizational and that emotion and cognition have to be studied together. Emotional development is both organized in its own right and also influenced by general developmental organization. Although, in detail, Bridges (1932) conclusions are criticizable in that she gave no indication of how emotional differentiation might have occurred, she did point to the orderliness of emotional development.

Sroufe argues that there are a number of what he terms 'organizers' that contribute to the eight stages of emotional development that he believes to describe what happens in the first two years of life. The social smile is the starting point, the first organizer beginning the relationship between an infant and familiar surroundings. Next come cognitive and motivational advances which allow experiences to become co-ordinated. By the end of the first year there are emotional responses to the loss or recovery of objects that are not visually present. The third organizer is an awareness of a separate self and the final one is the conglomerate development of the capacity for fantasy play, role playing and identification.

The eight stages of emotional development described by Sroufe (1979) are based on much of the research available at the time. Briefly, they are:

(1) Passive non-responsivity.
(2) A vulnerable turning towards the environment, ending with the social smile.
(3) Positive emotion, with awareness, anticipation and laughter, from three to six months.
(4) Active participation, from seven to nine months, with attempts to elicit social responses and initiate interaction. At this stage the child becomes aware of his or her emotions.
(5) Attachment, with increasing preoccupation with the caregiver and eventual clear communication.
(6) Practising, from 12 to 18 months with exploration and mastery.
(7) Formation of a self-concept.
(8) By 24 months there is play, fantasy and imagination.

In the midst of the emergence of these, or other, possible stages, how is it possible to be certain that emotion is present in children. An obvious difficulty comes if it is assumed that expressions and experiences are closely linked, or even isomorphic, and that expressions are identical in children and adults. The problem, though, is that the absence of expression does not necessarily mean the absence of experience. However, other than some sort of empathy, the other cues come from behavioural observation, for example, turning away and gaze aversion in fear.

Specific emotions

The development of pleasure and joy in the first two years of life, as particularly evidenced by the smile has already been discussed. There are changes from reflex to being more active, with arousal and relaxation being important. Sroufe argues that pleasure only comes from smiling when meaning is attached to it. Laughter is more concerned with mastery of the environment and stimuli which might also be threatening. The meaning of an event in relation to the child becomes increasingly important.

Bronson (1972) suggests that *wariness* is a negative reaction to the unknown in the first half year. *Fear* develops quite separately at about nine months and involves a negative categorization of an event. *Anger* emerges somewhere between six and nine months, and by the end of the first year there is a wide range of angry reactions. Then in the second year there develops angry defence, negativism and aggression.

Basically Sroufe (1979) would argue that it is at about three months that the first true emotional reactions emerge, although, as will be seen later, work in the last few years might suggest otherwise. By nine months, the infant has definitely become an emotional being. At this time the meaning of an event for the infant makes it responsible for emotion. Emotional tones now exist and there is awareness of the emotion itself. Memory is also developing its emotional aspects.

There is a dearth of work on emotional development after the first two years of life, with little other than speculation about the years of middle childhood and adolescence. With the recent interest in lifespan development, some researchers have turned their attention to the important matter of emotion in the aged, a topic hitherto almost totally ignored. For example, Sato (1983) reports an investigation of anxiety-provoking situations in a group of people approximately 70 years old. They rated their reactions to a number of situations and the three characteristic factors which emerged were threat to the ego, extrinsic threat, and threat to existence. They were also emotionally suppressive, had some encounters which prompted intense, chronic anxiety and found economic threat hard to cope with. This type of research is only a beginning and clearly needs to be developed much further.

Recent approaches

As mentioned earlier, during the last few years research into emotional development has taken a new turn. What follows represents some of the best of this research and the ideas which have developed from it.

Malatesta (1982) describes three studies in which she stresses discrete emotions as reflected in particular experiences and expressions. Results with infants (based on detailed observations and questionnaires of mother/infant interactions) showed that three- to six-month-olds *learn* to make their emotional facial expressions similar to those of their mothers. This implies that emotion in very young infants is *not* undifferentiated. Results also showed that mothers attempt to shape infant emotional expression by modelling and by making contingent responses. These studies also demonstrated that infants are very responsive to nonverbal emotional messages which seem both to arouse and to maintain attention.

Malatesta (1982) argues that 'the expression of emotion is subject to social influence and that the impact is probably substantial'. Also, some emotions appear to be more important than others for particular individuals as they grow and mature, something which may well hinge on constitutional factors. However, Malatesta draws special attention to the idea of *emotion socialization,* considering the learning of the rules which govern emotional expression and how such rules might change with age. Malatesta hypothesizes that preverbal infants are heavily dependent on their 'mother's' nonverbal expression in modifying their own. Thereafter, verbal instructions probably increase in importance as well and children continue to become emotionally socialized through observational learning and differential attention to their own emotional expressions, and sex-role patterns begin to have their effects. Malatesta also engages in interesting speculation about the continued process of emotional socialization through to old age.

Lewis and Michalson (1982) also consider the manner in which emotion might be socialized, resting their analysis on the view that the most important role in emotional development is played by a child's social environment. They consider in some detail the significance of the mother as the major (though not necessarily the sole) socializing agent and the possible importance of biological factors. They argue that models of emotional development which are based on the idea of socialization 'suggest *that experience and state may not be connected in a one-to-one fashion and that the socialisation task is to connect them*' (their italics). Socialization accomplishes a match between the cultural expectations of experience with particular emotional states seen in emotional expressions in particular situations elicited by certain stimuli. As an example, Lewis and Michalson suggest that children may experience fear 'only to the degree to which they have been socialised' rather than automatically through being in a fearful state. The emotional socialization itself they believe to depend on the interpretation, labelling and interactive behaviours of others. In their view then, it is the socialization process which brings about the differentiation of emotions into the highly complex cognitive-based matters that they become in the developing child.

Continuing to take this type of theoretical perspective, Fogel (1982) considers questions such as whether emotion in infants occur in predictable sequences, *must* there be sequences of emotion, and what makes an infant's emotional experiences change in the course of development? Fogel builds his studies on Field's (1977; 1980; 1981) *optimal-stimulation* model of emotion and interaction. Field's model has it that on those occasions when the adult gives too much or too little stimulation, the infant withdraws. The optimal amount of stimulation will depend on various characteristics of the infant. Also important in this context are Sroufe and Waters's (1976) influential data which show that infants' arousal levels fluctuate regularly but not too far from some optimal level. There is a gradual increase in emotional tension and then its release. Sroufe and Waters found that their heart rate measures of tension (arousal) relate to behaviours such as smiling.

On the basis of his researches following these models, Fogel himself (1982) constructs a model of emotional sequences in early mother–infant interactions. The model predicted a sequence of high-intensity infant emotion (smiles and eye gazes) at the start of interaction. This would be followed by withdrawal, all leading via more experiences to the infant gradually gaining more control over the sequences of arousal. Fogel accounts for these developmental changes with a theory of affective tolerance, developed by Epstein (1967) and Solomon (1980), whereby individuals gradually come to be able to reduce that arousal to an originally highly arousing stimulus, without disengaging themselves from it entirely. This is thought to occur through a simultaneous development of a physiological tolerance for the arousal and an 'addiction' to the stimulus.

Cognition

It is apparent from the previous section that at least the study of emotional development is at last reaching an impressively sophisticated standard. It is also apparent from all of the foregoing discussions that those who work in this area are making increasing reference to cognition in their accounts of emotional development. It would seem not possible to have a meaningful uncognitive theory of emotional development. The assumption is that cognition underlies the unfolding of the emotions through processes such as recognition, causality, intentionality and meaning. These are cognitive control systems.

Of course, this is the point at which Piaget's ideas bear on emotional development. These ideas are more implicit than explicit but are well described by Cichetti and Hesse (1983). According to Piaget, certain aspects of emotion do not change in development. For example, his work implies that virtually all emotions and emotional expressions are present at birth (a notion which makes the whole idea of emotional development problematic). As a further example, the functions of the emotions in the first two years of life appear to remain constant, although the situations in which emotions are expressed become increasingly complex.

Emotional change is, however, prompted by motor and cognitive changes. The emotions of children gradually approximate the meanings which adults give to them. Generally, Piaget implies that infants display more complex sequences of emotion because they become more complex cognitively.

While it is increasingly clear that emotion and cognition are inextricably intertwined, in their development as well as more generally, the problem is exactly how they are related. Piaget's position is one of parallelism, with cognition and emotion as complementary, non-causally related with the structure coming from cognition and the energy from emotion. However, it is clear that emotions are more than just energy. Cichetti and Hesse (1983) argue that interactionism is far more likely than parallelism, a view which is endorsed here. Cognitive development may well precede emotion and emotional development may well precede cognition.

The relationship between emotion and cognition within development is also considered by Buck (1983) within the context of emotional education. He argues that there should be situations that by their nature prompt attempts at emotional understanding and mastery. For example, the novel feelings a child might experience from neurochemical changes that might occur when he or she first feels angry with a parent or first encounters sex. If it is assimilable, the situation should be attractive.

Buck also suggests that the readiness to comprehend these types of experience will depend on cognitive development, a point which he believes to have implications for emotional education. Although emotional education is largely ignored except to urge suppression, the general ambience of a culture may well reflect the emotional education of its young. Buck argues that the various types of emotional responding are associated with different types of social learning. For example, instrumental responses should be related to the individual's expectations about what is the appropriate behaviour. Expressive behaviour and subjective experience would be related to actual emotional states. Reports of subject experience should reflect labels and interpretations and physiological responding should reflect the intensity of the prior condition of arousal in similar situations.

RESEARCH—ANIMAL

There has been a wide range of research into emotional development, using infrahuman species. This is probably due to the ethical problems involved in the experimental manipulation of emotion in children and the fact that for a number of years psychologists did little to develop observational techniques at the human level. The problem, of course, concerns the extent to which it is possible to extrapolate from this research to human emotional development. Bearing this in mind, what follows is only a brief overview of this research area. To do more in a context in which the relationship between emotion and cognition seems crucial would be vacuous. However, there may well be some pointers here for human development.

Heritability and emotionality

Research into heritability and emotion rests on two assumptions: (1) There are differences in emotionality or emotional reactivity between individuals. (2)

Some variations in behaviour are due to genetic variation. Here the term emotion is in a context of species-typical adaptivity, referring to processes concerned with both self- and species-preservation, these being the usual fighting, escaping or avoiding, eating, reproducing and caring for the young. Whether or not behavioural differences within a species are due to genetic variation, namely heritability, is an empirical question.

There are two procedures designed to investigate the effects of heritability on emotionality. First, there is the selective breeding of animals to minimize or maximize particular behavioural characteristics. If defecation in a strange environment is accepted as an index of emotionality, as it sometimes has been (see Chapter 5) then Hall (1951) demonstrated within 12 generations of rats that, that emotionality is heritable.

The other main research strategy in the study of heritability involves comparisons between inbred strains of animals. Bruell (1965), for example, found significant differences in the times which it took different strains of mice to emerge from a tunnel. He interpreted this as indicating that one strain was more timid, or emotional, than the other and that in consequence it is possible to infer that timidity must have been heritable in the original parent population. Of course, the mice may have been fortuitously bred with different visual capacities which might have led them to differ in tunnel emergence.

The use of these two fundamental techniques has produced research into the heritability of many types of behaviour. For example, aggressiveness in dogs and chickens, and frequency of turkey mating. These are merely instances, there has been much research demonstrating the heritability of many different forms of emotional behaviour. However, one overall point is that emotional reactions appear to be species-typical; within any species any differences are never qualitative—although Man is perhaps an exception to this rule.

Innate fear

The problem of innate fear is mentioned for two reasons. (1) Because there is always much conjecture (although little useful research) about built-in fears in children. (2) It highlights the broader controversy over the nature/nurture question which existed for many years between ethologists and psychologists. Recently, however, there has been something of a rapprochement in that heredity and environment are seen as interacting, one being clearly unable to exist without the other, their affects being interdependent.

The discussion of innate fear began with reports from a number of ethologists (see Thorpe, 1956) that many birds that are nest-reared show fear if a cardboard shape representative of a flying bird of prey (usually regarded as a hawk) is passed over them. When its direction of 'flight' is reversed, that is it becomes long of neck and short of tail, no fear is shown. The usual argument has been that this apparent fear remains intense over some time during the birds' early life, in the absence of any obvious reinforcement. Traditionally, stress has most commonly been put on an 'innate' explanation (i.e. there exists a 'blueprint' for a hawk) but with little information on the precise conditions of the early environment, although the effect has been supported by more precise studies.

Gray (1971) gives the most searching recent discussion of the degree to which fears might be innate or acquired. He suggests that the stimuli which promote fear can be classified under four general headings: those which are intense, those which are novel, some which stem from social interaction, and those which indicate special evolutionary dangers.

Reviewing the hawk/goose type of evidence, Gray argues that although there are some pointers in the direction of innate factors, the likelihood is that under conditions of natural rearing young birds will see more goose-like than hawk-like shapes. It is, therefore, possible that they show a fear reaction to a hawk because of its novelty.

The question of stimulus intensity is obvious and so will not be dealt with further. However, on the question of social interaction, Gray maintains that an important source of stimuli which elicit fear is the recognition of threat by observation of the behaviour of conspecifics—a point which does not necessarily bear on the innate/acquired question. Finally Gray argues that fear *may* be caused by stimuli which have previously been responsible for the deaths of large numbers of the species. Thus, for example, fear of the dark or of heights may well be inherited through its evolutionary usefulness.

Critical periods

By now, there is an extensive literature on critical periods in development, imprinting and early experience in general, although not all of it is relevant to emotional development. Moreover, these three topics are intertwined; for example, it is impossible to consider the evidence concerning critical periods without going on to the broader question of early experience. However, for the sake of convenience, they are separated in this discussion.

Scott (for example, 1967; 1968) has done much to further the importance of the concept of the critical period in development. The evidence from his work with dogs revolves around the notion of there being, early in life, a critical period for socialization, during which the animal is maximally sensitive to social stimuli. Scott maintains that a young puppy shows 'distress vocalizations' when it is removed from the objects and/or situations which it has experienced during its critical period. This emotional distress can only be relieved by the presence of other puppies or familiar surroundings. Scott regards this as a simple innate response. More important, he views it as a response which *maintains* an attachment to another member of the species. This thesis leads to the prediction that if other negative emotions are produced an intensification of the attachment should result. Scott takes his argument one stage further by suggesting that many animals form emotional attachments to certain familiar physical surroundings—a phenomenon he terms *primary localization*.

Imprinting

Imprinting refers to the formation of specific attachments by young precocial birds. It is generally regarded as developing from the approach and following responses and not to be simply explicable by recourse to the principles of conditioning. (Although it should be noted that the capacity to be reinforced is greatly enhanced by proximity to the source of reinforcement.) The usual example of imprinting involves a young chick which follows the first moving object which it encounters—normally the mother. However, in numerous studies the young of various species have been induced to follow virtually anything, from wooden blocks to rows of lights that become illuminated in rapid succession. In the limiting case, even approach and following do not seem to be crucial for imprinting to take place; it is merely necessary for the young animal to see an apparently moving object within some critical period. However, the basic conditions are as have been outlined, immediately suggesting the conclusion that under 'natural' conditions imprinting is a highly appropriate way for the young of a species to become attached to older members, on whom they are in any case dependent.

Of the four main theories to account for the end of the critical period (see Sluckin, 1964) two have obvious relevance to emotion. (1) Sensitivity ends with maturation. (2) Sensitivity is inhibited through socialization. (3) Sensitivity ends with the growth of timidity. (4) Sensitivity ends because a state of low anxiety also ends.

Early experience and emotionality

The typical procedure in studies of the effects of early experience on later emotionality involves subjecting animals as young as possible to conditions such as handling by the experimenter or electric shock. After this, they are reared individually under standard laboratory conditions. As adults they are tested in situations believed to allow a measure of emotionality, the 'open-field' test for example. The degree to which they behave emotionally is compared with that of untreated control animals. The degree to which control subjects are untreated is a determinant of how firmly any conclusions can be drawn.

In seeking to account for such effects, Denenberg (1964) argues strongly against the usefulness of the concept of critical periods. Instead he considers the problem of finding a common factor in studies of the effects of early stimulation. He suggests that any stimulation between birth and weaning reduces 'emotional reactivity'. The greater the infantile stimulation, the less the emotionality in adulthood. Thus Denenberg's main hypothesis:

'emotional reactivity is reduced as a monotonic function of amount of stimulus input in infancy'. (1964, p.338; italics his)

There are a number of lines of evidence which support this general proposition, although they are usually concerned with either handling or shock. For example, rats that are handled more in infancy, as adults are more active and defecate less than control rats in open-field tests (for example, Denenberg and Smith, 1963). Rats handled and shocked in infancy and later deprived of water (such deprivation being a novel situation) drink less than controls (Levine, 1957; 1958; 1959). Or rats stimulated in infancy are bolder than unstimulated controls as adults in emergence-from-cage tests, and handled rats are less emotional than non-handled on measures of avoidance learning. Denenberg (1964) also suggests that emotionality provides motivation, that is, the more emotional animal is more highly motivated.

It is clear that early experience affects later behaviour. Also emotionality appears to be a reasonably useful hypothetical construct to account for the mediation of these effects. However, the generality of early experience effects, particularly at the human level, is an open question. Few species have been studied and few sources of stimulation used. Intensity of early stimulation is likely to be an important variable, but it has appeared in few investigations and then has provided scant support for Denenberg's hypothesis suggesting a monotonic relationship between stimulus input and emotional reactivity. Finally, Denenberg argues that intensity of infantile stimulation is a major parameter affecting later differences in 'chronic' (i.e. general level) or arousal. Again, however, this is simply trying to explain one rather unwieldy concept (emotionality) by another, and in the absence of more precise definition and firm evidence should be treated with caution.

Affection, fear and aggression—Harlow

Harlow (for example Harlow and Harlow, 1962; 1970; Harlow and Mears, 1983) is accorded a section to himself in this discussion of emotional development since: (1) his approach is unique; (2) he normally studies rhesus monkeys, results from which can perhaps be more meaningfully extrapollated to the human level. Harlow regards social and emotional development as being intimately connected. He suggests that there are three fundamental patterns of social response, which make their developmental appearance in the sequence: affection, fear, aggression. Anything which distorts this sequence may distort social–sexual development.

Affection

Harlow believes emotional attachment to develop in the first month or two of life owing to the satisfaction of hunger, and comfort, warmth and support from the mother. He suggests that the grooming and caressing of their young by adult females is a reflection of reciprocal emotional satisfaction.

By the second month of life, infant monkeys show interest in their peers. Contacts lengthen, turn into play and lead to the development of emotional attachments. Harlow regards this new type of attachment as growing with the decline of mother–infant attachment; it is not simply generalization. Harlow argues, but with only discursive, observational support, for the ubiquitous nature of peer affection in primates, including humans. Early on, sexual differentiation is unimportant, but after three or four months, male monkeys become progressively more dominant and females more passive. In the juvenile period (one to two years in monkeys) friendship pairs are usually like-sexed—the human parallels are clear. Harlow suggests that culture merely emphasizes and moulds sex differences which already exist. Peer affection is the main factor in learning effective adult social and sexual adjustment—learning the appropriate place in the group.

Fear

Harlow affirms that fear in rhesus monkeys only begins after the first two months of life. They scream, cling to or run to their mothers if shown unfamiliar places, objects or humans, objects moving towards them, or unusual and loud noises. If they are separated from their mothers they cry and clasp themselves. The development of fear is partially dependent on experience, since it involves perception of potential danger.

Aggression

Harlow states that playful *attacks* are obvious from the start of social play. Free aggression towards peers does not appear until about ten to twelve months in monkeys raised in a group, but earlier in those raised in isolation. The latter also inflict worse injuries on one another. Once the dominance hierarchies have been established in socially raised monkeys, there is relative peace. Monkeys raised in isolation often show uncontrolled or undiscriminated aggression, or sometimes incapacitating fear. Harlow concludes that affectional relationships are necessary precursors to normal social aggression, which keeps physical injury at a minimum.

Much of Harlow's research has involved social isolation. Monkeys are raised from birth in stainless-steel chambers with diffused light temperature and air control and food, water and cleaning accomplished remotely. Typically, the monkeys see *nothing* living for either three, six or twelve months, after which they are placed in individual cages and a few days later they have their first social experiences. Often, they are put together in a playroom with another isolate plus two cage-reared monkeys for half an hour per day, five days per week, for six months.

The main response to removal from isolation seems to be fear. This fits well with work on imprinting. The three-month isolates recovered (became normal) in a few days or weeks. In the six- and twelve-month animals the fear remained predominant. They did not defend themselves against attack and they did not form social attachments. In the six-month group, minimal play was observed, in the twelve-month group none. When six- and twelve-month animals of the same age were put together, the twelves were attacked by the sixes with very accentuated aggression. After these tests the monkeys spent two years in standard laboratory cages and were then tested with strangers, either large, powerful adult monkeys, normal peers, or normal one-year-olds. All the experimental monkeys were terrified, but this was punctuated by isolated, extreme, violent, suicidal, aggressive attacks. It seems that the fear and aggression had intensified with time. These results perhaps point to the three-to-six-month period being critical in a monkey's development.

Further support comes from Harlow's observations that even monkeys that were reared with their mothers, but whose peer experiences were somewhat delayed, showed a measure of this fear and aggression. Also, very immature, long-lasting clinging was seen in monkeys raised with no mothers but continually in contact with peers. If four monkeys are reared together with no mother, they spend most of the time sitting clinging in a line, like carriages in a train, to use Harlow's analogy.

The emotional inadequacies in monkeys reared in isolation also extend to their sexual behaviour. The separate behaviours involved in copulation are evident, but they never become integrated into a whole unless the monkeys are taught by an 'experienced' adult. The sex drive seems to be as strong as in normal monkeys but the behaviour is typically autistic and onanistic with short bursts of aggression.

On the basis of this and similar work, Harlow argues that there are two independent but interchangeable affectional systems—one based on peer socialization and the other based on mother–infant socialization. Also, for fear and aggression to develop 'normally', the positive affectional system must develop first.

CONCLUSIONS

As was stated at the start of this chapter, for many years emotional development, particularly during the first two years of life, seemed to have been so well described by Bridges (1932) that very few investigators looked any further. At the human level some work was conducted on the important but obvious matters of smiling and crying, deprivation and attachment. The range of research was wider at the infrahuman level but its relevance to human emotional development is difficult to determine. Also, at either of these levels, theoretical contributions were slight.

Fortunately, during the last few years the situation has improved considerably. Techniques for the observation of human interaction have become far more sophisticated and a number of investigators have produced theories of some penetration concerning emotional development. Furthermore, a start has even been made on the study of emotional development as it occurs throughout life, after the first two years.

Emotional development clearly depends on an interaction between genetic and environmental influences, the nature-nurture involvement which typifies all studies of development. Most of the earlier research points to this interaction. However, more recent investigations (for example, by Malatesta) far in advance of any that have been made previously point strongly to the importance of social interaction to the initial development of emotions. They might apparently unfold in the approximate order described by the early researchers, but the influences on this seem to be largely social. Indeed, it is very difficult to separate social and emotional development. We are born with the capacity to respond emotionally, and from this emotional responses become refined through social experience. Early learning then is crucial to emotional development, but whether or not at the human level this in any way depends on critical, sensitive periods in development remains to be seen.

If it is accepted that emotional development is heavily dependent on social development, then it follows that it is also intimately linked to cognition and cognitive development. This conclusion is reinforced by each of the recent theories of emotional development. The major point which they have in common is an emphasis on the importance of cognition. In fact, the implication is strong that it is simply not possible to account for emotional development without also considering cognition.

At the theroetical level, the most useful contributions to an understanding of emotion have been made by Plutchik (1983) and by Izard and Malatesta (1984). Plutchik provides a very useful list of matters which any theory of emotional development should take into account. Izard and Malatesta put forward a series of twelve postulates which together form the basis of a full theory of emotional development. These stress the importance of neurophysiology, expressive behaviour and emotional experience and not only derive from Izard's influential, more general theory of emotion, but also depend on much of the recent research findings in the area. Again, at various levels, this promising theory stresses the basic importance of cognition to an understanding of emotional development. As with all other aspects of emotion, an understanding of its development relies more and more on its interplay with cognition. We may be born with the capacity for emotional arousal, but it is through social cognition that this arousal becomes refined and enriched into the distinct emotions.

7

Social Aspects of Emotion

Emotion is a social phenomenon. For the most part the stimuli for emotional reactions come from other people and emotion occurs in the company of others. Even if our emotional state is generated by memories, these are usually of other people or of the impact they may have had on us. In spite of this, for many years social psychologists only focused on emotional expression and its recognition. This is of course an integral part of emotion, and is interesting in its own right. In addition, the problems which beset the study of expression and recognition and the attempt which have been made to solve them are instructive for more general analyses of emotion. They have even led to some of the comparatively full theories of emotion (for example, Izard, 1972; 1977). More recently, social psychologists have also turned their attention to the more genuinely social aspects of emotion and have begun to explore emotion in relationships, from friendship to love. Also, they have begun to emphasize the importance of cross-cultural comparisons.

Whenever we interact with another person, whether face-to-face or otherwise, we are continually expressing emotion. Simultaneously, we are monitoring and interpreting the other person's emotional expressions. He (or she) is doing the same. It is fair to say that it is this complex and possibly often unconscious process which gives social interaction much of its subtlety and depth. Our emotional expressions are providing stimuli to anyone with whom we might be interacting. He or she in turn responds to these stimuli, observing, judging, and classifying, and then perhaps engages in some 'answering' expression. It is with how we express ourselves emotionally and with how accurately we identify such expressions in others that the social psychologist has been concerned. It is worth noting here that the identifying response is not made to the emotional expression itself, but to the *meaning* behind it. For example, a frown can be an expression of emotion. However, it is the state which is underlying the frown which we try to interpret. A thought about the complexities of this will show that in this chapter we are dealing with a particularly awkward and difficult area of research.

Frijda, who has produced excellent reviews and analyses of this field (for example, 1969; 1970), suggests that the recognition of emotion may be broken down into three aspects. He means that when we express emotion we refer to three events, and when we recognize emotion we use three systems of identifying response. (1) We recognize emotions by the *situations* in which they occur. If we are asked to describe fear, for example, we refer to some recent situation in which we 'felt' afraid. (2) Emotional expression *anticipates action*. We observe an emotional expression in another person and ask what behaviour is likely to follow it. (3) We *experience* emotion. The meaning of any expressive behaviour may be bound up in our subjective emotional experiences or attitudes. The observer may represent this experience to himself in some empathetic way, or even make fractional empathetic expressive movements himself.

The first part of this chapter will survey the major work in this area, drawing attention to some of the difficulties which have beset it and highlighting some of the better research and theory. Analyses will also be made of research and theory into emotion in relationships. There are two points which should be borne in mind when appraising this field; in a sense they are both methodological. (1) Although we are directly within the sphere of the social psychologist, emotional expression and recognition is only one aspect of communication, and communication is also of concern to others, notably the clinician and the ethologist. Often, the research methods of such people differ from those of the social psychologist. This sometimes makes evaluation and comparison difficult. (2) The problem which any social psychologist has to face somewhat more squarely than does the 'individual' psychologist is that of artificiality. Do results gleaned from laboratory studies of social behaviour tell us very much about social behaviour in real-life settings? This problem is intensifid for the investigator of emotional expression. How does one produce 'real' emotion in the laboratory. How does one measure the way in which it is judged? Is the identification process the same as that which we use from day to day? How does the investigator even decide what to study? How does one decide whether or not some observed facial behaviour is pertinent to emotion? To take the most extreme example, how is it possible even to begin to study the emotions that we experience in our close relationships and cope with the artificiality/reality problems.

There are several interesting reviews of emotional expression and recognition; each has its own emphasis; Berscheid (1983)—relationships; Davitz (1964)—social-psychological; Ekman, *et al.* (1972)—social-psychological; Frijda (1969; 1970)—social-psychological; Izard (1972; 1977; 1980)—social-psychological; Knap (1963)—clinical; parts of Vine (1970)—human ethological; also the thorough reader should begin with Darwin's (1982) *The Expression of Emotions in Man and Animals*.

FACIAL AND VOCAL EXPRESSION OF EMOTION

Basic research and problems

The facial expression of emotion has been studied in many ways, the main problem being the choice of stimulus material. The solution to this has varied from posed photographs (more typical of the early studies) or schematic drawings through fully acted live expressions to spontaneous expressions. Typically, during recognition, subjects have been asked to provide verbal labels for the emotions expressed, or they have been given rating scales to complete or have had to match the photographs of emotional expressions to stories. Laboratory studies using animals report even more ingenious measures (for example, Miller *et al.*, 1959a; 1959b; see below). Another difficulty concerns the number of responses which have been required of a subject. In describing the emotion one has seen, one may have two adjectives to choose from, or a hundred. These may have a checklist or the possibility of a free description. One may be asked to respond strictly in terms of the emotional expression or be allowed to concentrate on the situation as well.

Similarly, various strategies have emerged for the study of the vocal expression of emotion. Here, the main problem has been to devise a method for cutting out the verbal content of speech while leaving nonverbal aspects. There are three solutions to this. (1) Subjects have been asked to express various emotions while reciting the alphabet, which on the face of it seems an awkward task. (2) Or they have been asked to express the same few neutral sentences in different ways. (3) Or, finally, electronic filtering techniques have been used on recorded speech. Again, as with studies of facially expressed emotion, the task set to the subject and the number or type of responses required have varied enormously.

Any evaluation of investigations into emotional expression and the degree to which its recognition is accurate is made difficult by this multiplicity of factors. Studies vary according to the task the subjects are given, the selection of responses which they are allowed, and the type and number of stimuli with which they are presented. This means that few definitive statements can be made about the accuracy of emotional recognition, which in any case is a problematic concept. However, some general statements can be made. For example, most studies based on spontaneous emotional expression in adult subjects lead to the conclusion that the performance of judges of the emotion is better than chance (for example, Coleman, 1949; Dittman, 1962; Ekman, 1965a; 1965b; Ekman and Oster, 1979; Frijda, 1969). Also most studies of vocal expression of emotion agree that emotional meanings can be communicated by vocal expression, although it is discrimination rather than recognition which is successfully achieved. (See Davitz (1964) and Frick (1985) for review.)

On the general question of accuracy, Ekman *el al.* (1972) suggest that to make a good judgement of accuracy of expression it is necessary to develop criteria based on at least four related sources of information: (1) antecedent events; (2) concomitant responses (physiological and bodily); (3) consequent events (such as self-reports and the behaviour of other people); (4) consensus of opinion by trained judges. As might be expected, there are few studies which have taken into account all such measures.

Ekman *et al.* (1972) also suggests that four major questions should be asked concerned the generality of any results which come from studies of the facial expression of emotion, be these based or spontaneous emotions expressed in artificial or natural conditions. (1) Is the finding germane to other settings? If so, which. (2) Is the finding relevant to the facial behaviour of people in general? If not, what are its limitations? (3) Is the finding general across time or is it transient or occasional? (4) Is the finding specific to the judges used (particularly if they are trained observers) or would anyone make similar judgements. Clearly, these are excellent questions to ask, but very few investigators have asked them. To ask them on their behalf demonstrates the somewhat limited nature of much of the research in this area.

Earlier research

Coleman (1949) provided an exhaustive study of facially expressed emotion. His two basic procedures involved the elicitation and recording on film of facial expressions of emotion and the subsequent identification of these from the eye or mouth regions or from full face. Judges were provided with a list of the situations used and in each case were asked to identify the situation which led to the expression. Although identifications were no better from the mouth region or the eye region, some expressions were identified better from one than the other. Identifiability depended on the subject, the facial region viewed and whether the expression was acted or natural. From subjective report, Coleman concluded that the method used for identification could best be described as empathy. Frijda (1969) provides further examples of similar work.

This would seem to be the right point to introduce the important work of Woodworth and its development by Schlosberg. Woodworth (1938) re-analysed data from earlier studies, and proposed a six-point scale of emotional recognition: (1) love, mirth, happiness; (2) surprise; (3) fear, suffering; (4) anger, determination; (5) disgust; (6) contempt. Woodworth and Schlosberg (1955) turned this into a circular rather than linear scale with contempt alongside love, mirth and happiness. Finally, Schlosberg (1952; 1954) proposed a dimensional representation of emotional expression and recognition. This implied that all emotional expression could be represented according to the three dimensions of: (1) pleasantness/unpleasantness; (2) attention/rejection; (3) activation level (sleep/tension). These analyses all seem quite reliable and led to considerable developments in the study of emotional recognition. They will be returned to later.

By the 1960s this type of investigation although providing useful information, had raised more questions than it had answered. Then, with a series of basic studies, Davitz (1964) broke much new ground. Further, R.E. Miller and his coworkers produced a series of investigations which, with an interesting technology and animal subjects, lent support to the human studies.

Davitz—earlier work

Having reviewed previous work on facial and vocal expression of emotion, Davitz (1964) devotes the remainder of his book to a description of the research undertaken by his group. He suggests that the field of vocally expressed emotion is open for research, having shown little more than its probable occurrence. He poses two basic questions concerning facially expressed emotion. (1) To what extent is it innate or to what extent acquired? (2) To what extent does it depend on individual differences? Two earlier research strategies had been directed at the nature/nurture question in emotional expression. There had been a few studies based on the proposition that if learning is important to expression then cross-cultural recognition of emotion should be poor. Also, another type of study had concentrated on subjects blind from birth. It is not worth reiterating these here.

Previous work on individual factors had been more or less restricted to sex differences with no general effects being found. Also, other than a few studies which had shown low positive correlations between intelligence and the ability to identify facial expression, there had been very little work on personality variables.

In describing the contribution of Davitz's group to this area, Beldoch's (1964) work will be mentioned in detail as it provided the basis of many of the other studies. He constructed tapes of male and female speakers reciting an emotionally neutral passage in ways expressive of various emotional states. He presented these tapes twice to 58 subjects. From their responses he produced a final tape containing those items most often correctly identified and representative of 10 emotional meanings. He followed the same procedure with musical tapes created by musicians in the same way—i.e. aimed at the expression of 10 emotions—and also with abstract art created for this purpose. All this stimulus material was then presented to 89 subjects with an adjective checklist (ACL), a questionnaire concerning their general background in these three media, a self-report scale of sensitivity to the emotional expressions of others and a simple test of verbal intelligence.

Beldoch found significant correlations between the ability to make correct judgements in all three media, and also with vocabulary scores. Background, training and interest contributed nothing and the ACL did not distinguish between high and low scores. However, scores of sensitivity to emotional expression on the self-rating scale were positively related to those on the speech and graphic art material.

Levy (1964) using 'content-standard' material derived from Beldoch, found significant correlations between the judgement of vocally expressed emotion, the recording of similar items then judged by others and subjects' recognition of tapes of their own expressed feelings one–two weeks later. Levy considers her results as implying a general 'communication factor'.

Davitz himself takes up this idea of a general communication factor. In his first study, he found no reliable correlations between personality and the ability to identify vocal expressions of emotion. But in a further study, he found that this ability did correlate with general auditory ability, abstract symbolic activity, verbal intelligence and knowledge of the vocal characteristics of emotional expression. He tentatively suggested that general emotional communication is perhaps some sort of symbolic process. He is, however, well aware of the dangers of reading too much into purely correlational results (see also later discussion of Frick (1985)).

The other studies reported in Davitz (1964) each make a cogent contribution, but there is little point in itemizing them in detail here, since the interested reader will find Davitz' book rewarding in its own right. However, two particularly relevant findings will be mentioned. Levitt (1964) studied the relationship between the ability to express emotional meanings vocally and facially. Levitt found significant correlations between facial and vocal expressive abilities, although full (vocal/facial) presentations were no better than facial communications alone. These results again provoke conjecture as to whether emotional communication is a matter of a general factor and/or a number of specific factors.

In what is probably the most interesting paper presented in the book, Blau (1964) devised a test of various commonly held hypotheses about the ability of the blind to communicate. For example, that the blind differ from the sighted in their ability to identify feelings from nonverbal cues, that blind females are better at this than blind males, that the blind pay more attention to emotion than the sighted and that they can make much fuller descriptions of sounds and are more confident in their judgements of feelings and sounds. He studied 57 blind adolescents and 66 sighted adolescents, both groups being comparable in other ways. The blind were significantly better than the sighted at judging sounds, but controlling for this ability, the sighted groups were found to be no better at judging feelings. In fact, where members of the blind group sometimes score better than the sighted, this was later shown to be dependent on differences in mental age. There were no sex differences, but the blind paid significantly more attention to affect and were the more specific reporters of sounds. However, they were not more confident than the sighted in their judgements of sounds and feelings. Blau concludes that sensory compensation exists to an extent, but not sufficiently to make the blind any better at judging emotion.

Although the research techniques reported by Davitz resulted in such interesting exploratory findings, he is aware that they are not above criticism. The main question is whether or not they lead to results which are at all representative of real life. Most of the studies he describesd rely on experimental instructions rather than actual emotion states; nevertheless, the overall findings are reasonably consistent. Also, he sets a fairly stringent operational definition of what he means by communication, and sticks to it. But Davitz does not make too strong a claim; he simply regards this work as a start and not necessarily representative of fine-grained, sensitive, everyday nuances of the communication of emotion.

Current perspectives

Since the seminal work of Davitz, there have been some impressive developments in the research and thought put into emotional expression and its recognition. Izard's (1972), 1977) influential views are predicated on analyses of emotional expression, and are described at many points throughout this book. Much of the upsurge of work in this area has coincided with a recognition of the importance of the face in human interaction, an obvious point but one that for many years was not addressed squarely.

With particular reference to emotion, recent research on the face is fully discussed by Ekman and Oster (1979) and Salzen (1981). Each summarizes a profileration of studies across a wide range of methods and across a wide range of cultures, but all concerned with the perception and recognition of discrete categories of emotion or of a limited number of dimensions, with evidence in support for both.

There are a number of different aspects to these studies. For example, cross-cultural studies (also see later in this chapter) show that observers recognize facial expressions in a similar way regardless of their culture and that the members of various cultures show similar facial expressions when ëperiencing similar emotions, unless there is interference from display rules specific to the particular culture.

From a developmental perspective recent research on facial expression shows that expressions resembling many adult expressions (for example, distress and disgust) are present from early infancy. Also, there is imitation of adult emotional expression from a very early age, preschoolers can recognize common facial expressions and emotional expression has an important role to play in the development of social communication.

Recent research as summarized by Ekman and Oster (1979) also demonstrates that facial expression can give accurate information about the pleasantness and unpleasantness of emotional states, but it is possible to disguise facial expressions to mislead the observer. Finally, the evidence is increasingly strong that it is feedback from facial expression that helps us to determine what we are feeling, particularly in its intensity.

As an alternative to research on the face, a recent review and analysis by Frick (1985) is made from a communication starting point and is concerned with the role played by prosodic features, mainly from expression through voice. The particular features that appear to be important are those such as pitch and loudness, and Frick argues that the evidence suggests that they may communicate transient emotional states and/or emotional attitudes towards the message or the audience. These effects also obtain cross-culturally.

The general types of findings in this area of research suggest for example, that an increase in activity or arousal correlates with increased pitch and a faster rate of speech. With aggression, sometimes pitch is lowered and sometimes raised, pitch is lowered during disgust and contempt and raised during fear and in some instances of nervousness. Suggested reasons for the links between emotion and the prosodic aspects of speech remain speculative, ranging from the possibility of an epiphenomenal relationship to both being the result of biological given, coming, for instance, from the muscular setting of the vocal structures (for example Izard, 1977).

CONCEPTUALIZATION OF EMOTIONAL EXPRESSION AND RECOGNITION

Research bearing on the theoretical analysis of emotional expression has usually been based on one of two approaches. These can be called *component* studies, in which facial behaviour as a response is put in a context of its relationship to the measurement of emotion, and *judgement* studies in which facial behaviour provides the stimuli to be judged.

Again it is Ekman *et al.* (1972; Ekman and Oster, 1979) who have some very cogent points to make about these research strategies. They suggest that any failures in accuracy or agreement by judges of emotional expression does not necessarily mean that the components of facial behaviour are unrelated to the eliciting stimuli, although it could be meaningless. However, failures in judgement observed in such studies may be due to defects in the task, in the sampling of observers, in the sampling of facial expression, in the recording, or in the sampling persons.

Ekman argues that the best research strategy is to combine both component and judgement procedures and then to determine how much information an observer can interpret, what facial behaviours relate to his inferences and what facial behaviours vary with emotion but are not recognized as such by observers.

There are three main ways in which emotional expression and recognition have been conceptualized. (1) Categories: emotions as expressed could be classed into any number of distinct, unrelated events. Tomkins and McCarter (1964), for example, assume that there are eight primary 'affects': interest, enjoyment, surprise, distress, fear, shame, contempt, anger. They also assume that each of these is primarily a facial response which is under the control of some innate subcortical programme. The main point about any categorization system is that the classes are unrelated and unordered. (2) Dimensions: from the dimensionality viewpoint, expressed emotions can be regarded as mixtures of pleasantness, activation, etc. (Statistical techniques based on factor analysis lead to the enumeration of distinct factors underlying behaviour. These may be conceived as occupying hypothetical n-dimensional space, each dimension being orthogonal to the remainder. Although this is easily understood with three dimensions, we need mathematical or philosophical analysis to conceive of more. Emotional expressions can be conceptualized in terms of such underlying dimensions.) This type of analysis can account for some of the more suprising similarities between emotional expressions (for example, between contempt and mirth). Equally well, it can account for differences and the various nuances of emotional expression in general. However, it quickly becomes unwieldy if too many dimensions are proposed. (3) Hierarchy: this refers to a combination of categories and dimensions. In a particular region of *n*-dimensional emotional space there may be differentiation between emotion in terms of the dimensions especially pertinent to that region. Emotions may be comparable as regards dimensions both within and between categories, although each category may have its own distinguishable qualities.

Are these ideas sufficient to define emotional expression? The answer must be no. Ideas of categories, dimensions or a hierarchy are abstract. And emotions as they are distinguished in the language cannot be distinguished in the same way from their expression. They are confused by observers. People use many different labels for any one expression, all of the labels sometimes being quite wrong. Also, different emotions can produce the same expression. This strongly suggests that there is something more or perhaps finer than is given by possible dimensions of emotion. The necessary richness could come from cognitive factors. However, if cognition is important, then emotion could not be fully recognizable from expressive behaviour, which may well be the case. Recognition and discrimination errors are commonplace.

Frijda (1969) explains the facial expression of emotion by the concept of 'positionality'. He defines this as: (1) tendencies to approach, withdraw and attend; and (2) the degree of control of activity. He regards these as usually but not necessarily being combined with possible cognitive determinants of emotion and argues that the naming of emotion follows from the recognition of positionality. Frijda also suggests that there may be a sort of balance between cognitive and behavioural factors in emotion; when one is high the other will be low and vice versa. However, why the behavioural components are sometimes well-differentiated and sometimes not is unclear. Also, for any one emotion, there are numerous behaviours and expressions which are considered to be appropriate. The problem is that many different states may share one expressive pattern, and that many different expressions may characterize one emotion. Analysis and conceptualization become difficult.

Dimensionality

The basic hypothesis underlying the idea of dimensionality in emotional communication is that errors in the recognition of emotion run parallel to similarities between expressed emotions, and these similarities are in fact proximities in multidimensional space. Thus, emotional recognition becomes a matter of placing emotions in this multidimensional space. This is extended by the similar idea that *named* emotions are also reducible to combinations of fewer dimensions than are immediately apparent. The concept of dimensionality has led to a search for the number of dimensions which will describe hypothetical emotional space more simply. Although Schlosberg set the scene, the three dimensions he proposed appear arbitrary and unsatisfactory. Other studies have found evidence for the pleasantness/unpleasantness (P/U) dimension and the sleep/tension (S/T) dimension, but often the attention/ rejection (A/R) dimension has been missing.

There have been two approaches to the study of dimensionality; (1) judgement of the meaning of emotional expression through the use of ACLs or rating scales; (2) judgement of similarity using paired comparison techniques or their extensions into triads or groupings.

Osgood (1955) provides a good example of the former. Subjects had to select one from 40 emotional-state labels which, in their estimation, best characterized a live, motionless protrayed by an actor. From an analysis of the frequency of usage of each label for each expression, Osgood plotted his results on three dimensions. There was a P/U dimension, an 'intensity' dimension (corresponding to S/T) and a 'control' dimension. Control can be regarded as a dimension peculiar to Osgood's experimental technique, since it distinguished expressions started by the 'actor' from those simply coming from the environment.

Frijda (1969) by contrast, in a rating-scale study found six main factors: (1) P/ U; (2) activation—but Frijda described this as corresponding to intensity rather than S/T since the low end was a lack of expression rather than sleep; (3) similar to Schlosberg's A/R but more like what might be called interest since the low end was disinterest rather than rejection; (4) Frijda found this dimension difficult to label, but suggested social evaluation or something akin to Osgood's control; (5) and (6) smaller factors, the first being described as surprise, the second as simple/complicated.

If emotional expressions can be reduced to dimensions, two questions require answering. (1) Do the dimensions delineate the 'meaning' or 'real' emotion which underlies expression, or, more mundanely, do they simply reflect the words used to describe emotional expressions? Frijda maintains that at least his first four dimensions correspond to expressive meaning. (2) How many dimensions are there? The only study to point to as large a number as Frijda's six factors is Osgood's (1966), which involved semantic differential-scale responses of judges. He found that his usual three dimensions could be divided further into nine interpretable clusters or factors, a number almost large enough to bring us back to a list of primary emotions: anger, amazement, boredom, quiet pleasure, disgust, sorrow, interest (expectancy) joy and fear.

Typically, studies using matching techniques for the judgement of similarities between photographs of emotional expression have found far few factors. However, such studies have normally used only a few posed expressions.

From the standpoints of their experimental requirements, the major differences between these two sorts of study is that when endeavouring to label an emotional meaning a subject has to make a discrimination, whereas when one is estimating similarities between emotions one must overlook any differences. From this point of view, Frijda (1969) maintains that pleasantness and interest are more important to the estimation of similarity than are intensity or artificiality.

The search for dimensions of emotion has been an important influence in the study of emotional expression. However, this is due more to the research which it has generated that to any fundamental theoretical contribution. Clearly, the parsimony implicit in the idea of dimensions could be significant in any analysis of emotion, but any economy is lost when, as has often been the case, too many dimensions are proposed. Also, it is sometimes difficult to compare dimensions between studies. Various research strategies and techniques of data analysis have been used and difficulty is often met with in describing and naming the dimensions when they have been found. Of course, naming is perhaps not important since dimensions are in any case mathematical/philosophical abstractions.

Finally, it should be remembered that, given the research techniqes most often used in this area of study, any dimensions of 'emotion' may simply be reflecting verbal behaviour. Also, none of the studies carried out to date makes it clear exactly what subjects are responding to; they may well be responding to dimensions or conversely to the actual categories of emotion. At present it is impossible to say whether the category, dimension, or category and dimension approach will be the most fruitful, although it is perhaps worth noting that each of them is concerned, in its way, with the cognitive structure of emotion.

OTHER ASPECTS OF EXPRESSION

So far, only studies involving the facial and vocal expression of emotion have been discussed. However, behaviour may reflect emotion in many ways, before considering other factors which might influence emotional expression in general, some of these will be mentioned.

In real life, it is clear that emotional expression extends in time and is carrried by many facets of the body, not just by the face or voice in a few moments. There have been some interesting investigations of body movements in emotional communication. Ekman (1965a; 1965b), Ekman and Friesen (1967a) and Dittman (1962) have all shown that bodily posture and movement contribute to the recognition of emotion, particularly its intensity. Body cues do not seem to be especially important for the P/U dimension. In extending this idea, Ekman and Friesen (1969) provide a novel slant on emotional communication. They suggest that nonverbal behaviour escapes the efforts that we make at deception and in fact allows our 'real' feelings to leak out. They propose that there are two types of deception, each of which contains much simulation. (1) We attempt to deceive others about our feelings. Even if we are discovered in our deception we may carry it through, with subtle changes, since open verbilization might prove embarrassing. (2) We may deceive ourselves.

This is a somewhat 'clinically' viewed blocking from self-awareness of feelings that might arouse anxiety if they were given free expression.

Ekman and Friesen regard these deceptions (which we all make) as having three dimensions: (1) saliency—the degree to which the deception is of obvious importance to the interactants; clearly a function both of the situation and the personality of those involved; (2) the roles adopted by the interactants—i.e. whether they are both deceiving and/or detecting, or one adopting each role, etc.; (3) collaboration or antagonism—an implicit or explicit pact (or lack of it) about the discovery and/or the continuation of the deception (psychotherapy is a collaboration to discover deception). They also suggest that each of us has a certain sending capacity for nonverbal signals; we can send them quickly or slowly, we can send many or few and we can make them easily visible or not. Ekman and Friesen maintain that according to each of these measures, the face is the best sender of nonverbal information, the feet and the legs are the worst and the hands and arms fall somewhere in between. Further, they stress the importance of external feedback. Nonverbal behaviour from B is perceived by A as being in response to his own nonverbal behaviour. Even so, it may be inappropriate to openly comment on this. For example, although we may comment if someone frowns in our presence, we shall probably not mention his squeezing his legs together. Finally, there is internal feedback-conscious awareness of what we are doing. Again, there is the progression face, hands, feet, this time in terms of the amount of nervous system feedback we obtain from the areas.

Ekman and Friesen's concluding suggestion is that the legs and feet are the worst senders of messages, they are the least responded to, they are the least in self-awareness and *therefore* they provide the best source of information about leakage or clues to the deception that is being practised on us. From this point of view, the face is the worst source of information and the hands and arms are again in between. Ekman and Friesen provide some support for these ideas with studies involving ratings of filmed interactions; the raters see only the head or the hands and arms or the feet and legs.

Related to this area of research is the question of the relationship between facial expression and psychotherapy. Apart from Ekman and Friesen's ideas, Haggard and Isaac's (1966) research on micromomentary facial expressions is also relevant. From an analysis of filmed psychotherapeutic interviews they observed a number of fleeting (1/8th—1/5th second) facial expressions, which cannot be observed under ordinary conditions, i.e. when the film is played at normal speed. They speculate with some force that such movements may well relate to the psychodynamics of the relationship between the patient and the person he or she was discussing at the time.

There has been discussion in the clinical literature of the importance of nonverbal behaviour in emotional communication. Although such discussions are speculative and concern data which come from rather dubious research techniques, they are nevertheless suggestive. For example, Jorgensen and Howell (1969) analysed head and shoulders audio-visual tapes of four experimentally naive females during stress and relief phases of structured interviews. Two of the four described themselves as outgoing (expressive) and two as unemotional (suppressive). 162 judges and the subjects themselves were shown the films and had to rate the emotions they saw expressed as 20 semantic differentials.

Jorgensen and Howell draw four main conclusions from their results. (1) Males and females made equally good judgements. (2) Suppressive individuals were judged more accurately than were expressive, although this result may have been due to the narrowest range of emotions they expressed being in accord with generally conservative judgements. (3) Pleasant emotions were better judged than unpleasant. (4) The best judgements of the pleasant emotions were made with no face and no soundtrack and the best of the unpleasant emotions came from the written transcripts alone (no face and no sound). Finally it should be stressed that although results such as these are interesting and suggestive they are based on relatively crude research techniques, although Izard's (1972; 1977) analyses in this area are an exception.

CONTEXT AND CULTURE

During normal everyday life, expressive behaviour is perceived in context; this would seem to be an important aid to judgements of emotion. Evaluations are made on the basis of information about body type, facial characteristics, purposive actions, the situation, behavioural constants, personality, age, sex, cultural group, and so on. Much of the standard research involving such variables is not pertinent here. However, before discussing the *general* role of context in judging emotional expression, it is important to mention recent work involving cross-cultural comparison in such judgements.

Izard (1972; 1977; 1980) and Ekman *et al.* (1972) have provided the most penetrating analyses of the cross-cultural investigation of emotional expression. Izard quotes powerful evidence that 10 basic emotions are interpreted in a similar manner across a wide range of cultures. There are interest–excitement, enjoyment, joy, surprise–startle, distress–anguish, disgust, contempt, anger–rage, shame–humiliation, fear–terror and anger. He regards this as confirming a degree of universal facial expression which is fired by an innate neural programme.

These general results are also supported by research on preliterate children and on mixed emotions and by the writings of cultural anthropologists. Investigations involving the labelling rather than the recognition of emotion also support the idea of universality although not so strongly. The difference in accuracy between recognition and labelling is possibly due to differences in the structure of the task, the relative infrequency with which people practise labelling and the possibility that some sense is lost in translation, particularly of idiosyncratic responses.

Izard assumes that emotions have served adaptive functions thoughout human history. For example, anger is described as adaptively mobilizing energy and mounting vigourous defences, fear motivates an escape from danger, and guilt promotes a heightening of personal responsibility, all of which could well have had adaptive consequences. There are various theories which seek to account for the apparent universalities in facial expression. For example, facial expressions may stem from defensive movements of the muscles which surround the facial sensory organs, although this could not account for the development of the positive facial expressions. The main cultural differences in emotion are not in the expression but in attitudes towards emotions and experiences; for example, there are display rules which restrict the time and circumstances of emotional expression.

To return to the general matter of context there would seem to be a two-stage process at work: (1) an evaluation of (Frijda's) general positional activity pattern; this is made from the actual emotional expression; (2) the more precise specification of this pattern from contextual cues. Cline (1956), for example, demonstrated the possible importance of context in judging emotional expression. He manipulated the context by making schematic drawings, unarguably a very artificial technique but nevertheless one from which putative conclusions can be drawn. He found, for instance that the drawing of a face was perceived as angry, jealous and unhappy when paired with a smiling face, but aloof, independent, domineering and unafraid when paired with a frowning face. Out of context it was judged to be glum.

It was once thought that the context was the only way in which we can recognize emotion and at best the expression itself was secondary. However, it is now clear that expression does give important clues, although perhaps when there is an obvious context available such expressive cues may become less important. This point implies that contextual cues may possibly conflict with expressive cues.

If contextual and expressive cues are dissonant, which is dominant? Flores d'Arcais (1961) gave the first answer to this by using films with either correct or incorrect soundtracks. Expressive cues were dominant. This finding has been confirmed in a series of studies by Frijda (1969). His basic experiment involved the use of photographs with either concordant or discordant descriptions. The design called for free ratings of the photographs and also ratings including the information given by one or other of the descriptions. Ratings shifted in the direction of the expression rather than the situation. Interestingly, the discordant description seemed quite acceptable to the subjects. It may be that in real life such apparent paradoxes are not uncommon.

It is a simple matter to suggest factors that might influence the dominance of expressive over contextual cues when the two conflict, for example, ambiguity in the cues, the nature of the expressive cues, the nature of the contextual cues, and so on. It is more difficult to specify the process of judgement when there is such conflict. The obvious answer is a sort of compromise. But, as usual, it is Frijda (1969) who provides the more subtle and more interesting explanations.

He suggests that the person making the judgement forms various hypotheses until he or she has an aggregate of them. He believes that 'gap-filling' hypotheses are often produced, i.e. possible additional factors are hypothesized to have their effects between a particular situation and a facial expression which may not accord with it. If the discordance persists, then Frijda posits four possible ways of reducing it. (1) Divorce the emotion from the situation. (2) Divorce the emotion from the situation and accept the situation. (3) Divorce the expression from the emotion. (4) Deny the situation. There are obvious resemblances between these ideas and those proposed for the reduction of cognitive dissonance.

Ekman *et al.* (1972) reach a conclusion rather different from Frijda's, namely that no definitive statement can be made about the relative influence of facial expression and context on the judgement of emotion. They feel that on different occasions either can be dominant. They suggest that investigators in this area need to address themselves to three research questions. What are the parameters of facial expression and context that determine their relative influence? What cognitive mechanisms resolve any discrepancies between face and context? What is the nature of the occasions when either the face or the context gives more information than the other?

OTHER LINES OF RESEARCH

Empathy

Stotland's (1969) consideration of the social and physiological aspects of emotion rests on the intuitively reasonable assumption that we share other people's feelings. This sharing of feeling does not necessarily imply any sympathetic *behaviour* on the part of the observer. Stotland defines empathy as 'an observer's reacting emotionally because he perceives that another is experiencing or is about to experience an emotion'. He regards this as a state of physiological arousal, with strong subjective concomitants and he suggests that even if an emotional response pattern has not been convincingly demonstrated physiologically, it exists subjectively. He argues that emotions are dichotomized into positive and negative and then any further differentiations occur via subjective report. It is then a little difficult to see why he brought physiology into the picture at all.

Stotland distinguishes empathy from those situations in which our experiences may carry implications for the welfare of those who might observe them. For example, when his or her father frowns a child might expect unpleasantness to follow. This is not empathy: the other's perceived emotions are acting as discriminative stimuli (sources of information) about the observer's possible or probable fate. Stotland also distinguishes empathy from predictive empathy. In the latter he suggests that the observer does not have to *experience* the emotion he is perceiving to predict what it may be. However, he also argues that predictive empathy and nonpredictive empathy must share any factors which influence the perception of another's emotional state. Also, they may interact.

There is an interesting distinction between Schachter's (1964) views and those of Stotland. Schachter proposes that we use the behaviour of others to interpret our own, perhaps amorphous, feelings. Empathy is the reverse of this; we perceive another's emotion and then change our own emotion state—both physiologically and subjectively. Rather than contradicting each other, these directions of influence may happen in sequences or in different conditions.

Stotland's (1969) experimental procedure typically involves five or six subjects observing another, pseudo-subject, undergoing some positive or negative experience while under instructions to empathize in various ways. The observers' reactions are measured by palm sweating and vasoconstriction; and also by self-ratings of their feelings immediately after the emotion-producing stimulus had ceased (a limited but inevitable measure in such studies). Stotland concludes from his results that an interpersonal process which leads us to imagine ourselves in the position of another leads us to empathize, although exactly how this occurs depends on the relationship between the observer and the observed.

Such results are interesting and the general research strategy is promising. However, the findings often show a lack of consistency between the physiological measures and the self-ratings. Also, as has sometimes been the case with investigators of emotional expression and recognition, Stotland goes further than is justified by his data.

The language of emotion

Davitz (1969); 1970) makes one of the more fruitful approches to the social psychology of emotion. He deals with a problem which sprang from the final stages of Davitz (1964): 'What does a person mean when he says someone is happy or angry or sad?' Davitz believes that this should be answered descriptively—a belief which characterizes the social psychology of emotion in general. His answer leads him, by a completely different route, to a concept of dimensionality reminiscent of Frijda's.

Davitz (1969) suggests that the meaning of the various emotions depends on our experience. He argues for a study based on language. A problem which all psychologists must face is having to use everyday terms in a more rigorous, restricted context; the everyday connotations of words simply cause confusion, 'anxiety' perhaps being the best example. Davitz therefore aimed to produce a dictionary of emotional terms, drawn from what he calls 'commonalities of meaning'—verbal descriptions of emotional states. Clearly, such an aim is likely to result in enormous subjective confusions. Davitz is aware of this but hypothesizes that any common ground may appear in mathematical abstractions from the basic data.

Davitz asked 30 people to imagine a time when they experienced a given emotion and then to describe it. From this, and from judgements about information relevant to the emotional experiences, he ended with 556 statements which referred to (in decreasing order of frequency) physical sensations (for example 'I feel soft and firm') relations to the external world (for example, 'Everything seems unimportant and trivial'), cognitive events (for example, 'My thinking is rapid'), relations to others (for example, 'I feel outgoing'), self-reference (for example, 'I feel aimless'), impulses to behave or to control behaviour (for example, 'I want to be tender and gentle with another person') and formal aspects of the experience (for example, 'It's a steady, ongoing feeling').

Terms for labelling the emotions were taken from *Roget's Thesaurus*. The 400 words obtained in this way were read to 40 subjects who were asked to say which of them they would use to label an emotion; 137 of these were well agreed on, of which 50 were chosen on the basis of their coverage of the vocabulary of emotion. Each subject was asked to think of a critical experience for each of these emotions, describe it and then use the checklist to find each statement which agreed with the experience. Next, 50 subjects used this large checklist, each describing a range of emotional situations. Although these subjects were taken from both sexes and from negroes and whites, they were all highly verbal graduates; this is a clear limitation to the generality of Davitz's findings. Arbitrarily, Davitz included in his final definition of a term any statement which had been checked by at least one-third of the subjects in their descriptions. Finally, each of these was given to 20 judges with instructions to rate (on a four-point scale) their adequacy in describing both the emotion and their own experience of it. Davitz then presents his reader with the actual list of phrases and his resultant dictionary of emotional meaning.

One obvious advantage of Davitz's dictionary is that it gives a vocabulary which can be simply used for phenomena which are normally very difficult to describe. On the other hand, as Davitz shows himself to be well aware, it must represent an oversimplification. He oversimplified further by carrying out an analysis of 215 items that each appeared in the definitions of at least three emotions. He found 12 clusters which were then factor analysed, the results suggesting four dimensions of emotional meaning. These are activation, relatedness to the environment, the hedonic tone of an emotional state, and a sense of competence in relating to the environment.

From this extensive analysis, Davitz (1969) produces a tentative theory of emotion which can be reduced to six main propositions. (1) Emotion is partly concerned with private (experienced) events—a clear phenomenological, subjective viewpoint. (2) Emotion embraces specific states which are labelled, and each label refers to experiences about which there is reasonable common ground within a culture. This proposition comes more directly from Davitz's dictionary. (3) The language of emotion reflects experiences but is also directly influenced by linguistic considerations; people make mistakes in their descriptions of emotion, and, in fact, learn to label the emotion from the situation (see (5) below). (4) Definitions of emotional states fall into 12 clusters, which can fit into four dimensions of emotional experience: activation, relatedness, hedonic tone and competence. (5) Labelling emotion depends on experience. Any change in experience will change the label and the state. (6) Emotional states come about from stimuli which are psychologically relevant to the four dimensions of emotional meaning.

Davitz is aware that these propositions fit neither phenomenology, nor a psychoanalytic approach, nor behaviourally orientated ideas. In fact, as a theory it leaves much to be desired, since it is both lacking in formal properties and is not well-anchored to empirical fact. However, he quotes studies to show that his proposals do lead to productive research and the ideas are, once again, clearly relevant to a cognitive analysis of emotion. Moreover, Davitz's (1969) contribution of the dictionary of emotional meanings, gave a fresh approach to the social psychology of emotion and may provide the impetus for some fundamental research.

Ethology

Recent advances in the ethological approach to emotional expression brings us back full circle to the Darwinian starting point. Interestingly, modern ethology has been extended to man as well as animals. However, the study of animals is instructive since it perhaps points to the origin of emotional expression. Tail-wagging in dogs and purring in cats are obvious examples of this. Ethologists believe such responses to have a communicative function; to act as releasers for the co-ordination of social behaviour.

Eibl-Eibesfeldt (1970) argues that, evolutionarily, expressive behaviour is often derived from other behaviour that has been accompanied by frequent arousal or activity. For example, in many species social grooming always indicates that social contact may proceed. Sometimes it has become ritualized into expressive movements. The lemur, for instance, greets other lemurs with the movements it uses to comb its fur. Similarly, Eibl-Eibesfeldt maintains that behaviour which once led to attack has evolved into gestures of threat. It may, for example, be reduced to preparing to jump, or to jumping and falling short. One unfortunate aspect of such evolutionary arguments is that they tend to lead to useless speculations about similar mechanisms in man. To take the last example, a man stamping his feet in anger can be said to be showing incipient, but ritualized, attack movements; a point which can be neither proved nor disproved.

The ethological suggestion is that ritualization—the modification of behaviour to make it communicative—is the main process underlying the evolution of expressive movements. The changes that it produces in behaviour are regarded as all-important to signalling. Eibl-Eibesfeldt (1970) describes eight changes in behaviour which accompany ritualization. (1) Behaviour changes in its function. (2) Ritualized movements change their *apparent* motivation. (3) Movements become simpler but exaggerated both in frequency and amplitude. (4) Movements 'freeze' into postures. (5) The actual behaviour occurs to a greater range of stimuli. (6) Orientation changes. (7) The behaviour becomes stereotyped and occurs with a constant intensity. (8) The variability of behaviour is suppressed. He also suggests that these changes are often accompanied by the development of conspicuous bodily structures. Although these speculative ideas may appear to make good sense from the viewpoint of biological adaptivity, it is difficult to see how they may be substantiated. However, at the descriptive level, there are many possible examples of the process (see Eibl-Eibesfeldt (1970) for review). For instance, many carnivores feed their young by pushing food into their mouths, and also often greet one another, by pushing together their muzzles and rubbing them. (In this case, the ethologist would maintain that the latter has evolved from the former by a ritualization process.) Also, both apes and man sometimes feed their young with a mouth-to-mouth method and greet one another by kissing. More interestingly, Eibl-Eibesfeldt suggests that ritualization may begin to occur within ontogenesis as well as phylogenesis. He supports this by the exaggerated, rhythmic and stereotyped behaviours seen in zoo animals; these often seem to be directed towards 'begging' for food, for example. However, there are many alternative explanations of such stereotyped behaviours (see Strongman, 1985).

Modern ethologists also provide classifications of expressive behaviour. Again, to take Eibl-Eibesfeldt's (1970) work as an example, he classifies expressive movements according to their function. His major division is between intraspecific and interspecific releasers. The intraspecific group are: (1) signals that promote group cohesion; these are precise signals which regulate interaction and attraction, for example courtship behaviour, submissive gestures and behaviour which establishes and maintains contact; (2) communication about the external environment; for example, warning and distress is signalled in squirrels and birds, and chemically in some fish; also there is the famous bee language in which the direction and distance of a food source from the hive is communicated; (3) intraspecific threat signals; for example, certain bird songs, a gorilla's chest-beating, various ritualized attack behaviours. Eibl-Eibesfeldt subdivides interspecific expressive releasers into two: (1) contact readiness, in which many members of different species live near to one another to mutual advantage; (2) threat postures, for example, back-arching in cats.

An important (although implicit) thesis in recent ethology is that an obvious way to overcome the difficulty of laboratory studies of emotional expression in man is to study them using more 'naturalistic' techniques. Brannigan and Humphries (1971) exemplify this approach. They criticize the more traditional photograph-based studies of emotional expression by pointing out that their validity depends on the correctness of the basic definitions of the emotion on which they are based. Also, of course, the expressions are not occurring within their usual dynamic context. They suggest further that the actual expressions which have been studied have not received enough ethological analysis. Such analysis is complex, but they argue that a sound ethological description of an emotion should be the starting point. This approach has recently led to some excellent research in the area of emotional development (see Chapter 6).

Emotions in Relationships

By far the most exciting recent developments in the social psychology of emotion have moved completely away from the question of the actual expressions of emotion and the ways in which these expressions might be recognized. Emphasis is again on communication but at a different level. At last, attempts are being made to grasp the nettle of the nature of emotion as it occurs in human relationships, even those which culminate in love. Psychologists have been understandably reluctant to study these facets of emotion; their complexity is off-putting. However, it is fitting that the attempt should be made, since in everyday terms this is probably the most important part of emotion.

Although a number of investigators have begun to turn their attention to relationships, by far the most penetrating analysis of the role of emotion in relationships has been made by Berscheid (1983). It is with a summary of some of her ideas that the remainder of this section will be concerned.

Berscheid characterizes interactions as involving causal connections between the chains of events that make up the interactants' lives. Also, she follows Mandler (1976; 1984) in suggesting that it is interruption of event sequences that brings about emotion. The extent to which the potential to experience emotion in a relationship depends on the connections *between* two chains of the events within each.

Initially, there is usually a great deal of interruption and hence emotion in relationships, but gradually as the two chains of events become more meshed, so this settles down and the relationship becomes more tranquil (or humdrum). If there are awkward, emotion-provoking parts of the interaction which the people concerned work at by severing, then the emotional investment decreases and the relationship deadens. This is the case, for example, when couples begin to take separate holidays or evening activities.

If an emotionally tranquil relationship, which is nevertheless based on considerable emotional inverstment, is suddenly severed, the extent of the trauma depends on how rapidly an alternative way of completing the interrupted sequences can be found. For example, those who establish new relationships before a divorce cope more ably. All of which means that people tend to be more aware of what is wrong with a relationship than what is right.

One difficulty with Berscheid's type of analysis is to account for positive emotion in relationships, since interruptions of another's sequence of events would seem likely to generate a negative reaction. Mandler, however, suggests that events which interrupt but which seem controllable lead to positive emotions. Also, if an event is judged to facilitate rather than interfere with an organized sequence of events/behaviours, it is likely to generate a positive emotional reaction—for example, a sudden windfall.

Berscheid's suggestion for the emotional background to romantic love is that one person must have the power or resources to remove an interrupting stimulus for another. A partner must have plans and be unable to complete them as easily alone as with the other's help. Young people typically have more unfulfilled plans than older people and so are more likely to experience the positive emotions of romantic love. For many people (but not all) in mid-life, plans cease because they are fulfilled or because it is too late and so there are mid-life crises and feelings of being emotionally dead. From this type of analysis it follows that it is perhaps only those who dream in life and continue to strive for goals who stay alive emotionally.

There are many more aspects to Berscheid's compelling analysis of the magnitude and quality of emotions in close relationships; for now, one further example must suffice. The main cause of the breaking up of relationships is a change in the causal conditions that surround them. In present times, it is relatively easy to disagree with a partner and to fulfil plans without the partner because there are so many possible alternatives. The irony is that the most enmeshed relationships are, because of their closeness, the most vulnerable to these effects.

Of course, the main influential change that can occur outside the relationship is the effect of a third person. Berscheid suggests that jealousy occurs under three conditions: (1) X's plans are interrupted by events in Y's chain. (2) A partial causal source of this is Z outside the relationship. (3) The causal source is also perceived to be within the partner, Y. Again the irony is that close relationships are more vulnerable to these effects than those which are more distant. In this context, an external person who looks to mesh well with a partner is the most likely source of jealousy. Also, it is perfectly possible to love two people at once, if they fulfil different needs or even if they fulfil the same needs in different ways.

CONCLUSIONS

The majority of the research that falls within the particularly social aspects of emotion has been concerned with expression and recognition. It allows the conclusion that there exists some immediate, apparently intuitive, perception of expressive meaning. But this by no means accounts for all the findings in this field. Although the recognition process occurs very quickly, much knowledge and experience must intervene. Clearly, the recognition of emotion is determined by a very complex process. This process depends on the integration of many cues, from facial expression through body movement to the situation and the more static features of the interactants; whilst at another level, the process depends on whatever hypotheses we may hold about life. Frijda (1969) offers the most complete formulation: (1) the understanding of a situation and its implications; (2) a store containing factual and emotional implications; many possible emotions connected with varying probabilities assigned to each situation; (3) we are 'set' for a person in a situation to experience a particular emotion; (4) a store of emotional knowledge; emotions and their scale values—from which we also get our own emotional expression; the system must be able to register expressive behaviour and code it; (6) a working out of expressive meaning; (7) a comparison of expressive meaning and situational suggestions; (8) a combination of (4) and (6); (9) an emotion is selected from the store in (4); (10) an adjustment is made if the selected emotion does not conform to expectations; (11) a mechanism to resolve any continuing discordance; (12) the selected mechanism then defines a new emotion; (13) finally, there is the construction of situation components to fit with the selected emotion.

Frijda (1970) simplifies this formulation to three main points: (1) categorizing an observed behaviour pattern in terms of a set of general dimension of emotion; (2) further differentiation; (3) the specification of probable emotion from situational cues or suppositions. Frijda suggests that his view of emotional expression is also applicable to emotion in general. But the relationship between expressive behaviour and emotion is too complicated for this sort of direct inference to be made. It is clear that every emotion can be carried by many different expressions, which sometimes have very little in common. Often there is little hope of the recognition of the emotion out of context. On the other hand, all the complex combinations of expression make sense in their situation context.

It should be said that in spite of the various attempts to define dimensions of emotional meaning, the process is much more complicated than simply inferring the dimensions of emotion directly from the dimensions of the recognition of emotional expression. And in real-life situations with all their other cues, our recognitions and even the recognition process itself *may* be quite different from those suggested by laboratory studies.

In spite of these conclusions, the importance of the facial expression of emotions is beyond doubt. Its most significant aspects concern the relationship between facial behaviour which is associated with emotion and that which is not, the social interactional consequences of emotional expression, and the degree to which facial expression should play a necessary part in any theory of emotion. Facial expression may fill an informational gap which is left in any primarily visceral and cognitive theories of emotion. It allows emotion to be distinguished, allows emotions to change quickly, and also gives more possibility for subjective feedback than is given by the viscera alone. Thus it is reasonable to argue that any theory of emotion, should, like Izard's (1977) or Mandler's (1984) not only indlude visceral physiological arousal and cognition, but also facial expression.

Izard rests his compelling analysis of facial expression on two assumptions. (1) Emotion is a complex of the physiological, muscular and phenomenological and has a biological and psychological function for the individual and a social function in interaction. Also the three levels of emotion are both independent and interdependent. It is feedback which permits an integration of these components into a process and which also allows differentiation between the emotions. (2) The relative importance of facial and bodily activity in emotion has changed during the course of evolution, such development being paralleled in ontogeny. The general point here is that the importance of the face in emotional differentiation and communication increases with a phylogenetic and ontogenetic development, this being in accord with a similar development of the facial muscles.

Of particular importance in this context is ontological development. On this matter Izard argues that in early infancy emotional expression is underlain by undifferentiated excitement in the striate muscle. However, by the end of the first year the facial muscles are developed fully enough to allow the expression of any emotion. Thereafter the role of the face in emotion changes, whereas posture for example remains constant. Also the suppression of facial patterning hinges on cognitive development. Here Izard suggests that there are learned proprioceptive patterns of particular facial configurations, with memory perhaps substituting for the actual pattern on occasion. Furthermore, in Western culture at least, the expression of strong emotion is increasingly discouraged by parents and peers throughout a child's development. Such repressed expression may well show up in micromomentary movements. Izard even goes so far as to argue that if parents severly punish a young child's facial expressions, this causes a significant repression and leads to constricted emotions and a considerably attenuated emotion; characterized mainly by primitive undifferentiated disturbance in other areas (e.g. the viscera).

Izard assumes that feedback from facial expression generates increased hypothalamic activity and a correspondingly more intense emotional experience than would be given from a memory image alone. The experienced emotion would be more precise and complete.

Finally, Izard points to the importance of facial expression in communication, especially between parents and young children, even suggesting that the first means of communication are the smile and frown. So facial expression is significant in both brain–body communication and in interpersonal communication.

Izard then, has made the most thoroughgoing analysis of the role of facial expression in emotion. It is worth noting that this analysis, like all of the others in this field, including the broader matters of emotional communication in social relationships, relies heavily on cognitive concepts. Once again looking at yet another aspect of emotion, the role of cognition appears to be crucial.

Further, Leventhal and Tomarken (1986) have recently cast doubt on the belief in peripheral feedback mechanisms which are integral to thought in the area of emotional expression. They suggest it is just as viable to consider a model that has feeling and expression mediated by a central motor mechanism. This could occur through the activation of emotion memory, for example. This idea clearly warrants attention, which of course it is given in Leventhal's (1982) own theory.

8. Abnormal Emotion

One of the traditional ways of regarding psychopathology in general is to assume that it is partly a matter of emotional malfunction. By definition, emotion is implicated in all of the ffective disorders. Schizophrenia is described as often involving emotional change. The neuroses are characterized as dependent on anxiety in extreme forms. Psychopathy rests on an apparent lack of emotion. Frequently any type of abnormal behaviour, such as excessive eating or drug-taking is believed to stem from 'emotional problems'. The mentally retarded are assumed also to be emotionally disturbed.

Emotion then is seen as playing a central role in abnormal behaviour or mental disorder, perhaps because of a long-held tendency to denigrate emotion by viewing human beings as rational and intelligent, somehow above any primitive emotional impulses, which every effort should be made to ignore. If they become so insistent as to be impossible to ignore, or so extreme as to interfere with normal life then the result is termed abnormal. The abnormality in emotion, then, may be occurring at a number of levels—particularly in the interaction between the person and the environment and in the form of the emotional reaction, any that is especially high or low being seen as abnormal. Or, of course, any abnormality may be laid at the causative feet of emotional problems. The idea which probably underlies this view is that since emotions are essentially uncontrollable passions they must lie behind abnormality. By contrast, controllable rationality could not be the cause of emotional problems.

A number of writers have pointed out the shortsightedness of this approach, arguing instead that without emotions man would not have evolved and that due attention should be paid to emotional abnormalities and techniques for their control (for example Leeper, 1970; Peters, 1970; Izard, 1972; 1977). In fact, it is even reasonable to say that an individual with emotions so suppressd as to be regarded as nonexistent is extremely dangerous. It is therefore important to attempt to gain an understanding of abnormalities in emotion and of what can be done about them therapeutically.

Izard's (1972, 1977) is probably the best-worked-out general view. He puts together research on the significance of muscular tension in maladjustment with his own work on the importance of the striate muscle (mediating facial expression) in emotion and argues that emotion must therefore be central in individual dysfunction. He suggests that if emotion follows its natural course then it will lead to function or action, which in turn is regulated by cognition or verbal expression. Unwanted muscular tension might stop this action and lead to maladaptive behaviour. Izard even goes so far as to suggest that our understanding and control of emotions will determine whether or not civilization advances, arguing that neurosis, psychosis and even violence come from over-intellectualism and an ignoring of the emotions.

Following the traditional links between abnormal emotion and mental illness, one way to tackle this chapter would be to give a potted summary of all mental disorders. However, there would be little profit in this in the search for an understanding of emotion. Another approach might be simply to take each emotion in turn and consider its extreme forms. This would also be inadequate. However, there are certain conditions which are so commonplace in any discussion of abnormality that they must be considered, in particular anxiety and depression. Also, there is a background of work that is concerned with the links between emotions and the bodily responses sometimes referred to as symptoms. This leads to an important consideration of psychophysiology, emotion and pain and psychosomatic disorder. Finally, there have been some interesting analyses made of emotion in psychopathy and in the mentally retarded. These topics will be considered in turn in the attempt to come to grips with abnormal emotion. Following this will be a brief discussion of some of the possible roles of emotion in therapy.

The usual practice in this text has been to discuss empirical research before considering the relevant theory. However, in the case of abnormal emotion, theories and theoretical issues are rather limited in number and reasonably straightforward to grasp. Some of them will be described now in the hope that they will help to provide a stance from which to view the remainder of the chapter.

THEORETICAL CONSIDERATIONS

Emotion and personality

Within pyschology, there has been a longstanding link between personality and abnormal behaviour, an understanding of the former often being regarded as important to the study of the latter. Perhaps one reason for this is the impact of the early psychoanalysts on both fields. A very brief comment therefore might be useful on some of the links between emotion and personality (see Keen (1977) for a much fuller exposition).

To Freud and Jung, emotion, like all behaviour has multiple referents, in other words, it means many things simultaneously. Since psychologists seek the meaning of interpersonal events, it is reasonable to ask what emotions mean. But this can be from the viewpoint of the individual or from the viewpoint of the psychologist. Within a personality theory framework, although it is possible to identify something as an emotion, specifically anger, this does not answer the question: Why is he or she angry now? This would get at the meaning of the anger.

Keen (1977) argues that personality theory helps in the study of emotion by providing a context which is more general than a particular emotion and yet more specific than a single emotion in general. From this type of perspective, emotions are private experiences, occurring only in a context of a person who is behaving in a situation. So, although emotion might be invisible, its context is not, which will help in its interpretation and in a search for its meaning. Personality theory, then, assists the study of emotion by providing a framework within which to deal with contextual data that help to find the meaning of an emotion.

In an interesting recent analysis, Watson and Clark (1984) link personality dispositions to the experience of aversive emotional states, a condition sufficiently negative to perhaps be regarded as abnormal. They sample a wide range of data which suggest that there are stable individual differences in mood and self-concept which characterize some people as experiencing high negative affectivity and others as low.

Those with high negative affectivity report distress, discomfort and dissatisfaction, regardless of the situation. The condition is related to state anxiety and occurs in individuals who are more introspective and self-honest than others. These are individuals who focus on the negative side of others and of the world. People with low negative affectivity are content and less honest about themselves. They do not much dwell on self but when they do, tend to like what they find. They have a positive view of other people. Watson and Clark suggest that there are two types of low negative affectivity person, those who are truly self-satisfied, well-adjusted and happy, and the others who deny their unpleasant or undesirable self-perceptions. Abnormal emotion is likely to be experienced by those who are high in negative affectivity, and by those who are low for reasons of denial. It is perhaps interesting to note that in this brief consideration of some of the links between emotion, personality and abnormality, the implications are of some type of cognitive involvement. The possible relationship between abnormal emotion and cognition are also considered by Rachman (1981) in his discussion of Zajonc's (1980) ideas (see Chapter 4).

Gellhorn and Loufbourrow

Although it is a quarter of a century old, Gellhorn and Loufbourrow's (1963) theory is still the only general theory of abnormal emotion. They review fields such as experimental neurosis, sensory deprivation and stress. In each case they argue that the hypothalamus is crucially involved. For example, they suggest that the hypothalamus is unable to cope with the reduced sensory input characteristic of sensory deprivation or that prolonged stress produces hypothalamic changes which may ultimately prove pathological. They maintain that in neurosis and experimental neurosis the two divisions of the hypothalamus are simultaneously activated; this produces automatic imbalance, which in turn leads to neurosis. The premorbid balance determines the extent of the reaction, in some cases there being no neurosis at all. They suggest that such effects occur following exposure to severe and unexpected pain, 'emotional excitement', particularly where life is threatened, and strong conflicts. Each of these will change behaviour, via their effect on the hypothalamus; the automatic changes may persist for years with the behavioural aspects varying from stuporous to manic, convulsive to compulsive.

Gellhorn and Loufbourrow support the role of the hypothalamus in emotion by their analysis of the physiological mechanism involved in such states as hypertension, peptic ulcers, nausea and fever. They believe that all evidence points to the importance of the hypothalamically controlled autonomic balance. For example, the SNS is predominant in sympathotonics, so disposing to hypertension. Gellhorn and Loufbourrow argue that the experience of different moods is the reflection of various states which exist between the extremes of hypothalamic action on the cortex, from emotional excitement (sympathetic – ergotropic) to sleep (parasympathetic – trophotropic). Also involved are positive feedback systems, such that if the skeletal muscles are somehow relaxed then emotional reactivity and possibly neurotic symptoms will be reduced (as in some aspects of behaviour therapy). Finally, they suggest that the physiological and pathological states of altered hypothalamic balance are characterized by changes in automatic reactivity and by changes in the whole personality. These effects will result partially from altered hypo-thalamic–cortical discharges. This picture is complicated further by the influence of the hypothalamus on the endocrine system.

Gellhorn and Loufbourrow extend their argument with the suggestion that there is an interrelationship between emotional disturbance, automatic changes and behaviour disorder. At this point their thesis weakens. They maintain, for example, that the fact that many investigators have emphasized the emotional aspects of psychoses and neuroses also points indirectly to the hypothalamus. Also, they suggest that perception depends on emotion and hence on the various links which exist between the hypothalamus and cortex. Anxiety modifies perceptual thresholds and perceptions are distorted in psychoses and neuroses. They argue that psychosis is characterized by two symptoms, which again point to the hypothalamus. (1) The psychotic will often not react to physical pain—the hypothalamus is pain-sensitive. (2) The catatonic schizophrenic state known as waxy flexibility can be produced by bilateral hypothalamic lesions.

In outlining the possible role of the hypothalamus and emotional responsiveness in the functional mental disorders, Gellhorn and Loufbourrow stress Walther's (1956) idea of the autonomic–affective syndrome, which shows fluctuations in mood, restlessness, anxiety and various autonomic disturbances. They argue that this syndrome is the response of a labile hypothalamic system to acute emotional stimuli and bodily stress and that a gradually developing imbalance from similar circumstances will produce hypertension or gastric ulcers. Walther also observed the autonomic–affective syndrome to precede functional psychoses and to occur transitorily during remission from a psychosis and on awakening from an insulin coma. This all supports the idea that 'mood' is determined by the state of the hypothalamus and its autonomic balance. Mood is determined by the hypothalamic–cortical discharge, and by the rate of secretion of various hormones.

Gellhorn and Loufbourrow's theory can be simply illustrated by their analysis of abreaction which involves reviving a memory of supposedly repressed unpleasant experiences and expressing the emotions related to them. This is believed to relieve the pressure on the personality: a release of emotions through reliving the experience. It is usually brought about by the administration of cortical depressants. Again, there is strong emotional excitement, then exhaustion, and then finally the disturbances disappear. Gellhorn and Loufbourrow suggest that the hypothalamic action which typifies intense excitement is enhanced by a cortical depressant since this releases the hypothalamus from cortical inhibition. After an abreaction there is some evidence for a physiological oscillation until the balance is restored; this is supported by the alternating laughter and crying which is seen at this stage. Thus, to Gellhorn and Loufbourrow, an abreaction consists of an intensive hypothalamic–cortical discharge, lessened hypothalamic–cortical interactions and the re-establishment of normal relations and excitability.

This has only been a brief description of some of Gellhorn and Loufbourrow's (1963) fundamental arguments. They range far wider than it is possible to show here. However, whatever the topic they touch on, it is with the same guiding principle: the conviction that the hypothalamus, its interactions with the cortex and the balance between its ergotropic and trophotropic systems are crucial to all aspects of emotion, particularly pathological emotion. At times they become highly speculative, but nevertheless provide a reasonably solid theoretical starting point for the study of pathological emotion.

Eysenck

Eysenck's (1976) theory is narrower than that of Gellhorn and Loufbourrow, being restricted to a consideration of the neuroses, but is worthy of consideration for its freshness of approach and interesting implications. To do justice to its description, it is first necessary to summarize the analysis he makes of the work of Watson and Mowrer. Eysenck points to three basic criticisms which can be levelled against Watson's view of neuroses as CERs. (1) The only study on which it was based was the famous one with Raynor which has never been replicated. No-one attempted to take genetic influences into account. (2) Eysenck points out that many neuroses do not develop from a single traumatic event. (3) There is direct evidence for strong fears other than those mentioned by Watson.

However, Eysenck suggests that these criticisms can be dealt with by substituting frustration for pain, the CER model then possibly pointing to the causation of neurosis. Again, though, he raises two objections. (1) Unreinforced conditioned responses extinguish; so then should neurotic reactions. It appears, though, that many neurose do not extinguish. In this regard Mowrer's two-factor theory is of some help, in which the original conditioning can be viewed as 'protected' by the second stage of instrumental conditioning in which relief from anxiety produced by the avoidance of the CS (conditioning stimulus) leads to a conditioned avoidance reaction. However, this still cannot account for all neuroses and the sometimes massive resistance to extinction. (2) Eysenck points out that there have been several attempts to explain the problems of the absence of extinction in neurotic behaviours, but that even if these were successful they could not account for the commonly observed enhancement effect in which a CS produces *more* and *more* anxiety with no reinforcement. Eventually, under these conditions the CRs (conditioned responses) are *stronger* than the original URs.

These difficulties lead Eysenck to his incubation model of neurosis. He argues that there are two possible outcomes of the presentation of CS alone. The CR might extinguish or might be enhanced, the latter being an incubation of anxiety or fear response. He believes it necessary to postulate two classes of CR which lead to these responses—those with drive properties and those without. Those which do not produce drive extinguish and those which do, lead to enhancement (incubation). Eysenck is not arguing that a CS with drive properties (for example, anxiety) is reinforced without the US. Rather, he is arguing that the US produces the anxiety originally, and the CS does not. Pairing the two leads to identical effects; both produce anxiety. Hence a positive feedback cycle develops, the CS-only reinforcing itself and incrementing the CR.

Eysenck points out that there is much experimental evidence in support of this theory, both from animal studies and from those with neurotic humans. These also point to the time and duration of the CS-only presentation as an important parameter in determining whether extinction or enhancement will ensue. He argues that important sources of influence are personality (particularly extraversion/introversion and neuroticism with their genetic basis and implications for conditioning), and the strength of the UR.

However, Eysenck also points out that incubation plus individual differences may still not be enough to account for all neurosis, and suggests that Seligman's (1971) idea of preparedness may give the final link. This suggests that whilst certain fears may not be innate, phobias are likely to be highly prepared to be learned by humans. If this is so they are also likely to be selective (to particular CSs) resistant to extinction, easily learned and probably noncognitive. Preparedness *may* interact with incubation.

It is easiest to finalize Eysenck's theory by presenting a brief summary of the conclusions he draws from it. (1) Maladaptive, unreasoning fears which can be innate or learned through modelling sensitize a person to certain types of stimuli and facilitate the conditioning of fear to these (preparedness). (2) The main process of such learning is classical conditioning, traumatic or repeated presentations of CS and US. (3) The main US in human conditioning is not pain but frustration. (4) CRs may extinguish with non-reinforcement (CS-only). (5) Sometimes CS-only leads to incubation or the enhancement of the response, more frequently the greater the CR—this is neurosis. (6) Incubation only occurs in CSs which have drive properties, which through positive feedback makes it functionally equivalent to the US. (7) The prime examples of CRs with drives linked to CSs are fear and anxiety (and possibly sex). (8) The most favourable conditions for CS-only leading to incubation are: short presentations of strong USs, high N versus low N scores and introverts versus extraverts. (9) CRs which develop from this process are stronger than the original URs and allow for the slow growth of neurosis. (10) The incubation model of neurosis is not open to the objections which can be made to the other learning models of neurosis.

Psychophysiology, symptoms and pain

Within the broader aspects of abnormal emotion, there are possible links between psychophysiological measures, the relationship between physical symptoms and emotion, and pain and emotion. This in turn leads on to a consideration of the important topic of psychosomatic disorder.

Research on abnormal psychophysiological responses has been concentrated mainly on anxiety. There have been two main approaches (1) Stimulation has been used to induce anxiety in normal subjects or psychiatric patients. (2) Differences have been measured between anxious and the normal.

The best results in this area come from cardiovascular measures. For example, in patients with anxiety states there is a general rise in heart rate (for example, Lader and Wing, 1966).

Lader (1969) points to the important problem of reactivity. If the resting levels of various physiological measures are studied there is no consistent relationship between anxious patients and normal subjects. Add stimulation and the differences become obvious, but tend to go in *both* directions. Anxious patients are sometimes more reactive than controls and sometimes less, although they do adapt more slowly to the experimental situation than normal subjects (for example, Kelly, 1966). Further, Lader (1969) suggests that anxiety can be seen as one of many states that can be distinguished as arousal becomes more intense. So, psychophysiological measures reflect the level of arousal and therefore the intensity of the emotion. But of course, he is forced to say that there are no *definite* physiological patterns yet delineated for the different emotions.

The possible relationships between emotion and psychophysiology, as instanced by anxiety, have implications for the manner in which people perceive their own physical illness. Studies by Pennebaker (1982) suggest that people perceive specific constellations of symptoms associated with specific emotions. These appeared to be unconscious links with similarities between people.

If symptoms and emotions are linked, is there a causal connection? The possibilities are fairly obvious. Sensations of symptom produced arousal may be labelled as a particular emotion, a perceived emotion might precede the sensation, or symptoms and emotion might merely occur together but be independent (or even identical). Pennebaker's studies suggest that the perception of emotion or symptom can occur in either order and either state can be causally related to the other. He argues that emotion provides a way of categorizing symptoms/sensations. This type of idea is really concerned with 'implicit psychophysiology', showing that we *can* match sensations and emotion, although we would normally not do so.

A further question in this context concerns the possible nature of a physiological link between emotions and symptoms. Various studies are reported by Pennebaker in which Ss are shown emotionally arousing stimuli (or tape or slides) and asked to rate the degree of physical symptoms they might experience if they had actually seen such things, or to actually rate various symptoms. Results show, for example that perceptions of temperature and stomach mobility related directly to Ss ratings of gruesome and sexual slides. However, monitoring of actual skin temperature and stomach mobility did *not* relate to the other measures. Emotions and symptoms can be linked independently of underlying physiological processes (for example, Skelton, 1981).

If physiology is not directly involved, what is the nature of the specificity between emotions and symptoms? One possibility is that people may infer an emotion—symptom link through a linguistic convention which was originally dependent on a physiological basis. Also, misattribution research (see Chapter 6) supports the idea that not only can people report which symptoms are associated with which emotions, they also use this information on deciding on their emotional experience. Pennebaker argues that the more complex the emotion the more that situational information is necessary to perceive it. He also speculates about the psychotherapeutic possibility of using drugs to induce particular symptoms and hence, through this, particular emotions.

Perhaps the most problematic aspect of extreme physical symptoms or sensations is that involving pain with its mixture of physical discomfort or hurt and consciousness. It is possible to view pain from all levels, ranging from the cellular to the experimental and social. People find it difficult to give phenomenological descriptions of pain and when they make the attempt, it is usually mixed with emotion. The basic paradox in pain is that although it usefully signals imminent damage it also, less than usefully, can impair sleep, appetite and the ability to think.

The relationship between emotion and pain varies enormously across situations, individuals and emotions. Examples of common links are fear following an unexpected, acute pain, an adaptive increase in vigilance and concern to escape. If pain lasts, the emotion involved appears to be distress, but if it continues unrelieved the result can be anger and aggression, particularly if the pain stems from the thoughtlessness of another person. Also there is an unusual link between pain and guilt in that pain can relieve guilt.

Analyses of the relationship between emotion and pain typically bring cognition into the account (for example, Izard, 1977), particularly in discussions of pain tolerance and attitudinal influences on pain. Tomkins (1963) lists a number of interactions between emotion, cognition and pain. For example: (1) unnoticed pain stimuli may be painless; (2) pain may appear quite different within a context of sexual excitement; (3) pain tends to be attenuated by any strong competing emotion.

Psychosomatic disorders

The links between physical symptoms, pain, emotion and cognition reach their most complex with the psychosomatic disorders, which have medical, organic symptoms, but an aetiology closely bound up with psychological variables. Although there have been many models and definitions of psychosomatics, most of them include specific reference to emotional disturbance (particularly anxiety) since the symptoms are seen in structures innervated by the ANS, the stomach, bronchioles and skin for example. (Instances of the more common disorders are asthma, peptic ulcers and hypertension.) However, it should be said at the outset that it is impossible to determine the extent of the emotional involvement, the degree to which emotion is a causative factor. Sternbach's (1966) view is that *all* illness is psychosomatic, but that some diseases have more obvious emotional aspects than others.

There have been many explanations offered for psychosomatic illness. For example, one viewpoint is that, biologically, emotions have come to energize us for survival. Nowadays, however, violent physical responses gain social disapproval. Hence, we experience emotion from physiological change, but have no opportunity to discharge our energy behaviourally. Organic changes persist and pathology results. Alternatively, it has been argued that psychosomatic disorder results when physiological responses in emotion are either too great or too small. This leads to excessive or inadequate adaptation. Finally, from the psychoanalytic viewpoint, it is said that if a person regresses for example, the inappropriate emotions associated with an earlier stage in his development lead to specific symptoms and pathology results.

These various ways of accounting for psychosomatic disorder can be categorized into two major groups, the biological and the psychological. The biological theory of psychosomatics most relevant to emotion suggests that patterns of autonomic reactivity are inherited. This is based largely on the work of such as Lacey et al. (1963) and Lacey and Lacey (1958), which shows consistent individual variation in automatic reactivity. They demonstrate that there are hierarchies of autonomic reactivity which are maintained whatever the stress might be. However, it could be that such differences are learned.

There are many psychological theories of psychosomatic disorder, but they can be exemplified by Mahl (1950). He points to the importance of fear (anxiety) in this context, and sees it as usually preventing the expression of behaviour. For example, a conflict between dependency and anxiety will lead to ulcers, between anger and anxiety to hypertension, and fear of separating or crying in children will lead to asthma. Mahl's theory is specific to ulcers and is based on studies with dogs, monkeys and students. For instance, he compared students who were to sit an examiniation later in the day with those whe were not. He found more free hydrochlorine acid in the 'anxious' than the 'non-anxious' group. Confirmation of this comes from Brady's (1958b; 1963) studies on 'executive' monkeys. Monkeys were studied in pairs, one being trained to respond to shock for both of them. Only the executive monkey developed ulcers. Although this work is open to alternative interpretations (Seligman, 1975) it is still reasonable for Mahl to suggest that acute anxiety leads to sympathetic dominance and therefore a decrease in stomach acid, but that in chronic anxiety the parasympathetic nervous system becomes dominant and acid is secreted. This is supported by research which shows that acid is only secreted after prolonged anxiety. To account for some individuals developing ulcers and others not, such a theory must also depend on the inheritance of physiological dispositions.

In making observations during the Second World War, Grinker and Spiegel (1945) showed that, in the field of battle, moderate anxiety facilitated performance. On the other hand, excessive anxiety results in inefficiency. Perceptions were distorted and the men became overreactive. They describe this as tending to lead to psychological and physical regression and dependency, which often became intensified towards the end of stressful stimuli. Various postwar studies confirmed these observations. This led Grinker (1953) to develop an influential analysis of psychosomatic disorder based on the assumption that anxiety is a basic cause of all types of behaviour.

At the start of this work Grinker was unable to find freely anxious people, so he had to manufacture anxiety. He did this in terms of four phases: alertness, apprehension, free anxiety and panic, the last two being seen as neurotic or pathological. Substances which needed to be broken down in the liver were injected and a measure taken of the amount of hippuric acid secreted. The rapidity and degree of the breakdown was used as an index of the extent of anxiety. As anxious patients were treated, so the amount of hippuric acid which they secreted fell. Grinker (1953) then moved on to an analysis of what he called 'system anxiety', i.e. he attempted to break down anxiety into its parts. He gradually developed what he believed to be reliable measures. These were based on: (1) observing patients diagnosed as anxious and developing specific verbal descriptions of their various degrees of anxiety; (2) interviewing the patients and taking statements as to their level of anxiety; (3) having the patients rate their own anxiety. After this, anxiety was manipulated individually, this being determined by what the interviewer had found to be most likely to disturb the patient. The best method was usually to block dyadic communication, although there were many methodological problems with this technique.

Grinker's analysis points to the possibility of anxiety having a central place in the aetiology of psychosomatic disörders. He (1953) also proposes that it is the individual conditioning of responses in the young organism that is critical for psychosomatics, rather than specific emotional constellations. Although Grinker made a considerable contribution both to the study of psychosomatic disorders and to the study of anxiety, the concepts involved remain somewhat obscure and nebulous.

Lader (1972) provides an extremely thorough analysis of the relationship between psychophysiology and psychosomatic disorder, in which he emphasizes arousal and response specificity rather than anxiety. His starting point is with the idea that both psychophysiological investigation and psychosomatic medicine assume a psychophysical parallelism—the assumption of a simultaneity of function rather than causal links. This promotes investigation of the relationships between behavioural and physiological events. Hence, within the framework of psychosomatics, it would not be said that anxiety causes tachycardia, but rather that verbal reports of anxiety accompany tachycardia, both in response to the same stimulus, a point clearly relevant to Pennebaker's (1982) analysis of emotion and symptoms.

Lader argues that two main concepts relate psychophysiology and psychosomatics—arousal and response specificity. He suggests that arousal helps our understanding by functioning as a construct between physiological measures and any concomitant emotions, with heightened arousal being a necessary condition for the experience of emotion. This will be reflected in any psychophysiological measure but to be meaningful must also be consistent with self-reports and observed changes in behaviour. Of course, Lader cannot deny the low intercorrelations which obtain between measures of arousal, but suggests that to use psychophysiological measures of arousal it is important to make clear distinctions between individuals, within individuals on one occasion, on different occasions and on any one occasion under different conditions.

The idea of psychophysiological response specificity is central to understanding of psychosomatic dysfunction since it gives a theoretical basis for variation in vulnerability of physiological systems from person to person. In support, Lader mentions Lacey's ideas on three types of response stereotypy (see also Fehr and Stern, 1970). There are: (1) intrastressor stereotypy, in which each subject shows a similar psychophysiological response pattern to a repeated stimulus; (2) interstressor stereotypy in which some subjects show similar patterns to different stimuli; and (3) situational stereotypy in which response patterns are related to the type of stimulation rather than to idiosyncrasies of subjects.

These ideas lead to the view that different somatic processes play different roles in different types of behaviours. This is related to an analysis of psychosomatic disorder with the notion of symptom specificity, namely that the particular physiological mechanism involved in some somatic complaints in some psychiatric patients, is especially susceptible to activation by stress.

From this discussion of the functions of arousal and response specificity Lader proposes a model of the psychophysiological basis for psychosomatic disorder. This is represented in Figure 8.

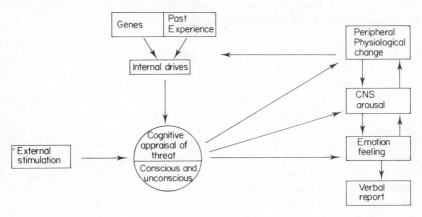

Figure 8. Lader's model of the psychophysiological basis of psychosomatic disorder.

In the terms of this model, environmental stimulation (unconditioned or conditioned) interacts with individual factors to produce general arousal. Appraisal follows and a specific emotion is experienced. These interactions may be conscious or unconscious and the emotions may therefore be rational or irrational.

Lader calls upon four factors to account for the individual response patterns in the concomitant psychophysiological changes. (1) Emotion is partly dependent on previous experience and physiological patterns vary according to the emotion. (2) Individual differences in responses to emotionally neutral stimuli are also very variable. (3) There are individual differences in the intensity of physiological responses; bodily systems are differentially involved. (4) The awareness of peripheral changes varies from bodily system to bodily system, hence there is differential feedback from these systems.

The final step in the argument inevitably brings in a discussion of severe or chronic environmental events. In Lader's view these interact with internal factors and produce high arousal and intense emotion. The physiological changes which accompany this may be morbidly severe in one bodily system. Also, there is a loss of adaptive responses when arousal is very high. All of which becomes self-perpetuating. If this process goes on for long enough then anatomical changes occur and psychosomatic illness appears.

There is a reasonable amount of empirical support for these carefully conceived ideas of Lader's, which clearly have important therapeutic implications particularly if they are considered in conjunction with the work of

Miller (for example, 1969) and others on the operant conditioning of autonomic responses, and biofeedback in general. Why, for example, should not *any* bodily disorder be capable of control in this way? Finally, it is again worth noting that this discussion of psychosomatic disorder and emotion has both implicitly and explicitly relied on cognition.

ANXIETY

Undoubtedly the central concept in any discussion of abnormal emotion is anxiety. It has probably had more written about it than has been written about any other emotion. In any discussion of anxiety there are usually characteristic problems. The most obvious of these is that of definition. There are many definitions of anxiety all of which leave unanswered questions. For example, is anxiety a convenient shorthand for certain behaviours which typify particular circumstances? Or is it an internal state which causes and can therefore be used to account for, some abnormal behaviour? What is the distinction between normal and abnormal anxiety? In reading what follows it will be helpful to bear in mind questions such as these.

Clinical descriptions of anxiety

Mayer-Gross *et al.* (1969) give a complete description of anxiety from the clinical viewpoint. In this context, anxiety reactions are regarded as normal adaptive responses which carry unpleasant emotional overtones. They are described as involving a strong expectation of danger, threat and distress for which an extra effort will be needed, but about which nothing can be done at the time. Physically, there is increased ANS activity, a rise in the output of adrenalin and a rise in blood pressure and heart rate. The skin becomes sweaty and pale and the mouth dry. Respiration is deep and frequent and the muscles lose tone. Rate of defecation and urination increases. If this state continues for some time, then fidgety movements begin to appear and digestion and sleep are affected. Sleep and concentration worsen and irritability, short-temperedness, frustration and impatience increases. From such a description it is difficult to decide whether we are dealing with a bodily state, a complex of feelings, or a set of behavioural and physiological responses.

Anxiety is regarded not only as the most common neurosis but also as basic to the other neurosis. It is often believed to occur as a secondary reaction to depression and it is implicated in specific phobias which tend to develop after stress in someone already suffering from an anxiety neurosis. Prolonged anxiety inevitably leads to physical debilitation, which in turn will often lead to hypochondriasis; an hysterical reaction may then result. Sometimes 'depersonalization' is seen in those anxiety states which are also symptomatized by agoraphobia.

Anxiety is regarded as coming about through organic conditions or as an accompaniment to some psychoses. Genetic and constitutional factors become implicated since it it associated both with immaturity and advanced age. For example, tendencies to anxiety are usually described as lessening markedly when the normal individual moves from adolescence to adulthood. Also, in any anxiety neurosis there is usually some precipitating factor, which may vary from organic to psychological stress. It is thought to be more likely to occur in those who are unsure of themselves, who doubt their ability to achieve and to cope and who magnify their own failures, worries, tensions and apprehensions. At best, these are people who need a great deal of support from others; they are immature, dependent and sexually cool.

The measurement of anxiety

If it is assumed that anxiety is a state of the organism then at present it cannot be measured directly. However, it is usually regarded as being reflected both behaviourally and physiologically and measures have been developed accordingly. Also many scales have been constructed which aim to measure subjects' self-reports of reactions to specific situations, which of course must be the aim if anxiety is viewed as a cognitive variable (for example, Mandler, 1976; 1984).

At the human level Eysenck (for example, 1969) is the major advocate of the usefulness of this view of anxiety. He argues that if anxiety is a drive then it should be governed by laws which apply to drives in general. These are seen most easily via the Yerkes–Dodson law which proposed a curvilinear relationship between drive and performance. Intermediate drives lead to optimal performance, optimal drive level depending on the difficulty of the task being performed. Although there are many examples of this relationship in the literature (for example Easterbrook, 1959; or Eysenck, 1964) they lack clarity and there is no single study which demonstrates the inverted U relationship to exist within one subject.

Such propositions imply that anxiety may be produced by particular situations and have its effect on virtually anyone who experiences it. However, anxiety-producing stimuli do not have similar effects on everybody: some seem to be habitually more anxious than others, reacting more strongly to situations which would not be productive of anxiety in others. Eysenck believes that studies of anxiety as a personality variable are best conducted via his own two-dimensional model with neuroticism (stability/unstability) and extraversion/introversion as the two orthogonal dimensions. He suggests (1967; 1969) as does Gray (1971) a strong hereditary basis for these dimensions and argues that they accord well with psychiatric classifications. For example dysthymic neurotics are introverted and unstable, whereas psychopaths are extraverted and unstable. He believes that these dimensions have a firm physiological basis.

A problem with the studies from which Eysenck's views on anxiety derive is that it is difficult to determine whether the results are due to differences in extraversion/introversion or stability/unstability. Also it is not clear how emotionality (neuroticism) is related to anxiety. Finally, it may be wrong, as Pichot (1969) argues, to equate a disposition to anxiety with pathological anxiety. It may be that 'anxiety disposition' is a proneness to respond to real danger maladaptively, and that anxiety states are the result of non-objective danger, coming from psychological conflicts for example (see discussion below of Spielberger's work on state and trait anxiety).

Some light is thrown on this area of study by Cattell (for example 1963) who suggests that anxiety is an underlying state which is reflected in many ways, introspective, behavioural and physiological, 'typical' measures for each of which he has developed. Whichever way he collects his data, they suggest, through factor analysis, that they depend on one main factor which can best be labelled anxiety. He argues in fact that factor analytic studies separate anxiety from neuroticism and stress reactions.

Theories of anxiety

There are two distinct levels to the many theoretical accounts which have been made of anxiety. There are broad theories which attempt to address anxiety in all of its facets and there are those which are restricted to an attempt to explicate the causes of anxiety. It would be counterproductive to list all of the theories of anxiety, so there follows a brief description of a few representative examples at each of these levels.

Anxiety and affection

Bowlby (1961; 1969) discusses the role of affectional bonds, particularly between mother and child, in the formation of pathological anxiety. He argues that two sorts of behaviour are related to subjective feelings of anxiety: escape and attachment. Escape is the result of sudden, strange events; attachment occurs when the members of a 'bonded pair' become separated from one another. Without discussing all the evidence it can be said with reasonable conviction that some children who experience an unsettled early home life are far more anxious than control children who have had more settled home lives. Also, they tend to be more aggressive and antisocial. Such separation anxiety only becomes pathological when it is extreme, although it is difficult to define what 'extreme' is in this context. Bowlby argues that such extreme reactions result from long or repeated periods of separation in strange surroundings.

Anxiety and genetics

Slater and Shields (1969) provide a review of studies designed to assess genetic influences on anxiety. Such studies range from selective breeding in animals, family studies and twin studies. They find for example that about 15 per cent of the parents and siblings of anxiety neurotics are also anxious, and that 50 per cent of the co-twins of anxiety neurotics are similarly diagnosed. However, only the usual conclusions can be drawn, namely that a predisposition to anxiety is best accounted for by an interaction between hereditary and environmental factors.

Experimental neurosis

The learning theory approach to anxiety has already been described. One specific form which this takes is that of work on experimental neurosis (see Lazarus (1972) and Wolpe (1961; 1966) for reviews). The basic question is that if neurosis (and hence anxiety) is learned, then how does this learning occur? In answer to this, Wolpe, for example, suggests that neurosis develops through simple conditioning.

Wolpe's view depends very much on the early demonstrations of so-called experimental neurosis in animals. These demonstrations led to the development of two methods for producing the effects: (1) subjecting animals to ambivalent stimuli when they are under the influence of a powerful drive; Pavlov (1928), for example, in a conditioning study made a circle of positive stimulus and an ellipse of negative stimulus; when he altered the semi-axes of the ellipse so that they more and more approximated circularity, his dogs responded with what can be described as generalized anxiety; (2) presenting animals with aversive stimuli in confined places.

Wolpe argues that if work on experimental neurosis can be extrapolated to the development of neurosis in humans under 'natural' conditions they will have to show three common features of learning. (1) Neurotic behaviour will be similar to that seen in the precipitating situation. (2) The neurotic response will occur in the presence of the original stimulus. (3) There will be stimulus generalization. Each of these features was shown in Wolpe's (1966) work on neurotic cats. From the human viewpoint, anxiety is thought to be important in any neurosis. The starting point for a neurosis is usually regarded as a single or recurrent anxiety producing event or a chronic anxiety situation. The stimuli present at this time are those most likely to become conditioned to neurotic anxiety responses. Also stimulus generalization is clearly evident in neurotic anxiety.

These are three representative examples of the hypotheses which have been put forward to account for the causation of anxiety. They differ markedly from one another and each has its limitations. However, the evidence for each is sufficient to suggest that it has some force. Indeed, the idea of experimental neurosis has led to the development of the very important therapeutic technique of desensitization. Anxiety is a complex topic and is likely to have complex causes.

The two broader theories of anxiety to be summarized now have been chosen because they seem to be particularly well conceived. However, for more comprehensive reviews see: Fischer (1970); Hoch and Zubin (1950); Lader (1969); Lazarus et al. (1952); Malmo (1957); Spence (1958); Spielberger (1966); Taylor (1956).

In his very useful attempt at theoretical clarification of anxiety, Spielberger

(1966) suggests that conceptual ambiguity has surrounded the term because it has been typically used in two different ways: (1) as a complex response—a fluctuating state, varying in intensity; (2) as a personality trait, in which there are individual differences. On the basis of factor analytic studies, Cattell and Scheier (1958; 1961) identified two distinct anxiety factors, which they labelled (1) trait anxiety and (2) state anxiety. Trait anxiety refers to stable, individual differences in relatively permanent personality characteristics and state anxiety to a transitory, fluctuating state.

In the field of transitory anxiety, most work seems to have focused on delineating the state and outlining the conditions which may invoke it. Krause (1961) concludes that it can be inferred from six types of evidence: introspective reports, physiological signs, gross behaviours such as bodily posture, speech, etc., task performance, clinical intuition, and responses to stress. However, he suggests that the most important of these is introspective report, since most researchers argue that all one needs to be satisfied that anxiety is present is this plus some physiological or behavioural indices. Martin (1961) describes anxiety as a complex response pattern which should be carefully distinguished from its eliciting internal or external stimuli. This concentrates attention on physiological/behavioural patterns which distinguish anxiety/fear from other emotions. This formulation also carries the implication that it is important to differentiate anxiety from the cognitions and behaviours which are learnt to reduce it, although recent theoretical developments would suggest that it is ill-advised to leave cognition out of any analysis of emotion.

Work on personality anxiety has mainly centred on subjects chosen because they differ in measured anxiety level. For example, patients with high chronic anxiety have been compared with non-anxious controls in stressful and non-stressful conditions. Using this method of investigation, Malmo (1950; 1957; 1959) concluded that the chronically anxious show much more reactivity and variability than normals, irrespective of stress. Also, many questionnaire-based studies have been carried out on normal populations (for example Spielberger and Smith, 1966). They suggest that subjects with high manifest anxiety scale scores have higher than average responses in situations involving some stress, but not otherwise. Trait anxiety may therefore be measuring anxiety proness. However, in more general terms, state anxiety is seen as an empirical reaction occurring *now* at some given intensity. Trait anxiety is a latent dispostion for a certain type of reaction if this is cued by the necessary stressful stimuli.

Spielberger (1966) proposes an interesting trait-state conceptualization of anxiety. He suggests that anxiety as a state is characterized by subjective, conscious feeling of apprehension and tension, with ANS arousal. Anxiety as a personality trait is more like a motive or an acquired behavioural disposition, predisposing the perception of a threatened environment and also predisposing disproportionate responses to these threatening situations. He suggests further that the arousal of anxiety states involves a series of events: (1) an external stimulus of internal cue; (2) if there is a cognitive appraisal of danger or threat, then an anxiety state develops; (3) the sensory and cognitive feedback may make the anxiety state act as a signal which initiates a behaviour sequence to deal with the danger or avoid it; (4) Also, cognitive or motivational defence processes have been effective in reducing past anxiety states by altering appraisals. (There are clear similarities between this view of anxiety and recent more general view of emotions.) Anxiety traits, on the other hand, reflect residues of past experiences which have determined individual differences in anxiety-proneness, the most important aspect of this probably being during childhood and involving parent/child punishment situations. Finally, he suggests that anxiety-trait level will only affect some anxiety-state responses, depending on the stressfulness of the situation.

Spielberger's ideas have been described in some detail since they represent a worthwhile attempt at synthesis in a very woolly theoretical field. They gain impetus because they were suggested by two distinctly developed areas of enquiry. Even so, they are speculative and the lack of a general definition is very apparent. Also, whether or not we are considering transient anxiety as well as anxiety as more permanent characteristic, the status of the concept remains obscure. We cannot say if it is best to regard it as a state of the organism or a set of physiological and behavioural responses. If we define it in terms of responses, then it is difficult to say whether it is best left there or whether these responses should be seen as symptomatic of some underlying (causal) condition. Also, the distinction between 'normal' and pathological anxiety remains hidden. The differentiation implicit in much of the foregoing discussion is one of degree; the more extreme forms of transitory or personality anxiety are considered abnormal. The difficulties with this viewpoint are: (1) the arbitrariness involved in drawing the demarcation line; (2) the question of whether or not different determinants might underlie normal and abnormal anxiety.

In his general texts on various theoretical considerations of emotion, Mandler (1976; 1984) also puts forward an interesting theoretical analysis of anxiety. He suggests that anxiety is a cyclical distress experienced by the newly born human infant, a fundamental distress, the crucial aspect of which is the perception of a variable and intense automatic visceral activity. The distress is not necessarily stopped by escape or avoidance; and at times it even reverberates, signalling more distress. There is *no* specific event antecedent to such distress, according to Mandler.

Secondly, Mandler suggests that anxiety is sometimes controlled by specific inhibitors, which eventually leads to the possibility that any organized activity will ward off the distress involved in anxiety. Thus, whenever the individual is helpless, anxiety results. This brings Mandler to the concept which has been central to his ideas for many years, that of interruption. Given the foregoing, then it follows that any situation that interrupts, or threatens an interruption of organized sequences of responses and that does not offer any alternative responses, will produce anxiety. He also argues that broad social and cultural variables can influence anxiety in four ways. (1) By providing people with organized sequences of responses that are very likely to be interrupted. (2) By interrupting organized response sequences. (3) By providing alternative response sequences. (4) By providing inappropriate alternatives to interrupted sequences.

In summary then, Mandler hypothesizes that anxiety has its ontogeny in the original distress experienced by the newborn. This has no antecedents but can be inhibited by specific responses such as sucking and rocking. Later these give way to an organized sequence of behaviour. The interrupted sequences of behaviour lead the organism to be helpless, which in turn alters arousal to anxiety, although interruption is only one condition which might produce helplessness. Mander's general point here is that disorganization and helplessness may well result in the same emotional state. Finally, if helplessness is extreme and ongoing, it may turn into hopelessness and depression. Clearly, Seligman's (1975) ideas are directly related to Mandler's, although he is concerned with learned helplessness, which Mandler views as an antecedent of the unattainability of a desired state.

Anxiety—conclusions

From this review of some of the research and theory into anxiety it must be concluded that much of the work is not of high standard. It tends to be descriptive rather than explanatory, with the descriptions themselves being made at many levels. It is not possible to give a precise definition of anxiety nor to distinguish normal anxiety from pathological anxiety. This is simply a reflection of the general field. There is a vast literature on anxiety, the surface of which has been barely scratched here, and it represents work carried out from many standpoints and according to many whims, idiosyncrasies and personal commitments to particular viewpoints.

It may be that, as Izard (1972; 1977) points out, those interested in abnormal emotions have not conceptualized conditions such as anxiety adequately. They have tended to treat them as global undifferentiated concepts, possibly because their main source of data has come from disturbed individuals in which negative emotion is so predominant or so confines them, that it seems undifferentiated. It would seem that anxiety is far too complex to be treated as an entity. Izard argues that it is an admixture of at least fear, distress, shame (shyness, guilt) and interest, all of which in his terms are differentiable emotional states. Perhaps it should be dealt with as such.

DEPRESSION

Depression has been chosen as the other main abnormal emotional condition to discuss in this chapter, since, like anxiety, it is relatively common, and also because it can take many forms, sometimes being categorized with the neuroses and sometimes with the psychoses. Again like anxiety, it is clearly a very complex emotional disorder, but also one which is experienced by all of us in mild form as part of everyday life. The reader is referred to Beck (1967) and Becker (1974) for a much fuller exposition of general depression and to Cantwell and Carlson (1983) for a discussion of childhood depression.

Description and classification

Although depression is exacerbated by many other conditions such as hypochondriasis and anxiety, it commonly has five sets of characteristics: (1) a sad, apathetic mood; (2) a negative self-concept involving self-reproach, self-blame, and so on; (3) a desire to avoid other people; (4) a loss of sleep, appetite and sexual desire; (5) a change in activity level, which may take the form of agitation, but more usually involves lethargy.

Beyond these typical characteristics attempts have been made to classify depression further. For example, a common distinction is drawn between psychotic and neurotic depression. This is both a matter of degree—psychotic depression is more extreme in all characteristics than is neurotic depression—and kind—psychotic depression is also characterized by delusions. The second common distinction is between endogenous and exogenous depression, the former being thought to be caused by a physiological malfunction and the latter environmentally. As might be imagined, it is often difficult to make this distinction with any confidence. In fact, the general question of the diagnosis of depression is awkward. The usual example is of a man whose wife has died. If he immediately shows the characteristics described above this is viewed as normal grief; if he still has them two years later, then it is depression. As ever, there is the problem of where the line is drawn.

Mendel (1970) took up some of these problems of whether or not to diagnose depression as normal. He points out that reported links between life events and depression might not provide causal links but may only be correlational. Typically, depression is seen to result from illness or a worsening of abilities. Rather than the direct causal explanation, environmental stress may be interacting with underlying predispositions. So since Mendel, the terms endogenous and exogenous depressionhave been applied to different patterns of reaction. Endogenous depression is seen as more severe than exogenous, being particularly characterized by slowed motor responses, a very deep depression, a lack of reactivity, a general loss of interest, insomnia in the middle of the night, and a lack of self-pity—conditions which do not characterize so-called exogenous, or environmentally generated, depression.

Theories of depression

It will be clear from the following, that theories of depression once again reflect the usual ways in which emotion in general has been viewed.

Psychoanalytic

The psychoanalytic theories of depression are best exemplified by Freud. He suggested that if a child's oral needs are over- or under-satisfied then he may develop an excessive dependency for self-esteem. Then, if he loses a loved person, he introjects the lost person into himself with full identification. As some of his feelings towards the loved person will have been negative, so he now comes to hate and be angry with himself. At the same time he resents the desertion of the loss because he feels guilty at the sins he committed against him. Then he mourns to separate the self from the lost person. In over-dependents this can develop into self-punishment and self-blame and lead to depression. The bonds are never lost and self-castigation continues, as does self-anger. So Freud sees depression as anger turned against the self.

Of course, there are many criticisms that can be made of such a loose theory. For example: What causes depression in those who have not lost a loved one? Why is love not turned inwards as well as anger? Where is the evidence that people interpret the death of someone as rejection? How much is too little or too much gratification at the oral stage?

Cognitive

Cognitive theories of depression can be exemplified by Beck (1967) whose starting point is that thoughts and beliefs cause emotional states. He argues that people become depressed through making a logical error; they distort events into self-blame. An event which is normally seen as just irritating (for example, spilling a drink) is seen as another example of the utter hopelessness of life. So, the depressed person only draws illogical conclusions about himself.

Beck describes such illogicalities as 'schemata'. So the depressed person interprets all events from the schema of self-depreciation and self-blame. Beck describes him as making four types of logical error: (1) arbitrary inference where there is no evidence for a conclusion drawn (I am useless because the shop was closed when I went to buy something); (2) selective abstraction in which a conclusion is drawn from only one element of the many possible (it is my fault that the firm I work for is full of unintelligent people); (3) Over-generalization, or the making of a massive conclusion from a trivial starting point (I am completely thick because I did not understand that one point); (4) magnification and minimization which simply involves errors in judging performance (I told one white lie and completely lost all integrity).

From Beck's viewpoint then, emotional reactions come from cognitions, and the interpretations of the world made by depressed persons do not accord with reality. He provides some correlational evidence that depressives do indeed think in this way. To endorse his thesis it must also be shown that the cognitive errors which depressives appear to make are *not* the result of their emotional disturbance.

Physiological

The basic point underlying physiological theories of depression is that if a genetic basis can be proved for the predisposition to depression then physiology must be an important link in this. The evidence on this point is only suggestive.

Nevertheless, two main types of physiological theory of depression have been put forward. The first is argued on the basis that there is a disturbance in the electrolyte metabolism of depressed patients. Sodium and potassium chlorides are particularly important in the maintenance of potential and the control of excitability in the nervous system. Normally there is more sodium outside the neuron and more potassium inside it, but in depressed patients this distribution is disturbed.

The second physiological based theory views depression as resulting from an inhibition of neural transmission. This is thought to occur in the SNS and to involve its neural transmitter—norepinephrine.

The major problem with these theories is that they mention no mechanisms to link psychological and physiological factors in depression.

Learning

The main idea behind the various learning theories of depression is that it is a condition which is mainly characterized by a reduction in activity which occurs when a large and accustomed reinforcement is withdrawn. There is no recourse to concepts such as unconscious mourning. Often it is argued that the depressed behaviour itself may be reinforced by attention and sympathy.

The most influential learning-based theory of depression is that of Seligman (1975), which characterizes depression as learned helplessness. This is based on seeing anxiety as the initial response to stressful situations, which, if a person comes to believe as uncontrollable leads to the anxiety being replaced by depression. In a typical experiment of a series to test this hypothesis, Seligman gave dogs severe inescapable shocks and then put these and unshocked dogs in an avoidance apparatus. Those without previous experience with shock soon learned to avoid, whereas the previously shocked animals gave up and seemed to passively accept the shocks in the new situation. Seligman describes this as a sense of helplessness acquired in the presence of uncontrollable stimuli affecting behaviour in other similar stimuli *can* be controlled.

Thus learned helplessness in animals provides a model of depression in man, there being remarkable similarities between animal and human data on the symptoms of the two conditions. This inevitably leads to an examination of common causes, which is more difficult since there has to be a comparison of data derived experimentally in dogs and on the basis of clinical observations in humans. However, it is commonly remarked that one of the aspects of human depression is that the patient seems unable to control events; he seems unable to act to reduce his suffering or to obtain gratification.

Childhood depression

In many ways, recent research into childhood depression (Cantwell and Carlson, 1983) has led to the development of theories which parallel those already described. Two types of biological theory stress, respectively neuroendocrine mechanisms and biochemistry whilst a related type of theory assumes genetic vulnerability to childhood depression. At another level there are the life models of anaclitic depression and the almost psychodynamic approach of Bowlby (1969) for example. However, the learned helplessness model has also been applied to childhood depression, similar in some ways to the idea that it develops through cognitive distortions which stem from unfavourable life experiences.

Conclusions

This brief overview of depression permits little in the way of conclusion other than it is possible to account for it in many ways, each of which has its plausible aspects. At present, it is not possible to determine which type of theory is likely to lead to a greater understanding. Although Seligman's views on learned helplessness will probably remain influential, it seems increasingly important, as in most other aspects of emotion, not to leave cognitive factors out of consideration.

Clearly, Seligman is only attempting to account for depression which is reactive to environmental stress and which takes the form of lethargy rather than agitation. This is an obvious limitation of the learned helplessness hypothesis. Also there is a major difference between this view and that which regards depression as the result of reduced reinforcement. The latter view is noncognitive, simply regarding behaviour as a function of reward, with mood altering as a function of behaviour. The learned helplessness hypothesis highlights an individual's *perception* of the degree to which he is in control of the environment and hence has an important cognitive element.

PSYCHOPATHY

No discussion of abnormal emotion would be complete without mention of psychopathy, since psychopaths are usually described as emotionally flat and relatively free of anxiety. They are also incapable of learning avoidance responses frequently thought to be based on fear. Clearly then, their emotional reactions are unusual, not to say abnormal.

In an interesting analysis of psychopathy and emotion, Schachter and Latane (1964); but also see Mandler, 1984) distinguish two types of crime: (1) where motivation or passion becomes unbearably high, and (2) where fear is weak. They suggest that if the second condition becomes chronic, psychopathy results.

Schachter and Latane had their subjects rigorously selected by prison authorities using Lykken's (1957) procedures, including his anxiety scale—on which psychopaths should score very low. In the experimental situation, subjects faced an arrangement of lights and switches which represented a 20-choice point mental maze, a correct switch leading to the next choice, and so on. All errors were accumulated on a visible counter; some of these were punished with shock, which, however, could be avoided by the appropriate selection of switches. Epinephrine or placebo was injected just before the experimental run, and pulse, heart rate and questionnaire measures were taken. All subjects were given a pre-experimental talk but were told to expect no side effects from the hormone (Suproxin) injection.

Results comparing normals and psychopaths showed them to learn the positive maze tasks at the same rate. Also, this measure did not distinguish between epinephrine and placebo groups. However, normal subjects steadily learned to avoid shock, psychopaths did not. Avoidance seems to be mediated by fear, which is not present in psychopaths—a replication of Lykken's results. On the other hand, after epinephrine injections psychopaths learned the avoidance task very well, in comparison with normals. There was also a marked relationship between the degree of psychopathy and the post-epinephrine avoidance learning.

The obvious explanation of these results is that psychopaths are less sympathetically responsive, the implication being that they have a different physiological system from non-psychopaths. But this was not supported by the pulse-rate data. Further analyses showed that the greater the psychopathy the higher the pulse rate. Valins (1966) showed this to be due to *greater* automatic reactivity in the psychopath. Schachter and Latane also make the point that the best predictor of avoidance learning in their study was whether or not the subject was sensitive to epinephrine. They argue that psychopaths are more sensitive to epinephrine and that epinephrine sensitives should tend to behave psychopathically.

In discussing their results, Schachter and Latane conclude that a high automatic reactivity characterizes both those that are high in anxiety and those that are low. Schachter's other studies show that cognitive and situational factors influence whether a given physiological state will be labelled as an emotion. Hence, the psychopath, although ultrasensitive autonomically, also reacts to stimuli to which others would not. For him, little stands out from his environment. It may be that he has not learned to apply emotional labels to his states of arousal. On the other hand, the anxiety neurotic *constantly* interprets his world in emotional terms and gives cognitive explanations of what is occurring. Returning to the original idea of two types of crime. The psychopath would be expected to commit the 'cool' unemotional crimes, the 'normal' the passionful ones.

Valins (1970) interprets Schachter and Latane's results somewhat differently. His first suggestion is that the psychopath may simply not perceive his own bodily changes; there is no evidence to support this. Alternatively, he maintains that the psychopath may experience and perceive his bodily changes but nevertheless ignore them, not use them to appraise an emotional situation, an interpretation for which he has some experimental support. As with so many aspects of emotion, it seems impossible or at least inadvisable to consider the emotional reactions of psychopaths without dealing with cognition.

EMOTION IN THE RETARDED

An important but neglected apsect of abnormal emotion has been the study of emotion in the mentally retarded (see Strongman, (1985) for an extended discussion). Historically, the major thrust of research on this population has been concerned with so-called emotional disorders. Since the mentally retarded are clearly disordered, behaviourally and cognitively, within the guidelines provided by the traditional medical model, it has been assumed that their emotions are also disordered. Although at first sight this might seem to be a reasonable assumption, it is grossly ill-founded since it equates emotional disorder with psychiatric disturbance and tells us nothing about emotion. This surprisingly dated approach has continued into the 1980s, the most extreme example being that of a book by Szymanski and Tanguay (1980), entitled *Emotional Disorders of Mentally Retarded Persons,* which contains almost nothing which is recognizable to a psychologist as relevant to emotion.

In spite of this assumption of emotional disturbance in the retarded, there have been very few actual studies of it, by far the best of these being that of Gray *et al.* (1983). They demonstrated that the recognition of emotional expression is directly related to the degree of retardation, with somewhat different confusions and errors than those made by people of normal intelligence. Other than a small handful of such studies, knowledge about emotion in the mentally retarded is very limited. The reasons for this neglect of a potentially important area probably stem from the obvious difficulties of research, the pre-empting of attitudes by psychiatrically based assumptions about emotional disturbance, and reflect the general neglect of the retarded for many years.

Strongman (1985) makes the case that two main approaches have a potentially useful application to the understanding of emotion in the retarded. Although the behavioural analysis of emotion has declined in its general influence, its research techniques such as CER still offer considerable promise in the study of emotion in the mentally retarded. Similarly, within a broadly behavioural framework, recent work on emotional expression and recognition is directly applicable to the study of mental retardation.

Even more important in this context is recent research and theory into emotional development in infants, some of which is described in Chapter 6. This sophisticated research conducted within a naturalistic observational framework suggests a series of relevant questions to ask about the nature of emotional experience and expression in the retarded and leads to many exciting research possiblities. The questions concern matters such as the reliance of emotion in the retarded on socialization and interaction with primary caretakers and its relationships with cognition. The techniques of study transpose readily and this type of basic observational research on emotion in the mentally retarded could have significant implications for research, theory and therapy in this group. In the end, emotion in the mentally retarded may be shown to be undisturbed and, as a relatively primitive part of general functioning, possibly little different in some respects from emotion in the non-retarded.

A GENERAL THERAPEUTIC PROGRAMME

There are many aspects of therapy which could be examined in the context of emotion. However, attention will be focused on the work of Izard (1972) which is most directly relevant. On the basis of his own theory and evidence, he has developed a therapeutic programme which is concerned centrally with emotion. A number of fundamental principles lead him to suggest a new approach to psychotherapy. The principles are as follows, and have mainly been mentioned earlier in this text. (1) Fundamental emotions are innate and universal. (2) Fundamental emotions are recognized and labelled consistently by most people in most cultures. (3) Fundamental emotions provide people with the capacity for a common set of subjective experiences and expressions. (4) Emotional expressions have special communication value since they are universally recognizable. (5) This communication enhances understanding of subjective experiences and helps in the development of a therapist–client relationship. (6) The experiences and expressions of the fundamental emotions form the basis for understanding complex emotions, cognitions and actions. (7) Fundamental emotions generate cognitive labels which translate into a common set of meanings.

According to Izard, when patients are in the therapeutic situation they do not tend to characterize their life patterns by speaking of discrete emotions; they normally use general terms and descriptions. He suggests that the aim should therefore be to make this vagueness into discrete emotions. To this end the therapist should administer certain measures of emotion and then develop a hierarchy of situations for each emotion involved in the various problems of adjustment experienced by the patient. If the discrete emotions are not generally available then hierarchies involving stress broadly concerned might be used instead.

Having made such analyses the therapist should put the patient through a series of exercises which involve relaxation, the visualization of important life situations and an attention to internal emotional signals. The therapist should also check the involvement of the striate muscles and viscera (with psychophysiological measures) and persuade the patient to imagine increasingly difficult situations. Izard feels that this procedure would allow a delineation to be made of whatever discrete emotions were involved in the patient's problems. It would also allow the therapist to assess whether or not the patient receives usable signals from the striate muscles.

Moving on to the matter of emotional control, Izard suggests that any component of emotion or subsystem of personality is potentially usable. However, he feels that the best policy is to attempt to use those which relate to the striate muscles, particularly those concerned with facial expression and posture, since these can initiate, enhance, inhibit or truncate an emotion. One possibility, for example, is to generate one emotion which will inhibit another. He suggests two ways in which this might be achieved: (1) selective relaxation to inhibit unwanted aspects of expression; (2) role-playing or therapist–client interactions. He also mentions the techniques described above of counter-conditioning, self-assertion and desensitization as useful adjuncts.

There are two alternatives in Izard's view when dealing with a complex condition such as anxiety. It can be analysed into the discrete emotions involved, or it can be treated in a global way with behaviour therapy, although he argues that the latter by itself is not enough. For example, where the emotion process is incomplete or the neuromuscular component is dissociated from it, autonomic conditioning might be necessary.

In particular Izard sees emotion itself as an important means of the control of emotion, again, for example, using one emotion to inhibit another. Also cognitive control may be achieved by imaginal activity. Overall, he argues that it is best to have a combination of neuromuscular, emotional and cognitive control.

Izard outlines two main principles which normal personalities can use to increase their spontaneity and effectiveness and which therapeutic programmes should employ. (1) Each experience of emotion has an inherently adaptive aspect, so the adaptive action involved should be executed. (2) Emotional control can be achieved by the appropriate integration of emotion, cognition and action.

Concerning the integration of emotion, Izard argues that the therapist should work with stressful situations, in an attempt to move towards relief and once again an analysis of what is involved into discrete emotions. The patient should be taught whatever is essential for understanding the natural process of emotion, and also about bodily signals, particularly those which come from the striate muscles. He or she can use these in the control of emotions, either to relax or to assume postures (facial) other than those which he or she would normally in a given situation. Alternatively, the patient could be put through the enactment of a series of mildly emotion-provoking situations whilst engaging in progressive relaxation—a procedure which has clear foundations in progressive relaxation and desensitization.

Hence the first stage in therapy is for the patient to develop these skills. Then the patient should be trained to allow the signals from the striate muscles to impel and guide his or her actions (both verbal and behavioural). This will inhibit the build-up of tension and so serve an adaptive function. Notice that Izard is here advocating training, so he is straightforwardly saying that the use of cues from the striate muscles can be learned.

Izard's general point is that if emotional expression or action is suppressed or postponed then there is an increased likelihood of maladaptive functioning. Vicious circles are set up which may be exacerbated by repression. Therapy then takes the essential form of enacting more and more emotional situations in appropriate ways.

In his rather radical ideas for emotionally based therapy Izard is working towards the concept of an optimum personality. He seems to hold a concept of personality and behaviour which is very similar to self-actualization. He views all the subsystems in his theory of personality as being free to interact so as to capitalize on all their various inherently adaptive aspects. But in this freewheeling system emotions are given the most important role.

In the development of the optimum pesonality, Izard believes five processes to be involved: (1) emotional experience; (2) the differentiation in awareness of the discrete emotions; (3) emotional expression; (4) action which follows from the inherent adaptiveness of an emotion; (5) the optimal integration of emotion with cognitions and interactions between persons and the person and his environment. To allow Izard his own final word: 'personality functioning is optimally effective when the person's goal and the cognitive and motor processes constituting the goal-directed activities are congruent with the underlying emotional processes which initiate, sustain and guide the effort'.

CONCLUSIONS

The aim of this chapter has been to give some idea of research and thought about what happens when emotion goes wrong in some way that appears too injurious to the individual or to others. This is clearly an unusual state of affairs since it is virtually axiomatic that emotion is germane to survival. Also, some attention was given to the nature of emotion in those who might be experiencing disorders which are not defined by their emotional aspects but which nevertheless might have emotional implications.

Unfortunately, one conclusion that must be drawn is that there remains a long way to go in the understanding of abnormal emotion, be it the extremes of anxiety or depression or the emotional facets of psychosomatic disorders or psychopathy. One of the major difficulties is that apart from Gellhorn and Loufbourrow's early attempt and Izard's analysis of emotion-based therapy, broad theories of abnormal emotion have been scant.

Sometimes abnormal emotion springs from what, to the individual, are abnormal and extreme external situations and sometimes it seems to come from within. This is further complicated by the fact that within psychopathology the emotions might not be particularly abnormal in the statistical sense— if comparisons are made across individuals it might not even be an extension of normal emotion. Frequently, it is the interaction between the individual and his or her circumstances which are unusual. This may stem from an abnormal environmental situation and/or from an abnormal constitution which predisposes extreme reactions to relatively mild stimuli. Abnormal emotion may be little more than a corollary to this.

As with all aspects of emotion considered in this text, the one concept which keeps demonstrating its significance to an understanding of abnormal emotion is cognition. This is shown even in attempts to characterize emotion in the mentally (cognitively) retarded. It may be that what is abnormal in abnormal emotion is cognition, or the links between cognition and emotion, or the general process involved when the individual appraises the environment. Again it is the cognitive approach to emotion which at present offers most hope for an understanding of what is involved when emotion goes awry.

9.
The Individual, The Environment, The Culture

The preceding chapters, which make up the core of this book, have been aimed at providing a comprehensive view of emotion as psychologists currently conceive of it. It should be clear from this that there are certain principles that emerge and conclusions that can be drawn. Some of these will be discussed in the final chapter. However, this is not the whole story. Although there has been a burgeoning of theory and research into emotion, it could be argued that a great deal is still missing, both from the layperson's and from the scientist's viewpoint, not that these need be dissimilar. At one level, what is missing can be characterized as 'meaning' and at another as a consideration of some of the many areas of human existence to which emotion is of great significance and yet which have so far received scant attention in this text.

If non-advanced students or interested non-psychologists were to skim through this book, they would probably be surprised, if not bewildered or even aghast, to find little discussion of emotion as it impinges on them, personally. For example, there has been no space given to emotion and sex, or even of sex differences in emotion, both of which are matters of daily import in people's emotional lives. Similarly, there has been little mention of how emotion impinges on personality, or personality on emotion, nor of the manner in which the natural or the man-made environment helps to determine emotional reactions. Furthermore, what of emotion in the arts, in literature and drama, and in music? In fact, what of the interrelationships between emotion and culture and the general although difficult matter of emotion and aesthetics and creativity?

It is then with these types of topic that the present chapter is concerned, with the aim of helping in the general appreciation of the search for meaning which lies behind emotion. The progression in this search will be made from individual factors, through the impact of the environment, to the place of emotion in culture, and cultural factors in emotion. The list of matters included is not exhaustive, but is aimed at both stimulating and broadening interest in emotion, as well as showing that its more personally significant aspects can be, and, indeed, are being, studied.

THE INDIVIDUAL

Personality

The obvious starting point for a consideration of the links between emotion and personality is with Freud and Jung (see Keen (1977) for an extended discussion). In fact, other than in the work of Izard, very little can be found which is relevant to these links since the time of Freud. Within this psychodynamic tradition of personality, emotion is viewed as qualitatively different from thought, as motivational and hence more powerful than thought, as referring to invisible psychic processes and as expressing things which are not apparent to the conscious mind.

Emotion is believed always to involve more than the immediate situation, that is, something within the individual. Personality theory can also provide four focuses for the analysis of emotion—the body, the family, the rules and regulations of behaviour, and a questioning consciousness.

Bodily pleasure and pain is the basis of the pleasant/unpleasant dimension of emotion. The family provides the context for the basic emotional reactions to people. In this focus, fantasy is important, in terms of both cognition and emotion. Identification with the same-sex parent establishes sexual identity, but there are cross-sex impulses which are repressed, the result being anxiety. Jung's theory of personality is prospective and speaks of self-realization, whereas Freud's is retrospective and is concerned with the death instinct. Furthermore, Jung's archetypes involve a passionate, emotional engagement with the world whilst remaining at peace with the self. Emotions come to be seen as the expressions of things which are beyond conscious control.

According to Freud and Jung, there are a number of factors which determine that the various emotions are different. Instinct, for example, ensures that hate is aggressive and love is sexual. The ego, however, promotes relational, reflective and anxious emotions. Cognitive factors are crucial, in that they permit the making of subtle distinctions. The relationship between the individual and society is represented in personality, which determines both how much guilt and how much anxiety the individual feels.

Since Freud and Jung, the emphasis in personality theory has been either on the existential or matters interpersonal. These suggest new interpretations of contingencies of life to which people react emotionally. For example, the clinical literature abounds with the suggestion that it is dangerous to block emotional expression. Within this interpersonal framework, relation emotions such as love and hate become events that happen between people. Keen (1977) argues that any of the more recent approaches to personality theory suggest that cognition and bodily events both precede and follow perception and emotional experience, there being no discrete beginnings and ends to these processes.

Mandler (1984) makes the most searching recent analysis of emotion—

personality links. The study of personality is clearly concerned mainly with individual differences. Emotional experiences are also unique to the individual. Mandler suggests two approaches to analysing individual differences. The first is to devise personality scales that might characterize individual emotional reaction. The second is to search for particular cognitive systems within a culture which will allow individual prediction of emotional responses. An example of this is the psychoanalytic approach.

Personality tests provide one measure of cognitive interpretation. A good example is Eysenck's concern with the two major dimensions of personality tests—introversion–extraversion and neuroticism, which he discusses in terms of conditionability and emotionality. Mandler argues that introversion–extraversion characterizes people according to tendencies to view events as threatening, punishing or frustrating. Neuroticism (emotionality) is concerned with amount of arousal.

The psychoanalytic approach to the personality–emotion link has already been discussed to some extent. A fundamental aspect of it is that emotional structures are developed in the first few years of life, with prototypical cognitive schemas being built up which relate to coping with problems in the oral, anal and genital areas. By now, it is clear, as Mandler trenchantly observes, that the abstract nature of much of this type of theorizing renders it of limited value, particularly with respect to prediction. Even so, it should be noted that it does provide yet another perspective on possible relationships between emotion and cognition.

Mandler (1984) also takes an entirely different perspective to that of traditional personality theory on the question of individual factors in emotion. He considers the matter of a situation becoming emotionally significant when it is recognized as being personally relevant. An example would come from the graded reaction we might have to an accident depending on the extent of our involvement with its victim. Mandler argues that it is projection of the self into the situation, based on previous experiences, which leads to this effect.

In a similar vein, Mandler suggests that emotion might be related to degree of visual imagery. Those who prefer visual effects of imagery are more concrete than those who prefer the verbal mode of imagery. So high imagery people are more likely than others to be bonded to the immediate emotional demands of whatever their circumstances might be. In general, Mandler suggests that the evidence points to the hypersensitivity of visualizers and the calm, equanimity of verbalizers. He has made an interesting beginning in this analysis of what might be termed cognitive style and emotion.

Pain

Like emotion, pain is an extraordinarily difficult topic, involving obvious physical elements with subjective experience. It is not restricted to neural and physiological aspects, particularly where tissue damage is concerned. At the level of sujective experience, pain appears to be linked with emotion and is discussed here because of its obvious intra-individual aspects. Of course, like emotion it also has its social aspects, a signalling function concerned with the need for sympathy and help.

As mentioned in Chapter 8, Izard (1977) makes an interesting analysis of the relationship between emotion and pain, within the general context of vast individual differences, particularly since a given pain can activate more than one emotion. Four of Izard's examples will suffice to make the point. Fear follows acute and unexpected pain, as a clearly adaptive reaction which increases alertness and a keeness to escape. It is even possible that this type of pain is an innate releaser of fear. Distress occurs after lasting pain, again increasing concern to remove the cause and helping in sympathy and compassion.

If pain is unrelieved, it can lead to anger, although this depends to some extent on the environment. For example, pain stemming from someone else's thoughtless act can lead to anger. If pain and anger occur together, the threshold for striking out in aggression is very low. Finally, pain is related to guilt, in being able to relieve it under some conditions.

Of particular interest in the frame of reference which is being built not just in the present chapter but in this book as a whole, there is a long line of thought from Tomkins (1963) through to Izard (1977) which links pain, emotion and cognition. Izard refers to pain setting into motion a chain of perceptual–cognitive processes with the emotion–cognitive structures involving pain having an important effect on pain-tolerance, with parental attitudes towards pain being significant. In general, extraverted, field-dependent people are most tolerant of pain and neurotics are most likely to complain of pain, as do older people, those with more siblings and those from lower socioeconomic classes.

There are a number of standard interactions between pain, emotion and cognition, many of which are well known in the everyday world. For example, unnoticed pain stimuli may be painless, and pain may either pass unnoticed in a context of sexual excitement, or even in some conditions add to it. If pain is combined with a positive emotion it tends to be decreased, and it is even attentuated by any strong competing negative emotion, fear or anger for example. So pain need not be enhanced by fear. Finally, it would seem that pain typically elicits some other emotion. The links, then, between pain, emotion and cognition are intricate and again point to the compelling nature of accounts of emotion involving cognition.

Sex

Engaging in sexual intercourse, making love, lusting, being in love, always involve complex emotions. All of the intricate behaviours concerned result from arousal through brain processes, hormones, external stimulation, imagery and thought in massive interaction, all tempered by learning and experience. As with much of the recent work on emotion, the links between this and sex have been most thoroughly explored by Izard (1977) and Mandler (1984) and it is their ideas that form the basis of the present discussion.

The links between sex and emotion have their roots both in biological processes and in psychological processes, including the cognitive and the experiential. With his usual approach, Izard deals with the interrelationships of various emotions with sex, beginning with interest, which he terms an emotion, although others might disagree. It is obvious that the sex drive can dominate both cognition and action, an effect which is enhanced by interest or excitement. This produces urgency. In Izard's view, if interest is combined with joy and certain emotion–cognitive structures, the result is love. Of course, explicating the nature of such structures is the problem. Similarly, observations in sexual interest can lead to what is regarded as maladjustment, as in fetishism, for example.

Whereas interest or excitement interact positively with sex and enhance it, an emotion such as fear is incompatible with it. For example, in males fear may render an erection impossible, may make one collapse, or may lead to premature ejaculation. The effects on the female are just as inhibiting. Fears related to sex appear to be socioculturally determined, generally in modern culture the fear of being discovered in clandestine sex being replaced with the fear of failure. All of which builds up from self-doubts which depend on stereotypes which are more than a hint ridiculous.

Although attitudes have become far more liberal during the last quarter of a century, guilt concerning sex is still around. In Izard's view, this may not be a learned relationship. Guilt about sex tends to follow from ideas about commitment and responsibility which are adaptively important. However, if the sociobiologists are right, males should feel less guilt than females about sexual encounters that society in general might frown upon since they might very well be increasing their chances of spreading their genes. Guilt about sex tends not to be as strong as fear and so may not inhibit sexual performance. Rather it tends to regulate the rate of intimacy, as well as appearing to habituate with time and practice.

Under some conditions, sex can be related to other negative emotions such as anger, disgust or contempt, any of which can be very harmful. The possibilities range from angry arguments which end in lovemaking through to the apparently worsening problem of rape. Clearly, either disgust or contempt associated with sex can be harmful to the individual or to his or her partner.

At a more general level, Izard sees strong links between sex, emotion and cognitive structures. For example, sexual attitudes show considerable variation with age, probably owing to both socialization and parental modelling. Even more generally than this, there have been enormous changes in society in the direction of the liberalization of sexual attitudes and an acceptance of sexuality.

Mandler's (1984) discussion of emotion and sex is rather more searching than Izard's. He makes it turn on the basic differences which appear to obtain between sexual arousal and the arousal which is central to other emotional experience. His argument, which is endorsed by virtually everything which has been considered in this book, is that most emotions are determined by an interplay between sympathetic arousal and cognitive interpretation. However, during sex, an important role is played by parasympathetic arousal.

During the early stages of sexual arousal there is a unique series of responses, such as vaginal lubrication and tumescence. These are not only integral to sexual arousal, but are also parasympathetically determined and their perception, has a significant psychological function. Later, of course, at orgasm, sympathetic arousal takes over. Thus it is implied with good reason by Mandler, that we might expect the emotions involved in lust to be different in nature from others. Also, the interplay between sympathetic and parasympathetic arousal might well account for the inhibiting effects that emotions such as fear can have on sexual arousal.

In the most interesting part of his discussion, Mandler goes on to consider the possible relationships between romantic love and lust. Love remains imperfectly understood, although some psychologists are at least beginning to make the attempt, rather than leaving it to the poets. Whatever view one takes of love, psychologically it must be amongst the sympathetically aroused emotion conditions. If so, argues Mandler, then strongly aroused love may well inhibit the early stages of sexual arousal. Although the force of this argument can be seen, somehow it still does not compel, and it would be extraordinarily difficult to study empirically, even in the present liberalized climate.

Mandler also speculates about possible cognitive structures that might relate appraisals or interpretations to lust and love. For example, being pushed to love X rather than lust after X may inhibit the sexual response. Whereas, sexual responses may be related to X's with whom such a relationship is not possible. In Mandler's view, if different occasions and persons, that is, different cognitions, produce love and lust, whether this is culturally or individually determined, there will be difficulties. Sexual arousal will be problematic and interpersonal relationships impaired.

Interestingly, Mandler extends his love–lust argument to other emotions that may occur during sexual arousal. Romantic jealousy provides a good example, its determination being most appropriately seen as dependent on a situation which is evaluated as being likely to lead a loved one to be lost to someone else. It is probably Berscheid's (1983) analysis (see Chapter 7) of meshed relationships that offers the most cogent account of jealousy viewed from a situational cognitive perspective.

Clearly, the emotional aspects of sex are a very significant part of life, although they have been considerably under-researched. They are not well-understood, although it is apparent that they may have essential differences, particularly in their arousal and its interpretation, from the remainder of the emotions. Also, to date, almost no headway has been made in gaining an understanding of what is arguably the most important of the human emotions, or emotional complexes, love. However, since it is indisputable that a major, if not the major, component of love is cognition, the increasing and necessary concern with cognition by those who study emotion, may lead to more psychologists making the attempt to embrace love, at least with their theories.

Sex differences

For once, to leave aside the dispassionate objectivity of the writer of a textbook, and make a value judgement, even though a slight one, gender differences are trivial and boring for the most part. They tend to be built into research designs in case they show something. If they do, there is almost no theoretical import to them. If they do not, the researcher is then merely in a position to say that they were controlled for.

However, possible sex differences in emotion ought to be briefly considered, if for no other reason than to explore the foundations of one of the most commonly held stereotypes. After all, stereotypes must be based on something. The stereotype has it that, in comparison with men, women are illogical and emotional, at the whim of their feelings, which they find it very difficult to hide. Is this so?

Nicholson (1984) provides a straightforward summary of the evidence. For example, adult women cry more than adult men, although young boys cry more than young girls. Data from adjective checklists show that women view themselves as more anxious, moody and emotional than men, such differences also being seen in children. However, observational studies of children do not support this and it is also clear, for example, that boys are less prepared than girls to admit fear.

It is thought that women are more prone than men to psychosomatic disorders, which might point to their greater emotionality. Nicholson, however, points out that even if this is so it is neither neurotic nor illogical to be emotional, emotions in fact being essential to existence. Furthermore, medical practitioners tend to have different expectations about psychosomatic disorders in males and females, which may well help to confirm their diagnoses. Finally, it is also the case that women are more likely than men to admit to disorders that may be psychogenic. Of course, this in itself is a sex difference, but not in emotion.

However, women do seem more susceptible than men to neurosis, at least, they do if they are married and under 35. If they are single, they are less likely to be neurotic than if they are married, and are also less likely to be so than men. Apart from this there is very little evidence to support the view that women are more emotional than men. However, they do tend to pay more attention than men to other people's emotions, they are more affected by them, and perhaps might be regarded as more emotionally sensitive than men, although this is more speculative.

Nicholson spends some time considering the commonly held view that women cannot help being more emotional than men some of the time because of their periodic hormonal changes. Certainly, it is by now indisputable that premenstrual tension exists, but that not all women are affected by it.

However, in those that do suffer from it, their work is not much affected, even though it might seem to them that it is. Also, in some cases, those women that do periodically fluctuate in their emotions, may do so because of cultural expectations or suggestions rather than because of built-in propensities. Of course, there may also be periodic emotional differences in males, a possibility which has not been much researched.

Considering laboratory studies, Nicholson points out that if subjects are stressed by having to carry out a difficult task in noisy conditions, males and females do appear to react differently. Males show a larger physiological response than females, whereas females say that they have been more affected consciously by the experience. Thus, emotion-evoking experiences *may* affect males and females differently, from the primarily physiological for males to the primarily verbal/cognitive for females. Which of these is preferable, if either, is impossible to say.

Finally, within the context of sex differences in emotion, it is possible, indeed likely, that any differences or patterns that there might be, are changing, in Western society at least. As women gain more and more equality, so it is possible that they are reacting more like men emotionally. At present, if there are any differences, it is not possible to say wheather they are based on major biological disparities or sociocultural learning. If there are differences, and if these are changing, it might all be a function of the degree to which males and females will allow themselves to accept sex-role stereotypes. The problem with this argument, personally attractive though it may be, is that the degree of acceptance might in itself by partly determined by sex-role stereotypes or other sociocultural forces which are no less powerful than built-in biological constraints or predispositions.

THE ENVIRONMENT

It is indisputable that the environment has an emotional impact on the individual. By this, reference is not simply being made to stimulus–response relationships, but to the influence of the grand environment, be it natural or artificial, on the emotional state of a person. Even though this has been one of the most neglected areas of concern, it is clear from personal experience and the sharing of such experiences with others that the environment can have profound emotional effects. Under the simplest and most favourable conditions, emotions are difficult to describe. When they reach the ineffable extremes of the sublime, the task becomes almost impossible.

To date, there have been two approaches made to the study of the emotional impact of the environment. One has come from Mehrabian and Russell (1974), who take a singular approach to what they term environmental psychology, from a background in social psychology, particularly as it is concerned with nonverbal communication. Although their work is far-reaching and thorough, its singularity is perhaps attested to by its not yet having inspired similar research. The second approach is perhaps more promising and comes from a background of concern with the natural environment and our place within it, concerns which have not necessarily stemmed from psychology (for example, Ulrich, 1983).

Environmental psychology

For the most part, environmental psychologists have not been concerned with emotion. As mentioned above, however, the exception is Mehrabian and Russell (1974). They attempted to generate a theoretical basis for this area by developing measures to assess emotional and approach–avoidance reactions to the natural world. Reasonably enough, they took approach–avoidance as the basic dependent variable within studies of the environment, including such specific measures as physical approach, exploration, verbal expression of preference, and so on.

The emotional aspects of the environment–individual interaction are considered by Mehrabian and Russel to be intervening variables. Here they argue that semantic differential scales can be used to measure emotional reactions to the environment, therefore assuming that pleasure, arousal and dominance are the three basic human emotional reactions. This assumption is more or less forced by the use of the semantic differential, although Mehrabian and Russell also justify it through their non-factor analytic work.

They argue further that approach–avoidance tendencies to the environment are not only occasioned by the emotional responses it prompts, but also by the emotions which the person brings to the situation. So they developed measures of what they term trait emotions to study personality or individual differences in emotional predispositions. On the other side of the coin, they also developed measures for the description of environments. The final measure of this, which they consider not only to identify physical aspects of the environment but also to usefully characterize relationships amongst stimulus dimensions pertinent to emotion, is information rate.

Mehrabian and Russell develop various hypotheses concerning approach and avoidance and report various tests of them. They found a positive correlation between approach–avoidance and the pleasantness of environments. There was also support for an inverted U-shaped relationship between approach–avoidance and the arousing quality (information rate) of the environment. They argue that the pleasant–unpleasant dimension has traditionally been afforded too much importance and arousal has been relatively neglected. Their major point in this context is that in the modern, city environment there has been in recent times a rapidly accelerating increase in information rate. Environments are now massively arousing, particularly in urban areas where there is a massive concentration of stimuli. This is likely to be so stressful as to be maladaptive. There is little doubt that prolonged information overload can lead to fatigue and exhaustion: it is simply too much to cope with.

This type of analysis is supported by the tradition of work which has long suggested that high arousal generated by dwelling in crowded, unpleasant places makes interpersonal relationships suffer to the point of aggression and violence. It is as if the negative feelings generated by the environment are generalized to the other people within it.

The natural environment

Writing from a non-psychological background, Ulrich (1983) nevertheless puts forward an analysis of emotional responses to the natural environment which is likely to do much to prompt research in this direction. He views affect (which he both equates with emotion and does not distinguish sharply from mood) as being the basis of conscious experience in any environment. From a practical point of view, he believes that it is therefore important to use emotion as an indicator of an individual's interaction with the environment, in order to assist in environmental planning.

Ulrich makes his analysis very much influenced by Izard's (1977) views of emotion. However, he also considers aesthetic as well as emotional responses. He characterizes the aesthetic response as preference or an emotional response of like or dislike which is associated with pleasureable feelings and neuro-physiological activity. So, for Ulrich, aesthetic preference is emotion within the dimension of pleasantness.

Ulrich bases his theory on the assumption that emotions are adaptive and goes on to the question: What are the adaptive functions of emotional reactions to the landscape? If individuals respond to parts of the landscape with feelings of aesthetic pleasantness, is this in any way significant for survival?

There are three elements to the theory: (1) internal processes which generate emotion; (2) adaptive functions of emotions in the natural environment; (3) emotions in this context are related to behaviour. The assumption is also made that thought or cognition, as mediated in the neocortex, and emotion, as mediated in the limbic system, are separate systems.

Ulrich's theory is best represented diagrammatically (see figure 9).

The theory assumes that preferences in the natural environment are for gross configurations, gross depths, and general classes. The whole process of emotional appreciation occurs very quickly, even before proper identification has occurred, particularly if water or vegetation are involved. Various parts of the model can be strong or weak and there is a constant interplay between emotion and cognition. However, in Ulrich's view, in most (unspectacular) natural environments, it is only elementary cognition that is involved.

As mentioned before, Ulrich assumes that emotional reactions to nature are adaptive and that feelings are linked to behaviour. So, emotional reactions act as motivators, arousal changes that lead to behaviour. He argues that strong positive emotions sustain behaviour, adaptively. Or they might lead to a physiological restauration through feelings of pleasantness, interest or inhibition of stressful thoughts. This may well lead to an increased sense of competence.

Apart from putting forward his theoretical model of emotional responses to

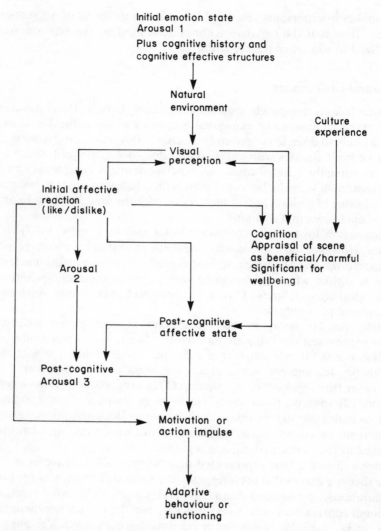

Figure 9. (Adapted from Ulrich, 1983.)

the natural environment, Ulrich also describes the results of studies in which there are high levels of intersubject agreement on the visual reactions to the natural environment.

Considering unspectacular scenes, a view is preferred if its complexity is reasonably high and has a focal point, its depth is moderately high and clearly perceivable, the surface texture of the ground is homogeneous, there is a deflected vista and the appraised threat is negligible. Preferences are even greater than this if water is present.

Conversely, there tends to be low preference expressed for a view if its complexity is low and its depth restricted, if its ground is rough, if there is no water and no deflected vista, and if it is appraised as highly threatening.

To Ulrich, the basic question, perhaps prompted by the work of Izard, is whether or not aesthetic, emotional preferences are culturally determined and hence different between societies. The studies he mentions are a little ragged, but like those of Izard, they tend to show similarities across cultures. This might have something to do with the universal characteristics of the nervous system and certainly accords with the apparent universality of emotion and cross-cultural similarities in cognition and perception.

Ulrich provides some interesting evidence that viewing natural scenes is emotionally restorative. This effect has been shown in people in different countries and from rural and urban backgrounds. Further, urban views appear to be actually detrimental to emotional wellbeing. These are interesting results and certainly endorse some commonly held views. Ulrich's theory is well thought out and thoroughly explicated. It could prove to be a very useful foundation for the future of what could become an important area of research. It is indisputable that the environment has an emotional impact on the individual and that, as far as emotion in everyday life is concerned, this is an important part of it.

THE CULTURE

The links between emotion and cultural pursuits such as literature, music, drama and art are highly significant. What are commonly called the arts depend on emotional impact; in fact it is hard to conceive of them existing without their influence on emotion. As with the relationship between emotion and the landscape, emotional responses within the arts are tied in with aesthetic preferences. However, beyond this they are also associated with creativity and with conscious attempts at manipulation by the artist, and in the case of music and drama, also by the performer. The aim of this section then is to explore some aspects of emotion in the arts, or more broadly, within culture. However, it is not intended to be exhausive but to concentrate on some of the more interesting facets of the arts. Of course, it almost goes without saying that since this is a very difficult area of study and since it is apparently somewhat removed from science, it has been neglected. Once again, as with the other facets of the present chapter, this is in spite of its obvious significance at the everyday level. There are very many aspects of the arts which are relevant to emotion, and indeed which many people would regard as relying on emotion for their effects. In order to illustrate this point, the relationships of emotion to literature, music and drama will be considered in turn. Following this, more general issues will be raised concerning emotion and the arts and questions of creativity and aesthetics.

Emotion and literature

That the literature of fiction both in form of prose and poetry is often concerned with emotion almost goes without saying. Frequently, it is aimed at portraying, describing and analysing individual emotions. Also, at another level entirely, it is manipulative of the reader's emotions. Of course, the writer adopts a very different manner to that of the psychologist. While the psychologist is concerned to portray the average person and so describe the human condition, the writer of fiction is more often concerned with the best possible example of whatever is being portrayed.

Frequently, in fiction, emotion is characterized as being precipitated by some or other startling event. Following this, the other influential factors often remain unstated but implied. Clearly though, the writer of fiction is as aware as the psychologist that emotion involves bodily, physiological arousal and behavioural, particularly facial, expression. Also, it tends to be taken almost as axiomatic that some process of cognitive evaluation precedes the experience of emotion.

After emotions have been experienced, then characters in fiction are typically shown as having to act on their feelings. In other words, fictional characters remain, even these days, in the grip of passion, and carry on fierce battles between the rational and the emotional sides of their make-up. Also though, emotion is often regarded as a motivator in fiction, as a force which drives the person to accomplish goals.

What of the manipulation of the reader's emotion rather than that of the fictional characters? This can occur in a number of ways. For example, it is readily apparent that an absorbing work of fiction prompts much in the way of vicarious emotional experience for the reader. This may be so whether or not the reader has similar experiences, non-vicariously. Furthermore, the experience of emotion through fiction can allow the satisfaction of a temporary escape from the less pleasant aspects of everyday emotional experience. Indeed, this is the essence of escapist fiction. From the crudest romance to the most spellbinding tale of high adventure, the reader is invited to suspend reality and to indentify with larger than life characters whose experiences reach commanding pinnacles of emotional satisfaction. In fact, the question of identification would seem to be crucial for the experience of vicarious emotion. If the reader can find no grounds for identification then a work of fiction assumes a curious emotional flatness. Such identification is perhaps closely allied to the projection and empathy which allows us to gain some understanding of the emotional experiences of those around us in the everyday world. No doubt, the emotional arousal occasioned by fiction has multiple causes and is idiosyncratic, and this is not the context in which to engage in further speculation. It is enough to say that the effects can be powerful, lasting and even harrowing. For the present purposes, it is more important to consider what picture of emotions and emotional life is portrayed by writers of fiction.

One way of determining what aspects of emotion are portrayed in fiction is through a content analysis. If this is carried out in psychological tests, the general finding is that apparently twice as much space is given to negative than to positive emotions (for example, Lindauer, 1968). One possible reason for this is that it may reflect the fact that negative emotions are more common than positive emotions in everyday life. Lindauer attempted to test this possibility by analysing the emotions mentioned in the titles of a very large number of plays, novels, short satires and öetry. This demonstrated a greater concern with positive than with negative emotions.

Lindauer's results prompt the question of whether the psychologist or the writer better portrays emotions, at this broad level. However, the picture is more complicated than this. Strongman (1983) analysed the content rather than the titles of a large number of short stories published in New Zealand and Australia. There was a general preoccupation with negative emotions, thus endorsing the psychological textbook writers. Interestingly, the same list of the eight most frequent emotions appeared in both the New Zealand and Australian literature, although in a different order of priority. In passing, it is worth noting that this type of content analysis of fiction might provide some interesting insights into national differences.

Although the content analysis of fiction, or even of factual material, may be said to debase either, at a very broad level it does give some indication of how writers and psychologists see emotion. The likelihood is that they view the balance between the positive and negative aspects of emotional life in a similar manner. This suggests that they are giving a fair reflection of emotional life and experience in the everyday world.

That emotion is a significant facet of the literature of fiction is indisputable. It is concerned both with the portrayal of emotional experience and with the manipulation of emotional reactions in the reader. The question of how such effects might be achieved will be returned to later. Meanwhile, preoccupations of both psychologists and writers of fiction with negative emotion has an interest possible basis in research into lateralization and emotion (see Chapter 3). There is evidence that spontaneous positive emotional expression is mediated in the left hemisphere and spontaneous negative emotional expression in the right. Yet, overriding this, the right hemispere remains dominant in emotion. This might indicate that negative emotions are more basic or more significant than positive emotions. At best, the negative emotions might simply be kept out of the way by things verbal (left hemispheric) and in the absence of this or of positive emotions, the natural, basic state is one of negative emotion.

This might account for their apparent preponderance, and be reflected in the writing of both psychology and literature.

Emotion and music

Much as with literature, it is frequently assumed that one of the major ways in which music has its effect is through its effect on the emotions. To those who listen to music this effect is an indisputable, integral part of the experience, although they would affirm that there is more to the experience than this. Also, from the observer's viewpoint, the sight of rows of people with closed eyes rapt in a performance of classical music or of crowds of young people banging their heads at a heavy metal concert makes the emotional aspect of music obvious.

The assumption that music not only reflects emotion but is also manipulative of it is also seen in the many attempts which are made to use it for what appear to be therapeutic purposes. It is thought that music might have calming effects, that it might alleviate anxiety or that it might have such a marked effect on the emotional lives of cows that milk yields increase. Some people play music to their plants for similar reasons.

The problem when considering the relationship between emotion and music comes when attempts are made to conduct empirical studies rather than to speculate. The sort of statement to be found in what is a disappointing literature can be exemplified by Ostwald (1966). Emotional excitement is thought to be generated by hot, bright, light, loud, fast, tense, rough and high music and emotional depression by cool, soft, low, dark, slow, slack and dull music. People are believed to become relaxed and happy with fast rhythms, consonant music and rising melodies. By contrast, they should become sad and pensitive with dissonant, descending music with drawn out notes. However, research to demonstrate these supposed effects unequivocally is lacking. Similarly, there have been very few actual demonstrations of the effects of music on anxiety, for example. Stanton (1973) showed that some highly anxious students gained better test results working with background music.

Although it may appear obvious to anyone who has experienced a shiver down the back during particular sequences of music that emotion is involved, and possibly at a very primitive basic level, genuine demonstrations of such effects are sadly lacking. For an effect which seems so basic, even atavistic, the literature on the topic is very poor indeed. In the end, it comes to highly speculative comments such as that music is an abstraction about emotion, a way of reflecting emotion symbolically. This may sound grand, but it is unsupported, even contestable and perhaps untestable. The field of emotion and music is open to investigation.

Emotion and drama

The state of affairs concerning the role of emotion in drama and the theatre is even more wanting than it is between emotion and music. There simply is no research in the psychological literature. However, once more the involvement of emotion in drama is obvious. Many plays are explorations of the emotional lives of their characters and much of the impact of the theatre is through the dramatic manipulation of the emotional reactions of the audience.

Although emotion in drama has been ignored by psychologists, it has not by those writers who are concerned with theatre. For example, Stanislawski (1929) discusses what he terms the emotion of truth. He regards the actor as a 'living, complex, emotion' who might, on occasion not complete a perfect bodily action or give a proper intonation. This leads to what he terms mannerism or awkwardness, the only way to guard against which is to develop a very strong sense of the truth of what he does. Stanislawski is also interesting in his descriptions of the problem faced by actors who have grown up and lived in societies which force the suppression of emotion when in the evening they have to 'leap into the life of the mad King, whose unrestrained passion sweeps like a storm across the moors'.

Writing at much the same time, Meyerhold (Braun, 1969) puts forward suggestions about the way in which an actor can build a way into a part physically and so manipulate his or her own emotions and hence those of the audience. 'From a sequence of physical positions and situations there arise those 'points of excitation' which are informed with some particular emotion. Throughout this process of rousing the emotions' the actor observes a rigid framework of physical prerequisites.'

Brecht addresses the whole problem of emotion much more directly, seeing the emotions as based on class, an idea noteworthy for its singularity. He suggests that works of art, particularly theatrical work of course, when handed down through time, allow successive generations to share the emotions of those that precede them.

This is sufficient to give the flavour of the types of analysis of emotion made by those who write about the theatre. It is clear that they are speaking in ways which would make the conventional scientifically based psychologist uneasy. They use unfamiliar concepts and dive into a sea of speculation, swimming strongly in apparent ignorance of the depths beneath them. The usual response to this on the part of psychologists is dismissive. Although understandable, this is shortsighted. They may have a point and it may be possible to search for it empirically, or even to couch their ideas in theoretical terms which are more acceptable. Certainly, there is no gainsaying the links between emotion, drama and the theatre, links which psychologists have almost ignored.

Emotion and the arts—general considerations

By far the most searching anlysis of the links between psychology and the arts has been made by Kreitler and Kreitler (1972). As part of their general treatise, they consider the nature of emotional involvement. This section relies heavily on their perspectives.

As a way of discussing the links between emotion and the arts, Kreitler and Kreitler introduce the concepts of set and empathy. Clearly, the experience of art is the result of stimuli from the art itself and the response of the spectator. The more responsive the spectator, the more intense is the experience and the more emotional involvement results. The strength of the response is thought to depend, amongst other things, on expectations or set, which of course, is a cognitive capacity. As a psychological concept, set is important in many spheres, believed to facilitate attention, for example, and to elicit and permit the completion of behaviour.

Many investigations of emotion show that emotional arousal depends on set, for example as generated by instructions. Similarly, Stotland (1969) shows that empathy can be generated by cognitive set. Within the area of art, there are many instances of people giving higher ratings to paintings or works of fiction that they believe to be those of prestigious artists, or to be highly rated in the opinion of a well-known critic. This is at the core of advertising and mass communication. If brand X is endorsed by a famous sportsman or by someone in a highly regarded profession, more people buy it.

Aesthetic meanings are partly shaped by social standards and habits, for example, dropping the name of a notable but highly intellectual or avant-garde writer or artist into a conversation. Sets are shaped from this by developing meanings associated with iedeas and from the influence of specific settings in which this might occur. For instance, drawings are judged differently in nicely appointed rooms than in dilapidated rooms. Similar contextual influences of aesthetic set come from things such as book bindings, the decor of a concert hall and so on.

According to Kreitler and Kreitler, emotion is a significant element in the experience of art. Art is essentially fictional, so what processes might mediate the intense emotional involvement? Their answer to this is empathy, which they characterise as a 'feeling into'. This is essentially a reaction which people have to other people undergoing emotional experiences. They go on to explore how and why empathy occurs and whether emotional involvement in art is a genuine example of it.

There are two basic theories the first involving a possible process of representation. In attempting to understand something, a spectator might dredge up memories which are relevant enough to prompt previous emotional experiences. In this sense, empathy would be dependent on cognition and imagining, with the emotional experience involved being therefore clearly attenuated. This view has links with the Schachter type of analysis of the cognitive interpretation of physiological states.

The alternative theory involves the idea of 'feeling into', in which the emphasis is on the actual emotional experience involved in empathy. It is reflected in a tendency to imitate the movements of others, with motor expression being regarded as an important aspect of emotion. So, during an emotional experience X moves. Y notices this and spontaneously imitates the movement, which leads to sensations, which have themselves been previously linked to emotional experience. Eventually then, Y is enjoying an experience similar to that of X.

The 'feeling into' theory of emotional empathy in art was formulated at the turn of the century, but developed by Lipps (1965). Kreitler and Kreitler point out that there is supportive research on imitation, but not that kinaesthetic imitation is automatic. They argue that it is necessary to have a combination of both theories. In this empathy would occur through the imitation of motional–dynamic features in an observed situation, which produces physiological arousal. This is identified by the observer as a specific emotion which is in accord with his or her interpretation of the the inner state and of the externally perceived situation.

Kreitler and Kreitler apply this type of analysis to the experience of art of a number of different types. For the present purposes, literature will be discussed at some length, although other areas of artistic expression will be touched on later.

As implied earlier, literature has great power to generate feeling into, via the events described, the situations and the characters. Frequently, this is accomplished through descriptions of gestures, movements and actions. It is assumed that the emotion generated in the reader would be weaker than that produced by similar stimuli in real life. The reason for this is that it is assumed that verbal descriptions of movements are not only weaker than visual, but are also longer, sequential and less spontaneous.

However, within fictional literature there are various techniques and devices for enhancing empathy. For example, there is selective description, particularly of expressive movements. There is the suggestion of nonverbal communication through verbal phrases and the amplification of movements through the sound of words and the melodies of sentences which may well evoke particular emotional tones.

It is also argued that in literature, stimuli to do with emotion evoke kinaesthetic imitation in the reading, which leads to physiological arousal. The reader actually makes incipient movements and bodily postures, over which he or she learns to exercise some control. The Kreitlers suggest that it is only when the physiological changes prompted by imitation are linked with cognitive elaboration that there is emotional experience. There are two processes which might allow such elaboration—simply expanding on and enhancing the material in the text, or identifying with the author.

The author depends on a sort of suggestive reporting to bring about a closure or sense of completion in the reader, which is similar to the way in which we attempt to understand people in everyday life. In literature, this is aided by fantasy which might interfere with understanding during reading, but extend it afterwards. If this type of interference does occur, empathy might well be replaced by some other emotion. Identificaiton with the author is assumed to contribute to contact with literary reality. To make this identification is to go along with the literary convention in which the writer suspends disbelief.

The difficulty with this type of argument (perhaps one of many difficulties) is that it can be distorted to account for almost anything. For example, Kreitler and Kreitler point out that novels began from a near–acted form of dramatic story telling. They began very much in the first person, only later giving way to more direct descriptions. Clearly, first person narrative is more likely than any other to prompt empathy or feeling into, more likely than is, say, third person narrative. Thus, with this shift in literary convention, there was probably a shift away from the easy means of feeling into. So, they argue, the reading public must have become trained in other ways.

Kreitler and Kreitler make a similar analysis of other forms of art. Sculpture, for example, like literature, is frequently concerned with human beings. When experts observe sculpture they tend to imitate the sculptural postures, even though they attempt to conceal the imitation. This inhibition does not, however, appear to reduce empathy. Similarly imitations can be observed in people who are studying paintings, although there appears to be a weaker tendency. However, there are clear fractional or implicit imitatory movements.

If dance is regarded as art, then it presents a simpler case for emotional empathy than those considered so far. There are obvious imitative movements which are reinforced by rythm and music and enhanced by cognition which follow from the interpretation of movements.

Of course, it could be argued that in contrast with dance, which is active, or obviously being engaged in by other humans, art forms such as sculpture and painting are more passive and may not depict anything human. How then can feeling into or imitation occur? In fact, seeing for instance, a tilted line actually causes a body tilt. Think, as an example, of the slightly awkward muscular strain which occurs on looking at photographs of the leaning tower of Pisa. There is much evidence in psychology (for example, Michotte, 1950) that people do project emotions on to inanimate objects. It is reasonable then to point out that one dimension of the meaning of such objects is expressiveness.

Kreitler and Kreitler pay some attention to music since it is a particularly difficult case to analyse in its relationship with emotion. For instance, any or each aspect of music—rhythm, harmony, melody, tone—could produce kinaesthetic responses. However, it is not possible to say that one of these elements is what is felt into. No studies have been successful in demonstrating that particular elements are associated with particular types of response. However, there must surely be a difference between the emotional impact of music and the emotion involved in an identification we might make with a fictional character.

The Kreitlers speculate that music does seem to evoke emotional responses through cognitive elaboration, the same concept they use to account for the emotional impact of other types of art. However, these effects do not seem to rely on any imaginal responses which come from any representational content the music might have. Studies show no clear relationships between the emotional intentions of the composer and what the resulting music suggests to the listener. This holds with what might appear to be obvious images such as the sound of thunder or of a cuckoo. In the end, such research as there is suggests that emotion and mood effects relate simply to the enjoyment of music, any effects tending to be idiosyncratic.

A final point which is worthy of mention from Kreitler and Kreitler's discussion of emotion and art is, if anything, a stress being placed on a sort of emotional distance. They regard a type of inhibition called 'disinterestedness' as being crucial to the experience of art. There are two main aspects to this. An object and its appeal may be separated from the self, at a distance from the practicalities of life. This is a positive condition and seems to help to intensify the subjective experience of the object. A second possibility concerns the detachment that results when a person concentrates so fully on a work that the result is an experience of richness and complexity. In this instance, there seems to be personal involvement at many levels at once. The difference between these two possibilities is that the distance involved is either external to the experience, or an integral part of it.

It is clear that the experience of art is extraordinarily complex, emotionally—much more so than has been considered here. A person does not simply make a single identification, but might simultaneously empathize with many figures, whilst also responding emotionally to his or her subjective experiences. The emotional impact of art is either enhanced or restricted through whatever social roles the individual might be playing or whatever sets he or she might have. All of these sources of influence change with culture and with time. Like empathy, which is a form of emotional closeness, emotional distancing is important for experiencing art. However, it has to be right: too great or too small a distance appears to detract from this experience, the exact nature of which probably depends to some extent on whatever process of empathy is occurring.

Aesthetics and creativity

Much of the foregoing discussion of art and emotion has been skirting round the difficult topics of aesthetics and creativity. Very few psychologists have been brave enough to tackle these topics, particularly as they relate to emotion. One exception has been Mandler (1982) who has been very consistent in not ducking difficult issues.

Mandler argues, and very reasonably in the light of what has been discussed in the last few pages, that art arouses through its interaction with the experiencing individual. Like Kreitler and Kreitler, Mandler places emphasis on set, which he refers to as anticipation. The work of art may or may not be in accord with whatever the anticipation might be, thus, in Mandler's usual terms, leading to some or other degree of interruption.

This aspect of things is basically concerned with the links between the information implicit in stimuli and emotional reactions. For example, there are suggestions that negative emotion results from the confirmation of expectations with low probability; the emotion becomes positive if the expectations are of medium probability and ends up as boredom when they are high probability. Another viewpoint is that emotional tension depends on competition between incompatible expectations. A further possibility is that the degree of arousal from a work of art varies with the discrepancies between stimulation and set.

Mandler argues that aesthetically meaningful experience in the emotional sense will depend to some extent on making more and more new interpretations and differentiations. Thus, the more complex the object or work, the more intense the possible emotional experience. A certain amount of artistic knowledge and training is related to the emotional experience of art. Thus, a piece of simple popular music will soon lose its emotional impact, whereas a more complex piece of music will not.

The essential ingredient in the emotionally positive side of aesthetic appreciation is novelty. This essentially cognitive characteristic can be in the form of new interpretations, new views or even, in Mandler's terms, new mental structures. However, in the extreme, novelty in art can lead to negative emotional reactions. Again, in Mandler's view, this is because the individual has no mental structures which can accommodate any attempts to analyse the work. With more familiarity and education, more should become assimilated and the reactions change to positive.

In a most interesting passage, Mandler argues that the creative person has to have, amongst other things, certain emotional characteristics. For example he or she should be able to tolerate the new, emotionally, and find such novelty attractive through cognitive interpretation. To Mandler, a creative work should involve destruction of existing structures, a sort of interruption. Also, he believes that creative individuals often have a parent of the opposite sex who was frustrated creatively. This is likely to push that parent into prompting the child to succeed where he or she had been blocked. Such a parent will be constantly interfering with the child's structures, destroying stability. Within a positive relationship, the development of new structures comes to be seen as an emotionally positive achievement. In this way, being creative (through destruction and production) is learned early in life and becomes associated with a positive emotional tone.

Mandler argues further that it is not just the early interactions that determine the emotional tone of creativity. Society also helps to form cognitive evaluations of feelings and actions. To view the destruction of the old as creative rather than aggressive depends on social values towards creativity and aggression.

CONCLUSIONS

This chapter has been concerned with some of the most interesting and yet least researched aspects of emotion. The probable reason for the dearth of research is the difficulty and complexity of the issues involved. However, this should not deter the psychologists for much longer. After all, only a few years ago there was a dearth of work on emotion altogether, for much the same reason.

Only certain topics have been covered in this discussion, emotion and personality, emotion and the environment in the sense of landscape, and emotion and the culture in the form of art and aesthetic appreciation. These were merely examples. Emotion is present in virtually every facet of day-to-day existence and deserves to be studied in these contexts rather than being ignored or taken for granted, either positively or negatively. For example, the role of emotion in sport, amongst either the participants or the spectators, is a fascinating topic. Also, what of the role and nature of emotion in childbirth or in dying? Does emotion have a place in religion? Is it possible or desirable to keep emotion out of certain aspects of life, such as politics or journalism? There are many rich, unanswered questions.

However, the only question which there is time and space to consider here is whether or not in the topics that have been considered in this chapter there is any common thread. The answer is clearly 'yes' and the thread is equally clearly the same one which has been running throughout the book—cognition. It is cognition that is the one aspect of psychological functioning that is impossible to ignore in the broad contexts which have been encompassed in this chapter. To understand the place of emotion in individual personality or in the experience of pain or sex, it is necessary to consider cognition. If one turns to the emotional impact of the environment, from the stimulus overload of urban life to the extreme experience of the sublime in the natural landscape, the one concept that can most easily help to explain the emotional effects is cognitive evaluations. Similarly, the experience of emotion in the arts again appears to depend on cognitions. The more complex the emotional experiences then the more obvious the cognitive involvement becomes.

Finally then, this brief chapter contains two fundamental points which it is important to reiterate before moving on to more general concluding comments. Although research and theory in emotion has profilerated in recent years, there remain many challenging areas which need basic research and thought put into them. Also, in whatever direction one turns in the study of emotion, one finds cognition.

10.

Conclusions

The aims of this final chapter are: (1) to summarize the current position in the various approaches which have been made to the study of emotion; (2) to discuss some of the problems which remain unresolved and which recent investigations have uncovered; (3) to draw conclusions and present a conceptual framework with the writing of this book and its previous editions; (4) to consider some of the implications of recent advances in the understanding of emotion, in particular with respect to emotional control.

The search for a physiological substrate to emotion has shown both the CNS and the ANS (plus hormonal and chemical change) to be implicated. Recent suggestions point to the CNS having the more significant role to play. Within the CNS, it is the evolutionarily 'older' parts of the brain (mainly the limbic system) which appear to be necessary to emotion. Their precise function and mechanism of action are still obscure. The indirect measures of psychophysiology have led to some well-conducted research on the ANS. However, the evidence for any physiological response patterning is disappointingly slight. All that can be definitely concluded is that the viscera are necessary to emotion, and that a better way of distinguishing between the emotions is through cognition.

There are many reasons for the absence of more precise conclusions at the physiological level. There is the problem of reductionism. It may be inappropriate, particularly in our present state of knowledge, to attempt a reduction of the study of emotion to the physiological level. Also, of course, there is the more obvious reason that emotion may not have an easily interpretable physiological basis. Two more subsidary but nevertheless cogent reasons are, firstly, that physiological research into emotion has run ahead of theory. It is comparatively more sophisticated and expert. Secondly, the attempts to produce a theory of emotion based on cognition and arousal begun to founder in the face of recent investigations. It begins to look increasingly likely that physiological arousal may not always be necessary to the experience of emotion. It is noteworthy, that in recent times those who have studied the physiological bases of emotion have ended by stressing cognition.

The cognitively based study of emotion has revitalized and indeed changed the entire field of study. The relationship between emotion and cognition is now so firmly established that it is beginning to be at the core of any understanding of emotion. The earlier, Schachterian suggestions of hypothetical interactions between physiological arousal and cognition, particularly the process of cognitive labelling, were extremely useful in leading to a large amout of interesting research. However, the theoretical basis of this research is clearly wanting.

Recent ideas, as put forward by theorists such as Izard, Mandler, Lazarus, Averill and, to some extent, Leventhal, have been concerned to analyse the nature of the cognitive involvement in emotion. In some ways these theorists have picked up and extended the earlier ideas of appraisal, evaluation and emotional meaning and begun to come to grips with them. Indeed it is here that the most searching accounts of emotion are to be found. Certainly, recent develpments in the cognitive approach to emotion have both improved the general understanding of it far more than has any other approach since psychologists first became interested in the subject. They have also led to innovative investigations in what appear to be fruitful areas, the obvious examples being studies of memory and emotion, and lateralization.

So much has happened in the study of emotion between the various editions of this book that the balance in its chapters has changed drastically. One of the results of this for the present edition is that the philosophical, phenomenological and behavioural approaches to the subject lie together within one chapter as rather uneasy bedfellows. The main reasons for this have been the upsurge in the cognitive approach and a more than corresponding falling away, almost to nothing, of the behavioural approaches. However, each of these three seemingly disparate areas has something important to offer those who attempt to understand emotion and yet each points in a similar direction for the future.

Recent philosophical approaches to emotion are very useful to the psychologist in that they are well enough argued to prompt stylistic caution in theorizing. The phenomenologists are to be congratulated for at least making the attempt to come to terms with the subjective experience of emotion. Sooner or later, psychologists of other persuasions will also be forced to make the attempt. The subjective experience of emotion will not go away simply by being ignored. The behavioural approaches to emotion have been made with an impressive methodological rigour which could well be emulated by others. Of course, the problem is that the data to which they give rise are often so rarefied as to appear to have little to do with human emotion at all. However, in spite of the differences between these three quite distinct types of standpoint, each in its own way, takes cognition into account. This is easy to see with the philosophers and phenomenologists, but is also apparent from the behaviourists by those who use more cognitive concepts sounding the more plausible.

Circumstances surrounding the study of emotional development have improved considerably during the last few years. Observational techniques have become more sophisticated and theories have become more penetrating. Apart from more positive outcomes, this has led to much less reliance on the the earlier, rather sterile, studies of emotional development in animals. Although it is clear that emotional development depends on nature–nurture interactions, recent investigations all point very strongly to the importance of social interaction during the first few months, even weeks, of life. Social and emotional development seem difficult to separate and, quite differently from the beliefs of the early investigators, very young infants are clearly capable of a wide range of emotional expressions if the social environment is right. Since the emphasis in emotional development is on social interaction, then once again everything is pointing in the direction of the importance of cognition.

Much of the research into the social psychology of emotion, and it is probably the area of greatest research endeavour, has been concerned with emotion expression and its recognition, particularly by researchers such as Ekman and Izard. A great deal is now known about emotional expression, even its cross-cultural aspects, and it is Izard especially who has made such thorough empirical and theoretical analyses. However, recent research has also begun into the very intricate but important matter of the nature of the emotional aspects of human relationships, a topic which at the everyday level, would seem to lie at the core of emotion. Again, looking at yet another facet of emotion, be it in facial or bodily expression or in social relationships, it is cognitive concepts which are drawn on most heavily in the accounts.

There remains a long way to go in gaining an understanding of abnormal emotion, particularly since broadly based theories are almost non-existent. It is even difficult to know what exactly is the nature of the abnormality and indeed whether it comes from within the individual or from without. In the end, abnormal emotion may be little more than an adjunct to either an abnormal environment or an abnormal constitution. Whether one considers anxiety, depression, psychosomatic disorders or psychopathy, the one concept which keeps proving essential to understanding is cognition. If emotion goes wrong in some way, the cognitive approach offers most hope in understanding how and why.

Clearly, the preceding brief overview points to an exciting set of circumstances in what for many years has been an under-researched and very piecemeal area of psychological study. The proliferation of research and theory into emotion during the last few years has not just added to existing knowledge in an incoherent manner. Almost all research and theory has pointed in the direction of the importance of cognition and indeed of the necessity to take it into account in any attempt to understand emotion. Not only is this evident within the traditional approaches to the subject, it also carries strong implications for other, interesting developments. For example, it now seems possible to carry out investigations in the fascinating areas of individual differences in emotion and of its role in the individual's interaction with the natural environment and the culture.

CONCEPTUAL FRAMEWORK

Apart from the present text, the most recent review of research and theory in emotions is that of Leventhal and Tomarken (1986). Although their review is somewhat selective rather than exhaustive, they draw some interesting conclusions. These will be discussed in this section as will some of the present author's conclusions concerning emotion. The aim is to provide a conceptual framework within which it might be useful to consider past and present research and anlyses.

Having given a detailed overview of developments in cognition–arousal theory, expressive behaviour, lateralization of emotion and memory, Leventhal and Tomarken attempt to look at the conceptual implications of the results for three issues. These are the biology of emotion, emotion and interpersonal communication and emotional development. They point out that it is now clear that at birth the infant has a range of emotional-expressive responses and that positive–negative emotion interhemispheric differences appear in the first year of life. They argue that, as what they term 'the machinery' underlying emotion becomes apparent, the arousal/cognitive labelling theory will disappear. This process is already well under way, but what at present remains unanswered are many questions concerning the nature of the innate CNS centres or patterns involved in emotion.

Leventhal and Tomarken (1986) also stress the importance of interpersonal communication in emotion since it was self-evident in a wide range of the studies they review. It is even crucial to the study of emotion and memory. In general, they argue that 'the universality of expressive behaviour and the lateralization of emotional processing suggests an innate, central-motor system for constructing expressions and feelings, with the critical function of cementing interpersonal relationships' (p.600). Further, 'Common sense and the data showing links between emotion and memory suggest that the emotion system undergoes elaborate development over the individual life span'.

Leventhal and Tomarken (1986) put these ideas within the context of Leventhal's three-level theory of emotion. The sensorimotor level is conceived of as an innate preparedness to respond to social stimuli which begins emotional interaction. When these processes are prompted socially, an emotion memory (schema) is formed. It is a nonverbal memory which integrates. The suggestion is that such emotional schema begin to develop in the first few hours of life, an important point since they are also seen as allowing the differentiation of self from others.

Later in development, meaning is given to new social situations and new emotional episodes are experienced through the stimulation of social interaction and its effect on cognition. Leventhal also sees possible important differences between the structure of and links within schematic and verbal memory. Through the stress on the integration of emotion with the self-concept, Leventhal and Tomarken argue that the study of emotion and personality may lead to interesting possibilities, a point which was also made in the previous chapter.

In previous editions of this book the final chapter contained an attempt to put forward a conceptual framework for emotion which derived primarily from a behavioural basis. In this context, emotion was portrayed as the response or responses which stimuli elicit from the individual. Their behavioural, physiological and subjective measurements could be made which would reflect the same basic emotional reaction. Clearly, in the light both of Leventhal and Tomarken's (1986) overview and of the directions in which the various chapters in this book have inexorably led, this behavioural framework is inadequate and now appears to be naive.

It is time perhaps to be a little bolder than previously and to attempt to draw some firm personal conclusions about emotion.

(1)   The evidence suggests that emotion is a psychological system which is separate from other psychological systems such as perception and yet which is linked to them in some ways.

(2)   Much as has been thought at the everyday level for many years, emotion is the system which gives the world, and our place within it, meaning. It is what provides the quality to life.

(3)   Emotion can occur without conscious awareness, but when it does then it is less relevant to questions of meaning and quality. When occurring preconsciously, it is similar to automatic behaviour. Of course, at this level, it may well be adding to emotion memory or emotional schema. These may have subsequent effects on the individual at the conscious level. However, even when emotion is being expressed automatically, although the individual is unaware of it, it may still act as an important social signal to which others respond.

(4)   The expressive aspects of emotion are crucial, not only as social signals for others to monitor, respond to and be regulated by, but also because feedback from the expressions helps in the creation of the emotional experience. However, although expression is a very important part of emotion it is not necessary to it. The evidence suggests that emotional experiences can occur at the subjective level without being reflected in expression, and might well not only affect the individual at the time or in the future. It is perhaps worth noting that a point such as this would either be anathema or nonsense to anyone attempting to give a behavioural account of emotion.

(5)   Physiological arousal, like expression, is a highly significant aspect of emotion but again is *not* necessary to it. The only way in which arousal may be regarded as necessary to emotion is if it is simply equated with the idea that everything must have its physiological underpinning. The evidence increasingly suggests that any such physiological mediation of emotion is in the central nervous system, although the autonomic nervous system and the

hormonal system are important to it as well. However, the evidence also points to the possibility of emotional experiences occurring in the absence of detectable physiological arousal, perhaps as purely cognitive activities mediated by emotion memory. It should be borne in mind that although the expressive aspects of emotion and physiological arousal might not be necessary to emotional experience, between them they do provide response patterns. Emotional response patterns may well have social and even individual implications.

(6) The subjective experience of emotion is very important to emotions, at times approaching crucial, but again it is not necessary. Common sense would suggest that without subjective experience, very little of importance in emotion remains for the individual. It is feelings that are important to people. However, common sense is not always very sensible. It suggests for example that we know our own minds (cognitions) in that we are aware of how and why we make the decisions we do. Cognitive psychologists have long since pointed to the incorrectness of this. Similarly, it is mistaken to assume that because the subjective experience of emotion seems significant when it occurs that it is necessary. Other indicants (e.g. physiological) demonstrate that under some conditions emotion can occur at a preconscious level which may not involve subjective experience, at that time.

(7) Having swept aside almost every aspect of psychological functioning as being not necessary to emotion, even though they might be important, only one remains—cognition. Recent research and thought all point to the inadvisability, not to say the impossibility, of accounting for emotion without considering cognition. Every chapter in this book, looking at emotion from all angles, moves inevitably in the direction of cognition. In my view, cognition is both central and necessary to emotion. That is, emotion cannot occur without cognition, in some form, even though this might only be fleeting appraisal. However, it might also take a far more complex form involving memory, mood and the more general intricacies of cognition.

Turning the coin over, the links between emotion and cognition can also be viewed from the other side. Although cognition is necessary to emotion, emotion is highly significant for cognition but not necessary to it. Emotional reactions and experiences may well influence cognitions and in some cases determine cognitions. However cognitions can and do occur in the absence of emotion. It is the present contention though, that emotions cannot occur in the absence of cognition.

In this context it does not seem relevant to consider whether emotion or cognition is the more important to human functioning, or even which comes first, in phylogeny, ontogeny, or even individual experiences. In some cases one will be more significant or dominant than the other and there is a constant interplay between the two.

As with cognition, for emotion the evidence begins to suggest strongly that there is an innate CNS basis, but that this is modified from infancy onwards by social experiences. Thus the complex interactions between emotion and cognition begin from the moment of birth (if not neonatally, although this seems unlikely).

The implications of this straightforward commitment to the importance of cognition to an understanding of emotion are very clear, and in a sense, they are already being reflected in the constantly expanding literature on emotion. Cognition should not be ignored. With the present state of knowledge, it makes no sense to take a solely or even a primarily behavioural or physiological view of emotion. As more links are forged between the structures of emotion and cognition and there is more exploration of the functional territory they share, so this should be concentrated on. This is not to argue that emotional expression, particularly as it occurs in a social context, or the physiological facets of emotion should be disregarded. However, it is to suggest they should be studied within a cognitive context.

For the most part, current research and theory implies that those who are concerned with gaining an understanding of emotion have reached similar conclusions to those of the present author. This is demonstrated not just in the more longstanding areas of study, but also in the changing balance of interests. For example, during the last few years there have appeared almost no investigations of emotion from a behavioural perspective. By contrast, the new areas of research which have appeared are very much driven by cognitive interests, the obvious examples being lateralization and emotion and memory. Similarly, all of the recent theoretical contributions have had at least a central, if not a necessary role for cognition, perhaps one of the few exceptions being the ideas of Zajonc. Even then, however, his concern with the possible links between emotion and cognition are self-evident.

One further implication of a stress in cognitive approaches to emotion should be mentioned since it suggests some exciting possibilities. Some of these have already been mentioned in the previous chapter. A cognitive perspective somehow permits the consideration of many areas which have been virtually ignored by psychologists since they became interested in emotion, and yet in which emotion is highly relevant. For instance, the question of individual differences in emotional experience and outlook can be reasonably viewed from a cognitive angle. Also, the fascinating matters of the place of emotion in cutural and artistic pursuits and indeed in any areas of creativity begins to appear at least possible to discuss if not to investigate, if a cognitive view is taken. If this has no other effect, it will at least make life easier for psychologists who are interested in emotion and who deal with the general public, since it is on such matters that they are always questioned.

Although a strong case has been made here for the necessity of accounting for emotion by cognitive analyses, any theory and research should, wherever possible, embrace all possible measures of emotion and of its effects. Knowledge of emotion should be gleaned from all sources, even those which do not easily fit within the framework of conventional science. In this way, the study of emotion can perhaps be accomplished without the topic losing too much of its everyday richness.

In spite of an obvious and exciting new impetus being given to the study of emotion, various problems remain. Or it might be more accurate to say that they have been generated by this new impetus. At the core of these problems is the question of what is the exact nature of cognitive involvement in emotion. When and how the interactions take place? What are the various forms that cognitive involvement in emotion might take? Also, there are basic problems that need to be answered concerning the expression of emotion. Again to strike at the heart of difficulty, is feedback from expression more or less important to emotional experience than CNS activity? Even more problematically, what is the nature of the subjective experiences of emotion? How can preconscious or unconscious emotion be studied at all? Although these and similar problems have been generated by the cognitively based approaches to emotion, fortunately these same approaches rest on an innovative enough tradition of empirical investigation to provide some of the ways of finding the answers. However, as well as this, psychologists interested in emotion should also leave themselves open to information that may be available from scientifically unconventional sources, such as literature. Indeed, this point might reasonably be made of psychology as a whole. It is now mature enough not to have to lean entirely on the crutch of conventional science.

EMOTION CONTROL

The point of this final section is to speculate a little about the possible education of the emotions. Although largely ignored by experimental psychologists, some theorists have been turning their thoughts to it. Certainly it seems to be a topic which has considerable ramifications, especially for therapy in the widest sense of the term.

Leeper (1970) suggests that emotions are perceptions of various life situations. He holds that one implication of this view is that society should give some attention to moving into an age in which we concentrate on the emotions.

Leeper argues that the human species has passed two great ages. In the first we learned very slowly the techniques which allowed us to cope with the simple but nevertheless huge problems of physical survival. Having done this we entered into an age of rapid scientific, technological and educational advance. In this second age the emphasis has been placed on the value of objectivity based knowledge. The individual has been taught to be self-effacing in the presence of what he or she has been taught to think of as objective reality. Traditionally, emotions have been seen as obstructing this ideal. As has been mentioned on a number of occasions in this book, the distinction has been made between intellectual and emotional functioning, with the latter being suppressed in favour of the former. If we are reacting emotionally then we cannot be aware of what is thought to be objective reality.

Within the context of emotion as motivation, Leeper believes that the outcome of the second age of man has been an emphasis on negative emotional motives such as shame and insecurity, whilst considering only very crude positive emotional motives. He suggests that one way out of this (undesirable state of affairs is that a third age be developed in which due recognition is given to the fact that people experience situations emotionally. The society, or its educators, would be in a position to concentrate on subtle emotional reactions and place any activities, however simple they might be, on a *positive* emotional basis. Leeper does not suggest how this might be achieved, but believes that he has taken the first step by pointing out that emotion is not merely a hindrance to objectivity but exists in its own and very significant right. Clearly, this view fits well with the conceptions of emotion which have been described in the present text. The cognitive approach prompts considerations of learning and education.

Peters (1970), whose basic view of emotion was discussed earlier, provides an even more substantial argument than Leeper in favour of educating the emotions, a matter which he regards as primarily a moral concern. He suggests that from the everyday viewpoint many emotions are also seen as virtues or vices, pity and envy for example. He holds that education implies the introduction of people to knowledge and understanding, to what is valuable, and to the pursuit of truth. Thus, anyone who is concerned with the education of the emotions inevitably assumes a moral standpoint, seeing some emotions as 'better', more worthwhile, more to be sought after, than others.

Taken at its face value, Peters' argument would seem to imply that emotional education is beyond the scope, or perhaps even the competence, of the psychologist. However, Peters points to two ways in which the psychologist would have something useful to offer. First, on the basis of research the psychologist should be able to say what people do and what they experience, and hence, to an extent, what they are *capable* of doing and experiencing. If, for example, it is decided that it be inevitable that people experience anger or rage from time to time (a point which has certainly not been established yet), then it becomes pointless to try to teach them not to. The emphasis could instead be on training them to be enraged at particular times and with particular people. Second, Peters maintains that those psychologists who are concerned with abnormal behaviour should be in a fair position to evaluate the worth of the various emotions. Some emotions are more appropriate for healthy development than others, some should be avoided, the experience of certain emotions might be seen as basic to a normal development of other emotions, and so on.

Education of appraisals

Like many more recent theorists, Peters' view of emotion is that it hinges on a process of cognitive appraisal. He suggests that when such appraisals are complex they subsume *belief*. For example, my fear of someone might be based on the belief that he intends to do me some harm, a belief which might be mistaken. Peters therefore argues that one way in which the emotions might be educated is to make certain that people do not make appraisals which are based on mistaken beliefs. This is actually educating the cognitions in order to control the emotions.

To train people in this way is more easily said than done. Like Arnold, Peters regards emotional appraisals as rapid immediate occurrences, which will naturally make them difficult to handle. Also, if someone is in a particular mood, then this may bias, on false grounds, any appraisal that he or she makes. Peters' answer to this sets him somewhat against Leeper, in that he suggests that it comes from training in objectivity, which is viewed as in some way synonymous with truth. In a sense, Peters is ducking the problem by suggesting that the emotions can be educated by educating rational, objective thought. He believes that it is the psychoanalysts who have taken us furthest along this path. Although he suggests that what the psychoanalysts do can be characterized as a re-education of the emotions, it can also be seen as an educated suppression of the emotions in favour of what is regarded as more objectively based behaviour. It is, however, possible to believe that Peters' argument has some force even though 'rational, objective' thought is not a necessary part of it. It may be that the cognitions involved are even at the preconscious level.

To go along with Peters for the moment, one aspect of the education of appraisals which he deems to be important is *sincerity*. This follows on well from his delineation of the aims of education. If an educator is concerned with knowledge and the pursuit of truth then he or she is concerned with sincerity. If people are insincere in their emotions then the truth is obscured. But Peters makes no prescriptions as to how sincerity in emotion might best be trained, although comparisons with those who write of the role of emotion in the theatre spring to mind.

At this point it is worth mentioning briefly that Arnold (1969) also makes a few suggestions about the education of intuitive, emotional appraisals. She simply holds that it is possible to reduce the intensity of either pleasant or unpleasant emotions and that we do this by the use of imagination on which in her terms our emotional appraisal depend. For example, Arnold believes that we can learn to dwell only on the positive aspects of something which we dislike or which is generally unpleasant to us; or that we can learn to live without some pleasures which we covet. But Arnold offers no precise directions as to how these ends are, or might be, met. Again, though, this approach to emotional education is clearly predicated on cognition.

Education of passivity

A second important element in Peters' view of emotion is passivity. He believes that emotions overcome us, passively, and that we can therefore do little to stop this. He regards this as being particularly the case with the more primitive appraisals which overwhelm us completely, thoroughly distorting our perceptions and judgements, even our self-perceptions and self-judgements.

Peters suggests three ways in which education might be applied to these more atavistic emotions. First, use could be made of conditioning or drugs. Peters brackets these together as having the effect of reducing some current condition so that more appropriate educational techniques could be brought into use. However, many psychologists would view conditioning techniques as being directly educational, or that all education could be construed in terms of conditioning.

Second, Peters proposes that we could be brought to have some insight into our irrational behaviours, which might encourage them to cease. Here, he is in fact referrring to what is the avowed aim of much of psychotherapy.

Finally, Peters develops a notion first put forward by Spinoza, namely that an emotion might best be controlled with another emotion. He suggests that certain appraisals such as that which leads to love or perhaps to empathy make little or no reference to self. If these are developed then they could well have an overriding function on the other, more primitive, emotions. He argues that to be most effective such appraisals should be developed into settled dispositions or sentiments.

A further way in which passivity in emotion can be controlled, according to Peters is that action patterns be developed to which emotional appraisals can be connected. In this way emotion is turned into motive. Here Peters is suggesting that instead, for example, of being overwhelmed by anger, we direct our appraisals into motives which leads to definite action. This implies that there be developed positive moral patterns of active emotion, rather than the vaguely negative one which Peters believes to be currently prevalent.

Peters also raised the interesting question of emotional expression which he views as a sort of half-way between the emotion felt and violent action. Thus it is better that we shake and fume and grow red with rage, rather than murder someone. Clearly, much of our social learning is concerned with developing ways of controlling the expression of our emotions, particularly its facial expression, so that it becomes socially acceptable. Here is an obvious way in which emotions can be educated and yet very little is known about such education. For example, nothing is known of the effects of extreme control, almost suppression, of emotional expression. Does it lead to a reduced capacity to *experience* emotion, or not? More basically, does it lead to reduced experiences rather than capacities?

Peters then expresses clear and well-thought out ideas on the various ways in which the education of the emotions might take place, and on the general importance of the aim. Naturally enough, however, Peters' views are couched in the terms of his general theory of emotion. This results in his ideas for educating the emotions having little to do with the emotions directly, but to be more concerned with the training of the various alternatives to emotional reaction. However, this is reasonable in the light of the recent concerns with the role of cognition in emotion.

Finally, it is clear that the views expressed above are in close accord with Izard's ideas concerning emotional therapy and education. He argues that the typical aim of socialization in our society is to suppress emotional adaptiveness and even to work against an understanding of the emotions. The pressures are to inhibit certain emotions with the aim of increasing the use of the intellect coupled with a hiding of emotional reactions. The implicit thesis seems to be that truth and knowledge come from reason and intellect with emotion acting solely as a hindrance to sound perception and judgement. Izard suggests that attitudes such as these make it very difficult to develop a fully integrated personality and also make effective therapy for behavioural (emotional) problems very awkward to pursue.

In their various ways and from their different starting points it may well be that Leeper, Peters, and Izard are right and that it is important to gain an understanding of, and some degree of effective education of, the emotions, rather than simply trying to hide them away. It is hoped that the present text has made a small contribution to this endeavour, particularly in its reflection of the significance of cognition to an understanding of emotion.

References

Ahern, G.L., and Schwartz, F.E. (1979). 'Differential lateralization for positive and negative emotion', *Neuropsychol., 17,* 693–8.

Amsel, A. (1958). 'The role of frustrative nonreward in noncontinuous reward situations', *Psychol. Bull,* **55,** 102–19.

Amsel, A. (1962). 'Frustrative nonreward in partial reinforcement and discrimination learning: some recent history and a theoretical extension', *Psychol. Rev.,* **69,** 306–28.

Amsel, A. (1967). 'Partial reinforcement effects on vigor and persistence: Advances in frustration theory derived from a variety of within-subject experiments', *The Psychology of Learning and Motivation: Advances in Research and Theory.* Academic Press, New York, London.

Amsel, A., and Roussel, J. (1952). 'Motivational properties of frustration: I. Effect on a running response of the addition of frustration to the motivational complex'. *J. Exp. Psychol.,* **43,** 363–8.

Arieti, S. (1970). 'Cognition and feeling', in M.B. Arnold (Ed.) *Feeling and Emotion.* Academic Press, New York, London, pp.135–43.

Arnold, M.B. (1945). 'Physiological differentiation of emotional states', *Psychol. Rev.,* **52,** 35–48.

Arnold, M.B. (1950). 'An excitatory theory of emotion', in M.L. Reymert (Ed.) *Feelings and Emotions.* McGraw-Hill, New York.

Arnold, M.B. (Ed.) (1960). *Emotion and Personality* (2 volumes). Columbia University Press, New York.

Arnold, M.B. (1968). *The Nature of Emotion: Selected Readings.* Penguin Books, Harmondsworth.

Arnold, M.B. (1969). 'Human emotion and action', in T. Mischel (Ed.) *Human Action,* Academic Press, New York and London, pp.167–97.

Arnold, M.B. (1970a). *Feelings and Emotions: The Loyola Symposium.* Academic Press, New York, London.

Arnold, M.B. (1970b). 'Brain function in emotions: A phenomenological analysis', in P. Black (Ed.) *Physiological Correlates of Emotion.* Academic Press, New York and London.

Aronfreed, J. (1968). *Conduct and Conscious: The Socialization of Internalized Control over Behaviour.* Academic Press, New York.

Averill, J.R. (1982). *Anger and Aggresion: An Essay on Emotion.* Springer-Verlag, New York.

Averill, J.R., Opton, E.M. Jr., and Lazarus, R.S. (1969). 'Cross-cultural studies of psychophysiological responses during stress and emotion'. *International Journal of Psychology,* **4,** 83–102.

Ax, A.F. (1953). 'The physiological differential of fear and anger in humans', *Psychosom. Med.,* **15,** 433–42.

Bard, P. (1928). 'A diencephalic mechanisms for the expression of rage with special reference to the sympathetic nervous system', *Homer. J. Physiol.,* **84,** 490–515.

Bard, P. (1929). 'The central representation of the sympathetic nervous system as indicated by certain physiologic observations'. *Arch. Neurol. Psychiat.*, **22**, 230–46.

Bard, P. (1934). 'Emotion 1. The neurohumoral basis of emotional reactions', in C. Murchison (Ed.) *Handbook of General Experimental Psychology.* Clark University Press, Worcester, MA.

Bard, P. (1950). 'Central nervous mechanisms for the expression of anger in animals', in M.L. Reymert (Ed.) *Feelings and Emotions: The Mooseheart Symposium.* McGraw-Hill, New York, 211–37.

Bard, P., and Mountcastle, V.B. (1948). 'Some forebrain mechanisms involved in expresion of rage with special reference to suppression of angry behaviour', Research Publication, *Assoc. Res. Nerv. Ment Dis.*, **27**, 363–404.

Beck, A.T. (1967). *Depression: Clinical Experimental and Theoretical Aspects.* Harper & Row, New York.

Becker, H.S. (1953). 'Becoming a marihuana user', *Amer. J. Sociol.*, **59**, 235–42.

Becker, J. (1974). *Depression: Theory and Research.* Halsted Press, John Wiley, New York and London.

Beckwith, L. (1979). 'Prediction of emotional and social behaviour', in J.D. Osofsky (Ed.) *Handbook of Infant Development,* John Wiley, New York and London.

Beldoch, M.M. (1964). 'Sensitivity to expression of emotional meaning in three models of communication', in J.L. Davitz (Ed.) *The Communication of Emotional Meaning.* McGraw-Hill, New York, pp.31–42.

Berscheid, E. (1983). 'Emotion', in H.H. Kelley *et al.* (Eds) *Close Relationships.* W.H. Freeman, New York and San Francisco.

Bindra, D. (1968). 'A neuropsychological interpretation of the effects of drive and incentive-motivation on general activity and instrumental behaviour', *Psychol. Rev.*, **75**, 1–22.

Bindra, D. (1969). 'A unified interpretation of emotion and motivation', *Ann. New York Acad. Sci.*, **159**, 1071–83.

Bindra, D. (1970). 'Emotion and behavior theory: Current research in historical perspective', in P. Black (Ed.) *Physiological Correlates of Emotion.* Academic Press, New York and London.

Blau, S. (1964). 'An ear for an eye: Sensory compensation and judgements of affect by the blind', in J.L. Davitz (Ed.) *The Communication of Emotional Meaning.* McGraw-Hill, New York, pp.113–27.

Block, J. (1957). 'Studies in the phenomenology of emotions', *J. Abnorm. Soc. psychol.*, **54**, 358–63.

Bloemkolb, D., Defares, P., Van Enckevert, G., and Van Gelderen, M. (1971). 'Cognitive processing of information on varied physiological arousal', *Europ. J. Soc. Psychol.*, **1-1**, 31–46.

Bousfield, W.I., and Orbison, W.D. (1952). 'Ontogenesis of emotional behaviour', *Psychol. Rev.*, **59**, 1–7.

Bower, G.H. (1981). 'Mood and memory'. *Amer. Psychol.*, **36**, 129–48.

Bower, G.H., and Cohen, P.R. (1982). 'Emotional influences in memory and thinking: Data and theory', in M.S. Clark and S.T. Fiske (Eds) *Affect and Cognition.* Lawrence Erlbaum, Hillsdale, New Jersey.

Bowlby, J. (1951). *Maternal Care and Mental Health.* World Health Organization, Geneva.

Bowlby, J. (1953). 'Critical phases in the development of social responses in man', in *New Biology,* Vol.14. Penguin, London.

Bowlby, J. (1960). 'Separation anxiety', *Internat. J. Psychoanal.*, **41**, 1–25.

Bowlby, J. (1961). 'Separation anxiety: a critical review of literature', *J. Child Psychol.*, **15**, 9–52.

Bowlby, J. (1969). 'Psychopathology of anxiety: The role of affectional bonds', in M.H. Lader (Ed.) *Studies of anxiety.* Headley Bros., Ashford, pp.80–6.

Brady, J.V. (1958a). 'The paleocortex and behavioral motivation', in H.F. Harlow, and C. Woolsey (Eds.) *Biological and Biochemical Bases of Behavior.* University of Wisconsin Press, Madison.

Brady, J.V. (1958b). 'Ulcers in "executive" monkeys', *Scient. Amer., 199*, 95–100.

Brady, J.V. (1960). 'Emotional behavior', in J. Field, H.W. Magoun, and V.E. Halls (Eds.) *Handbook of Physiology,* Vol. III. Williams & Wilkins, Baltimore.

Brady, J.V. (1962). 'Psychophysiology of emotional behavior', in A Backrach (Ed.) *Experimental Foundations of Clinical Psychology.* Basic Books, New York.

Brady, J.V. (1963). 'Further comments on the gastrointestinal system and avoidance behavior', *Psychol. Rep., 12*, 742.

Brady, J.V. (1970a). 'Emotion: Some conceptual problems and psychophysiological experiments', in M.B. Arnold (Ed.) *Feelings and Emotions: The Loyola Symposium.* Academic Press, New York and London.

Brady, J.V. (1970b). 'Endocrine and autonomic correlates of emotional behaviour', in P. Black (Ed.) *Physiological Correlates of Emotion.* Academic Press, New York and London.

Brady, J.V. (1975). 'Towards a behavioural biology of emotion', in L. Levi (Ed.) *Emotions: Their Parameters and Measurement.* Raven Press, New York.

Brady, J.V., and Hunt, H.F. (1955). 'An experimental approach to the analysis of emotional behavior', *J. Psychol., 40*, 313–24.

Brady, J.V., and Nauta, W.J.H. (1953). 'Subcortical mechanisms in emotional behaviour: affective changes following septal forebrain lesions in the albino rat', *J. Comp. Physiol. Psychol., 46*, 339–46.

Brady, J.V., and Nauta, W.J.H. (1955). 'Subcortical mechanisms in emotional behaviour: The duration of affective changes following septal and labenular lesions in the albino rat', *J. Comp. Physiol. Psychol., 48*, 412–20.

Brannigan, C.R., and Humphries, D.A. (1971). 'Human non-verbal behaviour. A means of communication', in N. B.urton-Jones (Ed.) *Ethological Studies of Infant Behaviour.* Cambidge University Press, Cambridge.

Braun, E. (1969). *Meyerhold on Theatre.* Eyre Methuen, London.

Bridges, K.M.B. (1932). *The Social and Emotional Development of the Pre-school Child.* Kegan Paul, London.

Brierly, M. (1937). 'Affects in theory and practice', *Internat. Psychoanal., 18*, 256–68. (As quoted in Rapaport (1950).)

Bronson, G. (1972). 'Infants reaction to unfamiliar persons and novel objects'. *Monog. Soc. Res. Child Dev.,* No. 37.

Brown, J.J., and Farber, I.E. (1951). 'Emotions conceptualized as intervening variables—with suggestions toward a theory of frustration', *Psychol. Bull., 48*, 465–95.

Bruell, J.H. (1965). 'Mode of inheritance of response time in mice', *J. Comp. Physiol. Psychol., 60*, 147–8.

Brunswick, D. (1924). 'The effect of emotional stimuli on the gastrointestinal tone', *J. Comp. Psychol., 4*, 19–79.

Buck, R. (1983). 'Emotional development and emotional education', in R. Plutchik and H. Kellerman (Eds.) *Emotion: Theory, Research and Experience'.* Academic Press, New York and London.

Bull, N. (1951). 'The attitude theory of emotion', *Nerv. Ment. Dis. Monogr.* No. 81.

Buytedjik, F.J.J. (1950). 'The phenomenological approach to the problem of feelings and emotions', in M.L. Reymert (Ed.) *Feelings and Emotions: the Mooseheart Symposium.* McGraw-Hill, New York, pp.127–141.

Campbell, R. (1982). 'The lateralization of emotion: A critical review'. *Int. J. of Psychol., 17*, 211–229.

Cannon, W.B. (1915). *Bodily Changes in Panic, Hunger, Fear and Rage* (2nd edn, 1929). Appleton-Century, New York.

Cannon, W.B. (1927). 'The James–Lange theory of emotion: a critical examination and an alternative theory', *Am. J. Psychol.*, **39**, 106–24.

Cannon, W.B. (1931). 'Again the James–Lange and the thalamic theories of emotions', *Psychol. Rev.*, **38**, 281–95.

Cannon, W.B. (1932). *The Wisdom of the Body* (*2nd edn*, 1939). Norton, New York.

Cannon, W.B., and Britton, S.W. (1927). 'The influence of emotion on medulliadrenal secretaion', *Amer. J. Physiol.*, **79**, 433–65.

Cantwell, D.P., and Carlson, G.A. (1983). *Affective Disorders in Childhood and Adolescence—An Update*. Spectrum Publications, New York.

Cattell, R.B. (1963). 'The nature and measurement of anxiety', *Scient. Amer.*, March. See *Contemporary Psychology*, 1971, W.A. Freeman, New York, pp.358–65.

Cattell, R.B., and Scheier, I.H. (1958). 'The nature of anxiety: A review of thirteen multivariate analyses comprising 814 variables', *Psychol. Rep.*, **4**, 351–88.

Cattell, R.B., and Scheier, I.H. (1961). *The Meaning and Measurement of Neuroticism and Anxiety*. Ronald Press, New York.

CIBA Foundation Symposium 8 (1972). *Physiology, Emotion and Psychosomatic Illness*. Elsevier, Excerpta Medica, Amsterdam and London.

Cichetti, D., and Hesse, P. (1983). 'Affect and intellect: Piaget's contributions to the study of infant emotional development', in R. Plutchik and H. Kellerman (Eds.) *Emotion: Theory Research and Experience*, Vol. 2. Academic Press, New York and London.

Clark, M.S., and Fiske, S.T. (Eds.) (1982). *Affect and Cognition*. Lawrence Erlbaum, Hillsdale, NJ.

Cline, M.G. (1956). 'The influence of social context on the perception of faces', *J. Pers.*, **25**, 142–58.

Coleman, J. (1949). 'Facial expression of emotion', *Psychol. Monogr.*, **63**, 1.

Cotton, J.L. (1981). 'A review of research on Schachter's theory of emotion and the misattribution of arousal'. *Europ. J. Soc. Psychol.*, **11**, 365–397.

Darrow, C.W., Pathman, J., and Kronenberg, G. (1946). 'Level of autonomic activity and electrocephalogram', *J. Exp. Psychol.*, **36**, 355–65.

Darwin, C.R. (1872). *The Expression of Emotions in Man and Animals*. Murray, London.

Davis, H. (1968). 'Conditioned suppression: a survey of the literature'. *Psychon. Mongr. Supp.*, 2 (whole of issue No. 30).

Davitz, J.L. (1964). *The Communication of Emotional Meaning*. McGraw-Hill, New York.

Davitz, J.R. (1969). *The Language of Emotion*. Academic Press, New York and London.

Davitz, J.R. (1970). 'A dictionary and grammar of emotion', in M.L. Arnold (Ed.) *Feelings and Emotion: The Loyola Symposium*. Academic Press, New York and London, pp. 251–58.

Deaux, E., and Kakolewski, J.W. (1970). 'Emotionally induced increases in effective osmotic pressure and subsequent thirst', *Science*, **169**, 1226–8.

Delgado, J.M.R. (1970). 'Modulation of emotions by cerebral radio stimulation', in P. Black (Ed.) *Physiological correlates of Emotion*. Academic Press, New York and London.

Delgado, J.M.R., Roberts, W.W., and Miller, N.E. (1954). 'Learning motivated by electrical stimulation of the brain', *Amer. J. Physiol.*, **179**, 587–93.

Denenberg, V.H. (1964). 'Critical periods, stimulus input, and emotional reactivity: A theory of infantile stimulation', *Psychol. Rev.*, **71**, 335–51.

Denenberg, V.H., and Smith, S.A. (1963). 'Effects of infantile stimulation and age upon behavior', *J. Comp. Physiol. Psychol.*, **56**, 307–12.

De Rivera, J. (1984). 'Emotional experience and qualitative methodology', *Amer. Behav. Sci.*, **27**, 6, 677–88.

256

De Toledo, L., and Black, A.H. (1966). 'Heart rate: Changes during conditioned suppression in rats', *Science, 152*, 1404–6.

Dittman, A.T. (1962). 'The relationship between body movements and mood in interviews', *J. Consult. Psychol., 26*, 48.

Dixon, N.F. (1981). *Preconscious Processing*. John Wiley, New York and London.

Drever, J. (1952). *A Dictionary of Psychology*. Penguin, Harmondsworth.

Duffy, E. (1934). 'Emotion: An example of the need for reorientation in psychology', *Psychol. Rev., 41*, 184–98.

Duffy, E. (1941). 'An explanation of "emotional" phenomena without the use of the concept "emotion"', *J. Gen. Psychol., 25*, 283–93.

Duffy, E. (1951). 'The concept of energy mobilization', *Psychol. Rev., 58*, 30–40.

Duffy, E. (1962). *Activation and Behaviour*. John Wiley, New York and London.

Dunn, J. (1982). 'Comment: Problems and promises in the study of affect and intention', in E.Z. Tronick (Ed.) *Social Interchange in Infancy: Affect, Cognition and Communication*. University Park Press: Baltimore.

Dusser de Barenne, J.G. (1920). 'Recherches expérimentales sur les fonctions du système nerveux central, faites en particulier sur deux chats donc le néopallium a été enlevé', *Arch. Neurol. Physiol., 4*, 31–123.

Easterbrook, J.A. (1959). 'The effect of emotion on cue utilization and the organization of behaviour', *Psychol. Rev., 66*, 183–201.

Eibl-Eibesfeldt, I. (1970). *Ethology—The Biology of Behaviour*. Holt, Rinehart & Winston, New York and London.

Ekman, P. (1965a). 'Communication threough nonverbal behaviour: A source of information about interpersonal relationships', in S.S. Tomkins and C.E. Izard (Eds.) *Affect, Cognition and Personality*. Springer, New York, pp.390–442.

Ekman, P. (1965b). 'Differential communications of affect by head and body cues', *J. Pers. Soc. Psychol., 2*, 726–35.

Ekman, P. (1984). 'Expression and the nature of emotion', in K. Scherer and P. Ekman (Eds.) *Approaches to Emotion*. Lawrence Erlbaum, Hillsdale, NJ.

Ekman, P., and Friesen, W.V. (1967a). 'Head and body cues in the judgement of emotion: a reformulation'. *Percept. Mot. Sk., 24*, 711–14.

Ekman, P., and Friesen, W.V. (1967b). 'Nonverbal behavior in psychotherapy research', in J. Schlein (Ed.) *Research in Psychotherapy*, Vol. 3. A.P.A., Washington.

Ekman, P., and Friesen, W.V. (1969). 'Non-verbal leakage and clues to deception', *Psychiatry, 32*, 88–106.

Ekman, P., and Oster, H. (1979). 'Facial expression of emotion', Ann. Rev., 30, 527–54.

Ekman, P., Friesen, W.V. and Ellsworth, P. (1972). *Emotion in the Human Face*. Pergamon, New York and Oxford.

Epstein, S. (1967). 'Toward a unified theory of anxiety', *Progr. Exp. Res. Pers., 4*, 1–89. Academic Press, New York.

Estes, W.K., and Skinner, B.F. (1941). 'Some quantitative properties of anxiety', *J. Exp. Psychol., 29*, 390–400.

Eysenck, H.J. (Ed.) (1964). *Experiments in Motivation*. Pergamon, Oxford.

Eysenck, H.J. (1967). *The Biological Basis of Personality*. Springfield, Illinois.

Eysenck, H.J. (1969). 'Psychological aspects of anxiety', in M.H. Lader (Ed.) *Studies of Anxiety*. Headley Bros., Ashford, pp.7–20.

Eysenck, H.J. (1976). 'The learning theory model of neurosis—a new approach'. *Behaviour Research and Therapy, 14*, 251–267.

Fantino, E. (1973). 'Emotion', in J.A. Nevin (Ed.) *The Study of Behavior: Learning, Motivation, Emotion, and Instinct*. Scott, Foresman, Glenview, Illinois.

Federn, P. (1936). 'Zur Unterscheidung des gesunden and krankhaften', *Narzimus, 22*, 5–39. (As quoted by Rapaport (1950).)

257

Fehr, F.S., and Stern, J.A. (1970). 'Peripheral physiological variables and emotion: The James–Lange theory revisited', *Psychol. Bull.*, **74**, 411–24.

Fell, J.P. (1977). 'The phenomenological approach to emotion', in D.K. Candland, J.P. Fell, E. Keen, A.T. Leshner, R.M. Tarpy, and R. Plutchik, *Emotion*. Brooks/Cole, Monterey.

Ferrier, D. (1875). The Gornian Lecture. 'Experiments on the brain of monkeys' (second series), *Phil. Trans.*, **165**, 433–88.

Field, T. (1977). 'Effects of early separation, interactive deficits and experimental manipulations on infant–mother face-to-face interaction. *Child Dev.*, **48**, 763–71.

Field, T. (1980). 'Interactions of high risk infants: Quantitative and qualitative', in D. Sawin, K. Hawkins, I. Walker and J. Penticuff (Eds.) *Current Perspectives on Psychosocial Risks during Early Interactions*. Bruner/Mazel, New York.

Field, T. (1981). 'Gaze behavior of normal and high risk infants during early interactions'. *J. Amer. Acad. Child Psychiat.*, **20**, 308–17.

Fischer, W.F. (1970). *Theories of Anxiety*. Harper & Row, New York.

Flores, d'Arcais. (1961). 'Forming impressions of personality in situations of contrast between verbal and minoric expressions', *Acta Psychol.*, **19**, 495–5.

Fogel, A. (1982). 'Affect dynamics in early infancy: Affective tolerance', In T. Field and A. Fogel (Eds.) *Emotion and Early Interaction*. Lawrence Erlbaum, Hillsdale, NJ.

Freeman, G.L. (1948). *Physiological Psychology*. Van Nostrand, New York.

Frick, R.W. (1985). 'Communicating emotion. The role of prosodic features', *Psychol. Bull.*, **97**, 3, 412–29.

Frijda, N.H. (1969). 'Recognition of emotion', in L. Berkowitz (Ed.) *Advances in Experimental Social Psychology, *4**, 167–223.

Frijda, N.H. (1970). 'Emotion and recognition of emotion', in M.L. Arnold (Ed.) *Feelings and Emotions: The Loyola Symposium*. Academic Press, New York and London, pp.241–50.

Fuenzalida, C., Emde, R.N., Pannebecker, B., and Sternberg, C. 'Validation of the differential emotions scale in 613 mothers', *Motiv. and Emot.*, **5**, 1, 37–45.

Fulton, J.F., Pribram, K.H., Stevenson, J.A.F., and Wall, P.D. (1952). 'Interrelations between orbital gyrus, insula, temporal tip, and anterior cingulate', *Trans. Amer. neurol. Assoc.*, **74**, 175–9.

Funkenstein, D.H., King, S.H., and Drolette, M.E. (1957). *Mastery of Stress*, Harvard University Press, Cambridge, Mass.

Gellhorn, E. (1964). 'Motion and emotion: The role of proprioception in the physiology and pathology of the emotions', *Psychol. Rev.*, **71**, 457–72.

Gellhorn, E. (1968). *Biological Foundations of Emotion*. Scott, Foresman, Glenview, Illinois.

Gellhorn, E., and Loufbourrow, G.N. (1963). *Emotions and Emotional Disorders*. Hoeber, New York.

Giblin, P.T. (1981). 'Affective development in children: an equilibrium model'. *Genet. Psychol. Mong.*, **103**, 3–30.

Giorgi, A., (1970). *Psychology as a Human Science: A Phenomenologically Based Approach*. Harper & Row, New York.

Goldstein, M.L. (1968). 'Psychological theories of emotion: A critical historical review from the standpoint of behavior theory', *Psychol. Bull.*, **69**, 23–40.

Gray, J.A. (1971). *The Psychology of Fear and Stress*. Weidenfeld & Nicholson, London.

Gray, J.M., Fraser, W.L., and London, I. (1983). 'Recognition of emotion from facial expression in mental handicap', *Brit. J. Psychiat.*, **142**, 566–71.

Grinker, R.R. Sr. (1953). *Psychosomatic Research*. Norton, New York.

Grinker, R.R. Sr., and Spiegel, J.P. (1945). *Men under Stress*. Blakiston, Philadelphia. ((1961). McGraw-Hill, New York.)

Grossman, S.P. (1963). 'Chemically induced epileptiform seizures in the cat', *Science*,

142, 409–11.

Grossman, S.P. (1967). *Physiological Psychology*. John Wiley, New York and London.

Grossman, S.P. (1970). 'Modification of emotional behaviour by intercranial administration of chemicals', in P. Black (Ed.) *Physiological Correlates of Emotion*. Academic Press, New York and London.

Haggard, E.A., and Isaacs, F.X. (1966). 'Micromomentary facial expressions as indicators of ego mechanisms in psychotherapy', in L.A. Gottschak and A.H. Averback (Eds.) *Methods of Research in Psychotherapy*. Appleton-Century-Crofts, New York, pp.151–92.

Hall, C.S. (1934). 'Emotional behavior in the rat: I. Defecation and urination as measures of individual differences in emotionality', *J. Comp. Psychol.*, **18**, 385–403.

Hammond, L.J. (1970). 'Conditioned emotional states', in P. Black (Ed.) *Physiological Correlates of Emotion*. Academic Press, New York and London, pp.245–59.

Harlow, H.F., and Harlow, M.K. (1962). 'Social deprivation in monkeys', *Sci. Amer.*, **207**, 136–46.

Harlow, H.F., and Harlow, M.K. (1970). 'Developmental aspects of emotional behaviour', in P.R. Black (Ed.) *Physiological Correlates of Emotion*. Academic Press, New York and London, pp.37–58.

Harlow, H.F., and Mears, C.E. (1983). 'Emotional sequences and consequences', in R. Plutchik and H. Kellerman (Eds.) *Emotion: Theory, Research and Experience*. Academic Press, New York and London.

Harlow, H.F., and Stagner, R. (1933). 'Psychology of feelings and emotions. II. Theory of emotions', *Psychol. Rev.*, **40**, 184–94.

Harris, V.A., and Katkin, E.S. (1975). 'Primary and secondary emotional behaviour: An analysis of the role of autonomic feedback on affect, arousal and attribution'. *Psychological Bulletin*, **82**, 6, 904–16.

Harvey, J.A., Jacobson, L.E., and Hunt, H.F. (1961). 'Long-term effects of lesions in the peptal forebrain on acquisition and retention of conditioned fear', *Amer. Psychol.*, **16**, 449.

Head, H. (1921). 'Release of function in the nervous system', *Proc. Roy. Soc.*, **926**, 184. (As cited in Cannon (1927).)

Hearst, E. (1969). 'Aversive conditioning and external stimulus control', in B.A. Campbell and R.M. Church (Eds.) *Punishment and Aversive Behavior*. Appleton-Century-Crofts, New York, pp. 235–77.

Hillman, J. (1960). *Emotion*. Routledge & Kegan Paul, London.

Hillman, J. (1970). 'C.G. Jung's contributions to "Feelings and emotions": Synopsis and implications', in M.B. Arnold (Ed.) *Feelings and Emotions*. Academic Press, New York and London, pp.125–34.

Hinde, R.A. (1985). 'Was "The Expression of the Emotions" a misleading phrase? *Anim. Behav.*, **33**, 992–5.

Hirschman, R.D. (1975). 'Cross modal effects of anticipatory bogus heart rate feedback in a negative emotional context', *Journal of Personality and Social Psychology*, **31**, 13–19.

Hoch, P.H., and Zubin, J. (Eds.) (1950). *Anxiety*. Grune & Stratton, New York.

Hoffman, H.S. (1969). 'Stimulus factors in conditioned suppression', in B.A. Campbell and R.M. Church (Eds.) *Punishment and Aversive Behavior*. Appleton-Century-Crofts, New York, pp. 185–234.

Hohmann, G.W. (1962). 'The effects of dysfunctions of the autonomic nervous system on experienced feelings and emotions'. Paper read at Conference on Emotions and Feelings at New School for Social Research, New York. (Quoted by Schachter (1964).)

Hohmann, G.W. (1966). 'Some effects of spinal cord lesions on experienced emotional feelings', *Psychophys.*, **3**, 143–56.

Hull, C.L. (1943). *Principles of Behavior*. Appleton-Century-Crofts. New York.

Hunt, H.F., and Brady, J.V. (1951). 'Some effects of electro-convulsive shock on a conditioned emotional response ("anxiety'), *J. Comp. Physiol. Psychol.*, **44**, 88–98.

Hunt, H.F., and Brady, J.V. (1955). 'Some effects of punishment and intercurrent anxiety on a simple operant', *J. Comp. Physiol. Psychol.*, **48**, 305–10.

Husserl, E. (1913). *Ideas* (1962 edition). Collier Books, New York.

Isaacson, R.L., Douglas, R.J., and Moore, R.Y. (1961). 'The effect of radial hippocampal ablation on acquisition of avoidance responses', *J. Comp. Physiol. Psychol.*, **54**, 625–8.

Israel, N.R. (1969). 'Levelling-sharpening and anticipatory cardiac response', *Psychosomatic Medicine*, **31**, 499–509.

Izard, C.E. (1960). 'Personality similarity and friendship', *J. Abnorm. Soc. Psychol.*, **61**, 47–51.

Izard, C.E. (1964). 'The effects of role-played emotion on affective reactions, intellectual functioning and evaluative ratings of the actress', *J. Clin. Psychol.*, **20**, 444–6.

Izard, C.E. (1965). 'Personal growth through experience', in S.S. Tomkins, and C.E. Izard (Eds.) *Affects, Cognition and Personality*. Springer, New York, pp. 200–41.

Izard, C.E. (1972). *The Face of Emotion*. Appleton-Century-Crofts, New York.

Izard, C.E. (1977). *Human Emotions*. Plenum, New York and London.

Izard, C.E. (1980). 'Cross-cultural perspectives on emotion and emotion communication', in H.C. Triandis and W. Lonner (Eds.) *Handbook of Cross-cultural Psychology*, Vol. 3. Allyn & Bacon, London.

Izard, C.E. (1982). 'Comments on emotion and cognition: Can there be a working relationship?', in M.S. Clark and S.T. Fiske (Eds.) *Affect and Cognition*. Lawrence Erlbaum, Hillsdale, NJ.

Izard, C.E., and Malatesta, C.Z. (1984). 'A development theory of the emotions' (preprint).

Izard, C.E., and Tomkins, S.S. (1966). 'Affect and behavior: Anxiety as negative affect', in G.D. Spielberger (Ed.) *Anxiety and Behavior*. Academic Press, New York and London.

Izard, C.E., Randall, D., Nagler, S., and Fox, J. (1965a). 'The effects of affective picture stimuli on learning, perception and the affective value of previously neutral symbols', in S.S. Tomkins and C.E. Izard (Eds.) *Affect, Cognition and Personality*. Springer, New York, pp.42–70.

Izard, C.E., Wehmer, G.M., Livsey, W., and Jennings, J.R. (1965b). 'Affect, awareness and performance', in S.S. Tomkins and C.E. Izard (Eds.) *Affect, Cognition and Personality*. Springer, New York, pp. 2–41.

James, W. (1884). 'What is an emotion'. *Mind*, **9**, 188–205.

Jaynes, J. (1976). *The Origins of Consciousness in the Breakdown of the Bicameral Mind*. Houghton-Mifflin, Boston.

Jorgenson, E.C., and Howell, R.J. (1969). 'Judged imposed emotional behavior', *Psychotherapy: Theory, Research and Practice*, **6**(3), 161–165.

Kagan, J. (1978). 'On emotion and its development', in M. Lewis and L.A. Rosenblum (Eds.) *The Development of Affect*. Plenum Press, New York.

Kamin, L.J. (1965). 'Temporal and intensity characteristics of the condition stimulus', in W.E. Prokasy (Ed.) *Classical conditioning*. Appleton-Century-Crofts, New York, pp.118–47.

Kammann, R., Christie, D., Irwin, R., and Dixon, G. (1979). 'Properties of an inventory to measure happiness (and psychological health)', *New Zeal. Psychol.*, **8**, 1–12.

Karabenick, S.A. (1969). 'Effects of reward increase and reduction in the double runway', *J. Exp. Psychol.*, **82**, 79–87.

Keen, E. (1977). 'Emotion in personality theory', in D.K. Candland, J.P. Fell, E. Keen, A.I. Lashner, R.M. Tarpy and R. Plutchik *Emotion*. Brooks/Cole, Monterey.

260

Kelly, D.H.W. (1966). 'Measurement of anxiety by forearm blood flow', *Brit. J. Psychiat.,* **112**, 789–98.

Kelly, G.A. (1955). *The Psychology of Personal Constructs,* Vols. 1 and 2. Norton, New York.

Kemper, T.D. (1978). *'A Social Interactional Theory of Emotions.* John Wiley, New York and London.

Kennard, M.A. (1955). 'Effect of bilateral ablation of cingulate area on behavior of cats', *J. Neurophysiol.,* **18**, 159–69.

Kety, S.S. (1966). 'Catecholamines in neuropsychiatric state', *Pharmacol. Rev.,* **18**, 787–98.

Kety, S.S. (1970). 'Neurochemical aspects of emotional behaviour'. in P. Black (Ed.) *Physiological Correlates of Emotion.* Academic Press, New York and London.

Kiesler, C.A. (1982). 'Comments', in W.S. Clark, and S.T. Fiske (Eds.) *Affect and Cognition.* Lawrence Erlbaum: Hillsdale, NJ.

Kinsbourne, M. (1982). 'Hemispheric specialization and the growth of human understanding'. *Amer. Psychol.,* **37**, 411–20.

Klages, L. (1950). 'The life of feeling'. Excerpts from *Grundlegung der Wissenschaft rom Ausdruck,* Bouvrer (6th edn, 1964). Translated by M.B. Arnold (Ed.) in *The Nature of Emotion* (1968). Penguin, Harmondsworth.

Kleinginna, P.R. Jr., and Kleinginna, A.M. (1981). 'A categorised list of emotional definitions, with suggestions for a consensual definition'. *Motiv. & Emot.,* **5**, 4, 345–79.

Kluver, H., and Bucy, P.C. (1937). '"Psychic blindness" and other symptoms following bilateral temporal lobectomy in rhesus monkeys, *Amer. J. Physiol.,* **119**, 352–3.

Kluver, H., and Bucy, P.C. (1938). 'An analysis of certain effects of bilateral temporal lobectomy in the rhesus monkey, with special reference to "psychic blindness"', *J. Psychol.,* **5**, 33–54.

Knapp, P.H. (Ed.) (1963). *Expression of the Emotions in man.* International University Press, New York.

Krause, M.S. (1961). 'The measurement of transitory anxiety', *Psychol. Rev.,* **68**, 178–89.

Kreitler, H., and Kreitler, S. (1972). *Psychology of the Arts.* Duke University Press, Durham, NC.

Krueger, F. (1928). 'The essence of feeling'. Abridged from 'Das Wesen der GErfuhle', *Arch. f. d. ges Psychol.,* **65**, 91–128. Translated by M.B. Arnold (Ed.) in *The Nature of Emotion* (1968). Penguin, Harmondsworth.

Lacey, J.I. (1970). 'Individual differences in somatic response patterns', *J. Comp. Physiol. Psychol.,* **43**, 338–50.

Lacey, J.I. (1956). 'The evaluation of autonomic responses toward a general solution', *Annals N.Y. Acad. Sci.,* **67**, 123–63.

Lacey, J.I., and Lacey, B.C. (1958). 'Verification and extension of the principle of autonomic response stereotypy', *Amer. J. Psychol.,* **71**, 50–73.

Lacey, J.I., and Lacey, B.C. (1970). 'Some autonomic-central nervous system interrelationships', in P. Black (Ed.) *Physiological Correlates of Emotion.* Academic Press, New York and London.

Lacey, J.I., Kagan, J., Lacey, B.C., and Moss, H.A. (1963). 'The visceral level: Situational determinants and behavioural correlates of autonomic response patterns', in P.H. Knapp (Ed.) *Expressions of the Emotions in Man.* International University Press, New York.

Ladavas, E., Nicoletti, R., Umilta, C., and Rizzolatti, G. (1984). 'Right hemisphere interference during negative affect: A reaction time study'. *Neuropsychol.,* **22**, 479–95.

Lader, M.H. (1967). 'Palmer skin conductance measures in anxiety and phobic states', *J. Psychosom. Res.,* **11**, 271–81.

Lader, M.H. (1969). 'Psychophysiological aspects of anxiety', in M.H. Lader (Ed.) *Studies of Anxiety*. Headley Bros., Ashford, pp.53–61.

Lader, M.H. (1972). 'Psychophysiological research and psychosomatic medicine', in Ciba Foundation Symposium 8 (1972), pp.297–311.

Lader, M.H., and Wing, L. (1964). 'Habituation of the psychogalvanic reflex in patients with anxiety states and in normal subjects', *J. Neurol. Neurosurg. Psychiat.*, **27**, 210–18.

Lader, M.H., and Wing, L. (1966). *Psychological Measures, Sedative Drugs and Morbid Anxiety*. Oxford University Press, London.

Lange, C.G. (1885). *The Emotions* (English translation 1922). Williams & Wilkins, Baltimore.

Latane, B., and Schachter, S. (1962). 'Adrenaline and avoidance learning', *J. Comp. Physiol. Psychol.*, **65**, 369–72.

Lazarus, R.S. (1982). 'Thoughts on the relations between emotion and cognition'. *Amer. Psychol.*, **37**, 1019–24.

Lazarus, R.S. (1984). 'On the primacy of cognition'. *Amer. Psychol.*, **39**, 124–29.

Lazarus, R.S., and Opton, E.M.Jr. (1966). 'The study of psychological stress: A summary of theoretical formulations and experimental findings', in C.D. Spielberger (Ed.) *Anxiety and Behavior*. Academic Press, New York, pp.225–62.

Lazarus, R.S., Deese, J., and Osler, S.F. (1952). 'The effects of psychological stress upon performance', *Psychol. Bull.*, **49**, 293–317.

Lazarus, R.S., Opton, E.M.Jr., Nomikos, M.S., and Rankin, N.O. (1965). 'The principle of short-circuiting of threat: Further evidence'. *J. Person.*, **33**, 622–35.

Lazarus, R.S., Averill, J.R., and Opton, E.M.Jr. (1970). 'Towards a cognitive theory of emotion', in M.B. Arnold (Ed.) *Feelings and Emotions: The Loyola Symposium*. Academic Press, New York and London, pp.207–32.

Lebrun, C. (1734). 'A method to learn to design the passions'. The Augustan Reprint Society. Publ. No. 200–201. (1980). William Andrews Clark Memorial Library, U.C.L.A.

Leeper, R.W. (1948). 'A motivational theory of emotion to replace emotion as disorganised response', *Psychol. Rev.*, **55**, 5–21.

Leeper, R.W. (1962a). 'The motivational theory of emotion', in C.L. Stacey and M.F. De Martino (Eds.) *Understanding Human Motivation*. Howard Allen, Cleveland, Ohio, pp.657–65.

Leeper, R.W. (1962b). 'Learning and the fields of perception, motivation and personality', in S. Koch (Ed.) *Psychology: a Study of a Science,* Vol. 5. McGraw-Hill, New York, pp.365–487.

Leeper, R.W. (1965). 'Some needed developments in the motivational theory of emotions', in D. Levine (Ed.) *Nebraska Symposium on Motivation*. University of Nebraska Press, Lincoln, Nebraska, pp. 25–122.

Leeper, R.W. (1970). 'Feelings and emotions', in M.D. Arnold (Ed.) *Feelings and Emotions: The Loyola Symposium*. Academic Press, New York and London, pp.151–68.

Leventhal, H. (1974). 'Emotions: A basic problem for social psychology', in C. Nemeth (Ed.) *Social Psychology: Classic and Contemporary Integrations,* Rand-McNally, Chicago, pp.1–51.

Leventhal, H., (1982). 'The integration of emotion and cognition: A view from the perceptual motor theory of emotion', in M.S. Clark and S.T. Fiske (Eds.) *Affect and Cognition*, Lawrence Erlbaum, Hillsdale, NJ.

Leventhal, H., and Tomarken, A.J. (1986). 'Emotion: Today's problems', *Ann. Rev. Psychol.*, **37**, 565–610.

Levine, S. (1957). 'Infantile experience and consummatory behaviour in adulthood', *J. Comp. Physiol. Psychol.*, **50**, 609–12.

Levine, S. (1958). 'Noxious stimulation in infant and adult rats and consummatory behaviour', *J. Comp. Physiol. Psychol.*, **51**, 230–3.

Levine, S. (1959). 'Differential emotionality at weaning as a function of infantile stimulation', *Canad. J. Psychol.*, **13**, 243–7.

Levine, S. (1962). 'Psychophysiological effects of infantile stimulation', in E.L. Bliss (Ed.) *Roots of Behavior.* Harper & Row, New York.

Levitt, E.A. (1964). 'The relationship between abilities to express emotional meanings vocally and facially', in J.L. Davitz (Ed.) *The Communication of Emotional Meaning.* McGraw-Hill, New York.

Levy, P.K. (1964). 'The ability to express and perceive vocal communications of feeling', in J.L. Davitz (Ed.) *The Communication of Emotional Meaning.* McGraw-Hill, New York, pp.43–55.

Lewis, M., and Michalson, L. (1982). 'The socialization of emotions', in T. Field and A. Fogel (Eds.) *Emotion and Early Interaction.* Lawrence Erlbaum, Hillsdale, NJ.

Lewis, M., and Rosenblum, L.A. (Eds.) (1978). *The Development of Affect.* Plenum Press, New York.

Ley, R.G., and Bryden, M.P. (1982). 'A dissociation of right and left hemisphere effects for recognising emotional tone and verbal content', *Brain & Cogn.*, **1**, 3–9.

Lindauer, M.S. (1968). 'Pleasant and unpleasant emotions in literature: a comparison with the affective tone of psychology', *J. of Psychol.*, **70**, 53–67.

Lindsley, D.B. (1950). 'Emotions and the electroencephalogram', in M.L. Reymert (Ed.) *Feelings and Emotions: The Mooseheart Symposium.* McGraw-Hill, New York.

Lindsley, D.B. (1951). 'Emotion', in S.S. Stevens (Ed.) *Handbook of Experimental Psychology.* John Wiley, New York, pp.473–516.

Lindsley, D.B. (1957). 'Psychophysiology and motivation', in M.R. Jones (Ed.) *Nebraska symposium on motivation.* University of Nebraska Press, Lincoln, Nebraska, pp.44–105.

Lindsley, D.B. (1970). 'The role of nonspecific reticulothalamocortical systems in emotion', in P. Black (Ed.) *Physiological Correlates of Emotion'.* Academic Press, New York and London.

Linville, P.W. (1982). 'Affective consequences of complexity regarding the self and others', in M.S. Clark and S.T. Fiske (Eds.) *Affect and Cognition.* Lawrence Erlbaum, Hillsdale, NJ.

Lipps, T. (1965). 'Empathy and aesthetic pleasure', in K. Aschenrunner and A. Isenberg (Eds.) *Aesthetic Theory: Studies in the Philosophy of Art.* Prentice-Hall, NJ.

Louch, A.R. (1966). *Explanations and Human Action.* Blackwell, Oxford.

Lubar, J.F. (1964). 'Effects of medial cortical lesions on the avoidance behavior of a cat', *J. Comp. Physiol. Psychol.*, **58**, 34–6.

Lykken, D.T. (1957). 'A study of anxiety in the sociopathic personality', *J. Abnorm. Soc. psychol.*, **55**, 6–10.

Lyon, D.O. (1968). 'Conditioned suppression: Operant variables and aversive control', *Psychol. Rec.*, **18**, 317–38.

Lyons, W. (1980). *Emotions.* Cambridge University Press, Cambridge.

McDougall, W. (1910). *Introduction to Social Psychology.* Luce, Boston.

McDougall, W. (1923). *Outline of Psychology.* Scribner, New York.

McDougall, W. (1928). 'Emotion and feeling distinguished', in M.L. Reymert (Ed.) *Feelings and Emotions.* Clark University Press, Worcester, MA.

MacLean, P.D. (1954). 'The limbic system and its hippocampal formation: studies in animals and their possible application to man', *J. Neurosurg.*, **II**, 29–44.

MacLean, P.D. (1957). 'Chemical and electrical stimulation of hippocampus in unrestrained animals. II: Behavioral findings', *Arch. Neurol. Psychoat.*, **78**, 128–42.

MacLean, P.D. (1970). 'The limbic brain in relation to the psychoses', in P.D. Black (Ed.) *Physiological Correlates of Emotion.* Academic Press, New York and London.

Mahl, G.F. (1950). 'Anxiety, HCL secretion, and peptic ulcer etiology', *Psychosom. Med.*, **12**, 158–69.

Malatesta, C.Z. (1982). 'The expresion and regulation of emotion: A lifespan perspective', in T. Field and A. Fogel (Eds.) *Emotion and EArly Interaction.* Lawrence Erlbaum, Hillsdale, NJ.

Malmo. R.B. (1950). 'Experimental studies of mental patients under stress', in M. Reymert (Ed.) *Feelings and Emotions.* McGraw-Hill, New York, pp.169–80.

Malmo, R.B. (1957). 'Anxiety and behavioural arousal', *Psychol. Rev.*, **64**, 276–87.

Malmo, R.B. (1959). 'Activation: a neuropsychological dimension', *Psychol. Bull*, **66**, 367–86.

Mandler, G. (1962). 'Emotion', in *New Directions in Psychology*, Vol. 1. Holt, Rinehart & Winston, New York, pp.269–353.

Mandler, G. (1976). *Mind and Emotion.* John Wiley, New York and London.

Mandler, G. (1982). 'The structure of value: Accounting for taste', in M.S. Clark and S.T. Fiske (Eds.) *Affect and Cognition.* Lawrence Erlbaum, Hillsdale, NJ.

Mandler, G. (1984). *Mind and Body: Psychology of Emotion and Stress.* W.W. Norton, New York and London.

Maranon, G. (1924). 'Contribution a l'étude de l'action émotive de l'adrenoline', *Revue Franc. d'Endocrin.*, **21**, 301–25. (As quoted in Fehr and Stern (1970).)

Martin, B. (1961). 'The assessment of anxiety by physiological behavioral measures', *Psychol Bull.*, **58**, 234–55.

Maslow, A.H. (1972). *The Farther Reaches of Human Nature.* Penguin, Harmondsworth.

Mayer-Gross, W., Slater, E., and Roth, M. (1969). *See* Slater and Roth (1969).

Mehrabian, A., and Russell, J.A. (1974). *An Approach to Environmental Psychology.* MIT Press, Cambridge, MA.

Mendel, S.J. (1970). *Concepts of Depression.* John Wiley, New York and London.

Meyer, P.A., and McHose, J.H. (1968). 'Facilitative effects of reward increase: An apparent "elation effect"', *Psychon. Sci.*, **13**, 165–6.

Michotte, A.E. (1950). 'The emotions as functional connections', in M.L. Reymert (Ed.) *Feelings and Emotions: The Moosehart Symposium.* McGraw-Hill, New York.

Millenson, J.R. (1967). *Principles of Behavioural Analysis.* Macmillan, New York; Collier-Macmillan, London.

Miller, G.A., Galanter, E.H., and Prihram, K.H. (1960). *Plans and the Structure of Behaviour.* Holt, New York.

Miller, N.E. (1951). 'Learning drives and rewards', in S.S. Stevens (Ed.) *Handbook of Experimental Psychology.* John Wiley, New York.

Miller, N.E. (1958). 'Central stimulation and other new approaches to motivation and reward', *Amer. Psychol.*, **13**, 100–8.

Miller, N.E. (1969). 'Learning of visceral and glandular responses', *Science*, **163**, 434–45.

Miller, R.E., Murphy, J.V., and Mirsky, I.A. (1959a). 'Non-verbal communication of effect', *J. Clin. Psychol.*, **15**, 155–8.

Miller, R.E., Murphy, J.V., and Mirsky, I.A. (959b). 'The relevance of facial expression and posture as cues in the communication of affect between monkeys', *Arch. Gen. Psychiat.*, **1**, 480–8.

Mirsky, A.F. (1960). 'Studies of the effects of brain lesions on social behavior in *Macaca mulatta:* methodological and theoretical considerations', *Ann. N.Y. Acad. Sci.*, **85**, 785–94.

Moruzzi, G., and Magoun, H.W. (1949). 'Brain stem reticular formation and activation of the EEG', *Electroenceph. and Clin. Neurophys.*, **1**, 455–73.

Mowrer, O.H. (1960a). *Learning Theory and Behavior.* John Wiley, New York.

Mowrer, O.H. (1960b). *Learning theory and the symbolic processes.* John Wiley, New York.

264

Murphy, L.B. (1983). 'Issues in the development of emotion in infancy', in R. Plutchik and H. Kellerman (Eds.) *Emotion: Theory, Research and Development*, Vol.2. Academic Press, New York and London.

Myer, J.S. (1971). 'Some effects of noncontingent aversive stimulation', in *Aversive Conditioning and Learning*. Academic Press, New York and London, pp.469–536.

Nicholson, J. (1984). *Men and Women*. Oxford University Press, Oxford.

Nisbett, R.E., and Schachter, S. (1966). 'Cognitive manipulation of gain', *J. Exp. Soc. Psychol.*, **2**, 227–36.

Nowlis, V. (1953). 'The development and modification of motivational systems in personality', in M.R. Jones (Ed.) *Current Theory and Research in Motivation*. University of Nebraska Press, Lincoln, Nebraska.

Nowlis, V. (1959). 'The experimental analysis of mood' (Abstract), XVth International Congress of Psychology. *Acta Psychol.*, **15**, 426.

Nowlis, V. (1963). 'The concept of mood', in S.M. Farber and R.H.L. Wilson (Eds.) *Conflict and Creativity*. McGraw-Hill, New York.

Nowlis, V. (1965). 'Research with the mood adjective check list', in S.S. Tomkins and C.E. Izard (Eds.) *Affect, Cognition and Personality*. Springer, New York.

Nowlis, V. (1970). 'Mood: Behavior and experience', in M.B. Arnold (Ed.) *Feelings and Emotions: The Loyola Symposium*. Academic Press, New York and London, pp.261–72.

Nowlis, V., and Nowlis, H.H. (1956). 'The description and analysis of moods', *Ann. N.Y. Acad. Sci.*, **65**, 345–55.

Olds, J. (1955). 'Physiological mechanisms of reward', in M.R. Jones (Ed.) *Nebraska Symposium on Motivation*. University of Nebraska Press, Lincoln, Nebraska.

Olds, J. (1958). 'Self-stimulation of the brain', *Science*, **127**, 315–24.

Olds, J., and Milner, P. (1954). 'Positive reinforcement produced by electrical stimulation of the septal area and other regions of the rat brain'. *J. Comp. Physiol. Psychol.*, **47**, 419–27.

Orbach, J., Milner, B., and Rasmussen, T. (1960). 'Learning and retention in monkeys after amygdalahippocampal resection', *Arch. Neurol.* (Chicago), **3**, 230–51.

Osgood, C.E. (1955). 'Fidelity and reliability', in H. Quastler (Ed.) *Information Theory in Psychology*. Free Press, Glencoe, pp.374–84.

Osgood, C.E. (1966). 'Dimensionality of the semantic space for communication via facial expression', *Scand. J. Psychol.*, **7**, 1–30.

Ostwald, P.F. (1966). 'Music and human emotions—discussion', *J. Mus. Ther.*, **3**, 3, 93–94.

Panksepp, J. (1981). 'Toward a general psychobiological theory of emotions', *The Behavioural & Brain Sciences*, **5**, 407–67.

Papez, J.W. (1937). 'A proposed mechanism of emotion', *Arch. Neurol. Psychiat.*, **38**, 725–43.

Papez, J.W. (1939). 'Cerebral mechanisms', Research publication, *Association for Research in Nervous and Mental Disorders*, **89**, 145–59.

Pavlov, I.P. (1938). *Conditioned Reflexes*. Translated and edited by G.V. Arup, Oxford University Press, London.

Pennebaker, J.W. (1982). *The Psychology of Physical Symptoms*. Springer-Verlag, New York.

Peters, R.S. (1969). 'Motivation, emotion and the conceptual schemes of common sense', in T. Mischel (Ed.) *Human Action*. Academic Press, New York and London, pp.135–65.

Peters, R.S. (1970). 'The education of the emotions', in M.B. Arnold (Ed.) *Feelings and Emotions: The Loyola Symposium*. Academic Press, New York and London, pp.187–204.

Pichot, P. (1969). Discussion of 'Biological aspects of anxiety', in M.L. Lader (Ed.) *Studies of Anxiety*. Headley Bros., Ashford, pp.26–7.

Plutchik, R. (1962). *The Emotions: Facts, Theories and a New Model*. Random House, New York.

Plutchik, R. (1965). 'What is an emotion?', *J. Psychol.*, **61**, 295–303.

Plutchik, R. (1966). 'Emotions as adaptive reactions: Implications for therapy', *Psychoanalyt. Rev.*, **53**, 105–10.

Plutchik, R. (1970). 'Emotions, evolution and adaptive processes', in M.D. Arnold (Ed.) *Feelings and Emotions: The Loyola Symposium*. Academic Press, New York and London, pp.3–24.

Plutchik, R. (1980). *Emotion: A Psychoevolutionary Synthesis*. Harper & Row, New York.

Plutchik, R. (1982). 'A psychoevolutionary theory of emotions'. *Soc. Sci. Inf.*, **21**, 4/5, 529–53.

Plutchik, R. (1983). 'Emotions in early development: A psychoevolutionary approach', in R. Plutchik and H. Kellerman (Eds.) *Emotion: Theory, Research and Experience*, Vol.2. Academic Press, New York and London.

Plutchik, R., and Ax, A.F. (1967). 'A critique of determinants of emotional state by Schachter and Singer', *Psychophysiology*, **4** (1), 79–82.

Plutchik, R., and Kellerman, H. (Eds.) (1983). *Emotion: Theory Research and Experience*, Vol.2. *Emotions in Early Development*. Academic Press, New York and London.

Posner, M.I. (1978). *Chronometric Explorations of Mind*. Lawrence Erlbaum, Hillsdale, NJ.

Posner, M.I., and Snyder, C.R.R. (1975). 'Attention and cognitive control', in R.L. Solso (Ed.) *Information Processing and Cognition: The Loyola Symposium*. Lawrence Erlbaum, Hillsdale, NJ.

Pribram, K.H. (1970). 'Feelings as monitors', in M.B. Arnold (Ed.) *Feelings and Emotions: The Loyola Symposium*. Academic Press, New York and London, pp.41–53.

Pribram, K.H., and Fulton, J.F. (1954). 'An experimental critique of the effects of anterior cingulate ablations in monkey', *Brain*, **77**, 34–44.

Pribram, K.H., and Weiskrantz, L.A. (1957). 'A comparison of the effects of medical and lateral cerebral resections on conditioned avoidance behavior of monkeys', *J. Comp. Physiol. Psychol.*, **50**, 74–80.

Rachman, S. (1981). 'The primacy of affect: some theoretical implications', *Behav. Res. & Ther.*, **19**, 279–290.

Ranson, S.W., and Magoun, H.W. (1939). 'The hypothalamus', *Argebn. Physiol.*, **41**, 56–163.

Rapaport, D. (1950). *Emotions and Memory*. International Universities Press, New York.

Reis, D.J., and Fuxe, K. (1969). 'Brain norepinephrine: Evidence that neuronal release is essential for sham rage behavior following brain-stem transection in the cat', *Proceedings of the National Academy of Sciences of the United States of America*, **64**, 108–12. (Quoted by Kety (1970).)

Reisenzein, R. (1983). 'The Schachter theory of emotion: Two decades later', *Psychol. Bull.*, **94**, 239–264.

Ryan, T.J., and Watson, P. (1968). 'Frustrative nonreward theory applied to children's behavior', *Psychol. Bull.*, **69**, 111–25.

Rylander, G. (1939). *Personality Changes after Operations on the Frontal Lobes. A Clinical Study of 32 Cases*. Munksgaard, Copenhagen.

Rylander, G. (1948). 'Personality analysis before and after frontal lobotomy', *Res. Pub., Assoc., res. nerv. mentl. Dis.*, **27**, 691–705.

Ryle, G. (1948). *The Concept of Mind*. Hutchinson, London.

Salzen, E.A. (1963). 'Visual stimuli eliciting the smiling response in the human infant', *J. Genet. Psychol.*, **102**, 51–4.

Salzen, E.A. (1981). 'Perception of emotion in faces', in G. Davies, H. Ellis, and J. Shepherd (Eds.) *Perceiving and Remembering Faces*. Academic Press, New York and London.

Sartre, J.-P. (1948). *The Emotions*. Philosophical Library, New York.

Sato, S. (1983). 'An investigation of anxiety-provoking situations among the aged', *J. Child Dev.*, **19**, 5–13.

Schachter, S. (1957). 'Pain, fear and anger in hypertensives and a psychophysiologic study', *Psychosom. Med.*, **19**, 17–29.

Schachter, S. (1959). *The Psychology of Affiliation*. Stamford University Press, Stamford, California.

Schachter, S. (1964). 'The interaction of cognitive and physiological determinants of emotional state', in L. Berkowitz (Ed.) *Advances in Experimental Social Psychology*, Vol.1. Academic Press, New York, pp.49–8.

Schachter, S. (1965). 'A cognitive-physiological view of emotion', in O. Klineberg and R. Christie (Eds.) *Perspectives in Social Psychology*. Holt, Rinehart & Winston, New York, pp.75–105.

Schachter, S. (1970). 'The assumption of identity and peripheralist–centralist controversies in motivation and emotion', in M.B. Arnold (Ed.) *Feelings and Emotion: The Loyola Symposium*. Academic Press, New York and London.

Schachter, S. (1971). *Emotion, Obesity and Crime*, Academic Press, New York and London.

Schachter, S., and Latane, B. (1964). 'Crime, cognition and the autonomic nervous system', in D. Levine (Ed.) *Nebraska Symposium on Motivation*. University of Nebraska Press, Lincoln, Nebraska, pp.221–73.

Schachter, S., and Singer, J. (1962). 'Cognitive, social and physiological determinants of emotional state', *Psychol. Rev.*, **69**, 378–99.

Schachter, S., and Wheeler, L. (1962). 'Epinephrine, chlorpromazine and amusement', *J. Abnorm. Soc. Psychol.*, **65**, 121–8.

Schaffer, H.R. (1958). 'Objective observations of personality development in early infancy', *Brit. J. Med. Psychol.*, **31**, 174–83.

Scherer, K.R. (1982). 'Emotion as a process: Function, origin and regulation', *Soc. Sci. Inf.*, **21**, 4/5, 55–70.

Scherer, K., and Ekman, P. (Eds.) (1984). *Approaches to Emotion*. Lawrence Erlbaum, Hillsdale, NJ.

Schlosberg, H. (1952). 'The description of facial expression in terms of two dimensions', *J. Exp. Psychol.*, **44**, 229–37.

Schlosberg, H. (1954). 'Three dimensions of emotion', *Psychol. Rev.*, **61**, 81–8.

Schneirla, T.C. (1959). 'An evolutionary and developmental theory of biphasic processes underlying approach and withdrawal, in M.R. Jones (Ed.) *Nebraska Symposium on Motivation*. University of Nebraska Press, Lincoln, Nebraska, pp.1–42.

Schreiner, L.H., and Kling, A. (1953). 'Behavioural changes following injury in the cat', *J. Neurophys.*, **16**, 643–59.

Schwartz, G.E., Ahern, G.L., and Brown, S.L. (1979). 'Laterialized facial muscle response to positive and negative emotional stimuli', *Psychophys.*, **16**, 561–571.

Schwartzbaum, J.S. (1960). 'Changes in reinforcing properties of stimuli following ablation of the amygdaloid complex in monkeys', *J. Comp. Physiol. Psychol.*, **53**, 388–95.

Scott, J.P. (1967). 'The process of primary socialization in the dog', in G. Newton and S. Levine (Eds.) *Early Experience and Behaviour*. Thomas, Springfield, USA.

Scott, J.P. (1968). *Early Experience and the Organization of Behaviour*. Wadsworth, California.

Seligman, M.E.P. (1971). 'Phobias and preparedness', *Behaviour Therapy*, **2**, 307–320.

Seligman, M.E.P. (1975). *Helplessness*. Freeman, San Francisco.

Siegel, P.S., and Sparks, D.L. (1961). 'Irrelevant aversive stimulation as an activator of an appetitional response: a replication', *Psychol. Rep.*, **9**, 700.

Siminov, P.V. (1970). 'The information theory of emotion', in M.B. Arnold (Ed.) *Feelings and Emotions: The Loyola Symposium*. Academic Press, New York, London, pp.145–9. (From an original report at the Congress of Psychology, Moscow, 1966.)

Simon, H.A. (1982). Comments, in M.S. Clark and S.T. Fiske (Eds.) *Affect and Cognition*. Lawrence Erlbaum, Hillsdale, NJ.

Skelton, J.A. (1981). 'Specificity of physical symptoms and emotion'. Unpublished doctorol dissestation, University of Virginia. (Quoted in Pennebaker (1982).)

Skinner, B.F. (1938). *The Behavior of Organisms*. Appleton-Century-Crofts, New York.

Skinner, B.F. (1953). *Science and Human Behavior*. Macmillan, New York.

Slater, E., and Roth, M. (1969). *Mayer-Gross, Slater and Roth: Clinical Psychiatry*, 3rd edn. Baillière, Tindall & Cassell, London.

Slater, E., and Shields, J. (1969). 'Genetic aspects of anxiety', in M.H. Lader (Ed.) *Studies of Anxiety*. Headley Bros., Ashford, pp.62–71.

Sluckin, W. (1964). *Imprinting and Early Learning*. Methuen, London.

Smith, W.K. (1950). 'Non-olfactory functions of the pyriformamygdalid-hippocampal complex', *Fed. Proc.*, **9**, 118.

Solomon, R. (1980). 'The opponent-process theory of acquired motivation: The cost of pleasure and the benefits of pain', *Amer. Psychol.*, **35**, 691–712.

Spence, K.W. (1958). 'A theory of emotionally based drive (D) and its relation to performance in simple learning situations', *Amer. Psychol.*, **13**, 131–41.

Spielberger, C.D. (1966). 'Theory and research on anxiety', in Spielberger (Ed.) *Anxiety and Behavior*. Academic Press, New York and London, pp.3–20.

Spiesman, J.C., Lazarus, R.S., Mordkoff, A.M., and Davison, L.A. (1964). 'The experimental reduction of stress based on ego-defence theory', *J. Abnorm. Soc. Psychol.*, **68**, 367–80.

Spitz, R.A., and Wolf, K. (1946). 'Anaclitic depressions', *Psychoanal. Stud. of Child.*, **2**, 313–42.

Sroufe, L.A. (1979). 'Socioemotional development', in J.D. Osofsky (Ed.) *Handbook of Infant Development*. John Wiley, New York and London.

Sroufe, L.A., and Walters, E. (1976). 'The ontogenesis of smiling and laughing', *Psychol. Rev.*, **83**, 173–89.

Staddon, J.E.R., and Innis, N.K. (1966). 'An effect analogous to "frustration" on interval reinforcement schedules', *Psychol. Sci.*, **4**, 287–8.

Stanislawski, C. (1929). 'Direction and acting', *Encyclopaedia Brittanica*, 14th edn., Vol.22.

Stanton, H.E. (1973). 'The effect of music on test anxiety', *Austral. Psychol.*, **8**, 3, 220–8.

Sternbach, R.A. (1966). *Principles of Psychophysiology*. Academic Press, New York and London.

Stotland, E. (1969). 'Exploratory investigations of empathy', in L. Berkowitz (Ed.) *Advances in Experimental Social Psychology*, **4**, 271–314.

Strauss, E. (1983). 'Perception of emotional words'. *Neuropsychol.*, **21**, 99–103.

Strongman, K.T. (1965). 'The effect of anxiety on food intake in the rat', *Quart. J. Exp. Psychol.*, **17**, 255–60.

Strongman, K.T. (1967). 'The effect of prior exposure to shock on a visual discrimination by rats', *Canad. J. Psychol.*, **21**, 57–68.

Strongman, K.T. (1969). 'Analysing emotional behavior', *New Scient.*, Aug., 242–343.

Strongman, K.T. (1970). 'Communicating with the eyes', *Science Journal*, **6**, 47–53.

Strongman, K.T. (1981). 'Emotional experience—a review', *Curr. Psychol. Rev.*, **1**, 17–33.

Strongman, K.T. (1982). 'Emotional influences on memory', *Curr. Psychol. Res.*, **2**, 69–74.

Strongman, K.T. (1983). VII. 'Contribution to psychohistory: Emotional tone of fiction and psychology', *Psychol. Rep.*, **53**, 147–50.

Strongman, K.T. (1984). 'Replacement—a theory of stereotypy', *Curr. Psychol. Res. and Rev.*, **3**, 3, 72–83.

Strongman, K.T. (1985). 'Emotion in the mentally retarded', *Aust. & N.Z. J. Dev. Dist.*, **10**, 4, 201–13.

Strongman, K.T., and Russell, P.N. (1986). 'Salience of emotion in recall', *Bull. Psychon. Soc.*, **24**, 1, 25–27.

Strongman, K.T., and Wookey, P.E. (1969). 'Frustrative reward', *J. Exp. Psychol.*, **82**, 183–4.

Strongman, K.T., Wookey, P.E., and Remington, R.E. (1971). 'Elation', *Brit. J. Psychol.*, **62**, 481–92.

Szymanski, L.S., and Tanguay, P.E. (1980). *Emotional Disorders of Mentally Retarded Persons*. University Park Press, Baltimore.

Tart, C. (1969). *Altered States of Consciousness*. John Wiley, New York.

Tart, G.T. (1972). 'States of consciousness and state-specific sciences', *Science*, **176**, 1203–10.

Taylor, J.A. (1956). 'Drive theory and manifest anxiety', *Psychol. Bull.*, **53**, 303–20.

Thierry, A.M., Javoy, F., Glowinski, J., and Kety, S.S. (1968). 'Effects of stress on the metabolism of noxepinephrine, dopamine and serotonin in the central nervous system of the rat. I. Modification of norepinephrine turnover', *J. Pharmacol. Exp. Therap.*, **163**, 163–71. (Quoted by Kety (1970).)

Thompson, R.A., and Lamb, M.E. (1984). 'Assessing qualitative dimensions of emotional responsiveness in infants: Separating reactions in the strange situation', *Inf. Behav. & Dev.*, **7**, 4, 423–65.

Thorpe, W.H. (1956). *Learning and Instinct in Animals*. Harvard University Press, Cambridge, MA.

Tomkins, S.S. (1962). *Affect, Imagery and Consciousness, Vol. 1, The Positive Affects*. Springer, New York.

Tomkins, S.S. (1963). *Affect, Imagery and Consciousness, Vol. II, The negative Affects*. Springer, New York.

Tomkins, S.S., and McCarter, R. (1964). 'What and where are the primary effects? Some evidence for a theory', *Percept. Mot. Sk.*, **18**, 119–58.

Tucker, D.M. (1981). 'Lateral brain function, emotion and conceptualization', *Psychol. Bull.*, **89**, 1, 19–46.

Turner, M.B. (1967). *Philosophy and the Science of Behaviour*. Appleton-Century-Crofts, New York.

Ulrich, R.S. (1983). 'Aesthetic and affective response to natural environment', in I. Altman and J.F. Wohlwill (Eds.) *Human Behavior and Environment*, Vol. 6, *Behavior and the Natural Environment*.

Valentine, C.W. (1930). 'The innate bases of fear', *Journal of Genetic Psychology*, **37**, 394–419.

Valins, S. (1966). 'Cognitive effects of false heart-rate feedback', *J. Person. Soc. Psychol.*, **4**, 400–8.

Valins, S. (1968). 'Persistent effects of information concerning internal reactions: ineffectiveness of debriefing'. Unpublished manuscript. (Quoted in Valins (1970).)

Valins, S. (1970). 'The perception and labeling of bodily changes as determinants of emotional behavior', in P. Black (Ed.) *Physiological Correlates of Emotion*. Academic Press, New York and London, pp.229–43.

Vine, I. (1970). 'Communication by facial–visual signals', in J.H. Crook (Ed.) *Social Behaviour in Birds and Mammals*. Academic Press, New York and London, pp.279–354.

Wagner, A.R. (1959). 'The role of reinforcement and nonreinforcement in an "apparent frustration effect"', *J. Exp. Psychol.*, **57**, 130–6.

Wagner, A.R. (1966). 'Frustration and punishment', in R.N. Haber (Ed.) *Current research in motivation*. Holt, Rinehart & Winston, New York, pp.229–39.

Wagner, A.R. (1969). 'Frustrative nonreward: A variety of punishment', in B.A. Campbell and R.M. Church (Eds.) *Punishment and Aversive Behavior*. Appleton-Century-Crofts, New York, pp.157–81.

Walker, A.E., Thompson, A.F., and McQueen, J.D. (1953). 'Behavior and the temporal rhinencephalon in the monkey', *Bull. Johns Hopk. Hosp.*, **93**, 65–93.

Walsh, R.N., and Cummins, R.A. (1976). 'The open-field test: a critical review', *Psychol. Bull.*, **83**, 3, 482–504.

Walter, W.G., Cooper, R., Aldridge, V.J., McCallum, W.C., and Winter, A.L. (1964). 'Contingent negative variation: An electric sign of sensorimotor association and expectancy in the human brain', *Nature,* **203**, 380–4.

Walther, R. (1956). *Das vegetative-affektive syndrom und seine Bedeut ung fur die Psychiatrie.* VE3 Verlag, Berlin. (Quoted in Gellhorn and Loufbourrow (1963).)

Watson, D., and Clark, L.A. (1984). 'Negative affectivity: the disposition to experience aversive emotional states', *Psychol. Bull.*, **96**, 465–90.

Watson, J.B. (1929). *Psychology. From the Standpoint of a Behaviourist* (3rd edn, revised). J.B. Lippincott, Philadelphia and London.

Watson, J.B. (1930). *Behaviourism* (revised edn). University of Chicago Press, Chicago.

Watson, J.B., and Rayner, R. (1920). 'Conditioned emotional reactions', *J. Exp. Psychol.*, **3**, 1–14.

West, L.J., and Farber, I.E. (1960). 'The role of pain in emotional development', in L.J. West and M. Greenblat (Eds.) *Explorations in the Physiology of emotion.* American Psychiatric Association, Washington.

Webb, W.B., and Goodman, J.J. (1958). 'Activating role of an irrelevant drive in absence of the relevant drive', *Psychol. Rep.*, **4**, 235–8.

Weiskrantz, L. (1968). 'Emotion', in L. Weiskrantz (Ed.) *Analysis of Behavioural Change.* Harper & Row, New York and London, pp.50–90.

Wenger, M.A. (1950). 'Emotion as visceral action: An extension of Lange's theory', in M.L. Reymert (Ed.) *Feelings and Emotions: The Mooseheart Symposium.* McGraw-Hill, New York.

Wolf, S., and Wolff, H.G. (1947). *Human Gastric Function.* Oxford University Press, New York and Oxford.

Wolpe, J. (1961). 'The systematic desensitization treatment of neuroses', *J. Nerv. Ment. Dis.*, **112**, 189–203.

Wolpe, J. (1966). 'The conditioning and deconditioning of neurotic anxiety', in C.D. Spielberger (Ed.) *Anxiety and Behavior.* Academic Press, New York and London, pp.179–90.

Woodworth, R.S. (1938). *Experimental Psychology* (revised end). Holt, New York.

Wookey, P.E., and Strongman, K.T. (1971). 'Emotional and instrumental effects of reward shift', *Psychol. Rec.*, **21**, 181–9.

Yarrow, L.J. (1964). 'Separation from parents during early childhood', in M.L. Hoffman and L.W. Hoffman (Eds.) *Review of Child Development Research.* Russell Sage Foundation, New York.

Yates, A.J. (1962). *Frustration and Conflict.* John Wiley, New York.

Young, P.T. (1961). *Motivation and Emotion.* John Wiley, New York and London.

Zajonc, R.B. (1980). 'Feeling and thinking. Preferences need no inferences', *Amer. Psychol.*, **35**, 151–75.

Zajonc, R.B. (1984). 'On the primacy of affect', *Amer. psychol.*, **39**, 117–23.

Author Index

Subject Index